For good old Lucy and Jack
Vic Satzewich

For Dimitra, Yiannnis and Petros
Nik Liodakis

Contents

Preface   ix
Acknowledgments   xii

1 **The Concepts of Ethnicity and "Race"   1**

Learning Objectives   1
Introduction   1
Ethnicity: Early Sociological Approaches   3
A Short History of "Race"   9
Racism   18
Summary   27
Questions for Critical Thought   27
Debate Questions   28
Annotated Additional Readings   28
Related Websites   28

2 **Theories of Ethnicity and "Race"   30**

Learning Objectives   30
Introduction   30
Primordialism and Socio-biology   32
Culture and Assimilation   35
Culture and Socio-economic Success   39
Conflict Theory and Political Economy   42
Intersectional Analysis   49
Critical Race Theory   50
Post-colonialism   53
"Whiteness"   55
Summary   57
Questions for Critical Thought   58
Debate Questions   59
Annotated Additional Readings   59
Related Websites   60

3 **The Dynamics of Nation Building: French/English Relations,
Aboriginal/Non-Aboriginal Relations, and Immigration
in Historical Perspective   61**

Learning Objectives   61

Introduction   61
French/English Relations in Historical Perspective   63
Aboriginal/Non-Aboriginal Relations in Historical Perspective   65
Immigration in Historical Perspective   73
Ethnicity, "Race," and the Canadian Census   84
Summary   89
Questions for Critical Thought   90
Debate Questions   90
Annotated Additional Readings   91
Related Websites   91

4   Immigration and the Canadian Mosaic   92
Learning Objectives   92
Introduction   92
Why Immigration?   93
Contemporary Immigration Categories: Debates and Controversies   98
Migrants on the Margins   113
Summary   119
Questions for Critical Thought   119
Debate Questions   120
Annotated Additional Readings   120
Related Websites   120

5   Understanding Social Inequality: The Intersections of Ethnicity,
Gender, and Class   122
Learning Objectives   122
Introduction   122
The Vertical Mosaic: Porter's Legacy   123
Evidence for Ethnic Convergence?   125
The New Colour-Coded Vertical Mosaic?   128
A Critical Assessment of Ethnic/"Racial" Inequality Research   136
Bringing Class Back In   142
Summary   147
Questions for Critical Thought   148
Debate Questions   148
Annotated Additional Readings   148
Related Websites   149
Notes   150

6   Diversity, Multiculturalism, and Quebec Interculturalism   151
Learning Objectives   151
Introduction   151

Meanings of Federal Multiculturalism   153
Contesting Multiculturalism   157
Quebec's Response: Interculturalism and Reasonable Accommodation   171
Summary   177
Questions for Critical Thought   177
Debate Questions   178
Annotated Additional Readings   178
Related Websites   179

7   Racism   180

Learning Objectives   180
Introduction   180
Organized Racism   182
Racism, Surveys, and Public Opinion   184
Institutional Racism   189
New Racism and Religious Hatred: Islamophobia and Anti-Semitism   204
Summary   209
Questions for Critical Thought   210
Debate Questions   210
Annotated Additional Readings   210
Related Websites   211

8   Aboriginal and Non-Aboriginal Relations   212

Learning Objectives   212
Introduction   212
Labels, Identities, and Group Boundaries   213
Comparing Collectivities: Between-Group Differences   224
Explaining Aboriginal Conditions   227
Stratification and Differences within Aboriginal Communities   236
Summary   241
Questions for Critical Thought   241
Debate Questions   241
Annotated Additional Readings   242
Related Websites   242

9   Transnationals or Diasporas? Ethnicity and Identity in a
    Globalized Context   243

Learning Objectives   243
Introduction   243
The Genealogy of Diaspora and Transnationalism   246
Diasporas   250
A Canadian Diaspora?   255

Transnationalism   258
Five Critical Comments   265
Summary   271
Questions for Critical Thought   272
Debate Questions   272
Annotated Additional Readings   272
Related Websites   273

Glossary   275
References   279
Index   301

Preface

For students of immigration, Aboriginal/non-Aboriginal relations, and wider patterns of "race" and ethnic relations, Canada is a sociological garden. Our country offers an extraordinarily rich and complex environment for examining some of the central issues associated with indigenous/settler relations; why people migrate; how they integrate into society; how they retain aspects of their cultures and identities; and how racism, discrimination, and multiculturalism work. Part of the reason that Canada is such an interesting country to study is that patterns of immigration and of "race" and ethnic relations defy simple description and explanation. Moreover, there seem to be so many paradoxes.

Many individuals around the world are interested in moving to Canada in order to find a better life for themselves and their children. Canada allows about a quarter of a million immigrants per year into the country so that they can pursue these dreams. It also makes the acquisition of Canadian citizenship relatively easy. If you have lived in the country for four out of six years, can speak and write in English or French, and can pass a multiple-choice test about your knowledge of Canada, you get a Canadian passport, earn the right to vote in elections, and have the same rights as a person who was born here and whose ancestors came to this country centuries ago. However, even though Canada needs and wants permanent immigrants, thousands of foreign workers are admitted into the country to live and work on only a temporary basis and are denied basic citizenship rights. In other words, we need and want immigrants, but at the same time, some people are considered only good enough to work in Canada but not good enough to stay, form families, and pursue the Canadian dream. It is not clear what makes an individual a good immigrant, and what makes another individual a good worker but not a good potential future citizen.

Economically speaking, some immigrants in Canada do spectacularly well. Frank Stronach came to Canada as a young and virtually penniless Austrian immigrant and has subsequently built one of the world's largest auto parts empires. Michael Lee-Chin, the child of Jamaican immigrants, was the CEO of one of Canada's largest wealth management funds. Lino Saputo moved to Canada from Italy in the early 1950s, founded what has become a global cheese manufacturer, and in 2014 was the sixth-richest man in Canada and the 298th-richest man in the world. While some may dismiss these examples as isolated Horatio Alger stories that have little relevance for the majority of immigrants to Canada, many other immigrants and their descendants earn high incomes, own businesses, run corporations, become respected professionals, live in palatial homes, and have lifestyles that many of us would envy. Their dreams associated with migrating to Canada have been fulfilled. At the same time, however, some immigrants do spectacularly poorly in Canada. They experience downward mobility when they arrive and face lifetimes of poverty, no work, or doing the dirty work of our society cleaning toilets and washing dishes. Stories of overseas-educated doctors, lawyers, nurses, and engineers who are unable to practise their professions in Canada and end up driving taxis in Ottawa, Hamilton, or Saskatoon because of sticky professional licensing requirements or demands for "Canadian experience" are not simply urban legends. The dream of a better life in Canada may be more relevant for their children than for them.

Canadians of different origins generally get along well with each other. Even though the characterization of Canada as a multicultural society that celebrates and tolerates diversity is a cliché, it is true that compared to residents of many other countries, Canadians of different backgrounds do not generally and routinely go around hurting or killing other people simply because they do not like the colour of a person's skin or where they come from. Canadians are encouraged to celebrate and maintain their ancestral identities, cultures, and religions. Intermarriage rates have increased over the past three decades. Many cities have multicultural festivals, and so-called ethnic restaurants do not cater just to members of their own communities—they have diverse clienteles. Some say that these phenomena are superficial indicators of tolerance and diversity, more a reflection of symbolic ethnicity than anything else, but the fact remains that we do not have large-scale ethnic, racial, or religious violence.

Yet we do have instances of racism and discriminatory treatment. In fact, it seems like the more we celebrate diversity and equality, the more allegations of racism in Canadian society creep to the surface. Many institutions in this country have been accused of racism. Some Canadians, including people in some of Canada's most powerful institutions (like the police) are deeply suspicious of the commitment of certain religious and ethnocultural communities to Canada and to Canadian values. Homeland politics and controversies sometimes play themselves out in this country with tragic consequences. The bombing of the Air India flight from Vancouver in 1985 is thought to be related to Sikh struggles for an independent homeland. In some quarters, Islam is considered fundamentally at odds with Canadian values such as equality and tolerance and as a breeding ground for terrorism.

Many of our national symbols and coveted cultural artifacts are derived from Aboriginal cultures. The Hudson's Bay Company and the 2010 Canadian Olympic team adopted—some would say appropriated—the Cowichan sweater as the official attire for the Vancouver Games. Many Canadians enjoy canoeing as a way of communing and reconnecting with nature, and our quirky national symbol, the beaver, is in some ways a tribute to the complex relations of economic and cultural exchange that early Europeans and First Nations engaged in during the course of the seventeenth- and eighteenth-century fur trade. Yet First Nations' standoffs, blockades, and protests over unfilled treaty promises and land grabs are all too common in this country. And poverty rates and poor living conditions in First Nations communities, as well as violence against First Nations women, are of truly scandalous proportions in this country.

The aim of this book is to help students analyze and understand some of the complex and paradoxical patterns of immigration, Aboriginal/non-Aboriginal relations, and "race" and ethnic relations in Canada. These patterns, as will be clear from this book, are full of ironies, contradictions, and tensions. In the book, we adopt a position of methodological and theoretical pluralism. We want to encourage students to think critically about these issues and not to accept certain claims made in the media and by other academics—or even by us—as unquestionable truths. Rather than attempting to review, summarize, and synthesize what is now a massive body of scholarly and activist knowledge in these areas, this book deals with major approaches to and explanations of a number of issues that are central to the field.

Chapter 1 discusses some fundamental concepts in the field of "race" and ethnic relations. Concepts are important because they help define our subject matter. We need them as building blocks to begin to understand and make connections among various issues.

Chapter 2 extends the discussion in the first chapter and considers various theoretical approaches to studying "race" and ethnicity. Theories like socio-biology, political economy, and critical "race" theory offer lenses through which we can begin to interpret and explain events in the world.

In Chapter 3, we argue that history matters when it comes to understanding contemporary patterns of immigration, French/English relations, "race" and ethnic relations, and Aboriginal/non-Aboriginal relations. While we are not simple historical determinists who argue that history explains everything, we do believe that in order to understand issues like land-claims disputes and allegations that the Canadian immigration system is racist, we need to have an understanding of the past.

Issues associated with the contemporary immigration system are discussed in Chapter 4. We consider the question of why Canada has immigration and discuss a number of controversies over different immigration categories. These questions include but are not limited to the following: Are family class immigrants a "drain" on the Canadian economy? Do new "safe-third-country" rules put refugees at risk? What types of biases exist in the Canadian immigration system?

Chapter 5 discusses the issue of economic inequality among immigrants, non-immigrants, and racial and ethnic groups. Even though there is evidence that the vertical mosaic in Canada is being recast along racial lines, we propose an alternative perspective to understanding inequality. Our alternative suggests that social scientists also need to study the internal class and gender differences within basic ethnic and racial categories.

In Chapter 6, we examine issues of diversity, multiculturalism, and interculturalism. We conduct an extensive and critical discussion of the Canadian federal government's policy of multiculturalism, and we show that multicultural policy is a favourite whipping boy for Canadians, with some claiming that it encourages too much diversity and others that it does not promote genuine diversity. We also consider Quebec's policy of interculturalism, and some of the tensions in that province stemming from the issue of "reasonable accommodation."

Chapter 7 focuses on the issue of *racism*. We review a number of controversies about, and examples of, racism in Canadian society. We question whether racism is a "whites only" phenomenon as well as claims that there is a new kind of racism that characterizes many Western societies. We provide examples of institutional racism and extensively discuss Islamophobia, anti-Semitism, racial profiling in policing, racism and new media, and whether safe schools policies put black and other minority youth at a disadvantage.

We turn our attention to contemporary Aboriginal/non-Aboriginal relations in Chapter 8. We examine the political constitution of Aboriginal identities and categories and some of the controversies associated with how First Nations are defined. We then examine how social scientists explain differences in health status and socio-economic achievement between Aboriginal and non-Aboriginal people. In doing so, we critically evaluate biological, cultural, structural, and historical explanations of these differences. We conclude the chapter with a discussion of an alternative way of thinking about Aboriginal people's position in Canadian society—a way of thinking that focuses, once again, on the internal divisions within a group. We suggest that Aboriginal communities are fractured by variables like gender, class, and political power.

Finally, in Chapter 9, we extensively discuss two new approaches to the study of immigration and ethnic relations. The concepts of *diaspora* and *transnational* are introduced, explained, and critiqued in this chapter. We provide a number of examples of what researchers mean when they describe a community as either transnational or a diaspora. We argue that while these two concepts provide a useful lens through which patterns of immigration and of "race" and ethnic relations can be understood, many of their proponents' claims are not entirely new or novel.

Acknowledgments

We would like to thank Lorne Tepperman and the late James Curtis for initially inviting us to contribute a volume to this series. We are pleased that Oxford University Press has decided to publish a fourth edition of this book. A number of individuals at Oxford University Press, including Amy Gordon, Christina Maria Jelinek, and Darcey Pepper, have been very helpful in seeing this book through the publication process. The various referees who read and commented on the manuscript provided valuable critical comments, and this book is better because of the time they took to review our work. We would also like to thank our students, who over the years have been the unknowing collaborators with us on this project. They have provided us with valuable informal feedback on the particular take on ethnic relations and immigration that we offer in this book.

1 The Concepts of Ethnicity and "Race"

Learning Objectives

In this chapter you will learn that

- the meanings of the terms *ethnicity* and *"race"* are historically specific—i.e., they mean different things to different people in different places at different times.

- ethnicity and "race" are important bases for the formation of social groups. Historically, they have shaped the formation of real or imagined communities of people.

- ethnicity and "race" are relational concepts. They are social relations. As such, they represent the lived experiences of individuals and groups and are important dimensions of social inequality.

- ethnicity is usually associated with people's cultural characteristics, mostly symbolic, such as their customs, beliefs, ideas, mores, language, history, folklore, and other symbols that hold the group together and assist others to recognize them as separate.

- "race" is an irrational way of dividing human populations into groups based on the members' physical characteristics. "Racial" categories have their roots in nineteenth-century Western pseudoscience, supported and justified ideologically by the Enlightenment. Colonization, exploitation, and slavery have warranted the material subordination of non-Westerners over the centuries.

- constructions of Self and Other are used by dominant groups for producing and maintaining group boundaries and the reproducing processes of exclusion of subordinate groups.

- identities are produced and maintained within institutions. Institutional completeness measures the extent to which ethnic groups form institutions by and for their members.

Introduction

Former prime minister Stephen Harper is no fan of sociology, especially when it comes to efforts to understand patterns of "race" and ethnic relations in Canada today. In April 2013, following the arrest of Chiheb Esseghaier of Montreal and Raed Jaser of Toronto, both of whom were suspected of conspiring to commit murder in support of terrorism and participation in a terrorist group, Prime Minister Harper was quoted as saying, "I think, though, this is not a time to commit sociology" (Fitzpatrick, 2013). He must have thought that his glib anti-sociology remark was pretty clever because a little more than a year later he used it again. This time, though, it was in response to the murder of Tina Fontaine, a First Nations girl whose body was pulled out of the Red River in Winnipeg in August. In response to calls coming from a number of quarters for a broader national inquiry into missing and murdered Aboriginal women, the prime minister said, "I think we should not view this as sociological phenomenon. We should view it as crime" (Ditchburn, 2014).

His dismissal of sociology implies that trying to understand the root causes of terrorism is pointless because terrorist threats need to be seen as criminal acts to be confronted with the full force of the law and security establishment. In his view, there is little to be gained by trying to understand the reasons why some people might embark on the path toward extremism. Similarly, to him, there is little need for a society to understand the factors that might lead some people to commit violence against Aboriginal women, and the best societal response is for the justice system to do its work and put offenders in jail. Action, particularly action that involves getting tough on crime, rather than research, is what is needed in order to solve these kinds of social problems. In both cases, former prime minister Harper seems to assume that trying to understand why people commit crime means excusing, or justifying, crime (Sullivan, 2014).

Though his attitude toward how to solve these problems—by treating them as crimes may seem like common sense to some, separating action from research is not that simple. Nor is it smart from a public policy perspective. After all, taking the correct or most effective course of action in any aspect of individual or social life ought to be grounded in an understanding of *why* things are the way they are. With respect to the threat of terrorism, some say that young men and women from **ethnicized** and racialized communities embark on their path to extremism because they face racism, discrimination, and stereotyping, and hence feel they are excluded from mainstream society. Others argue that Arab cultures and certain strands of Islam are inherently illiberal and socialize members into thinking that attacking infidels is not just acceptable but also a duty. Given these different assessments of what leads people to join extremist groups, what is the best course of action? Is it to undertake efforts to try to change Arab and Muslim values and attitudes to make them conform more to liberal, Western values? Is it to subject Arabs, Muslims, and others to more intensive and invasive security screening and monitoring? Or, is it to make sure that society does not erect barriers to full and equal participation because of stereotypical and inaccurate beliefs about certain "Others"? There is, moreover, considerable debate about whether the issue of missing and murdered Aboriginal women is a reflection of a broader problem of gender inequality in Canada, the low socio-economic status of First Nations women, or racism in its multiple forms. That racism arguably includes the general lack of respect men have for First Nations women and the general tendency for the police to not take seriously cases in which First Nations women go missing in the first place. Where should societal resources go to help counter this problem? Should the police be given more "race relations" training so that they can deal more sensitively with First Nations communities? Should more police be put on the streets in places where women are known to go missing? Should we throw away the key when an offender is caught and convicted of a criminal act against a First Nations woman in the hope that this will deter potential future offenders? Should we put money into social programs that help First Nations women find good jobs so that some do not have to resort to so-called risky jobs like prostitution that inherently put them in harm's way? Or, do more society-wide changes need to be implemented to make sexism and racism less socially acceptable?

Clearly, what action we take depends on what we think is the source of the problem. Taking action without a proper understanding of why people behave the way they do is not only a waste of time and resources but also allows the harmful and threatening behaviour to continue. Prime Minister Harper's reluctance to "commit sociology" might make for a good political sound bite but it also speaks to one of the aims of the sociological project, which is to explain how and why groups of people behave in ways that they do. As part of the sociological project, sociologists seek to both describe how the world works and to offer explanations for patterns of behaviour. Concepts and theories are a critical part of the sociological project because they point to potential relationships, patterns, and processes that are responsible for individual and group behaviour.

We begin this chapter by examining several meanings of the terms *ethnicity* and *"race."* We suggest that ethnicity and "race" are important bases for the formation of social groups. Ethnicity and "race" are relational concepts. We suggest that constructions of Self and Other are central to the understanding of the concepts of "race" and ethnicity. We proceed to the examination of how identities are produced and maintained within ethnic institutions. Institutional completeness measures the extent to which ethnic groups form institutions by and for their members.

Ethnicity: Early Sociological Approaches

Whether by need or desire, efforts to answer questions about who "we" are and how "we" differ from "them" go back a long time in the history of Western thought (Miles and Brown, 2003: 84–6). Indeed, such efforts go back at least to Herodotus; his *Histories* gives accounts of the Persian wars against the Greeks and contains lengthy passages describing many different ethnic groups: their languages, gods, customs, idiosyncrasies, geography, and contacts with other groups, as well as their history, politics, social arrangements, and economies (Herodotus, *Histories*, 1998). Today, sociologists pose these types of questions in terms of the concepts of "Self" and "Other." In other words, how do groups of people understand and define themselves (the Self), and how do they distinguish themselves from, and define and understand, other groups of people (the Other)? This simple distinction is critical to helping us understand the historical development and current usage of the terms *ethnicity* and *"race."*

The term *ethnicity* has its roots in the Greek word *ethnos* and means "people." Unlike previous generations of philosophers and scientists, who tended to be interested in ranking the characteristics of groups of people, early social scientists writing in the late nineteenth and early twentieth centuries tended to be more interested in questions surrounding the social processes involved in the formation of ethnic groups.

Émile Durkheim used the concept of **collective conscience** as a primary source of identity formation. In his book *The Division of Labour in Society* (1964 [1893]), he tried to explain what made pre-modern societies so cohesive and emphasized the importance of community or group sentiments over individual ones. Social solidarity is based on sameness and the conformity of individual consciousness to the collective. Furthermore, similarities among members or sameness within the social group lead members to differentiate between themselves and others (non-members) and to prefer their "own kind" over others. Durkheim believed that the collective conscience of people leads them to "love their country . . . to like one another, seeking one another out in preference of foreigners" (60). This is an "us" versus "them" feeling, important in social group formation, reproduction, and maintenance. It sets and reproduces over time clear boundaries between those who belong to the group (Self) and those who do not (Other).

Group formation is directly associated with social practices of inclusion/exclusion, which in turn are important in the production and distribution of scarce valuable resources such as wages, social status and status symbols, economic and political power, equality, voting rights and citizenship, access to social programs, human rights, self-determination, and autonomy. These practices constitute the basis upon which decisions about social rewards and social sanctions are made.

Though the study of ethnic groups was not central to Max Weber's (1864–1920) overall work, he did nonetheless offer definitions of the concepts of ethnic group, tribe, and nationality. His definition of ethnic group in particular has become influential in later debates in the field. His definition of ethnicity is not that different from the one offered by Herodotus. According to Weber (1978), common descent, tribe, culture (including language and other symbolic codes), religion, and nationality (a product of the Enlightenment) are important determinants of ethnicity. In distinguishing between (smaller) kinship and (larger) ethnic groups, Weber wrote,

> We shall call "ethnic groups" those human groups that entertain a *subjective* belief in their common descent because of similarities of physical type or of customs or both, or because of memories of colonization and migration; this belief must be important for the propagation of group formation; conversely, it does not matter whether or not an objective blood relationship exists. Ethnic membership differs from the kinship group precisely by being a *presumed identity*, not a group with concrete social action, like the latter. (1978: 389, emphasis added)

Weber used the term "*race*" to denote the common identity of groups based on heredity and endogamous conjugal groups. He argued that "racial" heredity had historically been a basis for delineating social groups. Customs as well as visible similarities and differences, however minor, could serve as potential sources of affection and appreciation or repulsion and contempt (Driedger, 1996: 5). Weber wrote that "almost any kind of similarity or contrast of physical type and of habits can induce the belief that affinity or differences exist between groups that attract or repel each other" (1978: 386). Cultural differences, both symbolic and material, produced and reproduced over time, also constituted the foundations upon which a "consciousness of kind" could be built.

Such cultural traits, in turn, "can serve as a starting point for the familiar tendency to **monopolistic closure**" (Weber, 1978: 386). Monopolistic closure simply means processes and practices, often institutionalized, whereby members of the in-group have access to the scarce valuable resources mentioned above, whereas non-members (the out-group) are excluded. The former monopolize; the latter are left out. Social boundaries have thus been set. From the often minor but not inconsequential "small differences" that are "cultivated and intensified" comes monopolistic closure. Cultural differences may become apparent "due to the peaceful or warlike migrations of groups that previously lived far from each other and had accommodated themselves to their heterogeneous conditions of existence" (Weber, 1978: 388).

Weber makes clear that these differences may indeed be minor, but what matters is the belief in them. Commenting on the early experiences of people who immigrated as part of the great labour migrations under industrialization and colonization, he suggested that even if cultural differences are superficial or do not really exist, belief in their existence

> can exist and can develop in group-forming powers when it is buttressed by a memory of an actual migration, be it colonization or individual migration. The persistent effect of the old ways and of childhood reminiscences continues as a source of native-country sentiment among emigrants even when they have become so thoroughly adjusted to the new country that return to their homeland would be intolerable. (Weber, 1978: 388)

For Weber, the tribe is the historical predecessor of the ethnic group. A characteristic of the tribe is the formation of extended kinship groups. As families of people banded together to produce and share resources, protect themselves, survive, wage war, and migrate, they formed the basis for the emergence of a common historical memory, mainly through oral histories, as well as the notion of the "people" (*volk* in German). Weber argued that this often-assumed common memory of the people had a "vague connotation that whatever is felt to be distinctly common [among ethnic group members] must derive from common descent" (Weber, 1978: 395).

Further, the *volk*-feeling eventually gave rise to the notion of nationality, a concept that emerged during the Enlightenment. Later, during the time of the French Revolution, the idea of "nation-state" became prominent. There appeared to be a progressive-at-the-time call for the formation of states on the basis of nations. Until then, large political entities were multi-ethnic and **multinational**. The Roman, Byzantine, Ottoman, Chinese, Austro-Hungarian, and Holy Roman Empires were all multi-ethnic. Initial notions of nationality based the concept on a common language. Weber has suggested that "in the age of linguistic conflicts, a shared common language is pre-eminently considered the normal basis of nationality" (Weber, 1978: 395). The term *nation-state* had become synonymous with a state based on a common language. Today, few modern states are exclusively unilingual. Nevertheless, in eighteenth- and nineteenth-century Europe there was a push for the formation of nation-states on the assumption that there were ethnic groups that had become large enough in size and had some historical claim to nationhood and by extension to the right to form their own state—a nation-state.

The links of ethnicity to nationality and the state are comprehensive and totalizing. But Weber also included religion in his definition of ethnic groups. Religion, seen as an ideological system of symbols, is an essential part of culture. As such, common religion is a strong source of group self-identification and solidarity. Religion constitutes the basis upon which group values, ideas, customs, morality, and "world outlook" (*Weltanschauung*) are formed. As part of ideology, religion can have important material consequences. For example, Weber argued that we could not understand the development of capitalism without a comprehensive analysis of the Protestant ethic (Weber, 1958).

Culture, Ethnicity, and Identity

Building on these early foundations, many sociologists today are interested in how ethnic identities are acquired and transmitted between generations. **Culture** can be defined as a set of dynamic social processes and practices; it is a collective response of socially constituted individuals to their ever-changing external conditions. It is not monolithic, static, uniform, or homogeneous. It is important to remember that the link between ethnicity and culture is tenuous at best. Ethnicity cannot be equated with culture (Li, 1988). There is no simple, one-to-one correspondence between individual people, culture, and ethnicity or "nation." **Assimilation** is the process by which members of ethnic groups are incorporated into the dominant culture of a society, and experience *in*culturation (Isajiw, 1999: 170). Many assume, as we will show in Chapter 2, that the offspring of immigrants who assimilate are more likely to enjoy upward social and economic mobility. But how are ethnic identities acquired to begin with? What are the processes and practices whereby, and the sites or social spaces where, individuals acquire their ethnic identity, especially in societies like Canada that are multicultural?

Kallen (1995) has argued that ethnic identity contains both subjective (micro-individual) and objective (macro-structural) factors. We can distinguish between individual and **collective ethnic identity**. Collective ethnic identity refers to the existence of a certain consensus within the group about what constitutes it as such and differentiates it from other groups, whereas **individual ethnic identity** refers to the relationship of individuals to their own ethnic collectivity—that is, the strength and scope of the group characteristics with which they identify (Kallen, 1995: 83–4). Ethnic identity is "seen as an outcome of the impact upon the individual or the ethnic collectivity of the interrelationship between the diachronic and synchronic dimensions of ethnicity" (1995: 79). **Diachronic dimensions of ethnicity** include the ancestry, homeland, and culture associated with one's ethnic group. They constitute the core of one's ethnic identity. Endogamy, the practice of marrying only within the same community, and processes of enculturation (learning your own culture) transmit over time the distinctive culture of ethnic group members from one generation to the next. **Synchronic dimensions of ethnicity**, on the other hand, are those dimensions that refer to the ways in which an individual or ethnic collectivity is defined, evaluated, and treated by others. Ethnic identity formation, then, is a reciprocal process that varies according to time and place, since its diachronic, core dimensions must be reproduced over time in any given place and are contingent on the synchronic social construction of ethnic identity by ethnic outsiders (1995: 79–80).

Institutional Completeness

Ethnic institutions are sites or social spaces within which ethnic identity is produced and maintained over time. Ethnic group identity may be evaluated in terms of the expressive, organizational, and instrumental strengths of the groups (Kallen, 1995: 88–90). Expressive strengths refer to ethnic group folk customs like music, costumes and dances, values and activities, religion, language use, and perceived socio-economic "performance," as well as demographic characteristics, such as size and potential for endogamy (age and sex ratios). In addition, ethnic closure may be seen as part of the expressive strengths of a group—i.e., the ability to "enforce the rules" and sustain ethnic boundaries over time (inclusion and exclusion), either through behaviour (regulation, endogamy, segregation) or ideology (sense of peoplehood, criteria for group membership, ethnocentrism). Organizational strengths refer to the actual institutions that ethnic groups create and include their range and scope (provincial, national, international, political, economic, social, religious), ethnic communications (print and electronic news media, the Internet, and so on), and credible ethnic leadership and its ability to mobilize the group around issues pertaining to individual or group rights and/or economic demands on governments. Instrumental strengths refer to a group's relative collective political power (size, voting patterns, political party membership, positions of power and authority), the relationship of the ethnic leadership to political and economic powers and institutions in Canada, and the collective economic resources of the group.

A key concept in the understanding and analysis of ethnic identity is that of **institutional completeness** (Breton, 1964; Weinfeld, 2001). It refers to the extent to which an ethnic group in a particular place and time forms organizations by and for its members (Herberg, 1989: 208–9). These voluntary organizations and institutions—be they educational, religious, economic, or social—cater to the needs of the ethnic group members. It is argued that "the presence of many institutions and organizations within an ethnic community generates a social life in the community, not only among the members of these [ethnic] organizations themselves, but one that extends beyond them to persons in the community who are not members of [the ethnic] organization" (Isajiw, 1999: 200).

Large numbers of organizations within an ethnic community imply high levels of institutional completeness for the ethnic group. They tend to minimize "unnecessary" contact with non-group members. The higher the degree of institutional completeness an ethnic group enjoys, the higher the likelihood that its members will retain their ethnic identity. The role of institutions is crucial to the development of ethnic group consciousness (Kallen, 1995: 86–7). First-generation members of ethnic groups—that is, those born outside Canada—endeavour to transfer their ethnic identity to subsequent generations. Second-generation Canadians are those with at least one parent who was born outside the country. Third-generation Canadians are those whose parents were born in Canada, and so on. Reitz (1980: 23) has argued that the participation of first-generation parents in ethnic organizations serves as a model of socialization for their offspring, who may be susceptible to rejecting their ethnic background or assimilating to the dominant culture. Their ethnic organizations and institutions may be alternatives to those of the dominant culture or complementary and parallel to them. For example, although individuals who identify with a specific ethnic group send their children to public school, they may also send them to an ethnic educational institution where they learn their own ethnic language, history, and culture as well. Jewish, Greek, Armenian, and Muslim day schools in Toronto and Montreal serve that purpose.

Ethnic institutions extend beyond schools and language classes. Although members of an ethnic group may do their banking with the big Canadian banks, many of those banks now offer services in languages other than English or French. Moreover, they may also do it at their ethnic credit union (there are, for example, Polish, Portuguese, Ukrainian, and other ethnic credit unions). Ethnic organizations may also provide services to their members outside of the mainstream institutions and organizations of the larger Canadian society. For example, many ethnic communities have their own social services organizations that care for their youth, the elderly, newcomers, women, the unemployed, and other members in need. These services are often not available to non-group members. Furthermore, in many large cities, ethnic group members have access to professional services offered by co-ethnic members. Dentists, lawyers, real estate agents, immigration consultants, and other professionals often advertise their services in ethnic languages on the radio, on television, in ethnic newspapers, or on the Internet. They do this to expand their clientele and their business, but in doing so they further add to the institutional completeness of the community because they provide another venue for individuals to use their language and to express and reaffirm their sense of identity and attachment to the community.

As Breton (1991) has argued, ethnic organizations are political entities. They are "encapsulated political systems" embedded in the larger Canadian socio-political and economic conditions. Ethnic groups have both external and domestic "affairs," and their institutions provide material and symbolic services to their members. The domestic affairs of ethnic organizations ordinarily include the provision of material services, such as accommodating new immigrants and the elderly, as well as symbolic services, such as activities that pertain to the maintenance and development of the group's dominant cultural norms and values. Examples of such activities are celebrations of historical events and heroes, commemorations of community victimization either in the home country or in Canada, language instruction, dances, theatrical performances, and musical concerts. The external affairs of ethnic organizations relate to (a) matters of government policies on immigration, multiculturalism, public education, human rights, the economy, and so on; (b) issues of discrimination and prejudice; (c) relations with broader societal institutions (e.g., mainstream mass media, unions, the police); and (d) relations with the country of origin and its representatives (Breton, 1991: 3).

Today, most people assume that the provision of material and symbolic services to members of ethnic groups by their respective ethnic organizations and institutions exists because of the Canadian policy of multiculturalism (see Chapter 6). This is not necessarily true. Historically, such provision predates both the policy and the ideology of multiculturalism in Canada. Even during the years of anglo- and/or franco-conformity before 1971, many ethnic organizations provided ethnic language instruction, assisted new immigrants to Canada, fought against prejudice and discrimination, and struggled to maintain elements of their own culture in Canada and transmit them to the new generations. Multiculturalism, then, is not a prerequisite for community action in these areas. Many ethnic communities, even in countries without an official policy of multiculturalism (e.g., Germany, France, Italy, Greece, South Africa, Argentina), engage in similar activities (Liodakis, 1998).

In Canada, ethnic organizations have tended to emerge first as mutual benefit associations to meet the symbolic needs of their members, to contribute to group cohesion, and to assist newcomers in coping with the new social and economic conditions—often of hardship—that their members face on arriving in Canada. Herberg (1989) has gone as far as arguing that ethnic institutional completeness is "the most essential influence on a group's cohesion because it includes all the . . . arenas within which ethnic culture must be utilized and applied if it is to survive. . . . [E]thnic culture must be practiced in public situations, be relevant to these public and 'formal' interactions, and even be necessary for their conduct as something more than arbitrary personal norms if ethnoculture is to survive in Canada" (1989: 213).

A Short History of "Race"

While *ethnicity* is usually defined in terms of the cultural characteristics of group members, *"race"* has been historically defined in terms of physical or genetic characteristics, or as an **ascriptive characteristic**. We use quotations around the term "*race*" to denote that the term is a socially constructed category for classifying humans, with no real biological referent and, as we will argue below, with little analytical, *sui generis* value in the social sciences. In the past, the physical characteristics of humans that have been used to classify groups have included skin colour, eye colour, hair type, nose shape, lip shape, body hair, and cheek-bone structure (Hooten, 1946, in Driedger, 1996: 234–5).

When we ask our students how many "races" there are, the usual answer is that there is only one, the human "race." But when we begin to discuss the legacy of colonialism or issues of inequality among social groups, it is hard to avoid using terms like *white, black, visible minorities,* and *Aboriginals,* among others—terms that connote "*race*" as something that is real.

According to Banton (1987: 1), the term "*race*" appeared in written English for the first time in a poem by William Dunbar in 1508. Since then, the meaning of the term has undergone a number of changes. Prior to the late nineteenth century, the term "*race*" meant lineage, or line of descent, and it was attributed to social groups with a common history (Banton, 1987: xi). By the beginning of the nineteenth century, there was a shift in the meaning of "*race*." Part of this shift was the result of the historical intersection of colonialism and science. Banton (1977) argues that European scientists became preoccupied with the explanation of the physical and cultural diversity of the newly "discovered" peoples and groups that had been brought together as a result of colonial expansion, and of apparent European technological superiority over others. The concept of "*race*" was increasingly used to explain physical, social, moral, and intellectual variation among peoples. In seeking to explain those human differences, European scientists were unable to leave their prejudices outside of the laboratory doors. They inevitably drifted into the social evaluation of those presumed differences, and so the problem of racial classification became intimately tied to the issue of racism.

"Race" and Scientific Racism

Banton argues that the term *racism* should properly be confined to the world of scientific ideas. He also warns us against extending the term to situations in which racial referents are absent and to the world of folk or everyday beliefs (Chapter 7 returns to these two particular issues in more detail). Banton defines **racism** as "the doctrine that a man's behaviour is determined by stable inherited characteristics deriving from separate racial stocks having distinctive attributes and usually considered to stand to one another in relations of superiority and inferiority" (Banton, 1970: 18). Banton argues that the first systematic expressions of biologically informed racism appeared in the form of the doctrine of racial typology that was advanced by certain European scientists in the mid- to late nineteenth century.

By Banton's definition, one of the first true racists was Robert Knox, the Edinburgh anatomist who published *The Races of Men* in 1850. Knox's work signified a change in the social meaning of "*race*": away from vertical lines of individual and collective descent to basic "horizontal" differences between discrete groups of people. European scientists who came after Knox and who held to the doctrine of racial typology believed that much of human history and many of the variations in human culture could be explained by reference to innate biological differences between groups and that "races" could be arranged along a continuum of superiority and inferiority. Although the scientific theories that advanced the doctrine of racial typology took different forms depending on the scientist and the context, they had certain basic assumptions in common. That doctrine held that (1) there exist distinct and permanent types of *Homo sapiens*; (2) the physical appearance and behaviour of individuals is an expression of a discrete biological type that is permanent; (3) cultural variation is determined by differences in biological type; (4) biological variation is the origin of conflict both between individuals and between nations; and (5) "races" are differentially endowed such that some are inherently inferior to others (Banton, 1977).

Scientists make mistakes all the time. Hypotheses are proven false, data are misinterpreted, and variables are not measured properly. Banton argues that racism was one of these scientific mistakes; scientists wrongly equated biological difference with cultural difference and were not able to understand that the differences that existed between people were not intrinsically present but the result of broader environmental circumstances they lived within. Banton cautions us to be wary of explanations that attribute such theories, and the mistakes scientists make, to their personality traits:

> The inductivist explanation of scientific error is not only wrong but dangerous. It implies that men like . . . Knox . . . made mistakes because their hearts were not in the right place and that all we need today in order to avoid or combat racism is a pure heart. I believe that we also need a clear head. (Banton, 1970: 27)

In other words, it is too easy to simply say these mistakes were made because they were "bad white men."

Although some scientists began to have serious reservations about racially based theories of human development in the 1920s, scientific racism reached its zenith in Nazi Germany. Nazi "race" scientists were determined to prove the racial superiority of the Aryan "race" and the racial inferiority of Jews, blacks, Slavic peoples, Gypsies, and a wide range of others. According to Nazi sympathizer and physical anthropologist Alfred Baeumler, "race" is "a definite psycho-physical type which is common to a larger national and tribal circle of men, and maintains itself by hereditary descent. . . . Race is the alpha and omega of the life of nations in its entirety" (quoted in Montagu, 1964: 33).

It is important to recognize that theories linking "race," history, culture, and "national destiny" in the years that bracketed the Second World War were by no means confined to Nazi Germany (Montagu, 1964: 31). It is also important to recognize that these kinds of ideas were not confined to the level of scientific discourse.

Politicians, captains of industry, and members of the general public in many countries believed in and articulated racist doctrines that explained the past and possible futures of different communities. As we will see in Chapter 3, racial theories of human development and human capacities guided Canadian immigration policy until the early 1960s.

In the middle of the twentieth century, "race" thinking was ubiquitous in this country, and around the world. At the same time, many people understood that horrible atrocities had been committed during the war, in part in the name of "race." Individuals and organizations began to develop deep reservations about racial thinking, and the period after the Second World War produced some notable attempts at challenging the logic of racial categorizations and racist thinking, both on the level of science and on the level of public discourse. After the war, the United Nations Educational, Scientific, and Cultural Organization (UNESCO) played a leading role in challenging scientific racism by sponsoring a series of conferences where the aim was, among other things, to discredit Nazi-style racial ideology. Held in 1950, 1952, 1964, and 1967, these conferences were variously attended by internationally recognized scholars in the fields of anthropology, biology, population genetics, sociology, and zoology (Montagu, 1972). After each conference, UNESCO published a series of "statements" summarizing what "race" was, what it was not, and why rankings of groups along continuums of biological superiority and inferiority were wrong. The statements vary in their approaches and are subtly different from each other, but the common thread in these UNESCO-inspired conferences was that theories about the biological inferiority or superiority of groups of people and theories that claimed there was a deterministic relationship between biological and genetic characteristics and human culture were without scientific foundation. The 1950 *Statement on Race* is an example:

> 15 (2) According to present knowledge there is no proof that the groups of mankind differ in their innate mental characteristics, whether in respect to intelligence or temperament. The scientific evidence indicates that the range of mental capacities in all ethnic groups is much the same.
>
> (3) Historical and sociological studies support the view that genetic differences are not of importance in determining the social and cultural differences between groups of Homo sapiens, and that the social and cultural changes in different groups have, in the main, been independent of changes in inborn constitution. Vast social changes have occurred that were not in any way connected with changes in racial type.
>
> (4) There is no evidence that race mixture as such produces bad results from the biological point of view. The social results of race mixture whether for good or ill are to be traced to social factors. (Montagu, 1964: 365–6)

The scientists associated with the various UNESCO conferences worked hard to try to discredit scientific racism. Though by no means naive enough to think that racism could be eliminated simply by presenting and popularizing the true "facts" surrounding the nature of "race" and "race difference," the scientists involved in these projects nevertheless believed that a key part of challenging racism was to undermine its status as a scientific concept. However, one of the contradictions inherent in the efforts of scientists who participated in the conferences was that they did not effectively undermine the idea of "race" itself. They challenged notions of racial *hierarchy* and the idea that "race" determined cultural and historical development, but at the same time they left the concept of "race" intact. That is, they continued to endorse the idea that there was something out there that could legitimately and objectively be called "race." As a result, critics have argued that the UNESCO conferences did not go as far as they should have in undermining the scientific grounding of "race"-based thinking.

Modern Versions of "Race" Science

Even though many of the experts brought together by UNESCO after the Second World War thought that they were well on the way to putting nails in the coffin of racial categorizations, racism, and racial science, some scholars have continued the elusive search for biologically based differences in intelligence, and in social and sexual behaviour, and insist on continuing to call these differences "race" differences. In the mid-1990s in the United States, Richard Herrnstein and Charles Murray (1994) published *The Bell Curve: Intelligence and Class Structure in American Life*. This was a wide-ranging book that considered a number of complicated issues surrounding the relationship between environment, genetic makeup, intelligence, social inequality, and social behaviour. Herrnstein and Murray (1994) argue that human beings differ in what psychologists call the "general factor" of intelligence. Referred to as g, it is defined as "a general capacity for inferring and applying relationships drawn from experience" (Herrnstein and Murray, 1994: 4). As Herrnstein and Murray explain,

> being able to grasp, for example, the relationship between a pair of words like harvest and yield, or to recite a list of digits in reverse order, or to see what a geometrical pattern would look like upside down, are examples of tasks . . . that draw on g. (1994: 4)

They argue that American society is becoming increasingly stratified along differences in cognitive ability and that a cognitive elite is increasingly occupying positions of social, political, and economic power. In their view, the lack of cognitive ability is also related to a number of social problems, such as crime, vice, welfare dependency, unemployment, poverty, workplace injuries, and poor parenting styles. They argue that individuals with less g display more pathological forms of social behaviour than individuals with more general intelligence.

Herrnstein and Murray also argue, however, that general intelligence not only varies among individuals but also varies according to ethnicity and "race." Generally, they claim to have detected a pattern showing basic differences in intelligence among Asians, whites, and blacks such that Asians on average have marginally higher levels of general intelligence than whites. Asians and whites display on average significantly higher levels of intelligence than blacks. According to Herrnstein and Murray (1994), these racial differences in intelligence are the result of a combination of genetic and environmental differences.

Canadian psychologist Philippe Rushton has taken this line of thinking a step further and places even more emphasis on the biological basis for racial differences in behaviour than Herrnstein and Murray. He argues, for example, that "Orientals, whites, and blacks" differ in terms of sexual behaviour. In particular, these three groups differ in relation to what he calls "sexual restraint." Sexual restraint is a composite variable made up of things like rate of premarital sex, frequency of sex after marriage, and general level of interest in sex. He argues that blacks display less sexual restraint than whites, while "Orientals" display more sexual restraint than both whites and blacks. Whites are in between blacks and "Orientals" in their degree of sexual restraint (Rushton and Bogaert, 1987: 535–6). Rushton and Bogaert (1987) then go on to argue that blacks, whites, and "Orientals" also differ in their sexual anatomies. Black men have larger average penis sizes than white men, who in turn have larger average penis sizes than "Orientals." Women vary in similar ways. Black women have larger vaginas and longer clitorises than white women, who in turn have larger vaginas and longer clitorises than "Oriental" women (Rushton and Bogaert, 1987: 536).

Though Rushton and Bogaert (1987: 543) admit that environmental differences might explain some of the differences in degrees of "sexual restraint" among the three groups, they argue that the correlation between dimensions of sexual anatomy and sexual restraint is likely biologically driven. These patterns, they argue, are the result of the "variegated complex of human life history characteristics resulting from a trade-off between egg production and other adaptive behaviour such as parental care and social organization" (Rushton and Bogaert, 1987: 545). In short, blacks are less sexually restrained than whites. "Orientals" are most restrained because of supposed differences in their sexual anatomy. In other work, Rushton argues that blacks, whites, and "Orientals" differ in their cranial capacities and brain sizes, which accounts for differences in intelligence (Rushton, 1988). As Rushton once stated in an interview with *Rolling Stone* magazine, "Even if you take things like athletic ability or sexuality—not to reinforce stereotypes—but it's a trade-off: more brain or more penis" (cited in Rosen and Lane, 1995: 60).

The work of Rushton and of Herrnstein and Murray has been subject to intense critical attack. Rosen and Lane (1995: 58) dismiss it as the work of "disreputable race theorists and eccentric eugenicists." Others question the data and methods they use to arrive at their conclusions and their understanding of the fields of intelligence testing and genetics (Devlin et al., 1997; Fraser, 1995). While the criticisms are both complex and involved, critics of this type of research argue that Herrnstein and Murray and Rushton considerably overstate the degree to which intelligence is an inherited as opposed to environmental characteristic (Daniels, Devlin, and Roeder, 1997; Wahlsten, 1997) and considerably understate the degree to which socio-economic achievement is more conditioned by education, family background, and where one lives than by the notion of general intelligence (Cawley et al., 1997). Rushton's work on "race" differences in sexual behaviour is based on problematic data and on poorly grounded and stereotypical understandings of the diverse nature of human sexuality. Sexual practices, preferences, and identities vary as much within as they do between groups; Rushton seems to equate certain patterns of physical difference with inherent "race" difference.

The Human Genome Project

The debate about the existence and meaning of "race" differences has been undertaken with renewed vigour and respectability in the context of the Human Genome Project. With funding from a wide range of sources, the Human Genome Project began in 1987 as an attempt to trace the human genome and involved mapping the 3 billion nucleotides that make up the human DNA. Particular sequences of nucleotides combine to form the approximately 25,000 genes. Our genes provide the proteins to help produce human traits, such as the length of a person's index finger and the way the lungs work (Abraham, 2005). The project found, among other things, that humans were far more alike than they are different. In fact, the project found that humans share as much as 99.9 per cent of genetic material. Put simply, this means that individuals from different parts of the world are 99.9 per cent alike genetically speaking. This also means that only 0.1 per cent of genetic material accounts for differences among humans. This 0.1 per cent genetic variation is the basis for differences in skin colour, head shape, and predisposition toward certain diseases.

Scholars are divided on how to interpret the results of the Human Genome Project. Some scientists focus on the big picture and argue that the 99.9 per cent of genetic similarity that was discovered in the project confirms that "race" is an empty biological concept. Conversely, others suggest that even though the 0.1 per cent of difference in human genetic material appears small, it is nevertheless significant and further proof that there is something biologically real and relevant about "race." Indeed, a second research project, known as the Haplotype Project, has begun to draw out the significance of this 0.1 per cent difference. The project involves the mapping of genetic combinations in four populations: Utah residents with European descent, the Yoruba people in Nigeria, Han Chinese in Beijing, and Japanese inhabitants of Tokyo.

The advances associated with genetic mapping of the human genome raise a number of ethical questions about so-called race-based research. Ethicists are concerned about the long-term social consequences. Will insurance companies, employers, and others make decisions about individuals based on their genetic profile? To what extent will individuals with predispositions to particular types of disease be subject to unequal and discriminatory treatment?

These are not easy questions to answer. However, the other issue that needs to be raised is whether genetic mapping really undermines the view that "race" is a socially constructed label. The same observations about the socially constructed nature of "race" that were relevant in pre–genetic mapping days are still relevant today. There may in fact be a small proportion of human genetic difference from individual to individual. But they are precisely that—genetic differences. As a society, we still choose to label those genetic differences as "race" differences, but they are really genetic differences pure and simple.

Racialization

Many sociologists have opted to use the concept of racialization (Miles, 1982, 1984, 1993; Miles and Torres, 1996; Banton, 1979, 1987; Small, 1994; Goldberg, 1990) as a way of challenging the idea that "race" is an objectively measurable aspect of human difference. Though somewhat cumbersome, Miles and Brown (2003: 101) define **racialization** as social processes and practices whereby "social relations among people [are] structured by the signification of human biological characteristics in such a way as to define and construct differentiated social collectivities." The concept of racialization emphasizes the socially constructed nature of the concept of "race." As we have seen earlier in this chapter, many different variables have been used over the course of human history to define "racial" categories. "Race" has been variously defined as a lineage, as certain types of physical characteristics like skin colour or nose shape, and as certain genetic combinations. The point is that none of these are inherently correct definitions of "race." They are historically contingent ways in which societies have tried to make sense of certain kinds of differences. "Races" of people are not "real" in a biological sense (Allahar, 1998). "Race," simply put, is the term that human beings and societies have developed to describe and explain certain kinds of physical and/or genetic differences. According to sociologists who use this concept, the important question that needs to be studied is how and why certain groups and/or social relationships are defined and constructed in terms of "race."

Miles and Torres argue that there is a discrepancy between the popular, everyday, common-sense use of the term "*race*" and its social-scientific content. In criticizing "race" as an analytical category, they contend that social scientists ought to jettison the idea of "race" and refuse to use it as a descriptive and explanatory concept (1996: 32). The reason is simple. Social scientists tend to reify (treat as a thing) "race," "insofar as the outcome of an often complex social process is explained as a consequence of something named 'race' rather than of the social process itself" (1996: 32).

Case Study Box 1.1 Is Rachel Dolezal Black or White?

In June 2015, much of North America was obsessed with the racial identity of Rachel Dolezal. Dolezal was president of the Spokane, Washington, chapter of the National Association for the Advancement of Colored People when her mother told the press that her daughter is white and "is being dishonest with her racial identity." Though the Dolezal family story is complicated, Rachel eventually admitted on American national television that while she was in fact raised by her white parents, she had felt she was black since she was five years old. She also continued to insist that her racial identity is black. Though the NAACP initially defended her because they believe that the colour of a person's skin does not matter when it comes to civil rights activism, the organization eventually fired her on the grounds that the issue of her racial identity was undermining the institutional integrity of the organization. The widespread commentary on the case was polarized (Mimms, 2015). Some came to her defence by pointing out that there is nothing biologically real about "race," that it is a social construction, and that there is considerable variability in how societies use skin colour as a marker of "race" difference. Camille Gear Rich, professor of law and sociology at the University of Southern California, said in response to the controversy, "Like it or not, we have entered into an era of elective race—a time when people expect that one has a right and dignity to claim the identity of one's choice" (Rich, 2015). On the other side, she was the butt of jokes, and some argued that Dolezal was a liar and a fake and was illegitimately "passing" as black in order to bolster her status as an activist in the African-American community. The controversy that swirled around the question of whether she is black raises important and sticky questions about how "race" ought to be defined, racial authenticity, and who has the ability, and the right, to claim certain racialized identities.

How do we resist the temptation to use racist language and "explanations" and terms that are without scientific foundation? There is a major theoretical and practical difficulty here. Although, as we argue, "races" do not have a real social referent—that is, the biologically constructed categories do not correspond to real social groups—we lack a language, both academic and colloquial, that can capture the historical development and different, contextualized uses of "racial" terms. We must indeed reject the racist-inspired classificatory terms (*white, black, mongoloid,* etc.) and seek social-scientific definitions and explanations of social inequalities. But we still lack the appropriate language. Goldberg argues that

the discourse promoting resistance to racism must not prompt identification with and in terms of categories fundamental to the discourse of oppression. Resistance must break not only with *practices* of oppression, although the first task is to do that.

Resistance must oppose also the *language* of oppression, including the categories and terms of which the oppressor (or racist) represents the forms in which resistance is expressed. (1990: 313–14)

Racism

Few words in the English language carry the same negative connotations as the word *racism*. Racism has been identified as a cause of a number of the world's historical and current social evils, including slavery, genocide, human rights abuses, environmental degradation, and social inequality. In many cases, racism is also an epithet. To call someone a racist is to label a person as not only outside of polite society but also beyond the pale of civilization itself (Banton, 1970: 18–19). Indeed, a rather telling indicator that most people do not wear the term *racist* as a badge of honour is that even members of the Ku Klux Klan in the United States resist this label as a description of themselves (Reitz and Breton, 1994: 68).

Michael Banton (2002: 54) cautions that because the word *racism* has high rhetorical value it can be often over-employed in the characterization of individuals, organizations, or ideas. The problem is that using the term loosely and uncritically to describe too wide a variety of phenomena or social situations can inadvertently lead to the undermining of both its analytical and political power. If it is used too cavalierly to describe too wide a range of phenomena, it loses its meaning. It also becomes easy to be desensitized to the issue and then to dismiss genuine instances of racism as simply a form of complaining, or of "playing the race card" to attract illegitimate attention to racism.

One of the difficulties associated with analyzing racism is that there is no single agreed-upon definition of the term. Some might approach the definition of *racism* in much the same way as the definition of the proverbial duck; namely, that "if it walks like a racist, and it talks like a racist, then it is a racist." This approach, however, is not necessarily good enough for social scientists. Since the term is used in so many different ways and in so many different contexts to describe everything from individual actions, conscious and unconscious individual beliefs, conscious and unconscious organizational practices and policies, to media images and discourses, we should not easily dismiss the issue of definition.

Even though people believe that "races" of people exist as distinct biological groups, it is clear that "race" is better seen as a social construction; a concept that has been used to describe, categorize, and explain certain patterns of physical or genetic differentiation (Miles and Brown, 2003; Nagel, 2003). While physical and genetic differences among people exist, these are not "racial" differences. Even though we have reservations about the analytical utility of the concept of "race," this does not mean that racism is of equally questionable status as a social scientific concept. After all, people hold negative beliefs and act in discriminatory ways about other people on the basis of the belief that individuals are of a different "race" and/or that they are members of a biologically or culturally inferior social group. Even though those beliefs and actions are based on the myth of "race," the beliefs and actions are nevertheless real, as are their social consequences. Thus, questioning the existence of biologically based "races" should never be taken to imply that racism is not a problem (Satzewich, 1998b). This is why racism is something that exists beyond the level of science and scientific discourse. Racism is also a folk concept in the sense that it occurs in everyday life, at both an individual and institutional level. We want to examine the variety of definitions of *racism* and some of the debates about and contemporary forms of racism.

New Racisms

In the early 1980s British philosopher Martin Barker (1981) published a book titled *The New Racism*. In it, Barker argues, like Banton, that old, biologically informed expressions of racism were a thing of the past but that negative evaluations of racially defined groups were being masked in new, racially neutral language and rearticulated to make them more politically acceptable in public discourse. Since then, analysts in a number of countries have taken up this argument and elaborated on the new ways that racism is being expressed less overtly in different contexts and in different countries.

Britain

Barker argued that in Britain, new ideologies that emphasized that social problems were caused by people of different cultures coming into contact and living in close proximity to each other had come to replace previous views that "race relations" problems were caused by biologically distinct "races" coming into contact. He suggested that because of the general abhorrence in Britain of biologically based understandings of the link between "race" and social problems and conflict, conservative segments of British society developed a code language that allowed them to talk about "race" but in a way that would allow them to deny that they were being racist. This code language used politically neutral terms that played on racial themes, but it did so in ways that allowed individuals who expressed these ideas to avoid the racist label because they did not suggest biological inferiority. One of the most famous expressions of the new racism in Britain came in a speech by Prime Minister Margaret Thatcher in 1978:

> If we went on as we are, then by the end of the century there would be 4 million people of the New Commonwealth of Pakistan here. Now that is an awful lot and I think it means that people are really rather afraid that this country might be swamped by people with a different culture. And, you know, the British character has done so much for democracy, for law, and done so much throughout the world, that if there is a fear that it might be swamped, people are going to react and be rather hostile to those coming in. (cited in Barker, 1981: 15)

Thatcher, expressing sentiments that were quite widespread among conservative segments of British society in the late 1970s and the 1980s, was deeply ambivalent about immigration not only from Pakistan but also from India and the Caribbean and the negative consequences of that immigration. Her speech, however, was devoid of biological referents and instead focused on the negative evaluation of cultural differences. In Barker's view, these kinds of ideas were no less pernicious or racist than the old versions of racism based on biological notions of the racial inferiority of certain groups of people.

France

This kind of new racism is also present in France. According to Taguieff (1999), the New Right in France, represented by the National Front, has rearticulated racism to emphasize the notion of natural cultural differences between "race" and ethnic groups. Rather than expressing hostility toward non-European immigrants on the grounds of biological inferiority, they have appropriated much of the language of anti-racism by emphasizing their apparent respect for maintaining the cultural differences of both French people and new immigrants. For the National Front, immigrants from North Africa are bad for France not because they are biologically inferior. Instead, immigration from North Africa is allegedly bad for France—and for North Africans themselves—because it results in ethnic and racial mixing. Taguieff (1999: 209), quoting from texts published by radical right-wing groups in France, suggests that they have successfully turned the discourse of difference on its head. Taguieff cites claims like the following to demonstrate that notions of difference have replaced notions of inferiority as the rationale for maintaining a separation of the "races":

> The truth is that the people must preserve and cultivate their differences. . . . Immigration merits condemnation because it strikes a blow at the identity of the host culture as well as at the immigrants' identity. . . . It is because we respect ourselves and others, that we refuse to see our country transformed into a multi-racial society in which each one loses one's specificity. . . . Peoples cannot be summarily qualified as superior or inferior, they are different, and one must keep in mind these physical or cultural differences. (quoted in Taguieff, 1999: 209)

In Taguieff's view, the creation of group boundaries around notions of cultural difference is no less pernicious than the creation of group boundaries around notions of biological superiority or inferiority. The objectives of so-called old racism and new racism in France are the same—to exclude North African immigrants, either by voluntary return or involuntary repatriation. This would be for the good of both France and the immigrants themselves because they would lose their distinctive differences by assimilating into French society.

The United States

A number of American analysts have also argued that there are new forms of racism in the United States, which are replacing older, biologically informed expressions of racism (Kinder and Sears, 1981). Sociologist Nestor Rodriguez (1999: 373; see also

Sanchez, 1999) argues that increased immigration from Asia and Latin America has led to the emergence of a new American racism. This new racism, according to Rodriguez (1999: 376), is closely linked to the concept of *nativism*, which can be defined as a fear of "foreignness." Rodriguez outlines three anti-foreign sentiments that have characterized the new racialized American nativism. First, there is a fear of non-English languages based on the suspicion that the linguistic differences of immigrants will undermine the American nation. Second, there is a fear that racialized immigrants take advantage of multicultural ideology and affirmative action entitlements to strengthen their ability to retain distinct ethnic and racial identities. Many Americans feel that multiculturalism and affirmative action are "un-American" because they seem to contradict America's commitment to equality of opportunity and favour "non-Americans." Third, racialized anti-immigrant attitudes are informed by the fear that immigrants are a drain on public resources, particularly welfare, education, and health care services (Rodriguez, 1999: 377–8). According to Rodriguez (1999: 373), this new racialized nativism transcends both political divisions between liberals and conservatives and historical divisions between blacks and whites.

Other American analysts do not necessarily disagree with Rodriguez but suggest that anti-black racism continues to be the most powerful force in American society. Some suggest that this new form of racism is a form of "symbolic racism" (Kinder and Sears, 1981). Shull (1993) argues that in the 1980s and early 1990s, negative attitudes toward blacks were evident in the Reagan and Bush administrations' offensive against civil rights. Their attack on affirmative action, the appointment of conservatives to key administrative posts in the civil rights field, and budget cuts to the Civil Rights Commission, the Equal Employment Opportunity Commission, and the Fair Housing and Equal Opportunity Program were couched in non-racist language: promoting equality, freedom, and less government intervention in the lives of Americans. Although these measures were never politically framed or justified in old-style racist, anti-black terms, according to Shull (1993) they had particularly severe consequences for the income, employment, and housing conditions of poor black Americans. Rather than promoting the development of a "kinder and gentler society," these initiatives promoted a "kinder and gentler racism" (Shull, 1993).

Framing the issue more broadly than Shull, Kinder and Sears (1981) and McConahay (1986) suggest that the core of symbolic racism is the perceived value conflict between programs and philosophies that attempt to improve the conditions of minority groups in society and universal Western values of freedom and equality. As Brown explains, in the United States,

> it is thought that what upsets modern racists is not so much that Blacks may be going to the same school as their (White) children, but that the educational policy of enforced bussing to achieve better ethnic balances within city schools contradicts parents' "right" to choose the school for their children (1995: 219).

Canada

Henry and Tator (2010) build on the work of Barker (1981) and Kinder and Sears (1981) and argue that there is a peculiarly Canadian form of racism, which they term **democratic racism.** Like Barker, they argue that new forms of racism do not necessarily rely on or make reference to notions of inherent biological difference and/or inferiority. However, their definition of *racism* is even broader than that of Barker. Racism, in their view, is not simply about the negative evaluation of cultural difference. They suggest instead that democratic racism is more about value conflicts in Canadian society.

> Democratic racism is an ideology in which two conflicting sets of values are made congruent to each other. Commitments to democratic principles such as justice, equality, and fairness conflict but coexist with attitudes and behaviours that include negative feelings about minority groups, differential treatment, and discrimination against them. (Henry and Tator, 2010: 9–10)

Democratic racism is expressed "mainly through the discourse of domination, which includes myths, explanations, codes of meaning, and rationalizations that have the effect of establishing, sustaining, and reinforcing democratic racism" (Henry and Tator, 2010: 11). They identify a number of discourses of democratic racism that aim to undermine claims about the existence and seriousness of racism in Canadian society. While their list of examples of democratic racism is exhaustive, these are some of the main forms it takes:

- The discourse of colour blindness. This discourse involves white people insisting that they do not notice the skin colour of a racial minority person. In Henry and Tator's view, this is racist because it involves a "refusal to recognize that race is part of the 'baggage' that people of colour carry with them, and the refusal to recognize that race is part of the everyday values, policies, programs, and practices, is part of the psychological and cultural power of racial constructions" (2010: 12).
- The discourse of equal opportunity. This refers to ideas that suggest that "all we need to do is treat everyone the same, and fairness will be ensured" (2010: 11–12). This discourse is racist because it is premised on the belief that "white institutional power" does not have to be dismantled in order for Canadian society to become fair and equal.
- The discourse of blaming the victim. This discourse suggests that minorities themselves are the source of their own "problems." That is, the failure of certain groups to succeed in Canadian society is explained either in terms of inherent cultural differences with the dominant society or in terms of the lack of motivation to succeed (Henry and Tator, 2010: 13).
- The discourse of multiculturalism. This discourse involves the belief that tolerance and harmony can be achieved through accommodating diversity into

society in general and into organizations in particular. It is premised on the notion that the idiosyncrasies of others must be tolerated but that the dominant ways of doing things are ultimately superior. This is a form of democratic racism, in Henry and Tator's (2010: 15) view, because "declarations of the need for tolerance and harmony tend to conceal the messy business of structural and systemic inequality and the unequal relations of power that continue to exist in a democratic liberal society."

Henry and Tator (2010: 17) argue that many Canadians regard themselves as egalitarian and have little difficulty in rejecting the more overt, "in-your-face" expressions of racism. However, even though symbolic gestures are made toward inclusion and respect, these gestures are largely token efforts that mask a continued adherence to white supremacy.

Henry and Tator (2010) and researchers in other societies who advance the notion that new forms of racism have emerged to replace old, biologically informed forms offer a powerful condemnation of modern Western societies. However, we should not accept these broad definitions of racism uncritically. First, this kind of argument attaches simple motivations to complex ideas and discourses. For example, some people may genuinely believe that Canadian multicultural policy is an appropriate tool for the promotion of ethno-racial equity in this country. They may be naive or misguided but this does not necessarily mean that they are opposed to the concerns of people of colour and are using the ideology of multiculturalism to deny structural bases of inequality. Further, in the United States, some liberal objections to policies like affirmative action may be grounded in the belief that such policies are "patronizing to minority groups and undermine their subsequent academic or professional achievements" (Brown, 1995: 226). Second, these arguments tend to essentialize the category of whiteness (to be discussed in more detail below) and homogenize the category of ethno-racial communities. They assume that all members of ethnic/racial communities think the same way—that racism is a fundamental problem in Canadian society.

Third, there is no clear dividing line between "old" and "new" versions of racism (Brown, 1995: 225; Miles and Brown, 2003: 63). Many supposedly old versions of racism that were prevalent in the late nineteenth and early twentieth centuries also involved negative evaluations of cultural and religious differences. These differences were not necessarily understood as biologically grounded but rather as socially and contextually formed. For example, the Canadian federal government's policy of assimilating Aboriginal people in the late nineteenth and early twentieth centuries was not exclusively grounded in a biologically based understanding of their supposed inferiority. Rather, both the general assimilation policy and the programs that were designed to carry it out, such as residential schools, were grounded in the assumption that Aboriginal people could change and become culturally more like Europeans in their attitudes, beliefs, and values. Had Aboriginal difference been defined in purely biological terms, policies of assimilation would have made no sense.

White Racism: The Only Racism?

The preceding discussion is sometimes linked to the concept of "white racism." Either explicitly or implicitly, *racism* is seen as something that is inherent to only white people. Henry and Tator (2010: 11) argue that there is a dominant "white culture" in Canada and that this culture refuses to accept the reality of racism in the country. American sociologists Joe R. Feagin and Hernán Vera (1995) suggest that because of their power and privilege, white people in the United States are uniquely placed as both beneficiaries and defenders of racial hierarchies. Members of other communities may express negative attitudes about white people and even other minority groups. However, according to Feagin and Vera (1995: x), "what is often referred to as 'black racism' consists of judgments made about whites by some black leaders or commentators to the effect that 'no white people can be trusted' or 'the white man is the devil.'"

Feagin and Vera dismiss these ideas as not equivalent to "modern white racism" because unlike white people, black people in the United States are powerless to act on the basis of those ideas and deny privileges to whites or to other groups. They argue that in the United States, "black racism does not exist" (Feagin and Vera, 1995: x) because racism "is more than a matter of individual prejudice and scattered episodes of discrimination." "There is no black racism," they further claim, "because there is no centuries-old system of racialized subordination and discrimination designed by African Americans to exclude white Americans from full participation in the rights, privileges and benefits of this society" (Feagin and Vera, 1995: ix). In their view, "white racism can be viewed as the socially constructed set of attitudes, ideas, and practices that deny African Americans and other people of color the dignity, opportunities, freedoms, and rewards that this nation offers white Americans" (Feagin and Vera, 1995: 7).

Though they are correct to point out that racism has both individual and institutional dimensions, there are problems with their view that racism is the exclusive domain of white people. One problem is that this view assumes that all black people, or members of minority communities more generally, are powerless in the face of an insurmountable white power structure. Black and other minorities are not entirely devoid of power in American or Canadian society. Depending on the context, members of minority communities do hold positions of power within the social, economic, and political structures of society. Black people and other minority group members own businesses, run corporations, make decisions about hiring, and occupy positions of political influence. To assume, as do Feagin and Vera (1995), that black people are economically and politically powerless assumes, in stereotypical fashion, that black people form an underclass within American and Canadian society and that all black people or members of other minority communities are alike and occupy disadvantaged, socially marginal positions in political and economic relations. Not all blacks live in ghetto-like or working-class environments.

Furthermore, individuals within minority communities are not uniquely immune to racism or powerless to act on the basis of those beliefs. For example, surveys in the United States show that whites, blacks, Asians, and Hispanics display complicated negative stereotypes about each other. For example, in one survey, members of each of the four groups were asked to rate the other groups on three dimensions: perceptions of intelligence, perceptions of welfare dependency, and perceptions of their difficulty to get along with. In the survey, nearly two-thirds of Asian respondents thought that blacks were less intelligent than members of their own group. Forty per cent of white respondents and 30 per cent of Hispanic respondents believed that blacks were less intelligent than members of their own groups. On the other hand, nearly one-third of black respondents and 15 per cent of white and Hispanic respondents believed that Asians were less intelligent than members of their own group. Between 40 and 50 per cent of each of the three groups believed that Asians were hard to get along with (Johnson, Farrell, and Guinn, 1999: 395–6).

Arguably, the racism expressed by racialized group members against other racialized groups is just as socially consequential as white racism directed against blacks and other minority groups. Perhaps the best documented example of inter-minority group racism and associated conflict and hostility comes from the Los Angeles Riots in the 1990s. They were telling in that the conflicts and hostilities did not have clear and simple "racial" dividing lines (Feagin and Vera, 1995: 1). Though Feagin and Vera (1995: 1) argue that the conflicts in Los Angeles in 1992 were the result of "anger and rage at white racism," there is evidence that they were not just white versus black conflicts. Black and Hispanic rioters purposely targeted Korean-owned businesses, not just enterprises owned by individuals with "white" privilege. As explained by Johnson, Farrell, and Guinn, in Los Angeles, New York, and other major immigrant-receiving cities in the United States,

> Disadvantaged blacks in these communities see the Korean merchants as "foreigners" who are taking advantage of them by charging high prices, by refusing to invest any of the profits they earn either by employing local black [and Hispanic] residents or otherwise aiding the community, and by being rude and discourteous in their treatment of black customers. On the other hand, many of the stereotypic views that Koreans have of blacks are confirmed in their daily interaction with some of the most disadvantaged residents of inner-city communities. (1999: 406)

These tensions reached an ugly peak in the 1992 Los Angeles Riots. It would be a mistake, however, to dismiss these kinds of dynamics as not relevant to Canada because they happen south of the border. In Vancouver in 2003, a Filipino-Canadian teen was beaten to death by a group of Indo-Canadian youths in what the police describe as a "racially" motivated attack. According to a *Globe and Mail* report on the incident,

> The attack heightened tensions between Indo-Canadian and Filipino-Canadian youths. At [the teen's] ... funeral dozens of Indo-Canadian youths, many who didn't know the victim, attended as a demonstration of their respect and commitment to peace between the two ethnic groups. Police and community leaders urged calm amidst rumours that Filipino-Canadian youths were planning retaliation. (Fong, 2005: A11)

Some Filipino-Canadian community leaders were reluctant to blame other ethnic communities as the source of the problem and instead argued that systemic racism was to blame because it created "artificial conflicts" between racialized minorities. One commentator suggested that "if Indo-Canadian, Vietnamese-Canadian and Filipino-Canadian contributions are taught in school, we will have a better understanding of each other" (Fong, 2005: A11).

It is not clear that the responsibility for such incidents should be shouldered by "white society" for creating artificial conflicts between racialized groups. Some immigrants do bring the historically determined prejudices that they were raised with in their countries of origin to Canada and reproduce them among their Canadian-born children. Pre-existing prejudices, such as those that exist, say, between Dinka and Nuer people in South Sudan may play themselves out when they move to Canada and shape the way that members of the communities relate to each other here. These types of conflicts and hostilities can be understood only if racism is not assumed to be a "white only" phenomenon.

Moreover, even though it might be reasonable on one level to assume that groups that are the object of racism and discriminatory treatment might be more sympathetic to other groups that experience the same thing, this does not always happen (Noivo, 1998). In many ways, there is surprisingly little "transfer sympathy" among groups with common experiences of racism and discrimination. Edite Noivo's (1998) research on Greek and Italian landlords in Montreal in the mid-1990s shows that they and members of their community were racialized and experienced discrimination and prejudice when they arrived in Canada in the 1950s and 1960s. After having gained a solid foothold in Canadian society, however, they now articulate negative and racist attitudes toward new immigrants from Asia, Africa, the Caribbean, and Latin America. As one of her interviewees explained recalling his early experiences in Canada, "I used to be called a wop, macaroni, a *voleur de job*. . . . I was treated as an inferior, too hot-blooded and stupid, and people made racist jokes." Minutes later, in the same interview, he had this to say about more recent immigrants to Canada from Asia, the Caribbean, and Latin America: "These people are no good for this country, they don't like to work hard, they exploit the government, abuse our social system . . . and they'll never change because it's in their culture, that's how they are" (Noivo, 1998: 223).

Summary

We began this chapter with a historical account of the meanings of the terms *ethnicity* and *"race,"* arguing that they are historically specific. They mean different things to different people in different places at different times. Ethnicity and "race" are persistent bases for the formation of social groups. They have shaped in the past and continue to shape the formation of real or imagined communities of people. Ethnicity is usually associated with people's cultural characteristics, mostly symbolic, such as their customs, beliefs, ideas, mores, language, history, folklore, and other symbols that hold the group together and assist others to recognize them as separate. Identities are produced and maintained within institutional sites. Institutional completeness measures the extent to which ethnic groups form institutions by and for their members.

Many social scientists argue that "race" is an irrational way of dividing human populations into groups based on the members' physical characteristics. "Racial" categories have their roots in nineteenth-century Western pseudoscience, supported and justified ideologically by the Enlightenment. Colonization, exploitation, and slavery have warranted the material subordination of non-Westerners over the centuries. Irrational constructions of Self and Other are used by dominant groups for producing and maintaining group boundaries and the reproducing processes of exclusion of subordinate groups. Finally, we highlighted a number of different approaches to the definition of racism. While "old," biologically based racism may indeed be "dead" as Michael Banton suggested, it is clear that articulations of racism have changed and that new language is being used to define some groups as inferior, or as threats to what we have termed "the Self." In the remaining chapters, we offer a number of explanations of, debates on, and approaches to a variety of contemporary and historical issues related to understanding immigration, social inequalities, multiculturalism, Aboriginal relations, racism, and broader patterns of "race" and ethnic relations in Canada.

Questions for Critical Thought

1. Do "races" exist? If so, how many are there, and what are the criteria for dividing human populations based on physical characteristics? Why do we not define social groups on the basis of people's shoe sizes?

2. Why is it that, historically, claims for nationhood and/or the formation of states have been made only by ethnic groups (not "racial" groups)? What is the relationship between ethnicity and nation-state? Does the latter help to forge the former?

3. Can you think of any social processes of assimilation and/or government policies that may homogenize minorities in Canada?

4. Which ethnic communities in Canada today could be described as "institutionally complete"?

5. What could be the possible effects of membership of third-generation Canadians in ethnic institutions built by their parents and/or grandparents?

Debate Questions

1. What is the difference between *ethnicity* and *"race"*?

2. What, if anything, is different about racism today compared to the scientific racism of the past?

3. Is the adoption of a particular racial identity purely a matter of choice, as suggested by Camille Gear Rich?

4. Is "white racism" the only real racism? How does racism expressed by racialized minority groups different from white racism?

Annotated Additional Readings

Gellner, Ernest. 1983. *Nations and Nationalism*. Oxford: Blackwell. The author links ethnicity to nation and traces the historical formation of nation-states.

Goldberg, David Theo. 1993. *Racist Culture: Philosophy and the Politics of Meaning*. Oxford: Blackwell. Goldberg is the director of the University of California Humanities Research Institute. This book provides a sustained critique of the racialized discourse of modernity and post-modernity.

Hobsbawm, Eric. 1990. *Nations and Nationalism since 1780: Programme, Myth, Reality*. Cambridge: Cambridge University Press. This historical analysis of nationalism links ethnicity in modernity with the state and presents a prophetic look at the future of ethnicity and nationalism in post-modernity. States create imagined communities like ethnic groups, their language, and their (wrong) history—i.e., their myth.

Jablonski, Nina. 2006. *Skin: A Natural History*. Berkeley: University of California Press. This nuanced work provides a fascinating and comprehensive account of the biological and cultural aspects of human skin. Jablonski begins with a look at skin's structure and functions and then tours its 300-million-year evolution, delving into such topics as how the skin reflects and affects emotions and how environmental conditions have influenced its colours.

Steinberg, Stephen. 1989. *The Ethnic Myth: Race, Ethnicity, and Class in America*, 2nd ed. Boston: Beacon Press. The author argues that cultural "traits" that are often considered "ethnic" may be more directly related to class, locality, and other social conditions. This text offers a caustic commentary on the conditions of recent immigrants and a penetrating reappraisal of the black underclass in the United States.

Taylor, Paul. 2003. *Race: A Philosophical Introduction*. Cambridge: Polity Press. This book is a philosophical introduction to the field of "race" theory and to a non-biological and situational notion of "race." The book explores the many complex issues surrounding the concepts of "race," "racial" identity, and "race" thinking. It addresses such topics as "mixed-race" identity, white supremacy, the relationship between the "race" concept and other social identity categories, and the impact of "race" thinking on our erotic and romantic lives.

Related Websites

Anti-Racism Resource Centre
www.anti-racism.ca
A resource hub for educators, employers, students, youth, and anyone looking for info on race, anti-racism, and anti-discrimination.

The Canadian Race Relations Foundation
www.crrf-fcrr.ca/en
An agency dedicated to eliminating racism and discrimination in Canada.

The Canadian Sociological Association
www.csa-scs.ca
The national organization of professional sociologists dedicated to advancing research, publication, and teaching of sociology.

Raising Race Conscious Children
www.raceconscious.org
A website devoted to helping adults talk about race with young children.

Ukrainian-Canadian Congress
www.ucc.ca
The Ukrainian-Canadian Congress is a national-level umbrella organization representing Ukrainian Canadians.

2 Theories of Ethnicity and "Race"

Learning Objectives

In this chapter you will learn that

- concepts play a central role in forming hypotheses about the social world. Social scientists use theories that contain sets of interrelated and structured concepts in order to examine and explain social phenomena.

- there exist numerous theories of ethnicity and "race." Such theories are parts of broad conceptual frameworks and approaches to a variety of social phenomena.

- primordialist theories are closely linked with socio-biology approaches to ethnicity and "race."

- there is a great divide between culturalist theories that emphasize the role of culture in analyzing ethnic and "racial" differences and inequalities and critical political economy approaches that tend to focus on the role of social structures.

- intersectional analyses and standpoint theory seek to connect ethnicity and "race" with social class and gender. Together, they constitute fundamental bases of social inequality.

- critical race theories, post-colonial analyses, and studies of "whiteness" are rooted in the colonial experience. They are closely linked with the conflict perspective and seek not only to analyze racism and social inequalities but also to redress them.

Introduction

In the early 1990s, Rodney King was a household name in North America. In March 1991, King was pulled over by police officers in Los Angeles for speeding. When King stopped his car and came out, four police officers manhandled him. In the ensuing altercation, he was Tasered twice before the four officers eventually took out their nightsticks and repeatedly beat and stomped on him. In the space of a few minutes, King was nearly beaten to death. After he was taken to a hospital, it took three surgeons five hours to operate on him to repair a fractured facial bone, a broken ankle, and numerous cuts and bruises.

The police beating of Rodney King was caught on tape by George Holliday, a Los Angeles resident who lived in the neighbourhood where the beating of King took place. The vicious beating shown in the 12-minute video, which has been described as the first ever "viral video," shocked the world and raised serious issues in the United States and elsewhere about police brutality and racism. The repeated airing of the video eventually led the Los Angeles County district attorney's office to charge the four officers with the use of excessive force. In April 1992, a jury acquitted three of the officers of the charges and could not agree on the verdict for the fourth. Within a couple of hours of the not guilty verdicts being announced, parts of South Central Los Angeles had become a war zone. In the following five days, 54 people died in the rioting and several thousand were injured. More than 7,000 fires were started and over 3,000 businesses were vandalized and/or looted culminating in nearly $1 billion losses. What became known as the Los Angeles Riots riveted North American society; indeed, several smaller riots occurred in other American cities, and in Toronto on Yonge Street.

During the height of the rioting, Rodney King spoke publicly to the media and issued his now-famous plea, asking for calm, understanding, and social harmony: "People, I just want to say, can we all get along? Can we get along?" (Linder, 2001).

King's simple but heartfelt question captures, in a nutshell, what sociologists who study "race" and ethnic relations are interested in. That is, they study how and why different groups of people get along, or do not get along. King's question has surprisingly complex answers. In Chapter 1, we suggested that in order to understand and explain social phenomena we need to start with concepts. In this chapter, we suggest that the next step is to link those concepts to theories.

Social scientists use theories in order to analyze, explain, and often predict social phenomena. The term *theory* is derived from the Greek word *theoria*, which means to look at something—to contemplate it and examine it methodically. Alas, social scientists have divergent and often conflicting views on what theories are or what they should be. Some treat theories simply as loose sets of working concepts in order to classify and order our observations about the social world; others insist that theories must use their sets of clearly defined, interrelated, and structured propositions and concepts etiologically, that is, to uncover the causal mechanisms behind social phenomena (Mason, 1986). In general, theories are based upon hypotheses and empirical evidence in order to enter social reality, define it, and understand it.

Part of the role of theory is to act upon the social world in order to change it, in order to, hopefully, improve it. Theories search for the multiple causes of social relations. Could one social theory explain all social phenomena? Or, is a special theory required for each discernible social phenomenon or problem? Are special theories needed to explain ethnic and "racial" phenomena, say, separate from other theories that deal with issues of class, gender, or other dimensions of social inequality? The short answer to these questions is no. As Mason points out, most theories of "race" and ethnic relations "are best conceived as particular instances of more general processes of group formation, boundary maintenance, [and] identity structuring" (Mason, 1986: 11). The same can be argued for processes of conflict based upon "race" and ethnicity. In this chapter we present a short summary of several important theories of "race" and ethnicity. We discuss some of the influential contemporary schools of thought in the field, including socio-biology, the Chicago School, cultural theory, political economy, intersectional analysis, critical race theory, post-colonialism, and "whiteness."

Primordialism and Socio-biology

Primordial approaches to the understanding of "race" and ethnic phenomenon have a seductive, common-sense appeal because they emphasize that there is something natural and inevitable about groups of people wanting to "stick together." Literally, to be primordial means to be original, forming or constituting a beginning; an origin. Primordial approaches conceptualize ethnicity and "race" as being discrete, ascriptive characteristics that are given at birth and which derive from objective biological or blood ties. Group members are believed to share a genetic heritage. They are derived directly from kinship and clan biological structures of society and, as such, ethnic and "racial" groups are more or less fixed, permanent, and immutable. Ethnicity comprises primordial affinities and attachments with which individuals are born (Isaacs, 1975). It represents deeply rooted, old sentiments and impulses for other members of your "own kind." Fellow group members are sought because of an inherent need for belonging together with other, similar individuals. People's genetic inheritance, it is argued, gives rise to spontaneous feelings or urges of emotional attachment (Fleras, 2012). It is natural for people to form bonds with their "own kind" since we are "wired" by human evolution and survival requirements. Biological ties within groups give rise to similar types of behaviours by individual group members.

The socio-biology perspective is one variant of a primordial approach and is best represented by Pierre van de Berghe. In his controversial 1981 work, *The Ethnic Phenomenon*, he conceives the origins of ethnic bonding as extensions of kinship group solidarity. Kinship groups, he argues, tend to act together for self-preservation. Ethnic groups can be seen as "extensions of the idiom of kinship" or "in-breeding super-families." They band together, co-operate, and provide mutual aid to their related members because of their common biological ancestry. Sticking together, so to speak, ensures the long-term survival and propagation of the group. This bonding protects and promotes the evolutionary survival of one's own ethnic kind (Fleras, 2012). Van den Berghe (1981) argues that in order to maximize their chances of survival, individuals resort to inclusive fitness; they breed within their own kind. This term comes from biology and refers to a "propensity" of organisms to "leave behind" as many of their genes as possible. They achieve this by breeding within the group. Humans tend to do the same. He suggests that the basic mechanism of ethnic solidarity is nepotism, which is the tendency to exhibit in-group bias, or to favour members of the same ethnic or "racial" group. Ethnic nepotism "advances commonality of genetic interest as a type of interest distinct from others, such as class interests" (van den Berghe, 1986: 250).

Analysts and government officials often explain many of the modern-day world's recent conflicts with reference to versions of primordial theories. Some defined the 1994 Rwandan genocide as a reflection of longstanding ancient "tribal" warfare grounded in deep-seated differences between Hutus and Tutsis (see Mamdani, 2001, for a critique). Similarly, the conflicts in former Yugoslavia in the 1990s are often explained as reflections of inherent mutual hatreds involving Serbs, Croats, and Bosnians (Harvey, 2000). This view of the conflicts was reflected in many Western government efforts to understand what was going on in the region, and to figure out how to stop the killing. According to Lawrence Eagleburger, secretary of state in the George H.W. Bush administration and former US ambassador to Yugoslavia,

> I have said this 38,000 times, and I have to say this to the people of this country as well. This tragedy is not something that can be settled from outside and it's about damn time that everybody understood that. Until Bosnians, Serbs, and Croats decide to stop killing each other, there is nothing the outside world can do about it. (cited in Harvey, 2000: 9)

As Harvey (2000: 42) explains, the view that "violence escalates as group affinities and securities are challenged" was a predominant theme in North American and European government thinking about the conflict at the time.

As a number of critics have pointed out (Mamdani, 2001; Harvey, 2000), there are both logical and empirical problems with primordial explanations of such conflicts. In many cases, groups involved in conflict have also lived together for long periods of time in relative peace and harmony. If inherent primordial differences are responsible for conflict, then it is not clear why those groups ever live peacefully together. Second, in many cases, groups in conflict are virtually indistinguishable. Though nationalist leaders who fan the flames of hatred often claim to know "the Other" when they see them, or hear them speak (Mamdani, 2001), the physical differences between groups of people in conflict are often minute, and blurry.

But what about culture? As we saw in Chapter 1, the concept of culture is central in any definition of ethnicity. Although van den Berghe recognizes that the emergence and formation of ethnic groups cannot be reduced to biology and genes alone, he sees them as cultural events "*linked* (like the rest of culture) to a genetic process through the flesh-and-blood humans who undergo them. Ethnicity always involves cultural *and* genetic boundaries of a *breeding population,* that is, a population bounded by the rule or practice of *endogamy*" (1986: 256, original emphasis).

Case Study Box 2.1 raises the issue of primordialism in the case of both LGBT and straight dating websites. Is racial or ethnic filtering on dating websites a confirmation of socio-biology, or is it a reflection of culturally and structurally conditioned preferences?

Case Study Box 2.1 Love, Lies, and What They Learned

There are millions of Americans seeking love on the Internet. Little do they know that teams of scientists are eagerly watching them trying to find it.

Like contemporary Margaret Meads, these scholars have gathered data from dating sites like Match.com, OkCupid, and Yahoo! Personals to study attraction, trust, deception—even the role of race and politics in prospective romance.

They have observed, for instance, that many daters would rather admit to being fat than liberal or conservative, that white people are reluctant to date outside their race and that there are ways to detect liars. Such findings spring from attempts to answer a broader question that has bedeviled humanity since Adam and Eve: how and why do people fall in love?

"There is relatively little data on dating, and most of what was out there in the literature about mate selection and relationship formation is based on US Census data," said Gerald A. Mendelsohn, a professor in the psychology department at the University of California, Berkeley.

His research involving more than one million online dating profiles was partly financed by a grant from the National Science Foundation. "This now gives an access to dating that we never really had before," he said. (Collectively, the major dating sites had more than 593 million visits in the United States last month, according to the Internet tracking firm Experian Hitwise.)

Andrew T. Fiore, a data scientist at Facebook and a former visiting assistant professor at Michigan State University, said that, unlike laboratory studies, "online dating provides an ecologically valid or true-to-life context for examining the risks, uncertainties and rewards of initiating real relationships with real people at an unprecedented scale."

"As more and more of life happens online, it's less and less the case that online is a vacuum," he added. "It is life."

Of the romantic partnerships formed in the United States between 2007 and 2009, 21 per cent of heterosexual couples and 61 per cent of same-sex couples met online, according to a study by Michael J. Rosenfeld, an associate professor of sociology at Stanford. . . . Dating sites and academics have gotten cozy before; the biological anthropologist Helen Fisher of Rutgers, for example, is Chemistry.com's chief scientific adviser, and she helped develop the site, a sister site to Match.com.

But scholars are also pursuing academic research using anonymous profile content given to them as a professional courtesy by dating sites. Often the researchers supplement that with surveys and in-person interviews by recruiting online daters through advertisements on campuses, in newspapers and on Web sites like Craigslist.

Here's some of what they have learned. . . .

Guess Who's Not Coming to Dinner

"Stick to your own kind," goes the *West Side Story* refrain, a phenomenon that sociologists call homophily: love of the same. And they have observed this among online daters. But here is what they did not expect to discover: a very high rate of same-ethnicity dating.

"One of the theories of how the Internet might affect dating is that it might erode the tendency of people to mate with people like themselves," said Professor Rosenfeld of Stanford. "I really expected there to be more interracial relationships for meeting online. And it wasn't true."

Research on a major dating site between February 2009 and February 2010 by Professor Mendelsohn and his colleagues shows that more than 80 per cent of the contacts initiated by white members were to other white members, and only 3 per cent to black members. Black members were less rigid: they were 10 times more likely to contact whites than whites were to contact blacks.

"What you've got is basically the reluctance of white Americans to date and to contact members of other ethnicities, particularly African-Americans," he said. "We are nowhere near the post-racial age."

Professor Mendelsohn set out to study relationship formation, not ethnicity. Yet along the way he found that white more than black, women more than men, and old more than young prefer a same-race partner.

Some people indicated that they were willing to date different ethnicities, but they didn't. "What people say they want in a mate and what qualities they actually seek don't tend to correspond," said Coye Cheshire, an associate professor at the School of Information at Berkeley who has studied this with Mr Fiore, Professor Mendelsohn, and Lindsay Shaw Taylor, a member of the school's self, identity, and relationships lab.

Culture and Assimilation

Sociologists at the University of Chicago, writing in the early twentieth century, understood well the broad historical context of immigration and colonization that helped shape the United States. They studied the processes by which different ethnic groups came into contact with each other, the forms their contacts assumed, the nature of their competition, and the processes by which groups either maintained or lost their ethnic characteristics. Two sociologists of the Chicago School are especially important: W.I. Thomas, whom you may know from his famous dictum, "What is real in people's minds is real in its consequences," and Robert Park, who developed the theory of "the race relations cycle."

Thomas was influential in introducing the study of "race" and ethnicity to sociology (Parsons, 1991), studying the adjustment of recent immigrants to American society. With Florian Znaniecki, he published *The Polish Peasant in Europe and America*, a five-volume study that analyzed the experiences of Polish peasants after they had left their homeland and immigrated to major US cities like Chicago. They theorized that there should be a change in the experiences of Polish peasants after they had left the rural community settings of their country to seek a better life in a more "advanced," complex, and competitive society like that of Chicago. In essence, they were studying transitions and adaptations from feudal agrarian to industrial capitalist settings. Logically, they expected a social *reorganization* on the part of the peasants. The family unit, both a unit of production and consumption and a source of solidarity and support back home, suffered greatly in the competitive capitalist and individualistic environment of the tough Chicago labour markets. With few or no skills, the Polish peasant was competing not only with members of other ethnic communities but also with their ethnic compatriots for jobs, higher wages, and better opportunities. This internal and external competition often led to community disorganization, despair, and disarray, all characteristics of advanced industrial societies. In addition, they found that in subsequent generations, the family form changed to a smaller, less supporting structure (Driedger, 1996: 18). The experiences of Polish peasants, as analyzed by Thomas and Znaniecki, were arguably not different from the experiences of thousands of Canadian immigrants at the time who came to our industrial centres of Toronto, Montreal, or Hamilton.

As pressures for the Americanization of immigrants increased, Thomas argued against the forced abandonment of ethnic cultures, languages, religions, or other bases of ethnic identity. He did not support immigrants' fusion into the American melting pot. Instead, and against the current of the time, he called for the mainte-nance of ethnic languages and press, identities, institutions, communities, and or-ganizations, tolerance of ethnic differences, and reconciliation. Driedger suggests that Thomas was among the first to preach cultural pluralism, although Thomas himself never used the term (1996: 19). We can detect in his work the early seeds of multiculturalism, a Canadian value we recognize with pride and often use to differentiate ourselves from our neighbours.

Robert Park had a different focus. He studied the seemingly more complex processes through which "racial" groups come into contact and interact. He had considerable experience working with black people in the American South and rep-resented the interaction of whites and blacks in terms of a cycle, his now famous "race relations cycle," which is also applied to ethnic relations. The cycle included several stages and two different routes but one outcome: assimilation, in which the subordinate minority groups assimilate into the dominant majority group. Initially, there is *contact* between the two groups, creating *competition* for access to and ac-quisition of scarce and valuable resources. This competition can lead either to *ac-commodation* and eventually *fusion/assimilation* or to *conflicts* that in turn lead to accommodation and then fusion/assimilation. Underlying the cycle is the tenet that the "new" culture emerging from the fusion is good for both and certainly good for the "nation." Fusion also implies social harmony, even equality. This, in short, is the melting-pot theory of ethnic and "race" relations in the US (Park, 1914).

Writing in the early 1960s, Milton Gordon, another Chicago School sociolo-gist, expanded on Park's analysis by suggesting that assimilation is a seven-stage process. His seven stages included (1) cultural or behavioural assimilation (accul-turation into the cultural patterns of the host society); (2) structural assimilation (large-scale entrance into primary group institutions of the host society like clubs and sports teams); (3) marital assimilation (large-scale intermarriage); (4) identificational assimilation (developing a sense of peoplehood with longer-settled residents of a society); (5) attitude receptional assimilation (the absence of prejudice on the part of the host society); (6) behaviour receptional assimilation (the absence of discrimination on the part of the host society); and (7) civic assimilation (the absence of conflicts over values and power) (Gordon, 1964: 71). Gordon differed from Park by arguing that a group's progression through the process was neither inevitable, nor linear. That is, some groups could get "stuck" at an early stage of assimilation and some groups could go through one stage before another.

Though not part of the Chicago School of sociology, psychologist Gordon Allport's **"contact hypothesis"** of prejudice shares some resemblance to theories of assimilation. Allport (1954) was careful to argue that mere contact between members of different groups was not enough to reduce prejudice. Instead, he suggested that prejudice between groups can be reduced only if certain conditions are present (Pettigrew, 1998). First, in situations where groups come into contact, they must have "equal group status." Employers and employees do not have common status, and so if one ethnic or "racial" group tends to employ another, this unequal status may not necessarily reduce prejudice when contact increases. Second, in order for contact to reduce prejudice, groups require an active, "goal-oriented" effort. This is, in part, why participation in sports is often a successful way to improve intergroup relations since sports teams have winning as a common goal. Third, the attainment of the common goal has to be dependent upon both groups. And, fourth, if supported by relevant institutional authorities, contact can reduce prejudice (Pettigrew, 1998).

Allport's (1954) hypothesis has been described as "one of the most long-lived and successful ideas in the history of social psychology" (Brown, 1995). Despite this highly favourable endorsement and its common sense appeal, the "contact hypothesis" is not without its problems. As Pettigrew (1998) argues, the hypothesis does not really specify how and why contact under these conditions reduces prejudice, and it does not explain if and how the effects of contact are generalized to other situations individuals find themselves in, or to the groups more generally.

Park's and Gordon's approaches to understanding assimilation have also been criticized on a number of counts. Regarding Park's model, critics have pointed out that he might have accurately described the process of assimilation for European immigrant groups in the US, but visible minority groups may not be going through the process the same way. Further, assimilation may not be the end point of the process; in some cases, groups can end up in long-lasting, irresolvable states of conflict. Gordon's model has been criticized for his too simplistic understanding of stage two of the process: structural assimilation. That is, some groups might be able to become assimilated into "secondary" levels of society, the workplace, and the political system, but may have little interaction with members of the dominant society in the more informal settings of primary group life.

For a number of years in the 1970s and 1980s, assimilation theories fell out of favour within social science circles in the US and Canada. Government policies related to immigrants and Aboriginal people in both countries were often guided by the idea of assimilation, which many academics criticized for its forced qualities. However, the work of Alejandro Portes, and Richard Alba and Victor Nee, have helped put the concept of assimilation back into the theoretical debates about how to explain ethnic and racial group interaction. Much of the debate was rekindled by the problem of how to explain differences in how the children of immigrants made out in American society and whether the retention of ethnic identities by the second generation holds them back and prevents their assimilation into society. Portes introduced the concept of **segmented assimilation** in order to capture the idea that the society immigrants and their children assimilate into is not itself homogeneous. Portes (1995) argued that three outcomes are possible for immigrant children: (1) they become assimilated to the dominant culture (measured by their economic success); (2) they are integrated into ethnic enclaves (measured by their retention of ethnic identity); and (3) lower–social class immigrant children may develop marginalized identities and positions in the labour market (see also Boyd in Kalbach and Kalbach, 2000: 140–1). Immigrant children with higher economic resources tend to follow the first path; those with low or no resources tend to fall within the other two. In the US, Portes (1995), Portes and Zhou (1993), and Zhou (1999), researching black, Chinese, and Hispanic inner-city youth, have shown that immigrant offspring of Caribbean descent may reject their parents' culture, which may emphasize education and hard work as mobility mechanisms; they tend to be absorbed into the inner-city racialized underclass and eventually end up living in poverty. They call this "segmented" or "truncated" assimilation (Portes and Zhou, 1993). In contrast, the offspring of Cuban and Chinese immigrants, who tend to emphasize both the preservation of ethnic identity and economic advancement, are more likely to succeed within the ethnic enclave, if not in the mainstream (Portes and Zhou, 1993; Portes, 1995). This, of course, depends on the size of the ethnic economic enclaves and their capacity to employ large numbers of immigrant children.

While their argument is persuasive, the pattern may not be general. As Alba and Nee (1999) have argued, the vast majority of immigrants and their offspring are found in the larger, non-ethnic economy, and youth experiences—cultural and economic—may not necessarily carry over into adulthood. Mary Waters (2000) has analyzed the experiences of Jamaican, Barbadian, Trinidadian, and Guyanese immigrants in New York and compared them to Irish and Italian immigrants of the turn of the twentieth century. She has also examined relationships and differences among and within American blacks and black Caribbean immigrants. She found that the Caribbean immigrants who resist "Americanization" are the most likely to succeed. By preserving their own cultural identity and by resisting the African-American label, they have done well in education and earnings. For example, when analyzing food service workers, she demonstrated that having a transnational or Caribbean identity helps them to adapt more easily to the American reality of racialization and racism. Thus, attachment to an ethnic identity is not necessarily a barrier to assimilation. One of the groups she analyzed, the "ethnically identified," emphasized their Caribbean roots in order to differentiate and distance themselves from black Americans. They were predominantly middle-class suburban and performed well in school. They strongly believed that "whites" treat them as Afro-Caribbean, which they perceived as better treatment than that meted out to "blacks." They also felt that their ethnic values provided them with more opportunities for success. Thus, resisting assimilation into some aspects of American culture, particularly the underclass culture, provides better opportunities to the second generation (Louie, 2004: 197). In fact, Louie (2004: 326–9) argues that in the US, "becoming American" is now associated with less economic success. Often, then, the retention of ethnic identity may promote rather than hinder socio-economic advancement and help immigrant groups to combat discrimination and racism.

In Canada, Boyd (2002) has shown that results for ethnic groups tend to vary but that "visible minority" youth from low-resource homes, especially lone-parent families, tend to be disadvantaged and display the potential of segmented assimilation. They are likely either to be found in the ethnic economic enclave or to experience downward social mobility (Kalbach and Kalbach, 2000: 151). Arguing along the lines of Porter's 1965 blocked mobility thesis (see Chapter 5), Kalbach and Kalbach (2000) maintain that ethnic connectedness impedes the educational and economic achievement of individuals. Using 1991 census data, they show that individuals "in the more traditional ethnoreligious groups, who exhibit their greater ethnic commitment or connectedness through greater use of their ethnic language in the home, tend to report lower levels of educational and economic-status attainment than those who are less ethnically connected" (Kalbach and Kalbach, 2000: 199–200). In addition, those who immigrated to Canada at less than 13 years of age tend to exhibit better educational and economic status attainment than those who came later. Despite these findings, the relationship between ethnic identity retention and economic advancement in Canada is still the subject of debate. It is not clear whether ethnic identity holds people back, or whether individuals retreat into their ethnic community when they face discrimination in the wider society.

Culture and Socio-economic Success

The sociological interest in assimilation has given rise to a related theoretical perspective—or school of thought—that is interested in explaining the relationship between culture and socio-economic success and achievement. Briefly restated, the argument within this larger framework goes as follows: ethnic and "racial" groups share common values, beliefs, sentiments, ideas, languages, historical memories, symbols, religions, historical leadership, a past, and often ecological territories. They have specific ways of responding to their external conditions that vary and are shaped by their own environment. In other words, they have a common culture. Culture, then, is the key to understanding behavioural differences. Moreover, if we want to explain their differential socio-economic achievements, we should look into their culture. Culture is the *explanans* (that which explains) rather than the *explicandum* (that which must be explained). Cultural values and biological characteristics affect the psychological composition of group members and produce, it is claimed, "differences in cognitive perception, mental aptitude, and logical reasoning" (Li, 1999: 10). In turn, these differences affect subsequent educational and economic achievements. As a result, some groups do better than others in school and in the labour market. As with the primordial approach discussed earlier, there is a common-sense appeal to the argument that culture explains why some groups do better than others. Many decades ago, Vlassis (1942), referring to Greek Canadians, argued that they have a "national character" moulded by the sea (presumably applicable even to those coming from rural areas of Greece who had never seen the sea before boarding the ship that brought them to Canada). Further, Greeks are "adventurous, endeavouring to marry within their own race," "desire to attain the full status of Canadian citizenship," "possess an innate respect for law and order," "have an innate proclivity for education," and are "thrifty and enterprising," "proud and independent, hard working, courageous, persevering, and usually successful in business (mostly restaurants, confectioneries, and hotels) despite the fact that they begin with very meagre resources and with no experience, and are characterized by individuality and exclusiveness" (1942: 7–25).

In the 1950s, Rosen (1956, 1959) studied the relative upward social mobility of six groups—Greeks, Jews, white Protestants, French Canadians, Italians, and blacks—and "found" that the first three groups had higher mobility rates than the latter three because of what he claimed were differences in achievement motivation, achievement values, and educational aspirations. In the 1960s, anthropologist Oscar Lewis (1959, 1966), in attempting to explain the persistence of poverty among certain groups, developed another variant of this argument: the *culture of poverty thesis*. Living in poverty over extended periods of time becomes a culture within which generations are nurtured and from which they cannot easily escape. Wagley and Harris (1959) used "adaptive capacity" as an explanatory device. According to this line of thinking, some groups are able to adapt to their new external conditions better and more readily and perform better in education and the labour market than others because their own cultural values prepared them to do so. They argued that the French-Canadian and Jewish cultures had higher adaptive capacity than those of Canadian Aboriginal people and blacks. Hence, the former groups enjoyed higher socio-economic status than the latter.

Also in the 1960s, in his well-known book *The Vertical Mosaic* (1965[2015]), John Porter could not resist the temptation to rely on cultural explanations as well, although he emphasized structural conditions in explaining income inequalities. He distinguished between **behavioural assimilation** (acquiring dominant group cultural values) and **structural assimilation** (integration of minorities into the economic, social, and political life of the country). He argued that ethnic affiliation was a determinant of social class membership and prevented the upward mobility of certain groups, partly because they had not *assimilated culturally* to the new conditions of capitalist development in Canada. This was his famous *blocked mobility thesis*.

Though less popular today than in the past, this kind of approach nonetheless remains important in debates about the relationship between ethnicity, "race," and social inequality. In Chapter 8, we discuss in more detail how this kind of approach is used today to explain why Aboriginal peoples continue to lag behind other Canadians in terms of socio-economic achievement. For the time being, though, it is useful to offer some critical comments on this approach.

One of the problems with Rosen's type of argument is that he did not examine or show differentials *within* the groups he studied. Did all Greeks score high on his scales? Did all French Canadians score low? Were there not any highly motivated Italians in his sample? How could we explain, based on culture alone, French Canadians with high educational credentials? Presumably, if all members of a group share the same culture and have the same achievement motivation, values, and educational aspirations, there should not be any differences *within* these groups. Cultural accounts, then, do not explain why, for example, the supposedly "commercial-minded" Greek Canadians also tend to be overrepresented in the working class and have earnings as low as and often lower than those of "visible minorities" (see Chapter 5). Despite the "affinity for hard work and socio-economic advancement" displayed by Greeks in Canada (Chimbos, 1980: 43), not all "competitive-minded" Greek Canadians necessarily win in the economic "game." As we show in Chapter 5, there are great variations in socio-economic achievement *within* ethnic groups.

Culture no doubt plays some role in the educational and earnings potential of ethnic groups. Within every culture there are powerful beliefs and ideas about the importance of education, wealth, prestige, and power. There also exist customs and other social practices that may be conducive to social and economic advancement. But again, not all members of ethnic groups share them—at least not equally. Even though they may be from the same objectively defined ethnic origin, individuals from different regions, generations, social classes, gender groups, or professions may relate differently to these beliefs, customs, and practices. Peter Li (1999: 10–13) outlines yet other flaws in cultural approaches. He argues there are too many unquestioned assumptions about culture and the linkage between culture and ethnicity. There is no simple correspondence between people, culture, and "nation." Ethnicity cannot be equated with culture; the link is tenuous at best (Li, 1988). Moreover, centuries-old processes of international migration and colonialism and the development of modern capitalism have resulted in cultural heterogeneity among and within social groups and nations (see also Wallerstein, 1979). There is no cultural homogeneity based on territory, no common culture, tradition, ancestry, and so on. People with claims to common origins do not necessarily share the same experiences or culture. Even in ethnically/"racially" homogeneous societies—if they ever really existed— there were cultural differences among different gender groups, social classes, age cohorts, regions, and so on. The values and beliefs, or symbolic culture, of immigrants, even if it is "compatible" with the dominant values of a host society, cannot alone explain why some groups do better than others or why some members of the same group do better than others. The material elements of culture, and the structural economic, political, and social conditions within which cultures are formed are constantly changing, and these structural conditions can also play a powerful role in shaping how well members of ethnic groups make out in a society. Finally, culture is not static, monolithic, uniform, or homogeneous. It is a set of social processes and practices; it is a dynamic response of socially constituted individuals to their *ever-changing* external conditions (both material and ideological), largely determined by pre-existing social conditions and structures. Culture needs to be explained; it cannot be a tautology—that which explains and must be explained at the same time (Valentine, 1968).

For example, in the US, challenging the contemporary American image of Asian Americans as the quintessential immigrant success story—a success often explained in cultural terms—Louie (2004) conducted extensive interviews with second-generation Chinese Americans attending Hunter College, a humble learning institution, and Columbia University, an elite Ivy League school. All of the Hunter respondents came from "urban enclaves" like Manhattan Chinatown and ethnically mixed neighbourhoods in Flushing and Brooklyn. Most respondents at Columbia grew up in middle-class suburbs. Louie found large within-group differences in both groups in terms of income, neighbourhood, and parents' occupation. She concluded that "race," gender, and class do matter in opportunities and choices. Though most Chinese immigrant families value higher education and see it as a necessary safeguard against potential "racial" discrimination, she found that class differences do indeed shape the students' different paths to university education. Students whose parents had graduate degrees from elite universities back home or advanced degrees in America; whose parents had worked as engineers, doctors, or lawyers; and whose parents had houses in gated communities were more likely to attend the Ivy League school. Students whose parents had only grade-school education back home, had to work long hours in ethnic restaurants or in garment factories, and could only afford to rent apartments in ghettoized neighbourhoods went to tough schools that were "a waste of time" or changed schools frequently, often struggled academically, and witnessed their siblings and friends drop out of school, end up in jail, or die.

Conflict Theory and Political Economy

Conflict theory and the perspective of political economy constitutes another significant theoretical approach to issues of ethnicity and "race." Political economy analyses have emerged in order to explain both the historical development of the terms *ethnicity* and *"race"* and the social inequalities among and within such social groups (Cox, 1948; Solomos, 1986). The political economy perspective is a wide and varied corpus of literature that tends to share the following characteristics: (a) it tends to be rooted in the conflict theories of Marx and Weber and their contemporary variations and proponents; (b) as such, it focuses on the study of differential allocation of economic, political, and ideological power among individuals and groups in society; (c) in turn, it examines social relations based on the ownership and control of private property, as well as the historical development and manifold ideological and social manifestations and/or embodiments of these social relations; and (d) its approaches have as a central premise that people, in their relations to the means and objects of their labour and in the processes of the production and reproduction of their daily lives, engage in meaningful social action and practices. Political economy is fundamentally concerned with social change.

The overall perspective begins with the tenet that individuals belong to inherited social structures that enable but also constrain their social actions. These structures include those built on the social relations of class, gender, "race"/ethnicity, age, sexual preference, physical ability, and mental health/illness. Societies are characterized by the differential distribution of property, power, and other resources, both natural and sociopolitical. Who owns and controls what, when, why, and how are central concerns of critical political economy (Satzewich, 1999: 314). Analysis of intergenerational endowment of these resources is also imperative to the understanding of relations of social inequality. To paraphrase Marx, individuals are born into a web of unequal social relations, inherited from the past and beyond their immediate control at least until they understand them and try to change them. Although these social relations are malleable, it takes concerted social action—social praxis—to bring about social change.

In general the political economy approach perceives "race" and ethnicity as relational concepts. Goldberg argues that "race" (and, we argue, ethnicity as well) has been used as social status both in the Weberian sense and in the Marxist sense. As status, it is an

> index of social standing or rank reflected in terms of criteria like wealth, education, style of life, linguistic capacity, residential location, consumptive capacity, or having or lacking respect. Status has to do with one's ranking in a social system *relative to the position of others* [emphasis added], where the ranking involves criterial complex of self-conception and (de)valuations of others. Those who are conceived as "acting white" will be considered "white." (1993: 69)

At least historically, "race" and ethnicity have been defined as and often overlapped with class—class being both a fundamental economic relationship between groups and a structural condition within which these relations take place. The social composition of dominant classes corresponds with the dominant "racial"/ethnic groups. Although "race"/ethnicity cannot be reduced to class, they are nevertheless connected to it. One of the issues that political economy theorists have had considerable interest in is the explanation of racism. Let us look in more detail at some of these explanations.

Racism, Capitalism, and Class Relations

Karl Marx had little to say about racism in his analysis of the origins of capitalism and of the way that capitalist societies operated. However, subsequent generations of political economists have devoted considerable attention to the issue of racism and ethnic antagonisms. Political economists tend to argue that people do not hate each other simply because the colour of their skin differs; rather, in situations of conflict, "racial" and ethnic symbols are used to represent "some other, more fundamental reality" (Du Bois, 1992[1935]; Bonacich, 1979: 19). What is this "other reality"? Many political economists argue that "race problems begin as labour problems" (Bolaria and Li, 1988: 7). Political economists argue that contacts between different groups of people are structured not simply by the "innocent" mixing of populations but rather by economic imperatives associated with trade, colonization, migration, and the search for production sites and labour power. These economically inspired contacts form an important part of the basis for racial hostility and racism.

Some early versions of political economy focused on the specific issue of the relationship between racism and slavery. Slavery emerged not because of the belief in the existence of a superior white "race" and inferior black but rather because of the need for cheap, unfree labour. The construction of racial ideologies served as a justification for the allocation of one group of people—Africans—to positions of unfree labour in the system (Du Bois, 1992[1935]). According to American sociologist Oliver Cromwell Cox,

> Sometimes, probably because of its very obviousness, it is not realized that the slave trade was simply a way of recruiting labour for the purpose of exploiting the great natural resources of America. This trade did not develop because Indians and Negroes were red and black ... but because they were the best workers to be found for the heavy labour in the mines and plantations across the Atlantic. (1948: 23)

For plantation owners and slave traders in search of ever-cheaper sources of labour, racism operated to dehumanize Africans. Racism served as a justification for their exploitation and for their unequal treatment. According to political economists, defining certain groups of people as biologically inferior is a useful justification for poor pay and poor treatment. W.E.B. Du Bois's (1998[1899]) study titled *The Philadelphia Negro* was one of the first research projects undertaken in the US to systematically document the patterns of racism and discrimination present not just in the southern United States but also in the north. He found that patterns of employment, wages, jobs, and housing reflected continuing patterns of racialized segregation. Novel for its time for not focusing on the supposed racial inferiority of the black population as the explanation for their poor socio-economic position, Du Bois blamed capitalism for the discrimination that existed in US society at the time. In a later work, Du Bois argued that

The espousal of the doctrine of Negro inferiority by the South was primarily because of economic motives and the inter-connected political urge necessary to support slave industry. . . . The south could say that the Negro, even when brought into modern civilization, could not be civilized, and that, therefore, he and the other colored peoples of the world were so far inferior to the whites that the white world had a right to rule mankind for their own selfish interests (1935: 39).

Ashley Montagu (1964: 50), in a slightly different version of this argument, contended that racism emerged just as serious moral and ethical questions were being raised about slavery—when calls for the abolition of slavery were starting to be made more regularly in the United States and Europe. According to Montagu,

It was only when voices began to make themselves heard against the inhuman traffic in slaves, and when these voices assumed the shape of influential men and organizations, that, on the defensive, the supporters of slavery were forced to look about them for reasons of a new kind to controvert the dangerous arguments of their opponents. (1964: 39)

Supporters of slavery, according to Montagu, latched onto the idea of "race" and propagated the idea that blacks and whites were inherently different in their mental and physical capacities and that Negroes were inferior to whites: "the idea of 'race' was, in fact, the deliberate creation of an exploiting class which was seeking to maintain and defend its privileges against what was profitably regarded as an inferior social caste" (Montagu, 1964: 50).

Obviously, racism did not end with the demise of slavery. Political economists used broadly similar arguments in order to understand more modern forms of racism. Although the context was different, the underlying forces that sustained racism were the same. For some political economists, racism was employed as a weapon in the super-exploitation of certain groups of workers and as a strategy developed by employers to divide and conquer the working class (Castles and Kosack, 1973). Racist ideas were propagated by capitalists as a way of creating artificial distinctions between different groups of workers. By perpetuating ideas of racial superiority and inferiority, capitalists were able to sow discontent within the working class, reduce the unity of workers, and, as a result, better control them. Racism, according to this approach, deflects workers' attention away from the true source of their socio-economic problems—the capitalist system—and instead encourages them to focus on each other as the source of their problems. Racism, in other words, is a red herring that workers and others have bought into. As described by Bolaria and Li,

Race provides a convenient basis for generating low-cost labour, and racial discrimination serves as an effective barrier in preventing non-white workers from moving away from undesirable jobs. . . . Advanced capitalist countries rely on immigration as a means to recruit and to regulate the supply of cheap labour. Within the flow of immigration to industrialized nations are non-white workers from ex-colonies, who are recruited as guest workers, refugees and illegal immigrants, in addition to being admitted as regular immigrants. Their tenuous status, partly resulting from the political and legal conditions under which these immigrants are admitted, makes them exceptionally vulnerable to exploitation. (1988: 36)

One of the problems with this argument is that there is little evidence that racism is a capitalist conspiracy. It also wrongly assumes that workers and the working-class movement are empty vessels that are then filled with capitalist-inspired ideology.

Other researchers within the political economy tradition have tried to address these problems by focusing on the other side of the capital/labour dynamic. They focus on the dynamics of class conflict, and the other culprit in the search for the origins and development of racism is the white working class (Bonacich 1972, 1976). In capitalist societies, racism and ethnic antagonism emerge out of the dynamics of the relationships between capitalist employers, higher-paid labour, and cheap labour. According to split labour market theory, ethnic and racial conflicts are rooted in differences in the price of labour (Bonacich, 1979: 19). Employers try to hire workers at the cheapest price possible. For historical reasons, workers who move from rural to urban areas or from other countries have often been prepared to offer their labour power for a price below that of native-born and more established workers. For reasons connected more to accidents of history than to biology, non-white people have played the role of cheap labour, while white workers have tended to be higher priced (Bonacich, 1979: 20). The existence of these low-wage workers constitutes a threat to the social and economic position of higher-priced workers because employers try to replace expensive labour with cheap labour. According to this theory, higher-priced workers seek to reduce competition by imposing restrictions on where and under what conditions lower-priced workers can work. Racial hostility and **exclusionary movements** arise and attempt to limit job opportunities for cheaper, usually "non-white," labour. Racism and ethnic prejudices are the by-products of these kinds of competitive labour market dynamics. Indeed, Du Bois (1999[1935]) early on recognized that the fate of poor whites, white workers, and black workers were intertwined so that if racism was not effectively challenged by the former two groups, all three would continue to live and work in degrading conditions (Taylor, 2008).

Although the split labour market has existed in a variety of forms and places, perhaps the most extreme form was evident in South Africa during the period of apartheid (1948–94). Apartheid was characterized by a strict segregation of "races" in all spheres of life—education, work, leisure, and place of residence. While the origins of the apartheid system are complex, it came about when white workers sought protection from the competition of lower-priced black workers and were able to convince the governing authorities and employers that it was in all white people's interest to maintain a strict separation of "races." In the employment sphere, apartheid policies guaranteed more prestigious and better-paid jobs to whites and also dictated highly discrepant wages between blacks and whites. The job reservation system meant that no black could advance above a white in the same occupational area, and in some cases blacks were completely excluded from certain occupations (Marger, 1997: 406). One of the consequences of this policy was the virtual elimination of the class of poor whites from South African society: apartheid was essentially a policy by which black people subsidized white wages and white lifestyles. Drawing on notions of biological and cultural superiority, many whites believed that because they constituted "the civilized, Christian race," it was their duty "to use their control of the state to prevent racial friction and racial bastardization by ensuring that the races would be separated from one another" (Thompson, 1985, quoted in Marger, 1997: 409). According to Bonacich, the racial ideologies that accompanied the system of apartheid were essentially justification for the unequal treatment that black Africans experienced at the hands of whites.

Canada has also seen versions of the split labour market (Makabe, 1981), though less extreme than in South Africa. Agnes Calliste has documented the formation and reproduction of a split labour market on Canadian railways in the early and mid-twentieth century. She argues that black men were confined to lower-paying jobs such as sleeping-car porter, while better-paying jobs such as sleeping-car conductor were reserved for white men. According to Calliste, white union members and employers collaborated to keep black men out of better-paying jobs on railways. Black workers were kept in their inferior positions because they were desperately poor and needed the work and because it was a sign of status among whites to be served by black people. Furthermore, because of the social distance that existed between white and black people in Canada at the time, white people could commit indiscretions on trains without fear of social repercussion (Calliste, 1987: 3).

Though more compelling than earlier versions of political economy's analysis of racism, split labour market theory is limited in its historical scope. While it is useful for understanding and analyzing forms of racism in the past, racially based forms of employment discrimination are now very difficult to create and enforce in countries like Canada, where both domestic and international human rights norms prevent the development of policies or practices that explicitly put one particular ethnic or racial group at a disadvantage. Indeed, according to Calliste (1987: 11), black workers used the 1953 Canada Fair Employment Practices Act to challenge the discriminatory practices of both railway unions and railway employers.

Political economy lite

Though traditional versions of political economy that draw deterministic connections between the interests of workers and/or capitalists and the maintenance of patterns of social inequality no longer seem suitable for explaining contemporary forms of racism, softer versions of political economy that focus on the broad links between the expression of racism and wider materially based class relations and social conflicts remain relevant to the contemporary world. Economically driven contacts between different groups of people and struggles over markets, jobs, housing, and other resources often produce tensions and hostility (Mitchell, 2004). For example, Peter Li (1998a) argues that the controversies that occasionally arise in large Canadian cities over the development of "ethnic malls" reflect underlying class dynamics and class-based resentments. In Markham, Ontario, the deputy mayor warned in 1995 that the growing concentration of Chinese people in the city and the growth of malls catering to the Chinese community were causing social tensions and contributing to an exodus of white people from the city. Among other things, the deputy mayor called for restrictions on non-English language signs in the city. According to Li (1998a, 147), the hostility directed toward Chinese businesses had little to do with primordial and supposed "natural" hostilities between white and Chinese residents. Instead, it mainly had to do with the success that Chinese business owners were experiencing in suburban shopping areas where other small businesses were unable to survive. Part of the hostility, then, reflected the fear and concern of white business owners that they might not be able to survive in a competitive and changing marketplace.

The recent debate in Vancouver about rising housing costs is another good example of how economic conditions, and competition over scarce resources, can contribute to racial tensions. Some argue that the recent increase in housing costs in the city is largely due to wealthy immigrants from China and Hong Kong buying properties at inflated prices and hence bidding up the prices for all types of accommodation in the city. Some, particularly in the real estate community that benefits directly from high-value sales, say that blaming Chinese immigrants for increasing property prices is racist. Others say that they are being muzzled by political correctness and are not able to express their concerns about impact of increasing foreign capital in the real estate market without being labelled as "racist" (McSheffrey, 2015).

From this perspective, racism is not simply an idea that floats free and independent of wider social relations and conflicts. Rather, racism constitutes one of the ways that individuals interpret and give meaning to their lives, to their experiences and relationships, and to the tensions and contradictions that they face in the everyday world. In other words, people use "race" or biological and cultural attributes of themselves and others to explain and provide meaning to events in a complex and changing world.

This approach allows us to take the issue of racism seriously but without necessarily prejudging either the motives for or the consequences of racism. If ideas about the biological and cultural superiority of groups of people are used to make sense of the world, then we need to understand the motives and perspectives of those who articulate those ideas (Dunk, 1991; Hier and Greenberg, 2002). We also need to recognize that there is no a priori social consequence associated with such ideas. Racism has a variety of consequences, and these consequences depend on context, the power that individuals and organizations have to impose their ideas on others, and the degree of resistance that groups of people can mount to racism.

Intersectional Analysis

Today, many researchers are proponents of the *integrationist* or *intersectional* approach (Stasiulis, 1990, 1999). This perspective recognizes the multifaceted nature of social inequality and seeks to understand and explain the dynamic interaction of class, gender, and ethnic/"racial" forms of domination and subordination, as well as the different ways in which each dimension is experienced by people—separately as well as through the other dimensions. It is claimed that although these dimensions are necessarily treated as analytically distinct, their conceptualization as interlocking, mutually determining, and reinforcing categories, as well as their interconnections, have now become central to social analysis (Fleras, 2012). Despite the disagreements on the meanings and significance of class, gender, and "race"/ ethnicity, the trio is the new mantra of Canadian social researchers, as Agnew has suggested (1996: 3). Researchers now advocate the need to take into account all three when examining social inequality. For example, some researchers in the qualitative tradition have mainly examined the experiences of immigrant women of "colour" and the way in which they experience racism, compared to those of non-immigrant women (Ralston, 1991; Agnew, 1996). The central argument of this approach is that "race"/ethnicity, along with class and gender, are bases affecting individual and/or group identity, life experiences, and position in society. Ralston (1991), interviewing immigrant women, has found that "race," class, and language are interconnected and their combination has a significant and negative impact on their everyday life. Class, gender, and "race" are bases of the "multiple jeopardies" that confront minorities. This combination is the cause of the differential work experiences of immigrant and non-immigrant women (1991: 131). Agnew (1996), interested in the feminist movement in Canada, examined the compounding effects of "race," class, and gender on the lives of immigrant women from Asia, Africa, and the Caribbean. She suggested that the trio provides different bases for the political mobilization of immigrant women, which is necessary for social *praxis* and social change.

There is a lack of consensus on which of these bases of social inequality has the greatest impact on individual or group identity, life experiences, or social position. Stasiulis (1990, 1999), for example, has suggested that some black feminists see "race" rather than gender as the primary basis of their oppression. Gender is seen as more important than "race" among white feminists. Marxist and neo-Marxist scholars see class as the primary basis of social inequality. Stasiulis has argued recently that the intersectional theorizing of class, gender, and "race"/ethnicity is by no means dominant within the white feminist tradition. References to differences among women along class and "race" lines are, according to Stasiulis, "token mention"; she urges researchers to avoid "race" and gender essentialism (see also Jhappan, 1996). Most of these approaches are guilty of ignoring one or more of the simultaneous and interlocking axes of "racial," class, and gender power within what Patricia Hill Collins (2000) calls the matrix of domination (see also Stasiulis, 1999: 348).

The main conceptual anchor for a new intersectional theorizing ought to be the understanding of the simultaneity of racism, sexism, and class exploitation and the fact that they are interrelated systems of privilege and oppression (Stasiulis, 1999: 349). As described by Hill Collins (2000), the matrix of domination means that at the individual, collective, and cultural level of a society, systems of oppression are interlocking such that patterns of privilege and disadvantage can operate in complex ways. For example, US president Barack Obama is subject to some of the same racism experienced by other African Americans. But his position as a male head of state of one of the most powerful nations on earth gives him certain privileges that other African Americans do not have access to, and an ability to deflect some of the racism he experiences.

Hill Collins (2000) takes the concept of matrix of domination one step further in her presentation of "standpoint theory," a perspective first developed by feminist theorists to understand the different ways that knowledge is produced by men and women (Smith, 1987). According to standpoint theorists (Wylie, 2003), a person's position in the structure of domination produces different kinds of experiences, which in turn provide the basis for different ways of knowing about the world. Writing about the experiences of black women in the United States, Hill Collins (2000) argues that the everyday experience of working as a domestic in a white household gives a woman not only a unique set of experiences but also a unique perspective on the world, and of the nature of power and privilege. Though there are tensions between individual and collective levels of experiences, Hill Collins (2000: 249) argues that "groups who share common placement in hierarchical power relations also share common experiences in such power relations. Shared angles of vision lead those in similar social locations to be predisposed to interpret in comparable fashion."

Critical Race Theory

Close to the critical political economy and intersectional analysis approaches, in terms of focus if not always in terms of method, is **critical race theory** (CRT). This diverse body of work focuses on "racial" inequalities in the distribution of social goods such as work, education and training, housing, health, daycare and other social services, the legal system, and policing (Kobayashi and Peak, 2000). As a result, it has a broader focus on inequalities in the economy, within the state, and within civil society. CRT criticizes liberal notions of objectivity, meritocracy, neutrality, and colour-blindness as questionable constructs, which, although they permeate government rhetoric (and often societal ideology), in practice tend to favour whites. "Race" saturates a wide variety of social practices, policies, ideology, and values, often in coded, non-racialized language. Methodologically, CRT is also interesting because it maintains that the personal stories and experiences of minorities constitute facts; they are not subjective or biased (Pizarro, 1998).

CRT emerged in the 1970s in the United States when anti-racist lawyers started questioning the legal system and the way it treated black defendants and inmates. They were concerned with "racial" justice. They recognized that, despite some nominal rights gains in the late 1960s, the US justice system of litigation was resistant to progressive changes in favour of minority populations. Racism had become subtler and the labyrinth of US jurisprudence tended to undermine the rights of subordinate groups. Progressive lawyers and scholars began to criticize and challenge the liberal notion of the so-called colour-blindness of the law, since, under the disguise of neutrality, the conservative judiciary of the country continued to rule against minorities.

In Canada, generally, lawyers do not invoke the "race card"; our system is also generally based on the "colour-blindness" of the law principle. Many law scholars of "colour" have expressed their discontent with and frustration about the tendency of Canadian courts not to analyze but to exclude the role that "race" and racism play in discourses, practices, and the structure of the Canadian legal system. This is slowly changing. Though there are debates about its effectiveness, section 718.2 of the Criminal Code of Canada now recognizes that a person's unique life circumstance of disadvantage should be taken into account when judges sentence or set bail for Aboriginal offenders. Referred to as Gladue reports, the legislation instructs that courts investigate and consider issues stemming from an individual's or their family's experience of residential school, child welfare removal, and physical or sexual abuse in order to help judges determine the appropriateness of punishment for Aboriginal offenders (Nishnawabe-Aski Legal Services, 2015). Aylward (1999) has argued that, although most of the time Canadian courts erase the "race" issue, in certain Canadian police-brutality and jury-selection cases, raising the "race question" in courts has often proven successful for minorities. As Aylward (1999) shows, the Supreme Court of Canada has been persuaded that a "reasonable person" (in a case involving a black judge) would not be "colour-blind" but would be aware of the prevalence of racism in Canadian society. Aylward calls for *praxis* (action): raising the "race" consciousness of the people who participate in the delivery of justice in Canada. This is a prerequisite for "racial" justice. The issue is not only to analyze how Canadian society has been organized along "racial" lines and has formed enduring hierarchies, but also to change it for the better (Foster, 2008).

Case Study Box 2.2 First Nations Representation on Ontario Juries: Report of the Independent Review Conducted by the Honourable Frank Iacobucci

Former Supreme Court Justice Frank Iacobucci was appointed by the Ontario government in 2011 to conduct an independent inquiry into First Nations representation on Ontario juries. In the course of his review, Justice Iacobucci travelled

continued

across the province to hear from First Nations about their experiences of the justice system in general, and of the jury selection process more specifically. Justice Iacobucci identified a number of factors that were responsible for First Nations underrepresentation on juries. Consistent with critical race theory, some of his findings focus on the role that racism, both historical and contemporary, plays in explaining why First Nations are underrepresented in this, and other, aspects of the justice system.

> One of the biggest challenges expressed by many First Nations leaders and people is with respect to the conflict that exists between First Nations' cultural values, laws, and ideologies regarding traditional approaches to conflict resolution, and the values and laws that underpin the Canadian justice system. The objective of the traditional First Nations' approach to justice is to re-attain harmony, balance, and healing with respect to a particular offence, rather than seeking retribution and punishment. First Nations observe the Canadian justice system as devoid of any reflection of their core principles or values, and view it as a foreign system that has been imposed upon them without their consent. . . .
>
> Unfortunately, the criminal justice system represents deep-rooted pain and oppression for many First Nations peoples. The system is perceived not only as a tool to subjugate traditional approaches to conflict resolution in favour of assimilation into the mainstream society, but also as a mechanism by which a myriad of historical wrongs have been perpetrated upon First Nations. Today, First Nations peoples see themselves either as spectators to or victims of the justice system, whereas historically they were direct participants in the resolution of conflict within their own communities. To be asked to participate in Canada's justice system is seen by many First Nations people as contributing to their own oppression and, therefore, repugnant. . . .
>
> First Nations people often spoke of the systemic discrimination that either they or their families have experienced within the justice system as it related to criminal justice or child welfare. Negative experiences of the criminal justice system, along with historic limitations on the rights of First Nations, have created negative perspectives and an intergenerational mistrust of the criminal justice system. Such perceptions, by implication, extend to participation in the jury process. First Nations people generally view the criminal justice system as working against them, rather than for them. It seems counterintuitive to them to participate in it. . . .
>
> I heard numerous tragic stories of First Nations individuals' experiences with the justice system at various levels, and what they clearly revealed were pervasive systemic problems with the way in which justice is delivered, and is seen to be delivered, to First Nations individuals. Many persons accused of crimes plead guilty to their offences, rather than electing trial, in order to have their charge resolved quickly but without appreciating the consequences of their decision. In fact, many First Nations individuals explained that they have never known a friend or family member who, when charged, proceeded to trial. Many of these accused persons believe they will not receive a fair trial owing to racist attitudes prevalent in the justice system, including those of jury members. . . .
>
> Because my review was not a formal witness hearing inquiry, I did not ascertain the truth of these allegations. Quite frankly, that is not relevant. Even if they are only perceptions, they are instructive, because to First Nations people those perceptions inform their opinion about the justice system and that is the relevant and important consideration.

Source: *First Nations Representation on Ontario Juries: Report of the Independent Review Conducted by the Honourable Frank Iacobucci*, February 2013, 54–5. © Queen's Printer for Ontario, 2013. Reproduced with permission.

Post-colonialism

In Chapter 1 we provided a short account of the dominant ideas about "race" and ethnicity that permeated European philosophical circles during the Age of the Enlightenment. You will recall that "Self" and "Other" in imperial Europe involved notions of superiority of European colonizers and inferiority of the colonized. Members of European nations (white people) were perceived as being civilized, rational, artistic, and free. People of "colour," on the other hand, were thought to be irrational savages that deserved enslavement. This ideology was crucial in the development of capitalism: natural resources in the colonies were plundered, local cultures were destroyed, and colonized people were exploited and enslaved. In the middle of the twentieth century various regions of the colonized world gained national independence—often through armed struggles—from imperialist European countries (e.g., Algeria, Angola, Vietnam). The period of colonialism was over by the early 1970s. Given, however, the European grip on the economic, political, and cultural life of the old colonies, an era of neocolonialism had emerged during which new local elites often collaborated with the old colonizers, and increasingly the US, in order to gain political and economic control of the newly formed countries (e.g., in Latin and Central America, Africa, the Middle East, and the Far East). At the same time, these elites ran their countries in ways that also served the political and economic interests of the old metropolitan centres, especially those of big multinational corporations.

During the formation of new independent nation states in the so-called Third World, local cultures were in a process of revitalization and "soul searching." Questions of national identity came to the fore. What did it mean to be Algerian, Indian, Vietnamese, or Brazilian in the post-colonial era? A number of intellectuals who had been involved in the struggle for independence became prominent figures in local politics as well as in the production of new discourses, primarily through art and literature, about the history of colonization and its effects on the oppressed. This intellectual movement is known as post-colonialism. Although as a body of work it is very diverse, post-colonial theory has a few common sources of inspiration: it tends to come from power approaches inspired by the writings of Foucault, post-structural deconstruction (e.g., Derrida and Barthes), and psychoanalytical theories (e.g., Lacan). It focuses on issues surrounding the historical legacy of racism, the reasons for the persistence of racism, and how and why new forms of racism arise in the relatively young independent states. Our aim here is not to provide a detailed account of post-colonial theories but, as far as "race"/ethnicity is concerned, to offer a basis for understanding recent theoretical developments and debates on the subject.

Central to this approach is the idea that post-colonial societies are searching for their own identities that ought to be "uncontaminated" by universalistic or Eurocentric concepts and images. Even after the colonizers physically left and the formerly colonized nations were liberated, the presence of the colonizer remained in various economic, political, and cultural forms. The economic, political, and social life of the new states might have changed considerably, but the "consciousness" of that change remained. Kicking the colonizers out was, in some ways, the easy part. Overcoming the colonizers' intellectual legacy has been much harder. Thus, post-colonialism is a continuous process of resistance to European hegemonic cultural ideas and practices (including definitions of Self and Other), and, at the same time, involves the reconstruction of the local and more authentic identities of the colonized. It therefore questions many complex issues in the newly formed nation-states such as the use and meaning of language (oral versus written) and discourses; the roles of men and women (feminist liberation); nationalism (should old cultures be replaced by a new "sense of country"?); and hybridism, the forced mixing of cultures (Ashcroft et al., 2006). In this process of interrogation (examining cultures through literature), the dichotomous and oppositional concept of Self and Other is central. Post-colonialism generates an oppositionality brought about by (resistance to) colonialism. It uses the relational concepts of colonizer and colonized, oppressor and oppressed, and it examines the relationship between the (culturally) changed and the changer, the One (Self) and the Other.

Many internationally acclaimed scholars are important figures in the post-colonial approach (see Ashcroft et al., 2006). Space considerations do not allow us a detailed account of their work, but two writers are particularly influential: Frantz Fanon (1961, 1967) and Edward Said (1978).

Said's work *Orientalism* (1978) was concerned with issues of culture and focused on the history of the West–East relationship. For Said, **Orientalism** (the Western academic and literary study of the Arabs) was a discourse and a powerful political tool in the hands of the West used to misrepresent Arab cultures. Christian Westerners congratulated their own cultures and were hostile toward the Muslim East. Orientalists misrepresented Arabs as uniform, brutish, and exotic curiosities. Arab culture was suspended in time and place, seen as eternal, unchanging, and incapable of self-definition, self-government, or "serious" culture. Much of this portrayal was in the vein of eighteenth-century Enlightenment writers. Orientalism exalted European intellectual superiority and culture by negatively judging Arab cultures. This was a long historical and *relational* process by which the West defined itself positively by constructing *the* Arab (Other). Said's work was influential in post-colonial studies because it provided a powerful critique of the Western "gaze," the way Europeans looked, authoritatively, down upon Arab cultures. Much of the ideology that informs Arab–Western relationships even today is, arguably, informed by the Orientalist tradition that Said criticized.

Frantz Fanon can be also considered a pioneer because he laid some of the theoretical foundations of subsequent post-colonial works and inspired anti-colonial liberation movements worldwide. He argued quite forcefully (pardon the pun) for the use of violence by the colonized against the colonizers; he believed that colonization itself was a violent process with very traumatic effects on the colonized. In particular, he argued that the language of the colonizers and the whole system of power it represented denigrated the indigenous cultures of the colonized in order to replace them with the hegemonic language and cultural practices of the imperialist centres. English and French, for example, became master languages, languages of force, replacing local, fading ones. Those natives who learn the language of the oppressor are rewarded for their collaboration; those who resist it are reduced to poverty and despair. The latter are, potentially, the revolutionary force that will send the colonizer home. Writing from a psychoanalytic perspective, Fanon attempted to explain the white/black relationship, arguing that colonialism had left black people with self-perception feelings of inadequacy and inferiority to whites. Blacks had become self-alienated; they had lost their original identity and culture. Even their existence—their definition as beings (ontology)—was a result of white domination, language, and culture. Blacks were torn between white culture and their own. He wrote:

> It is implicit that to speak is to exist absolutely for the other. The black man has two dimensions. One with his fellows, the other with the white man. A Negro behaves differently with another Negro. That this self-division is a direct result of colonialist subjugation is beyond question. . . . To speak means to be in a position to use a certain syntax, to grasp the morphology of this or that language, but it means above all to assume a culture, to support the weight of a civilization. . . . To speak a language is to take on a world, a culture. The Antilles Negro who wants to be white will be the whiter as he gains greater mastery of the cultural tool that language is. Rather more than a year ago in Lyon, I remember, in a lecture I had drawn a parallel between the Negro and European poetry, and a French acquaintance told me enthusiastically, "At the bottom you are a white man." The fact that I had been able to investigate so interesting a problem through the white man's language gave me honorary citizenship. (Fanon 1967: 17–18, 38)

"Whiteness"

Fanon's writings have had a significant impact on new generations of social scientists who are interested in linking issues of individual and collective identity with wider structural forces within society. Following Fanon's and others' writings about whiteness in the 1960s, the study of "white"/"black" (Self–Other) dichotomy has recently found many institutional homes in departments and disciplines in numerous universities in North America. Colleagues in departments of English, cultural studies, history, women's studies, geography, anthropology, and sociology, and in interdisciplinary programs examine the construction of inferior Others and its effects on minorities by focusing on the "white"/"black" dichotomy. This in turn has generated a significant amount of interest in "whiteness" as both a socially constructed identity, and as a condition that shapes the ways that urban environments are built and social relations are understood (Satzewich, 2007). Understanding "whiteness" as an identity that is both claimed by and imposed on groups of people tends to be an issue mainly of interest to historians (see, for example, Roediger, 1991). Much of the stimulus behind the development of this approach is grounded in the recognition that the current tendency to equate "whiteness" with European origin or ancestry masks a complex social and historical process of racialization. Omi and Winant (1986: 65), for instance, claim that the processes of class and racial formation in American political culture produced "the institutionalization of a racial order that drew a colour line *around* rather than *within* Europe." However, Jacobson (1998: 7) counters that, in the US between the 1840s and the 1920s, "it was not at all clear just where that line ultimately *would* be drawn." Many of the European groups that we now think of as white were far from being considered white as little as two or three generations ago. For much of the late nineteenth and early twentieth centuries, scholars, politicians, trade union leaders, captains of business, and members of the public in North America and Europe considered Europe to be made up of a plurality of "races" that were inherently different from each other (Lorimer, 1978). Whether one analyzes the images and discourses of science, common sense, politics, or popular culture, there was considerably less certainty about the "racial" homogeneity of Europeans than there is now. Groups from the southern and eastern periphery of Europe were particularly prone to racialized othering, but so too were members of the working class and peasantry in various Western European countries (Guillaumin, 1995; Miles and Brown, 2003; Balibar and Wallerstein, 1991; Bonnett, 1998). The subsequent transformation of classes and nationalities of "Europeans" into "whites" was neither natural nor inevitable. Instead, it was the outcome of political, economic, and ideological struggles.

The second line of inquiry tends to examine whiteness as a condition. The condition of whiteness is variously referred to as "a gaze"—a "white" way of looking at the world—and as a "culture"—a "white" way of organizing social relations, government policies, and geographical spaces. Canadian geographers Audrey Kobayashi and Linda Peake argue that whiteness is a

> set of cultural practices and politics based upon ideological norms that are lived but unacknowledged. As a result, it "forecloses [a] broader examination of the present and thereby precludes action to transform it" (West, 1993: 39). Whiteness is indicated less by its explicit racism than by the fact that it ignores, or even denies, racist indications. It occupies central ground by deracializing and normalizing common events and beliefs, giving them legitimacy as part of a moral system depicted as natural and universal. . . . Geographically, human beings reciprocally shape and are shaped by their surrounding environments to produce landscapes

that conform similarly to ideals of beauty, utility, or harmony, values not immediately associated with "race" but predicated upon whitened cultural practices.
(2000: 394)

From this perspective one of the chief characteristics of the white gaze is a
refusal to recognize the reality of racism and a refusal on the part of white people
to recognize that they are disproportionate beneficiaries of the way the world is
organized, at least in the West. This is what Peggy McIntosh (1988) refers to as
"white privilege." Many aspects of society, including everything from the look of
certain public parks, neighbourhoods, and private houses (Mitchell, 2004) to law-
firm hiring practices and medical professional licensing procedures (Foster, 2008,
2009) are said to be infused with a dominant whiteness that provides white people
with an "invisible knapsack" of privileges they carry around wherever they go
(McIntosh, 1988).

The problematization of "whiteness" in recent scholarship about "race" and
racism has opened up new areas of inquiry. Whiteness studies are not, however, uncontroversial. The notion that whiteness is an objective condition that needs to be
overcome seems to be premised on a simplistic understanding of social inequality
and of advantage and disadvantage in capitalist societies. The conceptualization of
whiteness as an objective condition that carries with it a certain gaze, culture, and
set of aesthetics is further problematic because it homogenizes a group of people
with a diverse set of attitudes about racial issues. Individuals with purportedly
white skin tones or who are of European origin do not hold uniform beliefs about
minority- and racism-related issues, nor is it obvious that they have uniform preferences about urban designs, landscapes, or public spaces.

Summary

We began this chapter by posing a number of provocative questions about how to
understand the question of why different groups of people get along, or do not get
along, in Los Angeles. This question, we think, is intrinsically interesting. At the
same time, the questions are conceptually and theoretically loaded. Many of the
terms that we use to describe events in the world have both common-sense and
scientific meanings. Further, many of the explanations that social scientists offer
for events in the world seem to be part of common sense. A phrase like "racial conflict," though seemingly simple and obvious, is both theoretically and conceptually
loaded.

We have begun this book from the point of concepts and theory—not because we are necessarily fans of or cheerleaders for theory but because theories
and concepts are necessary for the analysis of social events and social processes.
They shape how we define, explain, and sometimes even try to predict events in
the world. In the remaining chapters, we offer a number of explanations of, debates

on, and approaches to a variety of contemporary and historical issues related to understanding immigration, Aboriginal relations, and broader patterns of "race" and ethnic relations in Canada.

As you can see from this chapter, there are many different theoretical approaches to the study of "race" and ethnicity in Canada. Some theories and approaches covered in this chapter are directly derived from broader traditions that you may already be familiar with, while others cut across two or more traditions. Political economy is most closely derived from, and aligned with, conflict theory. Approaches that focus on assimilation tend to cut across the theoretical traditions of symbolic interactionism and structural functionalism. Approaches that focus on the process of assimilation reflect symbolic interactionist concerns about identity formation and change while approaches that focus on the consequences of assimilation tend to reflect concerns about social stability and social integration. Studies of whiteness cut across conflict theory and symbolic interactionism. One strand of theorizing about whiteness focuses on how macro-level privileges are structured and maintained while another focuses on the micro-level privileges that accrue to whiteness. Intersectional theory, critical race theory, and post-colonialism arguably reflect the broader turn to post-modernism in the social sciences. These latter approaches tend to call into question Western and/or "white" institutions, practices, theories, and perspectives and focus on the multi-dimensional ways in which power relations and hegemony are configured and reconfigured. They also focus on other ways of seeing and knowing the world.

The influence and popularity of these perspectives depends, in part, on the topics being addressed and the broader values and assumptions of researchers. Socio-biological theories and approaches that focus on the existence of inherent biological or cultural differences as the drivers of "race" and ethnic relations tend to be favoured by more conservative-minded thinkers, while political economy, critical race theory, intersectional theory, standpoint theory, and post-colonialism tend to be favoured by those on the left. Alternatively, those interested in identity and assimilation might broadly be described as small "l" liberals for their emphasis on the ways in which various social conditions affect the identity choices that people make.

Questions for Critical Thought

1. Why is it that, historically, claims for nationhood and/or the formation of states have been made only by ethnic groups (not "racial" groups)? What is the relationship between ethnicity and nation-state? Does the latter help to forge the former?

2. Could culturalism be linked theoretically with primordialism and socio-biology? How? Read the culturalist arguments regarding the socio-economic performance of ethnic and "racial" groups and think of supporting or damning evidence from Canadian society.

3. How could primordialism and socio-biology explain increased rates of exogamy among human populations? If we adopt these social scientists' conceptualization of ethnic and

"racial" groups, can we make sense of Canadian cultural diversity? Conversely, why do certain ethnic groups exhibit high rates of endogamy? What could be considered advantages and disadvantages of endogamy?

4. In what ways is a political economy perspective useful in understanding patterns of "race" and ethnic relations in Canada today?

Debate Questions

1. W.I. Thomas and Robert Park were both Chicago School theorists. Compare and contrast their views on "race"/ethnicity in the United States. Which theorist is closer to the Canadian model of multiculturalism as you understand it, and why? Revisit this issue after you have read Chapter 7.

2. Does contact between groups reduce prejudice?

3. Read carefully the sections on critical race theories and critical political economy. What aspects of these theories are similar? Is critical race theory closer to culturalism or to political economy? Why?

4. Read carefully the section on intersectional analysis and attempt to determine which base of social inequality may be more important in influencing the socio-economic performance of ethnic groups: social class, gender, or "race"/ethnicity? Remember your answers and revisit the issue after reading Chapter 5.

Annotated Additional Readings

Back, Les, and John Solomos. 2009. *Theories of Race and Racism: A Reader*, 2nd edn. London: Routledge. This edited volume contains a great collection of essential sociological readings on theoretical and empirical issues of "race," both classical and contemporary.

Hill Collins, Patricia, and John Solomos, eds. 2010. *The SAGE Handbook of Race and Ethnic Studies*. Thousand Oaks, CA: SAGE. A collection of articles that examine various theoretical, conceptual, and empirical issues related to the study of "race" and ethnic relations.

Jenkins, Richard. 2008. *Rethinking Ethnicity*, 2nd edn. London: SAGE. A good overview of how ethnicity works in a variety of social and cultural contexts.

Rex, John. 1986. *Race and Ethnicity*. Milton Keynes, UK: Open University Press. This short volume situates "race" and ethnicity in sociological theory, examines their relations of social class, and discusses issues of colonialism and racism in capitalist metropoles.

van den Berghe, Pierre. 1981. *The Ethnic Phenomenon*. New York: Elsevier. The author interprets ethnic and "racial" phenomena in terms of the primordial origins of groups and the "selfishness of the genes." It is a controversial socio-biological argument. For this author, ethnicity and "race" are extensions of kinship elements. Ethnocentrism and racism are seen as extended forms of nepotism. Nepotism is supposedly grounded in the evolutionary "struggle of the genes" to perpetuate themselves.

Related Websites

Glossary of Political Economy Terms
www.auburn.edu/~johnspm/gloss
Created by Dr Paul M. Johnson of Auburn University, this website contains definitions for terms relevant to the study of political economy.

Marxism Internet Archive
www.marxists.org
This site contains most of the works of Karl Marx in electronic form. It includes the works of notable Marxists, historical archives, a library, search engines for a variety of subjects, and an encyclopedia.

Oxford Bibliographies: The Chicago School of Sociology
www.oxfordbibliographies.com/view/document/obo-9780199756384/obo-9780199756384-0007.xml
A site highlighting the approach to sociology and "race" and ethnic relations of the various members of the early Chicago School.

3

The Dynamics of Nation Building
French/English Relations, Aboriginal/Non-Aboriginal Relations, and Immigration in Historical Perspective

Learning Objectives

In this chapter, you will learn that

- the historical accommodations that English- and French-Canadian elites made in the late eighteenth and nineteenth centuries continue to have implications for contemporary Canadian society.

- Quebec society in the first half of the twentieth century was characterized by an ethnic division of labour in which "capital spoke English and workers spoke French."

- the provincial government in Quebec has control over its own immigration policy.

- Quebec's policy of immigrant integration is called *interculturalism*, whereas in the rest of Canada the policy is called *multiculturalism*.

- many of the contemporary issues faced by ethnic communities and Aboriginal peoples are rooted in historical processes and decisions made by policy-makers in the past.

- the historical patterns of Aboriginal/non-Aboriginal relations in Canada were structured by complex factors, including racism, economic expansion, and the process of state formation.

- decades-old treaties with Aboriginal peoples still have contemporary relevance.

- the federal government's policy of assimilation had a variety of negative consequences for Aboriginal peoples.

- various factors have shaped historical patterns of immigration control in Canada.

- a racialized hierarchy of desirability ranked potential immigrants to Canada until the 1960s.

- Canada abandoned "racial" discrimination in immigration policy in the 1960s, and this was the result of a combination of ideological, political, and economic factors.

- Census taking in Canada reflects a process of state formation where counting who lives in Canada reflects ideas about who belongs in the country and how resources ought to be distributed.

Introduction

In Canada, many of the issues and struggles that ethnic groups and Aboriginal peoples face today are rooted in the political and economic decisions, individual actions, and government policies and practices of many years ago. Let us take just three examples. First, 1,603 "specific claims" have been filed by various First Nations since 1970 against Indigenous and Northern Affairs Canada in Ottawa. Nearly 400 of those claims are still outstanding and under consideration by the federal government (Jimenez-Pardo, 2014: 1). These claims often revolve around decades-old disputes over unfilled treaty promises and the loss of reserve land through government negligence or malfeasance.

Second, growing support in Quebec for the Parti Québécois (PQ) in the late 1970s led to dramatic changes in the social and political landscape of Canada. In 1977, the PQ government of René Lévesque passed Bill 101, the Charter of the French Language. The legislation made French the official language of Quebec in the courts and in the legislature. It also restricted access to English-language schooling to children who had at least one parent educated in English in Quebec. The rationale for the charter was that francophones were a minority within both Canada and North America more generally and that active measures needed to be taken to protect the French language and culture in the province (Denis, 1999: 189). Three years later, the PQ government held a referendum, asking Quebeckers to give the provincial government a mandate to negotiate sovereignty-association—a form of separation—with the federal government. Even though 60 per cent of Quebeckers voted "no" in the 1980 referendum, the PQ nevertheless continued its push toward separation. A second referendum was held in 1995, with a thin majority voting against separation. As many as 120,000 English-speaking Quebeckers left the province between 1976 and 1986 (Rudin, 1993: 345) as a result of the passage of Bill 101 and the first referendum in 1980. Many of those who left Quebec moved to Toronto, as did the headquarters of many major Canadian corporations, such as Canada's largest insurance company at the time, Sun Life. Corporations moved their headquarters from Montreal to Toronto out of fear that, as anglophone-owned companies, they and their employees would face a hostile business climate in the province. These and other conflicts surrounding language and culture have long and complicated historical roots related to the founding of Canada. As we saw in the summer of 2009, plans to re-enact the battle at the Plains of Abraham in Quebec City were scuttled by the threat of violence. Some said this would "celebrate" the conquest of New France. Clearly, for those particularly conscious of their people's history, a historical defeat of their ancestors, even if it happened 250 years ago, touches a nerve.

Third, members of many ethnic communities in Canada have lobbied the federal government to apologize or provide compensation for events that occurred generations ago: Japanese Canadians successfully lobbied for redress over the internment of members of their community during the Second World War (Omatsu, 1992); Ukrainian Canadians have pressed for and won an apology and redress over the internment of Ukrainian Canadians during the First World War (Luciuk, 1994); Chinese Canadians secured an apology from Prime Minister Stephen Harper and compensation for the head tax that was imposed on Chinese immigrants to Canada between 1885 and 1923 (Li, 1998a); and Italian Canadians are lobbying for an apology and compensation for the internment of members of their community during the Second World War (Iacovetta and Ventresca, 2000). In 2016, Prime Minister Justin Trudeau apologized for the government's role in the *Komagata Maru* incident, which saw the forcible return to India in 1914 of a steamship carrying Indians who wanted to move to Canada.

For the purposes of this chapter, these examples illustrate the importance of a historical perspective in understanding contemporary issues and patterns of "race" and ethnic relations. They also point to the ways in which broader issues of "race" and ethnic relations have been central to Canadian nation building. The first section of this chapter focuses on French/English relations; the second focuses on broad patterns of Aboriginal/non-Aboriginal relations; the third focuses on historical patterns of immigration control; the fourth focuses on the role that census taking plays in the process of historical nation building.

French/English Relations in Historical Perspective

The "two-founding-nations" metaphor has been called into question as an accurate description of the historical forces that founded Canada. As critics have noted, a third nation, consisting of Aboriginal peoples, also played a significant part in nation building, as did immigrants from nations other than Britain and France. At the same time, however, it is clear that the French presence in Quebec and subsequent patterns of relationships between French and British settlers and their descendants have had a profound influence on the shape of Canada. These historical patterns continue to shape issues of "race" and ethnic relations in this country.

The Conquest

When the British won control of New France from France in 1763, they inherited both a problem and an opportunity. With France out of the way, Britain could further exploit the economic possibilities that the New World held; settlement and colonization would also be easier. But what would become of the some 70,000 French-speaking inhabitants of Quebec? French philosopher Voltaire quipped that New France was no big loss; it was nothing but "a few acres of snow." Much of the French-speaking political and economic elite left as a result of the British conquest but peasants, Catholic Church officials, and many large landowners stayed (Beaujot and McQuillan, 1982: 10–11). When the Quebec Act was passed by the British Parliament in 1774, British authorities were worried about an impending war with the American colonies. As a result, the British attempted to secure control over Quebec by legally recognizing the seigneurial system of landholding, by granting the Catholic Church the right to collect tithes, and by allowing French civil law to prevail. The hope was that these measures would satisfy the French-Canadian elite of landlords and Catholic Church representatives and that they would, in turn, act as agents of social control over the much larger French-Canadian peasantry. This approach met with success. American colonists tried to incite Canadians to join the struggle for independence from Britain, but few Canadians, including the newly conquered French Canadians, were willing to join their cause.

Racialized Understandings of French/English Relations

Britain lost the war with the American colonies in 1783, but it managed to retain control over the northern half of North America. The accommodations that the British made to French-Canadian society in 1774, however, came back to haunt them as a variety of conflicts arose within Quebec and between Quebec and the rest of Canada (Whitaker, 1993: 20–1). During the nineteenth and early twentieth centuries, conflicts between English and French populations of the country were commonly defined in racial terms. Lord Durham, who was sent by Britain to investigate the rebellions in Upper and Lower Canada in 1837, succinctly described the nature of "the problem." He stated that before he began his investigation,

> I expected to find a contest between a government and a people: [Instead] I found two nations warring in the bosom of a single state: I found a struggle, not of principles, but of races; and I perceived that it would be idle to attempt any amelioration of laws or institutions, until we could first succeed in terminating the deadly animosity that now separates the inhabitants of Lower Canada into the hostile divisions of French and English. (Durham, 1963: 22–3)

Lord Durham's construction of the "race" problem in Quebec did not put equal blame on both groups. Even though he thought that the French "race" had some quaintly redeeming qualities, he nevertheless saw them and their way of life as "hopelessly inferior" (Durham, 1963: 216). André Siegfried (1966), who wrote *The Race Question in Canada* nearly 60 years later, tended to spread the blame around. The problem was not the inferiority of the French "race" but rather the profound cultural and linguistic differences from the English "race."

Confederation to the Quiet Revolution

With Confederation in 1867, control over major economic institutions tended to remain in English hands. On the other hand, French was recognized as an official language in Quebec, and provincial governments, including that of Quebec, were given considerable authority over culture and education. The Catholic Church retained control over educational and religious matters and many other aspects of civil society. Political scientist Reginald Whitaker (1993: 22) described Quebec society in the first half of the twentieth century as one in which "capital speaks English and labour speaks French." By the early 1960s, however, the Catholic Church's control over civil society began to erode, and the old elite consensus began to break down. The 1960s witnessed a "Quiet Revolution" that involved dramatic changes to the social structure of the province. Some of those changes included secularization of the educational system, reform of the civil service, and nationalization of sectors of the Quebec economy. It also entailed a cultural and linguistic renaissance (Whitaker, 1993: 23–4).

The Quiet Revolution had a number of sources and a number of consequences (Whitaker, 1993). One consequence was growing support for more independence for the province of Quebec within Confederation. The majority "no" vote in the 1995 referendum on sovereignty settled the issue of separation for the time being. However, the spectre of another sovereignty referendum always seems to lurk in the background of provincial politics and of wider federal–provincial relations. Another consequence of the growing influence of the sovereignty movement in the 1970s has been Quebec's ability to negotiate successfully for more powers. This is important for understanding contemporary patterns of immigrant and "race"/ ethnic relations in at least two ways.

First, while provincial governments have always had some authority over matters related to immigration, in the postwar period, Quebec began to exert control over this policy field (Black and Hagen, 1993). In 1978, the Quebec government negotiated an agreement with the federal government that gave it some influence over immigration. By 1991, Quebec had its own immigration policy and control over the selection of independent immigrants as well as language training and adaptation programs for immigrants (Black and Hagen, 1993: 280). Two of the central aims of Quebec immigration policy are to increase the number of French-speaking immigrants in the province and to advance economic development. The Quebec government maintains overseas immigration offices in Paris, Hong Kong, and Mexico City for recruiting immigrants and processing applications.

Second, as we will discuss in more detail in Chapter 6, Quebec, like the rest of Canada, also has an official policy designed to facilitate the integration of newcomers to the province. Outside of Quebec, Canada's policy of immigrant integration is known as *multiculturalism*, but in Quebec the province's policy is termed "*interculturalism*." The differences between these policies are rooted, in part, in the unique historical position of the French language and culture in Canada.

Aboriginal/Non-Aboriginal Relations in Historical Perspective

Before Confederation, a number of European powers had interests in Canada, and those interests were varied. Some were attracted to the plentiful stocks of fish that could be found in the waters off the east coast of the country; others were interested in timber; others were interested in animal pelts. Eventually, among the European powers, the French and the English came to be the dominant contestants over Canada. Both were interested in the vast resources that the lands and waters contained, but they initially differed in how they pursued the exploitation and extraction of those resources.

In simple terms, the French initially chose to exploit the resources by encouraging the permanent settlement of French nationals on the land, mainly around the upper reaches of the St Lawrence River. The English, on the other hand, chose to exploit the resources through the establishment of fur-trading posts along major waterways and other bodies of water. These posts were staffed by English, Scottish, and Welsh labourers and traders. Initially, the settlement of colonists on the land was not a high priority for the English.

Early relationships between Aboriginal peoples and French and British settlers, government representatives, missionaries, and fur traders were complex. While Europeans did possess what would now be regarded as racist attitudes toward First Nations peoples, those attitudes and the policies based on them were moderated by two factors. First, various Aboriginal groups acted as important military allies of the French and the British (Allen, 1993). Second, there were relationships of mutual economic interdependence between Europeans and First Nations. Thus, negative attitudes and attempts at the social transformation of Aboriginal peoples were muted by the fact that these peoples were central to the success of the fur trade and the extraction of other resources from the environment and helped European powers establish military supremacy over North America.

Europeans had a more powerful material interest in treating Aboriginal peoples well during the fur-trade period than they did after the fur trade declined. Besides being important military allies, Aboriginal peoples were central to the reproduction of the social relations of the fur trade through their role as suppliers of food, clothing, and other goods that sustained European fur traders, through their supply of valuable trade commodities, and through the teaching of survival and transportation techniques that had been honed over the course of the centuries. The fact that Aboriginal peoples were not only useful military allies but also central to the operation of the fur trade created a strong incentive for Europeans to treat them with care, and perhaps even some grudging respect.

The Significance of the 1763 Royal Proclamation

When the English won the contest for Canada in 1763, British authorities had to articulate a more systematic policy for dealing with Aboriginal peoples in their newly consolidated territory. This policy, which some legal scholars regard as like a negotiated treaty (Borrows, 1997), was articulated in King George III's **Royal Proclamation of 1763**. Why should we pay attention to this proclamation? According to legal scholar John Borrows (1997: 169), the reason is that from 1763 to the present, the "principles derived from the Royal Proclamation have provided the procedural rules which govern the treaty-making enterprise in Canada" (see also St. Germain, 2001: 1). Thus, the proclamation shaped the kinds of strategies, structures, and options that subsequent government decision makers faced in their dealings with Aboriginal peoples. In turn, the decisions that followed from the principles laid out in the Royal Proclamation continue to carry social and political weight today.

For our purposes, there are three significant aspects to the Royal Proclamation. First, it recognized Aboriginal peoples' rights to land in "Indian territory" west of the Appalachian Mountains in the United States and in that part of Canada outside Rupert's Land and the old colony of Quebec (Frideres and Gadacz, 2012: 194; Borrows, 1997: 159–61). British subjects were not allowed to settle on or acquire Aboriginal lands. Second, the proclamation stated that no lands were to be taken from Aboriginal peoples without their consent. If land was to be given up by Aboriginal peoples, the authorities had to seek their agreement and there had to be compensation. Third, agreements to give up land could not be made between individual Aboriginal peoples and Europeans. Rather, land was to be surrendered to the government first, which could then keep it as Crown land, give it away, or sell it to someone else (Borrows, 1997: 159–60).

The principles outlined in the proclamation made sense in light of British priorities at the time. The British were concerned about the monetary cost of maintaining peace between colonists and Aboriginal peoples on the western frontier of European settlement. By outlawing European incursions on "Indian lands," the British hoped to reduce the potential for conflict on the frontier (St. Germain, 2001: 1–2). And while lands in eastern North America were already becoming filled with settlers, lands in western North America were still seen as important for the fur trade. As a result, the proclamation helped to prop up the fur trade by emphasizing that Aboriginal peoples should remain "undisturbed" on the lands of western North America so that they could continue to supply furs and other commodities to the traders.

The War of Independence undermined the status of the Royal Proclamation in the United States. The newly independent American government did not feel bound to this colonial document, and so it selectively rejected or maintained aspects of the proclamation that suited their interests. Thus, after 1776 the American approach to dealing with Aboriginal peoples began to depart from the British/Canadian approach (St. Germain, 2001: 2–3).

In Canada, as the fur trade declined and pressure for settlement grew, the guarantees contained in the Royal Proclamation eventually became more and more problematic for the authorities. Recognition of Aboriginal title to the land became a constraint on further westward expansion, economic development, and the process of state formation. The proclamation did, however, provide the broad outline of an approach to solving this problem, and the solution came in the form of land surrender treaties.

From the British/Canadian point of view, treaties were about how to extinguish Aboriginal peoples' title to the land in order to provide a legal basis for settlement, economic expansion, and the eventual formation of the Canadian nation. These motives were clearly articulated by the Canadian government, for example, in its approach to Treaty 8, which was agreed to by the Cree, Beaver, and Chipewyan nations and the government in 1899. As one government official explained, it is "Her [Majesty's] desire to open for settlement, immigration, trade, travel, mining, lumbering and such other purposes as to Her Majesty may seem meet" the lands in much of what is now northern Alberta, British Columbia, and the southern Northwest Territories (Canada, 1993: 291).

In Canada, land surrender treaties tended to take two forms. In southern Ontario much of the land was surrendered in exchange for one-time cash payments. For example, between 1790 and 1792, the Odawa and Potawatomi people sold the government some 5 million acres of land between Lake Erie and the Thames River for approximately 2,400 British pounds (Dickason, 1992: 190). But, on occasion, groups like the Six Nations of Grand River negotiated reserve land instead of cash payments.

As pressures for the settlement of western Canada grew following Confederation, the government's treaty-making strategy changed. The government felt that one-time cash payments were too costly and that smaller payments, to be made in perpetuity, would be a more economical way of acquiring Aboriginal lands. Beginning in 1871, the government embarked on an ambitious treaty-making process that, when concluded in 1930, covered northern Ontario, Manitoba, Saskatchewan, Alberta, and the present-day Northwest Territories. The 11 treaties that were negotiated between 1871 and 1930 are often referred to as "the numbered treaties." For a variety of reasons, treaties were not agreed to between government authorities and Aboriginal peoples in most of present-day British Columbia and the Yukon (see Figure 3.1).

While the specific terms of the treaties varied, they generally included the setting aside of reserve lands, cash annuities, and the provision of agricultural implements. For example, Treaty 8 provided for the creation of reserves, with one square

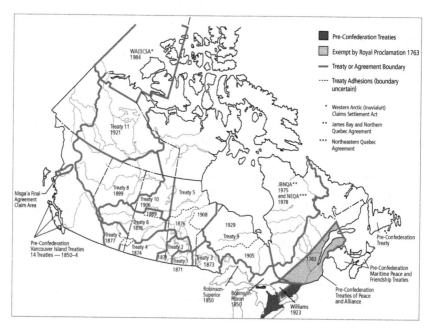

Figure 3.1 Historical Treaties of Canada

Source: Reproduced with the permission of Indigenous and Northern Affairs Canada.

mile allocated to each family of five. Chiefs were to receive $25 per year, while other band members would receive $5 each year in perpetuity. Chiefs were to receive a "suitable suit of clothing" every three years, and upon signing the treaty they received a medal and a flag (Canada, 1993: 292). Provisions were also made to supply hoes, spades, pitchforks, and other farm implements to bands that had taken up or were willing to take up farming.

The treaties also mentioned certain rights and obligations, which still have important implications today. For example, Treaty 6, which was agreed to in 1876 in southern Saskatchewan, contained a provision for a "medicine chest" at the Indian agent's office, while other treaties contained provisions for the supply of teachers in support of the education of Aboriginal children (Dickason, 1992: 282). Aboriginal people were also given the right to hunt, fish, and trap on Crown land.

The Continuing Relevance of Treaties

These decades-old treaties are still relevant to the understanding of contemporary patterns of Aboriginal/non-Aboriginal relations. First, Aboriginal peoples and the federal government currently disagree over the interpretation of the terms of the treaties. The federal government tends to favour narrow, literal interpretations of the obligations outlined in the treaties. Thus, in many reserve communities in western Canada, a "treaty day" is still held at which a $5 payment is made to each band member. First Nations, however, tend to see the treaties as living documents that need to be interpreted in light of changing times and social standards. For example, the commitment to provide teachers is interpreted by some First Nations leaders in western Canada as a long-term provision to support aspirations for the higher education of Aboriginal youth (Satzewich and Wotherspoon, 2000). This is why some claim that government support for post-secondary education is in fact a "treaty right."

Second, there have been instances of government negligence, malfeasance, or simple incompetence that resulted in Aboriginal communities not being given the amount of land they were entitled to as specified. In some cases, federal government officials deliberately under-counted the number of people in a band in order to reduce the size of the reserve allotment; in other cases, they were simply sloppy in arriving at a proper tally because they did not bother to include individuals who were away from the community at the time of the count. Some First Nations communities are currently seeking ways of addressing these kinds of historical wrongs or oversights through the courts.

Third, even though reserve lands were supposed to be provided to Aboriginal peoples in perpetuity, they were, on many occasions, coerced or tricked into giving up portions of their reserve land. In western Canada, government officials often responded positively to pressure from land-hungry farmers who wanted access to the good-quality land that fell within the boundaries of reserve communities (Carter, 1990: 185–8). These "surrenders" of portions of reserves are now the subject of legal dispute, with government representatives of the time accused of failing to act in a responsible manner to protect the interests of Aboriginal peoples and lands under their tutelage (Frideres and Gadacz, 2012: 194).

Fourth, treaties gave Aboriginal people the right of access to and the right to hunt and fish on Crown land. Currently, there are disputes about what the limits (if any) to those rights should be and whether they extend to the Métis and non-status Indians who did not agree to treaties with representatives of the federal government.

Assimilation Policy

From the government's perspective, treaties solved the problem of acquiring land so that the process of economic development and state formation could take place on a sound legal footing. However, treaties did not really resolve the question of how Aboriginal peoples were to be transformed into facsimiles of Europeans. That is, how could First Nations be transformed into a group of people with European values, attitudes, and orientations to life, work, and property? This is where government policies of assimilation came into play.

When the fur trade began to decline in the mid-1800s in western Canada and as pressure for settlement grew, Aboriginal peoples became more and more superfluous to economic development. While their skills and associated lifestyles were good for the fur trade, European authorities felt that their culture did not translate well when economic priorities shifted to the requirements of commercial agriculture and capitalist industry. Indeed, their presence as occupants of the land, along with their traditional lifestyles, constituted obstacles to socio-economic development. Thus, while European settlers, fur traders, missionaries, colonial administrators, and government officials may have always harboured racist and ethnocentric attitudes about Aboriginal peoples right from the days of early contact, only in the mid-nineteenth century do we really see the more systematic articulation of racist ideas and the emergence of government legislation and policies aimed at socially transforming Aboriginal peoples into something resembling white Euro-Canadians.

The titles of the mid-nineteenth-century pieces of legislation that were precursors to the 1876 Indian Act are telling indicators of the ways that those in power regarded Aboriginal peoples at the time. For instance, the 1857 Act for the Gradual Civilization of the Indian Tribes of Canada clearly suggested that they were in need of careful guidance to transform them from their uncivilized state. In not very subtle terms, the legislation implied that there was something faulty about Aboriginal peoples and their cultures but that these faults could be corrected through the mindful and benevolent actions of missionaries and the Canadian government.

Following on these assumptions, the federal government developed a variety of policies, strategies, and programs to transform Aboriginal people into Christians and to civilize and assimilate them. The government's resocialization strategies and techniques varied depending on the gender and age of the Aboriginal people. Among the many efforts undertaken to accomplish these ends from the late nineteenth century to the early 1960s, when the official rhetoric of the federal government changed from "assimilation" to "integration" (a subtle, and some say meaningless, difference), were policies and practices designed to eradicate traditional cultural and religious practices—including the residential school system. In 2015, Supreme Court Chief Justice Beverley McLachlin and Manitoba Justice Murray Sinclair both referred to government assimilation policies as a form of "cultural genocide" because those policies attempted to eradicate the identity and culture of Aboriginal peoples (Swartz, 2015).

The eradication of traditional cultural and religious practices was a major preoccupation of the Department of Indian Affairs between the late nineteenth and the mid-twentieth century (Pettipas, 1994; Backhouse, 1999). Egged on by missionaries offended by religious rituals involving body mutilation, the worship of non-Christian symbols and objects, and a seeming lack of respect for the notion of private property (Titley, 1986), ceremonies such as the sun dance on the Prairies and the potlatch on the British Columbia coast became objects of government surveillance and repression (Pettipas, 1994). An amendment to the Indian Act in 1895 made participating in or assisting in the organization of the following kinds of events indictable offences:

> Any Indian festival, dance, or other ceremony of which the giving away or paying or giving back of money, goods or articles of any sort forms a part, or is a feature, whether such gift of money, goods or articles takes place before, at, or after the celebration of the same, and every Indian or other person who engages or assists in any celebration or dance of which the wounding or mutilation of the dead or living body of any human being or animal forms a part or is a feature. (cited in Backhouse, 1999: 63)

Simple persuasion was not always successful in convincing Aboriginal people not to engage in these practices, and so jail terms and the denial of political positions and economic resources to participants were also used in the attempt to eradicate them (Backhouse, 1999; Satzewich and Mahood, 1994).

It is worth noting that Aboriginal peoples were not passive victims in these instances of state- and missionary-led repression. They continued to engage in the practices surreptitiously, and they modified them in ways to get around prohibitive legislation. Sometimes, in co-operation with whites in local communities (particularly merchants who wanted to include "exotic" Aboriginal dances at local country fairs), they challenged the legislation in the courts (Backhouse, 1999; Pettipas, 1994).

While prohibitions against religious and cultural practices were directed against Aboriginal adults, the government used other age-specific resocialization strategies. Industrial schools were established for Aboriginal children in eastern Canada in the 1840s, but what became known as the residential school system in

Canada was established following Nicholas Flood Davin's 1879 investigation into industrial school education in the United States. One of the features of the American model that impressed Davin was the use of a subcontracting arrangement in which the government gave per capita grants to churches to operate the schools (Titley, 1986: 75). Churches were eager to take on this responsibility because it gave them a source of revenue as well as a captive audience of potential new recruits to their version of Christianity.

The residential school system was premised on what sociologists see as a "classical" approach to resocialization. As is the case with resocialization in the military or in religious cults, government, religious, and educational officials recognized that the transformation of Aboriginal children was best accomplished in a setting where contact with their previous way of life was reduced to a minimum. That is, contact with friends, family, and previous customs and habits was severely curtailed. In taking children out of their homes and family environments, isolating them in schools often several hundred kilometres away from their communities, and discouraging contact between children, parents, and other relatives, the government and missionaries were attempting to minimize conflicting messages about appropriate forms of behaviour coming from home. Officials felt that this kind of educational environment would give them a relatively free hand to erase old patterns of culture, behaviour, and identity and to create in Aboriginal children new, European, and Christian attitudes, behaviours, and identities.

At the peak of the system in the 1930s and 1940s, approximately one-half of all Aboriginal children enrolled in school in Canada were enrolled in **residential schools** (Titley, 1986). The other children were enrolled in day schools and lived at home. Residential schools began to be phased out in the 1950s and 1960s.

Unfortunately, many of the children in the residential schools received more than just an education in the "3 Rs." Boys and girls in the schools also had to perform hard physical labour: chopping wood, washing clothes, and growing food. Some were subject to physical, emotional, and sexual abuse, and many First Nations individuals and communities continue to carry the scars associated with the residential school system. Given that they never experienced a normal family life while they were young, many individuals who attended residential schools feel that they now lack proper parenting skills (Schissel and Wotherspoon, 2003).

As with its approach to treaties, the strategies, policies, and practices that the government adopted in the past in an attempt to civilize and assimilate Aboriginal peoples continue to reverberate today. The residential schools were more often than not unsuccessful in their efforts at resocialization. Many children managed to retain their identities and attachments to their communities; others who went through the system eventually became leaders in their communities and pressed the federal government and churches for compensation for wrongs that were committed at the schools. A class-action lawsuit was won in 2006, which included compensation, an apology, and a truth-and-reconciliation process concluded in 2015. Those who opted out or who were not covered in the schools included in the lawsuit—including Newfoundland and Labrador schools, as well as day schools—are still awaiting trial as of this writing (Assembly of First Nations, 2006).

Immigration in Historical Perspective

After Confederation, economic and political elites in Canada understood that it was unrealistic to expect that the further development of capitalist industry and commercial agriculture could occur solely by using "assimilated" Aboriginal peoples as labourers and by encouraging them to become commercial farmers. As a result, elites realized that the non-Aboriginal population would have to increase dramatically in order for Canada to develop economically, socially, and politically.

There are two ways for a country to increase its population. One is to encourage its citizens to have more children. As can be seen in Figure 3.2, the other way to increase population in Canada has been through the promotion of immigration.

Understanding Immigration Control in the Early Twentieth Century

British elites in Canada realized from a fairly early date that individuals and families would have to be recruited from abroad in order to increase the size of the population and for Canada to prosper as a white settler society. The process of immigration, like the patterns of Aboriginal/non-Aboriginal relations, was therefore part of the process of state formation. Immigrants were not simply seen as economic agents whose main value was their contribution of brawn. Immigrants were also expected to become permanent settlers, to bring and/or form families, and to

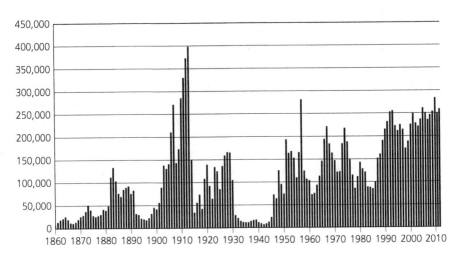

Figure 3.2 Canada, Permanent Residents, 1860 to 2013
Source: Canada. Citizenship and Immigration Canada. 2013.

eventually take up the rights and responsibilities of citizenship. As a result, there has always been an inherent tension within immigration policy—which is still with us today—between seeing and using immigrants as a convenient means of solving short-term labour market problems and seeing them as individuals and members of families and larger communities who will contribute to the reproduction of wider social and political relations in our society.

Over the years, a variety of competing social forces and ideologies have shaped the process of immigrant recruitment, selection, and control. Some employers wanted cheap labour, regardless of where it came from; workers feared competition for scarce jobs; social purity advocates focused on the moral qualities of potential immigrants; politicians thought about votes and winning elections; police forces were concerned about maintaining order and combatting real and imagined crime among immigrants; doctors worried about public health matters arising from immigration; government bureaucrats were concerned about how masses of newcomers could be educated, assimilated, and transformed into citizens; immigrants themselves wanted to escape poverty and oppressive political conditions, build new lives, and bring other family members to Canada.

Some commentators have focused on the racist nature of immigration control and immigration policy in the post-Confederation years (Henry and Tator, 2010). This focus is not wrong, but as intersectionality theory reminds us, broader considerations such as class, gender, health, and sexuality as well as political security also played important roles in regulating the flow of immigrants to Canada. These factors speak to the importance of looking at international migration in light of the process of state formation.

Class background, broadly defined, was an early focus of concern in post-Confederation immigration policy. For example, Canadian politicians, worried that Canada was being used by Britain as a dumping ground for its poor and unemployable surplus population, introduced legislation in 1879 to prevent the arrival of British paupers and destitute immigrants (Knowles, 1992: 47). Further, at the turn of the twentieth century, immigration officials were specifically interested in recruiting immigrants with agricultural backgrounds so that they could more easily take up homesteads on the Canadian prairies. At the same time, railroad, mining, and lumber companies were eager to recruit immigrants who were both tough and desperate enough to work in a variety of physically demanding jobs for relatively low pay (Avery, 1995: 30–1).

Women who were perceived to be of doubtful moral character were not permitted as immigrants. The **Immigration Act of 1910**, for example, prohibited the entry of "prostitutes and women and girls coming to Canada for any immoral purpose and pimps or persons living on the avails of prostitution . . . [and] persons who procure or attempt to bring into Canada prostitutes or women or girls for the purpose of prostitution or other immoral purpose" (Roberts, 1988: 12–13). For a time, the definition of coming to Canada for "immoral" purposes even extended to couples who had eloped to Canada (Roberts, 1988: 17).

Notions of physical and "mental" fitness also shaped immigration admissions. The 1910 Immigration Act prohibited the entry of (1) "the mentally defective," which included those defined as "idiots, imbeciles, feeble-minded, epileptics and the insane"; (2) "the diseased," which included those afflicted with "loathsome, contagious or infectious diseases"; and (3) "the physically defective," which included "the dumb, blind, or otherwise handicapped" (McLaren, 1990: 56).

Perceived political loyalty was also an important criterion of immigration control. In language that is strikingly similar to today's concerns about terrorism, a 1919 amendment to the Immigration Act defined the following behaviours as grounds for deportation from Canada:

> Every person who by word or act in Canada seeks to overthrow by force or violence the government of or constituted law and authority in the United Kingdom of Great Britain and Ireland, or Canada, any of the provinces of Canada, or the government of any other of His Majesty's dominions, colonies, possessions or dependencies, or advocates the assassination of any official of any of the said governments or of any foreign government, or who in Canada defends or suggests the unlawful destruction of property or by word or act creates or attempts to create any riot or public disorder in Canada, or who without lawful authority assumes any powers of government in Canada or in any part thereof, or who by common repute belongs to or is suspected of belonging to any secret society or organization which extorts money from or in any way attempts to blackmail, or who is a member of or affiliated with any organization entertaining or teaching disbelief in or opposition to organized government shall, for the purposes of the Act, be deemed to belong to the prohibited or undesirable classes, and shall be liable to deportation. (cited in Roberts, 1988: 19)

Assessments of those who constituted political threats to Canada changed depending on the circumstances. At times, people falling into the loosely defined category of "labour radicals" were barred from entry, and during the early postwar years, Canada was obsessed with preventing the arrival of Nazis, war criminals, communists, and communist sympathizers (Avery, 1995: 126–43).

"Race" and ethnicity were also critical. The first 60 years of the twentieth century saw sustained efforts by the government to control the immigration of people who were defined as unsuitable because of their "race," ethnicity, or country of origin. The social evaluation of immigrants was based on a racialized hierarchy of desirability in which some groups were seen as both good workers and desirable future citizens and should be encouraged to come; some were regarded as "racially" unsuitable for life in Canada and should be prevented from coming; and some were "in-between peoples" who, while perhaps posing certain short-term problems for Canada, could be admitted as a last resort. Within this context of **institutional racism**, British, white American, and northern European immigrants were at the top of the hierarchy of desirability. J.S. Woodsworth, an influential early twentieth-century commentator on immigration matters, once asked whether white Americans were "desirable settlers." Answering his own question, he had no doubts:

> Yes. Most of them are "well-to-do" when they come, and are bound to "make things go." The majority of them average up pretty well with our own Canadians. Of course, they are not British subjects, and some of them rather object to acknowledging allegiance to King Edward VII. But the King lives away in England. They soon become good Canadian citizens. Their children will be loyal British subjects. (Woodsworth, 1972: 65)

But not all people from "preferred" countries were given blanket free passes to enter. Canadian officials actively discouraged African Americans from moving north of the border (Shepard, 1991: 30–1). And, at times, a disadvantaged class background could trump the privileges of ethnicity/"race." Woodsworth, for example, had this to say about the English working class:

> Generally speaking, the Scotch, Irish and Welsh have done well. The greater number of failures have been among the English. This is due partly to a national characteristic which is at once a strength and a weakness—lack of adaptability. Someone has said that "the English are the least readily assimilated of the English-speaking nationalities." But the trouble has been largely with the *class* of immigrants who have come. Canada has needed farmers and labourers, and these should be resourceful and enterprising. England has sent us largely the failures of the cities. . . . [M]any of the immigrants are culls from English factories and shops. These cannot compete with other English-speaking people and often not with non-English, despite the latter's disadvantage in not knowing the language. (Woodsworth, 1972: 47–8; emphasis in original)

Eastern and southern Europeans were "in-between peoples." Even though broad racial distinctions marking "white" from "non-white" seem rather self-evident today, during the late nineteenth and early twentieth centuries it was not at all clear where the boundaries of "Europe"—and by implication "whiteness"—began and ended. In the United States and Canada (Roediger, 1991), assessments of the social desirability of European immigrants became more ambivalent and harsh as their origins approached the southern and eastern edges of Europe (Satzewich, 2000; Petryshyn, 1991).

Like other immigrants, immigrants from eastern and southern Europe had both their supporters and detractors. Railroad companies were keen on eastern European immigrants because they were a source of labour for railroad construction, and because they helped settle the West and provided a market for more rail traffic between eastern and western Canada. Among the better-known supporters of eastern European immigrants was Clifford Sifton, editor of *The Winnipeg Free Press* and Minister of the Interior in the early 1900s. Anxious to populate the Canadian west with farmers, Sifton saw in Eastern European men, women, and families a unique and seemingly "racial" ability to work hard on the land.

Others, however, were less than enamoured with the prospect of admitting immigrants from the southern and eastern fringes of Europe. They spoke unfamiliar languages, and some people were offended by their real and imagined customs and habits. Referring to immigrants from southern Europe, one Ontario member of Parliament stated rather bluntly in 1914 that "we do not want a nation of organ-grinders and banana sellers in this country" (McLaren, 1990: 49). At the other end of the scale of social desirability were non-European, non-white groups, who were defined as unable to assimilate and unsuitable as permanent settlers. Pre-war immigration legislation is full of examples of efforts to keep various "visible minority" groups out of the country and to limit the civil, political, and economic rights of those "undesirable" immigrants who did manage to find their way in and stay.

Chinese males were initially encouraged to come to Canada in the 1880s by labour-hungry contractors looking for cheap and disposable workers to help build the transcontinental railroad. Between 1880 and 1884, approximately 15,700 immigrants from China arrived in Canada, mainly in British Columbia, to work on railroad construction. These workers and those who came after them were soon caught in the crossfire between business-based pro-Chinese immigration sentiments and working-class-based anti-Chinese immigration sentiments. Nativists, labour unions, and other working-class organizations were concerned about competition in the labour market and the dilution of the white and British character of British Columbia and were opposed to capitalists who continued to want access to Chinese labour (Roy, 1989; Ward, 2002).

Caught between these competing forces, the government tried to resolve the conflict by keeping the door open to Chinese immigration while at the same creating obstacles that would reduce the rate of migration. The government needed to appear to be "doing something" to placate the politically influential anti-Chinese forces but at the same time did not want to alienate business owners in British Columbia and elsewhere by cutting off a valuable source of labour. Its preferred solution was the creation of the "**Chinese head tax**," which amounted to a bounty that Chinese male and female workers and family members had to pay the government when they arrived in Canada. The first head tax, introduced in 1885, was pegged at $50 per person. In 1900, the tax was increased to $100, and in 1903, it was raised to $500 per person. The head tax might have slowed the rate of immigration to Canada from China, but it did not stop it; indeed, the federal government collected approximately $23 million in revenues from the head tax when it was in effect (Li, 1998a: 42). By 1923, restrictionist forces were able to win the contest over Chinese migration, and the government introduced the Chinese Immigration Act, which barred further Chinese labour migration until after the Second World War (Li, 1998a: 89).

As with other immigrants, class background and gender were also important in regulating Chinese immigration to Canada. Chinese immigrants with wealth and capital who were interested in investing or establishing businesses in Canada were exempt from the head tax and the exclusionary provisions of the Chinese Immigration Act; even though few came, merchants of Chinese origin could still come to Canada after 1923, as could members of the diplomatic corps, students, and children born in Canada "to parents of Chinese race or descent" (Li, 1998a: 35).

Chinese women, on the other hand, were the object of special concern, entangled in contradictory discourses. Some government officials feared "racial inter-mixing." They felt that the absence of women within early Chinese communities in Canada would inevitably lead men within these communities to "debauch white women." Furthermore, intermarriage between Chinese men and white women would eventually lead to white "race" degeneration (Dua, 2004). Thus, some felt that the migration of women from China should be encouraged because Chinese men would form families with them, preventing future racial inter-mixing. At the same time, however, the presence of women from China was also seen as leading to the reproduction of "alien" cultures in Canada. Some Canadian immigration officials feared the creation of a second generation and tried to discourage the migration of Chinese women to Canada. The expectation was that once in Canada they would marry men of "their own kind," have children, "propagate the race" here, and undermine the status of Canada as a white settler society (Dua, 2004).

Immigrants from India were also the objects of concern during the early twentieth century. As with other waves of emigration at the time, poor peasants in India were looking for ways to escape from their dire circumstances at home, and Canada was seen as an attractive option. By 1908, a rather modest 5,000 immigrants from India had arrived in Canada. Upon their arrival, Indian immigrants became the object of widespread anti-immigration sentiments. However, like the Chinese, Indian immigrants had some champions within the business community of British Columbia. The owners of steamship companies made money from the fares they paid to reach Canada, and lumber and mining companies were always in search of cheaper and more exploitable sources of labour (Basran and Bolaria, 2003).

However, international political considerations introduced a wrinkle that made the regulation of Indian migration to Canada more complicated than it was for the Chinese. Whereas anti-Chinese legislation was blatantly "anti-Chinese," anti-Indian legislation was more subtle because of India's link with Canada through the British Empire. In theory, one of the official principles of the British Empire was that it "makes no distinction in favour of, or against any race or colour" (Bolaria and Li, 1988: 169). The Canadian government was concerned that blatantly anti-Indian immigration legislation would publicly embarrass the British and jeopardize their authority in India. As a result, it opted for legislation that appeared to be racially neutral but in fact was specifically designed to prevent the further migration of Indians to Canada. An order-in-council, passed on 9 May 1910, contained what is now known as "the continuous journey stipulation":

> From and after the date here of the landing in Canada shall be, and the same is hereby prohibited of any immigrants who have come to Canada otherwise than by continuous journey from the country of which they are natives or citizens and only through tickets purchased in the country or prepaid in Canada. (cited in Basran and Bolaria, 2003: 99)

On the surface, the wording of the order-in-council appeared to have nothing to do with Indian immigration. But despite the seemingly ethnically neutral language, its intent was to curtail further Indian migration to Canada. It was no coincidence that at the same time that the legislation was passed, the Canadian government persuaded Canadian steamship companies to stop making direct sailings between Canada and India. Thus, Indians who wanted to make the trip to Canada had to do so via Hong Kong, Japan, Hawaii, or some other location, which, according to the terms of the order-in-council, was not a continuous journey and was therefore not an allowable means of getting to Canada.

Indians saw through the discriminatory intention of the legislation and knew that it was specifically directed at them. In 1914, a Sikh businessman chartered a ship named *Komagata Maru* in Hong Kong to bring 376 Indian passengers to Canada, which was in direct contravention of the continuous journey stipulation (Basran and Bolaria, 2003: 100). On its arrival in Vancouver, the ship was refused permission to disembark its passengers. After a standoff that lasted for two months, the ship was escorted out of the harbour by the Canadian naval ship *Rainbow* and forced to return to India.

Other groups living in Canada were also targeted with restrictive policies by the federal government. They include Ukrainian Canadians who were interned during the First World War (Satzewich, 2002), Japanese Canadians who were interned and had their property confiscated during the Second World War (Sugiman, 2006), and Italian Canadians who were also interned during the Second World War (Iacovetta and Ventresca, 2000). These groups were targeted because they were perceived as "enemy aliens" and threats to the security of Canadian society during times of war (Principe, 2000).

As Case Study Box 3.1 discusses, these kinds of restrictive policies are now widely regarded as historical wrongs, and many groups who have been subjected to them have argued for combinations of apologies and compensation in order to correct those wrongs. The case study focuses on the debates within the Italian-Canadian community about the appropriateness of redress for some of their community members being interned during the Second World War.

Case Study Box 3.1 Italian Canadians as Enemy Aliens: Memories of World War II, Redress and Apology

I would say to [the Prime Minister]: Look it, you have an obligation to the children of internees. They suffered hardships because your underlings exploited the authority that they had by disallowing us assistance. If I didn't have my grandparents, either my mother would be washing floors or on the streets. One of the two. So I was lucky. So, what the problem is—I mean you don't even say you're sorry. Or thank you, or go to hell.—Attilio Girardi, son of internee Bruno Girardi, video interview, Columbus Centre Collection

I have more feelings towards people of Japanese descent [than Italian Canadians]. I figured they got a dirty deal when they were interned. Because to me it wasn't a selective internship for them. It was just everybody.—Rino Albanese, son of enemy alien Giovanni Albanese, video interview, Columbus Centre Collection

I would not expect to be compensated. I'm not of that school that thinks for every little thing that goes on you have to be compensated.—Nellie Cavell, enemy alien, Vancouver, video interview, Columbus Centre Collection

In as much as the soldiers have been honoured [in the Peace Tower in Ottawa], I think the people who have been falsely accused of something should be honoured in the same way. Their names should be written down as a memorial.—Sandy Corbo, granddaughter of internee Achille Corbo, Montreal, video interview, Columbus Centre Collection

Attempts at redress have been controversial among Italian Canadians. Some feel that Italian Canadians should receive financial compensation or, at the very least, be given a public apology by the prime minister in the House of Commons. Others believe that

Postwar Migration

While efforts were made after the Second World War to moderate some of the more discriminatory aspects of immigration policy, the basic philosophy behind immigration control remained the same: namely, that immigration to Canada was a privilege and not a right; that immigration needed to be carefully controlled; that the promotion of non-white immigration was not in the best long-term interests of the country; and that the economic benefits of immigration needed to be balanced by its "social" costs (Iacovetta, 1992). The philosophical framework for the early postwar immigration program was laid down in Prime Minister Mackenzie King's speech in the House of Commons in 1947:

> There will, I am sure, be general agreement with the view that the people of Canada do not wish, as a result of mass immigration, to make a fundamental alteration in the character of our population. Large scale immigration from the orient would change the fundamental composition of the Canadian population.

it is too late for an apology since the majority of internees and enemy aliens have passed away.

Redress initiatives began after World War II. Former internees in Hamilton and Montreal petitioned the Canadian government for lost wages, lost businesses, and emotional distress. They were unsuccessful.

In January 1990, the National Congress of Italian Canadians (NCIC) published a brief asking the federal government to compensate Italian internees wherever possible. They also requested that the government apologize to Italian Canadians for the treatment they received during the internment years. Later that year, Prime Minister Brian Mulroney expressed an apology at a luncheon held north of Toronto.

In Prime Minister Paul Martin's 2005 federal budget, the Canadian government set aside $25 million to address the claims of several communities seeking redress for internment, confiscation of property and businesses, and alienation. This was called the Acknowledgment, Commemoration and Education (ACE) Program. It was not the formal apology many had hoped for, nor would it provide compensation to the families affected. The fund was designated primarily for educational initiatives. When Prime Minister Stephen Harper's government took office in 2006, it replaced the ACE Program with the Community Historical Recognition Program (CHRP), which was established to formally distribute monies to community initiatives.

In 2009 Massimo Pacetti, Liberal MP for Saint Léonard-Saint Michel, introduced Bill C-302 in the House of Commons. The bill called for the creation of a foundation to develop educational materials on Italian-Canadian history—to be used in schools and cultural centres—and a commemorative stamp. Bill C-302 did not pass through the necessary stages to become law.

Source: www.italiancanadianww2.ca/theme/detail/redress_apology.

Any considerable oriental immigration would, moreover, be certain to give rise to social and economic problems of a character that might lead to serious difficulties in the field of international relations. The government, therefore, has not thought of making any change in immigration regulations that would have consequences of the kind. (Canada, 1947: 2644–6)

Admittedly, Canada did get rid of some of the more noxious and blatantly racist immigration legislation after the war, but many of the changes were largely symbolic. The Chinese Immigration Act was officially repealed in 1947, but the door still remained more or less closed through the application of other rules that restricted Asian migration to Canada more generally (Li, 1998a: 89–92). In a concession to Commonwealth solidarity, the continuous journey stipulation was repealed, and the door to immigration from India opened ever so slightly: in 1952, immigration from India was set at a quota of 150 per year, and five years later the quota was raised to 300 per year (Basran and Bolaria, 2003: 104). Small numbers of black women were allowed to enter Canada to work as domestics, typists, and nurses. Thus, despite the changes, the focus of the postwar immigration program remained on white immigrants from Europe and the United States.

Postwar immigration policy continued to give the Department of Citizenship and Immigration a tremendous degree of leeway to prevent the arrival of what it defined as undesirable and unassimilable immigrants. According to the **1952 Immigration Act**, the government could prohibit the entry of people for any of the following reasons:

1. nationality, citizenship, ethnic group, occupation, class, or geographical area of origin;
2. peculiar customs, habits, modes of life, or methods of holding property;
3. unsuitability having regard to the climatic, economic, social, industrial, educational, health or other conditions, or requirements existing temporarily or otherwise;
4. probable inability to become readily assimilated or to assume the duties and responsibilities of Canadian citizenship within a reasonable time after their admission. (Satzewich, 1991: 124–5)

If anything, the list is comprehensive in terms of the number of criteria for exclusion and for the flexibility it gave immigration officials to prevent the arrival of the "unsuitable immigrant." However, one variable notably absent from the list is "race." This was not accidental. In fact, in previous incarnations of the Immigration Act, "race" was a ground for exclusion. Why did it disappear from the books after the Second World War? Did it indicate that "race" did not matter in the selection of immigrants?

Part of the reason that the "race" category was taken out of the postwar act was that Canada and Canadians had gone to war in part to fight a regime that had committed terrible atrocities against Jews and others in the name of "race." Hitler and his National Socialist party had exterminated 6 million Jews because they believed that Jews were racially inferior. As more and more of the wartime atrocities flowing from racial ideology came to light in the immediate aftermath of the war, many countries around the world felt deeply uncomfortable that some of their own policies were based on the same underlying assumptions of Nazi racial doctrine. Thus, it was politically embarrassing for Canada to leave the category of "race" on the books as a ground for exclusion and risk unfavourable references and comparisons between Canada and the Nazi regime. By taking the "race" category out of the Immigration Act but leaving in a wide range of apparently non-racial grounds for possible exclusion, the 1952 Immigration Act gave the government and its officials a certain degree of flexibility and deniability when it came to public criticisms of immigration policy.

One area where this deniability came in handy was in the way that federal immigration officials dealt with the "problem" of immigration from the Caribbean. After the war, representatives of a number of Caribbean governments and

Canadian employer organizations lobbied the federal government to open the door to immigration from the Caribbean. Employers such as fruit and vegetable farmers in Ontario were having trouble finding and keeping European immigrants and Canadians as employees and became particularly interested in recruiting workers from the Caribbean. Newly independent Caribbean governments were also interested in finding opportunities for their nationals to migrate in order to ease unemployment problems and lobbied Canadian officials to permit more immigration from their countries (Satzewich, 1991: 148–9).

Federal government officials, however, were reluctant to admit black workers from the Caribbean, in part because of the old-style racist concerns that characterized pre-war immigration policy and control: namely, black people could not assimilate into life in a fast-paced, competitive, capitalist society; they were unsuited to climatic conditions in Canada; and their presence would cause the emergence of "race relations" problems. In 1952, the minister of immigration explained the position of his department on the issue of black migration to Canada:

> In light of experience it would be unrealistic to say that immigrants who have spent the greater part of their life in tropical countries become readily adapted to the Canadian mode of life which, to no small extent, is determined by climatic conditions. It is a matter of record that natives of such countries are more apt to break down in health than immigrants from countries where the climate is more akin to that of Canada. It is equally true that, generally speaking, persons from tropical countries find it more difficult to succeed in the highly competitive Canadian economy. (cited in Satzewich, 1991: 127)

What is interesting about the minister's statement was the disjuncture between the reality of immigration control, which was saturated by a concern over preserving the existing racial makeup of Canada, and the reluctance of Canadian government officials to admit publicly that "race" was a factor shaping whom they would allow into the country.

It took a decade and a half after the Second World War for the Canadian government to take the first genuine steps toward eliminating racist assumptions and practices from its immigrant admission criteria. In 1962 the federal government finally came clean and publicly admitted what most critics knew all along: that racist criteria were being used to select immigrants (Avery, 1995: 176). In 1967, further measures were taken to rationalize immigrant selection and make it fairer through the introduction of the points system. That system, which has evolved and changed over the years and which will be discussed in more detail in Chapter 4, involved the selection of immigrants on the basis of a combination of largely objective criteria such as age, educational background, English- and French-language abilities, and job skills and experience. It opened the door to a greater proportion of immigrants from Asia, Africa, the Caribbean, and South America coming to Canada.

Explaining the Deracialization of Immigration Control

Why were racist selection criteria publicly abandoned by the government in the mid-1960s? Some argue that the **deracialization of immigration** control in Canada was largely the initiative of liberal, enlightened, and forward-thinking bureaucrats in the immigration department who increasingly found racial discrimination distasteful (Hawkins, 1988). This bureaucrat-centred approach is problematic in that it assumes that there was a genuine interest on the part of these officials to eliminate racial discrimination in the early 1960s. Again, perception and reality collide: at the same time that the federal government was claiming it had eliminated racist selection criteria, racist attitudes within the bureaucracy continued to affect decision making about which groups should be let into the country and their conditions of entry (Satzewich, 1991).

A second, related explanation focuses on the liability that racial discrimination posed for Canada's international relations. After the war, Canada was emerging as a middle power, and Canadian officials were becoming increasingly involved in mediating international conflicts. The existence of a racially discriminatory immigration policy was an embarrassment and undermined the credibility of Canada in its efforts to act as a neutral international mediator and problem solver. Consequently, some argue that international political considerations played an important role in the public abandonment of racist immigrant selection criteria.

A third explanation focuses on the changing nature of the Canadian economy and changing assessments of where suitably qualified immigrants might come from in future. Some argue that the Canadian economy was undergoing a transformation from resource extraction to a more diverse industrial base. A resource extraction–based economy requires large numbers of relatively unskilled workers who do the heavy work of logging, mining, and the like. Technological innovations had reduced the demand for these kinds of workers, and white-collar employment became more and more important. Further, this argument suggests that European workers, particularly skilled workers, would be harder to recruit because there was growing competition for Europeans from countries like Australia and the United States and because the rising tide of economic prosperity in Europe made it more difficult to persuade them to leave in the first place. As a result, this argument suggests, the deracialization of immigration control was rooted not so much in ideological considerations but rather in hard-headed, practical economic considerations about the kind of workers the economy needed and a recognition that the search for that kind of worker would have to be global for the country to remain economically prosperous and competitive.

Ethnicity, "Race," and the Canadian Census

The three historical drivers of diversity outlined in this chapter touch on how that diversity is officially understood and counted. Though census taking is a seemingly innocuous process of counting how many people live in a country, it is also part of the ongoing process of state formation and reproduction. How a society counts its populations speaks not only to how the state recognizes who belongs but also how state resources are distributed.

The controversies in Canada about how to measure "race" and ethnicity in the census show that ethnicity and ethnic identity are not simply matters of individual choice, ancestry, and heritage but are also constructs shaped by larger political relationships and structures (Curtis, 2001). They also demonstrate that seemingly theoretical issues surrounding how concepts are defined are not important only to academics.

The Canadian census asks a number of questions in order to understand the family structure, economic position, demographic status, and "origins" of Canadians. The National Household Survey (NHS) contains questions about (among other things) education, marital status, age, occupation, income, linguistic ability, religion, nativity, Aboriginal origin, ethnic origin, and racial origin. In attempting to measure the ethnic origins of Canadians, the 2011 NHS asks the following question:

Q17. What were the ethnic or cultural origins of this person's ancestors?

An ancestor is usually more distant than a grandparent.

For example, Canadian, English, French, Chinese, East Indian, Italian, German, Scottish, Irish, Cree, Mi'kmaq, Salish, Métis, Inuit, Filipino, Dutch, Ukrainian, Polish, Portuguese, Greek, Korean, Vietnamese, Jamaican, Jewish, Lebanese, Salvadorean, Somali, Colombian, etc.

Specify as many origins as applicable using capital letters.

Starting with the 1981 census, individuals have been allowed to identify more than one ancestral origin, and, as a result, responses to the ethnic origin question have resulted in two categories of individuals: individuals who identify a single ethnic origin (for persons whose ancestors are of presumably the same origin) and individuals who identify themselves as having multiple origins (for persons acknowledging ancestors of different origins). Table 3.1 provides information on single and multiple ethnic origins of Canadians in 2011.

It is evident that Statistics Canada uses a definition of ethnicity based on a person's understanding of their "objective" ancestry or roots (Kordan, 2000). This definition does not take into account how individuals feel about their ancestry or their origins or how attached or connected they feel to their ethnicity. Nor does it measure what components of their ethnicity are important to them. As a result, the information in this table needs to be interpreted with care. For example, what does it mean when the census tells us that there are 1.25 million Ukrainians in Canada? At best, it means that 1.25 million Canadians identify their ethnic roots as Ukrainian. However, does this mean that there are 1.25 million "Ukrainians"

Table 3.1 Top 20 Ethnic Origins in Canada, 2011

Ethnic origins	Total responses	Single responses	Multiple responses
Total Population	32,852,320	19,036,295	13,816,025
Canadian	10,563,805	5,834,535	5,039,985
English	6,509,500	1,312,570	5,196,930
French	5,065,690	1,165,465	3,900,225
Scottish	4,714,970	544,440	4,170,530
Irish	4,544,870	506,445	4,038,425
German	3,203,330	608,520	2,594,805
Italian	1,488,425	700,845	787,580
Chinese	1,487,580	1,210,945	276,635
First Nations (North American Indian)	1,369,115	517,550	851,565
Ukrainian	1,251,170	276,055	975,110
East Indian	1,165,145	919,155	245,985
Dutch (Netherlands)	1,067,245	297,885	769,355
Polish	1,010,705	255,135	755,565
Filipino	662,600	506,545	156,060
British Isles N.I.E.*	576,030	128,090	447,945
Russian	550,520	107,300	443,200
Welsh	458,705	28,785	429,915
Norwegian	452,705	44,075	408,630
Metis	447,655	68,205	379,445
Portuguese	429,850	250,320	179,530

* not included elsewhere

Source: 2011 National Household Survey: Data Tables, Ethnic Origin", Statistics Canada, 2011 National Household Survey, Statistics Canada.

in Canada? Probably not. After all, not all Ukrainian-origin individuals currently think of themselves as Ukrainian, engage in activities that represent their Ukrainian origins, speak or understand Ukrainian, eat traditional Ukrainian food, follow traditional Ukrainian customs, or think that their Ukrainian origins are important to their lives in Canada today. Furthermore, only a small fraction of the individuals who identify their ancestry as Ukrainian belong to Ukrainian-Canadian ethnic organizations. Clearly, the Statistics Canada measure of ethnicity tells us nothing about the subjective attachments that individuals have to their ethnic ancestry (Isajiw, 1999: 47).

Another controversial aspect of the current ethnic origin question in the Canadian census is how to interpret the "Canadian" response to the question. Before "Canadian" was specifically identified as a legitimate response identity to the ethnic origin question in the 1996 census, few people in Canada identified their ethnic origin as Canadian. In 1991, just 4 per cent of individuals reported "Canadian" as their ethnic origin. However, in the 2001 census, more than 6.7 million individuals (23.7 per cent of the population) identified themselves as having a single Canadian origin. In the 2011 National Household Survey, almost 1 in 3 reported Canadian as a single ethnic origin (see Table 3.1).

Some dismiss the growth of the "Canadian" response between 1991 and 2006 as just a wording effect; that is, simply listing it as an option on the census questionnaire leads more people to mark it. As a result, it does not reflect any meaningful change in how Canadians identify their ancestry. On the other hand, some do consider this shift as a reflection of something more tangible than simply a recall or wording effect. Indeed, this has prompted some scholars to argue that Canadians are a newly emergent ethnic group not unlike other more traditional ethnic groups (Howard-Hassmann, 1999). As Howard-Hassmann (1999: 531) explains, English-speaking Canadians are an ethnic group because they share many customs, desires and ambitions, norms, and common values. In her view,

> An English-Canadian may be of any ethnic or racial background; he may have Ukrainian or Ghanaian rather than British-Protestant ancestry. While the parents' sense of place may be Ukraine or Ghana, the English-Canadians' sense of place will be his immediate environment, the town or city that he knows well enough to get around—the personal map of schools, shops, offices, relatives, friends. . . . His personal life history will have taken place in Canada, not abroad. Though he may eat foods different from other Canadians and worship at a mosque or a temple rather than a church, he will have attended the same schools, learned the same Canadian history and geography, and been present at the same lessons in family studies and sex education. (Howard-Hassmann, 1999: 531)

Not everyone agrees that the increasing proclivity on the part of Canadians to report "Canadian" as their ancestral roots represents the emergence of a new, pan-Canadian ethnicity that transcends old-world ethnicities and identities (Bourhis, 2003; Jedwab, 2003). In their analysis of the 1996 census, Boyd and Norris (2001) argue that it was mainly "old-stock" Canadians of British and French ancestry who were more likely to adopt "Canadian" as one of their ancestries. They also found that only 1 per cent of first-generation immigrants and 2 per cent of visible minorities reported "Canadian" as one of their ethnic origins. Furthermore, given that 54 per cent of Quebecers reported Canadian origins only on the census, some have suggested that the category conflates the French-Canadian notion of a *canadien* with the English-Canadian notion of an ethnic Canadian. In other words, the term *Canadian* in the census seems to mean different things to different people (Jedwab, 2003).

After a 55-year hiatus, the measurement of "racial origin" is once again part of the Canadian census. In 1951, the Canadian government stopped attempting to measure the racial origin of Canadians, in part because of the widespread discredit that the term "race" had after the Second World War (Bourhis, 2003: 17).

The introduction of a racial origin question in the Canadian census in 1996 was justified in part on the grounds that the information was needed to better monitor the success of policies like the federal government's employment equity policy. The aim of federal employment equity legislation, introduced in 1986, is to improve the employment opportunities of women, visible minorities, Aboriginal peoples, and the disabled. It seeks to correct the systemic discrimination that exists in the workplace by forcing federally regulated employers and federal contractors to develop employment equity plans and reports that outline the positive measures they intend to undertake to improve employment opportunities for the four target groups. In order to monitor whether the policy is successful, the government claims that it needs baseline data on racial origins so that it can track progress (Bourhis, 2003: 20).

The inclusion of a measure of "race" in the census has been controversial. Some argue that it contributes to the further reification of "race." As noted earlier, "race" is not a biologically real category but rather a socially constructed label used to describe and explain certain kinds of human difference. By attempting to measure the racial makeup of the Canadian population, Statistics Canada is helping to re-produce old and outmoded biologically based understandings of "race." Moreover, to the extent that the idea of fixed, biologically distinct "races" is a cornerstone of racist thinking, critics have suggested that the federal government is inadvertently promoting the racialization of public policy. As explained by Yehudi Webster, a professor of pan-African studies at California State University and author of *The Racialization of America* (1994), Statistics Canada's effort to measure the "racial" composition of the country is an "act of promiscuous stupidity":

> Politics are simply putting into law the racial concepts developed by 18th and 19th century racial theorists. The Canadian government clearly does not realize that when they put race in policy, they are helping to create the race consciousness that is the bane of American society. They are putting the stamp of officialdom on race con-sciousness. Canada will pay a heavy price down the road. (cited in Bourhis, 2003: 18)

Those who defend the collection of "race"-based statistics in the census, or in other areas such as the criminal justice system, argue that such data are necessary for the pursuit of social justice.

In 2011 the Conservatives scrapped the compulsory long-form census on the grounds that it was too intrusive and coercive in favour of a voluntary National Household Survey. The process leading up to the 2011 Canadian census created further controversy because the minority Conservative government made par-ticipation in the 2011 NHS—voluntary, rather than compulsory, as it was until the 2006 census. Many social researchers opposed this change and complained about possible data quality and historical comparability issues; Munir Sheikh, head of Statistics Canada, resigned over the Harper government's decision because he dis-agreed. The debate about changing the census was surprisingly controversial. The government found itself on the brink of collapse because so many Canadians were upset with how the census would record information. One of the first actions of the newly elected Liberal government in 2015 was the reintroduction of the compulsory aspect of the NHS.

In other countries, census taking is even more contested than it is here. In Nigeria, a census enumerator was killed and several others quit their jobs because of intimidation in the days leading up to the March 2006 census. Some ethnic group leaders in Nigeria boycotted the census, and leaders of other ethnic groups warned census takers not to even try to enumerate members of their community. Much of the controversy about the 2006 Nigerian census was not about the kinds of questions that were asked, but rather about the kinds of questions that were not asked. Specifically, the Nigerian census did not ask questions about an individual's ethnic origin or religious affiliation. Critics of the Nigerian census allege that this was a deliberate decision on the part of the federal government to maintain the traditional balance of power in the country and to continue to allocate resources disproportionately (Odunfa, 2006). The Nigerian constitution provides assurances that the "federal character" of the country must be reflected in every government appointment. According to Odunfa (2006: 2), "this means that the relative strengths of every ethnic and religious group must be taken into consideration in determining appointments in the civil service, the armed forces and political institutions." Muslim groups, who have traditionally been regarded as making up the majority of the population, were opposed to questions about ethnic origin and religion because the true facts about population size might undermine their claim to more state resources. On the other hand, Christian groups, traditionally regarded as a numerical minority but now believed to be a numerical majority, wanted to have ethnicity and religion included in the census in order to justify their claims for more resources. Without questions about ethnicity and religion, they regarded the census as a sham designed to maintain the unequal power relations between religious and ethnic groups in the country.

Just so you are not left with the impression that the absence of census questions about religion and ethnicity are peculiar to Nigerian society, you should also know that, by law, the American Census Bureau is not allowed to ask Americans about their religious affiliation, and the French government does not allow its census takers, private polling firms, or university researchers to conduct surveys that ask about a person's "race," ethnicity, or religion. Changes to the laws in these countries would no doubt generate heated debate there as well.

Summary

The recruitment of immigrants in the late nineteenth and early twentieth centuries and early measures developed to deal with the presence of Aboriginal peoples in Canada were part of the federal government's efforts to promote capitalist economic development, commercial farming, and the creation of a Canadian nation.

These economic and political priorities help set the wider context for the way that immigration and Aboriginal/non-Aboriginal relations in Canada were managed. The process of state formation involves more than the creation of political boundaries, government offices, and houses of parliament. It also involves the creation of citizens, national identities, and "populations" willing and able to be governed. As we have seen in this chapter, the creation of a governable population in this country was a complex matter. Different classes and groups of people had different ideas of who might constitute a good worker and a good citizen, what a good citizen looked like physically, and how individuals and groups who did not initially appear to possess the right qualities of citizenship might be able to acquire those qualities. Further, some groups were defined as racially unsuited to become part of the population and members of the emerging Canadian nation. As we will continue to show in later chapters, the policies and practices that emerged in this context produced outcomes that had powerful implications at the time and continue to reverberate today.

Questions for Critical Thought

1. How do Quebec's immigration and interculturalism policies differ from wider Canadian immigration and multiculturalism policies?

2. Why are the treaties agreed to by Aboriginal peoples and government officials many decades ago still relevant to understanding patterns of social conflict between Aboriginal/non-Aboriginal peoples today?

3. What factors have shaped historical patterns of immigration to Canada?

4. Critically assess the various explanations that have been offered for the deracialization of immigration control in the late 1960s.

Debate Questions

1. Are old treaties between the federal government and Aboriginal groups still relevant today? Why?

2. What could be some socio-economic and political reasons for immigration controls imposed in early twentieth-century Canada? Do you think that similar conditions may influence Canadian immigration policy in the near future? Why?

3. Consider carefully what has caused the shift of Canadian immigration sources from European to non-European countries, especially in the last three decades.

4. Is Canadian an ethnic category? Yes or no? Provide arguments for both sides, after reading carefully the arguments put forward by Howard-Hassmann and the subsequent critiques by Bourhis, Boyd and Norris, and Jedwab.

Annotated Additional Readings

Dickinson, John, and Brian Young. 2002. *A Short History of Quebec*. Montreal and Kingston: McGill-Queen's University Press. A good general overview of the history of Quebec society.

Iacovetta, Franca. 2006. *Gatekeepers: Reshaping Immigrant Lives in Cold War Canada*. Toronto: Between the Lines Press. An award-winning, highly readable, and empirically rich discussion of how various institutional authorities from social workers to immigration officials thought about and dealt with the arrival of immigrants in Canada in the 1950s and 1960s.

Miller, James. 2008. *Skyscrapers Hide the Heavens: A History of Indian–White Relations in Canada*, 3rd ed. Toronto: University of Toronto Press. This is a comprehensive history, including an extensive discussion of treaties and residential schools.

Satzewich, Vic. 1991. *Racism and the Incorporation of Foreign Labour: Farm Labour Migration to Canada since 1945*. London: Routledge. A discussion of postwar immigration policy with a central focus on the issue of racism.

Titley, Brian. 1986. *A Narrow Vision: Duncan Campbell Scott and the Administration of Indian Affairs in Canada*. Vancouver: UBC Press. Titley's book provides an excellent analysis of the federal government's policy of assimilation of Aboriginal peoples.

Related Websites

Indigenous and Northern Affairs Canada
www.aadnc-aandc.gc.ca
This is the website of the federal government department responsible for the administration of Aboriginal policy.

The Assembly of First Nations
www.afn.ca
The Assembly of First Nations is the main group representing the interests of status Indians in Canada.

Citizenship and Immigration Canada
www.cic.gc.ca
Citizenship and Immigration Canada is the federal government department responsible for immigration and multicultural policies.

Multicultural History Society of Ontario
www.mhso.ca
This organization is dedicated to examining the history of ethnic communities in Ontario.

Pier 21, Halifax
www.pier21.ca
Pier 21 is a museum and archive that commemorates immigration to Canada.

4 Immigration and the Canadian Mosaic

Learning Objectives

In this chapter you will learn that

- while Canada is a major immigrant-receiving country, many other countries around the world accept immigrants.

- immigrants are admitted to Canada for a variety of economic and demographic reasons.

- Canada's adherence to the "safe-third-country" principle is controversial because it may place vulnerable refugees in further danger.

- family class immigrants are not a drain on the Canadian economy.

- immigration officers have a tremendous amount of discretion in evaluating applications for permanent residence in Canada.

- some claim that this is one of the ways that racism continues to affect the selection of immigrants.

- many Canadians have ambivalent attitudes toward business-class immigrants.

- migrant workers are subject to exploitative working and living conditions in this country.

- non-status immigration is a growing concern in both Canada and the United States.

Introduction

Over the past five years, over 1.3 million new immigrants have come to call Canada home. Few other countries in the world admit more immigrants on a per capita basis than Canada. In 2011, 20.6 per cent of the population of Canada was born outside of the country. This was the highest proportion of foreign-born in Canada since 1931. In 2011, immigrants made up 46 per cent of the population of Toronto and 40 per cent of the population of Vancouver. Other large and medium-sized Canadian cities also have relatively significant immigrant populations: 26.2 percent of the population of Calgary, 23.5 per cent of Hamilton, 20.6 per cent of Montreal, 20.4 per cent of Edmonton, and 19.4 per cent of Ottawa-Gatineau was made up of immigrants, according to the 2011 National Household Survey.

As noted in Chapter 3, before 1962, Canada's immigration system was characterized by a distinct preference for white immigrants from Europe and the United States. While small numbers of visible minorities were allowed entry to Canada under highly restrictive quotas and other special arrangements during the early postwar years, there was a general feeling among government officials and many members of the Canadian public that non-white immigration was harmful to the long-term social, political, and economic stability of the country. In the early 1960s, the door to immigration began to open gradually to more and more immigrants from outside of the United States and the traditional European source countries. Between 1947 and 1955, Europe supplied over 85 per cent of all immigrants to Canada, but by 2014, Europe's share of total immigration declined to about 11.5 per cent. Now, as Table 4.1 shows, 7 of the top 10 sources of new immigrants to Canada are countries in Asia and the Middle East.

In this chapter, we consider a number of controversies and debates about the contemporary immigration system. We focus on the following questions: Why does Canada admit immigrants? Where do immigrants come from? Why are some people from other parts of the world admitted as immigrants and others admitted as **migrant workers**? To what extent does "race" continue to play a role in the process of immigration to Canada?

Why Immigration?

Why does Canada have immigration? Journalist Daniel Stoffman answers this question:

> There are the official reasons, the real reasons, and the ideal reasons. Officially, we could not survive without immigration and would be foolish not to have more of it. As no evidence exists to support the official version, Canadians are supposed to accept it on faith. They are "un-Canadian" if they don't. The real reasons Canada has immigration are that it helps the Liberal Party stay in power; it depresses wages, thereby transferring billions of dollars from workers to employers; and it benefits certain powerful industries, including the industry the program itself has created. (2002: 186–7)

Stoffman's provocative answer to why Canada has immigration is problematic, not least because the Conservatives, who won the 2006, 2008, and 2011 federal elections, also courted the so-called immigrant or ethnic vote during their terms in office. Former immigration minister Jason Kenney was widely regarded as the Conservative's "point man" for "all things immigrant and ethnic" (Black, 2015b). But more importantly, it assumes that immigration is unique to Canada and that there are peculiarly political circumstances here that lead us to admit relatively large numbers of immigrants. As noted above, Canada is undoubtedly one of the world's major immigrant-receiving nations; however, even though a central element of Canadian national mythology is that "Canada is a country of immigrants," other countries can legitimately make a similar claim. In 2011, the foreign-born made up 23.9 per cent of the population of Israel, 26.7 per cent of Australia, 27.3 per cent of

Table 4.1 Top Ten Sources of Immigrants to Canada, 2014

Source Countries	Number	Percentage Distribution
Philippines	40,035	15.4
India	38,341	14.7
China, People's Republic of	26,640	10.2
Iran	16,781	6.4
Pakistan	9,128	3.5
United States	8,496	3.3
United Kingdom and Colonies	5,764	2.2
France	4,717	2.2
Mexico	4,478	1.7
Korea, Republic of	4,463	1.7
Top 10 source countries	158,843	60.0
Other countries	101,561	40.0
Total	260,404	100.0

Source: Citizenship and Immigration Canada, 2014. Canada Facts and Figures: Immigrant Overview, Permanent Residents. Ottawa: Minister of Public Works and Government Services, http://www.cic.gc.ca/english/resources/statistics/facts2014/index.asp, p. 29.

Switzerland, 23.6 per cent of New Zealand, 16.8 per cent of Ireland, 13 per cent of the United States, 16.0 per cent of Austria, and 13.1 per cent of Germany (OECD, 2015). Moreover, immigrants and migrant workers make up significant portions of the population and labour force in a number of countries in Asia and the Middle East (Castles and Miller, 2003: 154–77). For example, in 2013 there were 2.3 million migrant workers living in Singapore, 3.7 million in Thailand, and 2.4 million in Malaysia (United Nations, Department of Economic and Social Affairs, 2013). Migrant workers in Singapore came from Malaysia, Thailand, Indonesia, the Philippines, Sri Lanka, China, Hong Kong, and Macau, and made up 34.7 per cent of the labour force in the tiny republic (Yeoh and Lin, 2012). In the Persian Gulf states in 2010, migrant workers made up about 32 per cent of the population in Saudi Arabia, 54 per cent in Bahrain, 68 per cent in Kuwait, 86 per cent in Qatar, and 88 per cent in the United Arab Emirates (Gulf Research Centre, 2013).

Since many other countries also admit migrant workers and immigrants, we should be skeptical of explanations of Canadian immigration that focus solely on factors unique to this country. There are undoubtedly unique social and political circumstances that lead to immigration to specific countries, but there are also wider social and economic considerations that lead to immigration in general, regardless of national context. These broader factors need to be understood in order to fully understand why immigration occurs.

There are a number of theoretical perspectives that seek to explain international migration (Massey, 1999). Some theories focus on the "push" factors that lead groups to leave their countries of origin, while others focus on "pull" factors that attract individuals to immigrant-receiving societies. Some theoretical traditions attempt to understand both sets of dynamics within the same framework. This chapter cannot discuss in any detail the complex push factors that lead people to leave their countries of origin. However, the significant factors include poverty, inequality, repressive political systems, and blocked opportunity for mobility (Massey, 1999).

The Political Economy of Immigration

From the perspective of political economy, immigration has traditionally been viewed within immigrant-receiving countries as a tool in the process of capital accumulation (Castles and Kosack, 1984). From this perspective, countries do not admit immigrants out of a sense of altruism or obligation to help people in difficult political, social, and economic circumstances in their countries of origin. Instead, national immigration policies are seen as mechanisms to supply workers for employers. Immigrants have been admitted and are of value for the role they play in the economy; in the words of Castles and Kosack (1984), immigrants are "tools that assist in the process of capital accumulation"—or, as Australian economist Jock Collins (1988) puts it, immigrants are "factory fodder."

Despite coming from different political starting points, there is a certain affinity between the analysis of immigration offered by political economists and by commentators like Stoffman. According to some of the early claims made within the political economy perspective, there are a number of reasons that immigrants are attractive to employers and central to the process of capitalist expansion. First, the cost of producing educated and skilled immigrant workers is borne in another country, thus resulting in significant savings for the receiving society. That is, in recruiting and admitting individuals who are already educated and trained, receiving societies like Canada save money that would otherwise have gone into educating and training native-born workers. One estimate suggests that between 1967 and 1987, Canada benefited to the tune of $42.9 billion in post-secondary educational training that immigrants brought with them to Canada (Devortez and Laryea, 1998; Li, 2003: 98). This is, incidentally, why some commentators argue that "south to north" migration is contributing to the brain drain from less developed countries and that immigration is in fact a form of neo-colonialism; it is likened to a form of development aid that poor, underdeveloped countries provide to rich, developed countries like Canada.

Second, political economists argue that because of their socio-economic vulnerability, immigrants are willing to take jobs that native-born workers avoid because the jobs are poorly paid, difficult, dangerous, or otherwise unattractive. Immigrants, according to this perspective, tend to do the "dirty work" of a society.

Third, political economists suggest that immigration is used by employers as a way to disorganize the working class. According to some versions of political economy, racism, ethnocentrism, and prejudice are mechanisms that employers use to promote disunity among workers. By promoting ideologies that identify immigrant workers as the source of native-born workers' socio-economic problems, employers are able to divide and conquer the working class and weaken efforts on the part of workers to organize collectively and pursue their wider common class interests.

Though originally developed in the 1970s, many of the broader assumptions of this classical political economy framework have been picked up by a number of Canadian scholars particularly critical of the recent neo-liberal turn in Canadian immigration. According to Abu-Laban and Gabriel (2002), neo-liberalism is a set of assumptions about the proper functioning of government in the era of globalization. These assumptions include "a more limited role for the state and, consequently, an emphasis on cutting back state policies and programs; a greater stress on individual self-sufficiency; and a belief that free markets are efficient allocators of goods and services" (Abu-Laban and Gabriel, 2002: 21). Critics of neo-liberalism argue that immigration policy-making has been hijacked by business interests and more recently by a security agenda. They contend that recent changes in the immigration system are rooted in part in a desire to keep Canadian industry globally competitive. According to Abu-Laban and Gabriel,

> large numbers of immigrants have always been selected on the basis of their ability to contribute to the Canadian economy. This is accentuated and consolidated in current developments. In response to the perceived economic imperatives of globalization, the "best" immigrants, and by extension prospective citizens, are those whose labour market skills will enhance Canada's competitive position in a world economy. (2002: 62)

There is evidence to support some of the broad contentions about immigration made by political economists, critics of the current immigration system, and commentators like Stoffman. Generally, employers in Canada and in other countries have historically been in favour of maintaining a robust immigration program and relatively open borders. As we saw in Chapter 3, capitalist employers have historically tended to be in favour of keeping the door open to immigrants, both racialized and white, in part because they know that immigrants are in a vulnerable position and are willing to take jobs that the Canadian-born avoid (Satzewich, 1989).

As we will see later in this chapter, Canadian employers have enthusiastically embraced the Temporary Foreign Worker, Provincial Nominee, Live-in-Caregiver, and Caribbean and Mexican Seasonal Worker programs to essentially fast-track the entry of workers to fill their specific labour needs. Farm labour, domestic labour, housekeeping, and childminding have been jobs that Canadian-born men and women have historically avoided. Farm work is arduous, relatively poorly paid, and not covered under many provinces' labour standards legislation. Domestic work is also characterized by long hours, poor pay, and the intense regulation of personal lives. Canadian-born workers are keen to leave these jobs when better job offers in other industries present themselves. As a result, farmers and middle-class families in need of workers have historically had to rely on the government's recruitment of immigrants to fill job vacancies in these relatively unattractive sectors (Satzewich, 1991; Bakan and Statiulis, 1997; Stasiulis and Bakan, 2005). It is important to remember, though, that this dynamic is not unique to Canada. At the same time, there is little evidence to suggest that racism is a conspiracy cooked up behind the closed doors of capitalist industry in order to disorganize the Canadian working class. Racism, as we will see in Chapter 7, is not the exclusive domain of one class, nor does it necessarily have only one logical consequence. As discussed in Chapter 3, racism in British Columbia in the 1910s and 1920s eventually resulted in restrictions on Chinese immigration and fewer opportunities for capitalists to exploit the labour power of Chinese workers.

Immigration: Broader Considerations

The political economy perspective has certain strengths and weaknesses when it comes to explaining why Canada, along with many other countries around the world, currently needs, wants, and admits immigrants. However, even with its strengths, it is not a complete explanation. Though broadly defined economic conditions and labour market factors drive much of the process of immigration, a number of other factors also shape contemporary immigration flows and patterns. First, demographic considerations underlie at least some of the current emphasis on the recruitment of new immigrants. Even though population aging may be somewhat exaggerated as an impending social problem (Stoffman, 2002), Canada, as well as many other economically advanced Western countries, is facing the demographic reality of declining birth rates and population aging. In this context, immigration is a means of mitigating some of the negative consequences of population aging, such as increasing tax burdens and worker shortages.

Canada is not alone in its concern over the "ticking time bomb" of demographics. Japan has been described by *The Economist* magazine as "the incredibly shrinking country" (*The Economist*, 2014). In 2013, the population of Japan declined by 244,000 people and a recent report suggested that if present trends continue, by 2060 the population of the country will have fallen to about 87 million, far below its current population of 127 million. Moreover, it is expected that about 40 per cent of the population will be 65 or older. Japan's demographic crisis is due, in part, to its low fertility rate: at 1.39 it has one of the lowest fertility rates in the world. The problem for Japan, though, is that there are social and ideological constraints involved with using immigration as a way to solve their demographic problem. Japan has had a deliberately restrictive immigration policy for many years because it prioritized maintaining the homogeneity of its society. As such, less than 2 per cent of the population is non-Japanese. Despite historically low levels of immigration, the Japanese government is currently floating the idea that it should begin to allow about 200,000 immigrants per year to help offset its demographic problems (*The Economist*, 2014).

Second, immigration flows are diverse, and not all immigration flows are about recruiting workers. While critics are right to be cynical about some of the claims made about the humanitarian nature of Canada's immigration program, Canada does have a record of humanitarianism in the field of immigration that it deserves to be rightfully proud of. Though the former Conservative government tested Canadians' commitment to humanitarianism by cutting health care benefits for refugee claimants, the move sparked a considerable backlash among many Canadians and was successfully challenged in the courts. The current Liberal government recently restored those benefits. Canada's refugee determination system is, moreover, ahead of the curve on many issues. To its credit, Canada was the first refugee-receiving country to accept gender-based persecution as a basis on which an individual can make a successful refugee claim. Canada also considers individuals in same-sex relationships as part of a family for the purposes of family class immigration.

Third, immigration policy is also formulated out of a complex set of pressures and social relations. Though business-based interests play a major role in shaping immigration policy, other groups like trade unions, church groups, non-governmental organizations, political parties, and bureaucrats themselves also play a role in shaping the overall direction of immigration policy (Hardcastle et al., 1994).

Finally, immigrants are more than just worker bees who create wealth that is appropriated by capitalist employers. Immigrants are human subjects with particular bundles of social, personal, and economic capabilities, characteristics, and potentials. Immigrants have been—and are—part of Canada's wider nation-building project, where the hope and expectation is that they will eventually become "Canadians," however ambiguous the term. Potential immigrants have been—and are—evaluated on the basis of their economic capabilities as well as their wider capacity to contribute to the social reproduction of Canadian society. As a result, assessments of the ability of immigrants to "fit in" or "adjust" to Canada have played an important role in regulating who gets in.

In sum, though simplistic, Stoffman's answer to the question of why Canada has immigration provides a useful foil to consider the broader reasons associated with why immigrants come to Canada. While there may be powerful political and economic interests behind certain recent policy changes and initiatives, immigration is a complicated process that does not lend itself to simplistic analysis.

Contemporary Immigration Categories: Debates and Controversies

Canada's immigration system is increasingly complex. It is made up of a patchwork of policies, programs, and mechanisms that allow people from outside of Canada to live and work in the country. The first distinction that needs to be made is between individuals who are provided with the right of permanent residence, and individuals who are provided with the right of only temporary residence. There are a number of ways that individuals can come to Canada as legal **permanent residents**, but, at

Table 4.2 Number and Categories of Immigrants Admitted to Canada, 2014

Family class		Economic immigrants		Refugees		Others		Total	
N	%	N	%	N	%	N	%	N	%
66,661	22.9	165,089	65.7	23,286	9.5	5,368	2.0	260,404	100

Source: Citizenship and Immigration Canada, 20143. Canada Facts and Figures: Immigrant Overview, Permanent and Temporary Residents. Ottawa: Minister of Public Works and Government Services, p. 5.

its simplest, permanent residents are categorized in government statistics as economic immigrants, refugees, or family class immigrants. Table 4.2 provides information on the number and proportion of immigrants in each category admitted in 2014. Each of these three broad categories of permanent residence contains various subcategories of immigration, with different rules and procedures for entry; each of these permanent residence categories also carries certain controversies. Debates have arisen over the philosophy and administrative practices behind each category, the hidden agendas, and the social and economic consequences of each category of admission. Though ethnic and racial considerations are no longer part of the official immigration policy, there are a number of ways that ethnicity and "race" are presumed to impinge on contemporary controversies surrounding immigration. In this section, we highlight and evaluate some of the controversies associated with specific **immigration categories**.

Refugees

In 2014, Canada admitted 23,286 refugees, who made up 9.5 per cent of the total flow of immigrants to Canada in that year. This was down from ten years earlier: in 2004, Canada admitted 32,686 refugees, who were 14.5 per cent of the total flow. There are two general ways that a person can become a refugee in Canada: (1) through resettlement from outside of Canada, and (2) through the in-Canada refugee protection process.

The first program is intended for people seeking refugee status from outside of Canada. In many cases, these people are the stereotypical refugees with whom we are most familiar because of heart-wrenching media images of squalid refugee camps or columns of refugees desperately trying to flee their country in times of war or ethnic cleansing. There are two subcategories of refugee that Canada admits under this program. The "convention refugees abroad class" refers to people who are outside their country of citizenship or habitual residence and have a well-founded fear of persecution for reasons of "race," religion, political opinion, nationality, or membership in a particular social group. The "country of asylum class" includes people who are outside their country of citizenship or habitual residence and are seriously and personally affected by civil war, armed conflict, or massive violations of human rights.

Canada works with the Office of the United Nations High Commissioner for Refugees (UNHCR), which determines the legitimacy of individual claims for refugee status under one of the above two categories. In 2014, it was estimated that there were more than 14 million refugees and asylum-seekers in need of protection and assistance around the world; another 32 million people were defined by the UNHCR as *internally displaced people* and under the protection of the UNHCR (UNHCR, 2014) because they were in refugee-like situations and also in need of protection but were not officially recognized by the UN as refugees or asylum-seekers (Castles and Miller, 2003: 5). In a sense, the UN-certified refugees constitute a pool from which Canada and other countries select refugees for resettlement. In Canada, charitable organizations, and groups of five or more can act as private sponsors of refugees. The Syrian refugee crisis has prompted many Canadians to sponsor refugees. A significant portion of the Liberal government's commitment to admit 25,000 refugees from Syria by March 2016 was made up of privately sponsored refugees. Individuals in many communities have banded together to provide support to refugees. In financial terms, each group of five sponsors is expected to provide at least $26,000 to support a refugee family during their first year in Canada. In addition to providing support for housing, those funds are expected to cover other living expenses such as food, furnishings, clothing, and educational supplies for children (Black, 2015a). Many other Canadians, including high school and university students, employees of various private enterprises, and corporations have undertaken various kinds of fundraising efforts or made significant financial commitments to help support the resettlement of Syrian refugees.

The in-Canada refugee protection process is the refugee determination system for individuals already in Canada. In its 1985 *Singh* decision, the Supreme Court ruled that non-Canadians, if they are on Canadian soil, are covered by many of the protections of the Canadian Charter of Rights and Freedoms (Pratt, 2005: 66). It also ruled that all refugee claimants in Canada have the right to an oral hearing to determine the legitimacy of their case. In that context, the federal government established the Immigration and Refugee Board (IRB) to adjudicate in-Canada refugee claims. Individuals who present themselves at a Canadian port of entry or a Canadian immigration centre in Canada can claim refugee status. Individuals qualify as a refugee if the Immigration and Refugee Board determines that the person is a convention refugee—a person outside their country of nationality or habitual residence and unable or unwilling to return to their country because of a well-founded fear of persecution for reasons of "race," religion, political opinion, nationality, or membership in a particular social group. Alternatively, individuals must prove that they are in need of protection because their removal from Canada to their country of origin would subject them to the possibility of torture, risk to life, or risk of cruel and unusual treatment or punishment (Citizenship and Immigration Canada, 2015).

In 2012, the federal government introduced a significant change to the way that refugee applications were reviewed in Canada. In particular, it introduced the concept of *designated countries of origin*; countries that in the government's view do not persecute their citizens and hence do not normally force people to leave.

Though individuals from a designated country of origin can apply for refugee status in Canada, they are subject to a fast-track process and, under certain circumstances, may appeal the decision of the Immigration and Refugee Board. Individuals from non-designated countries of origin are able to appeal a negative decision to the Refugee Appeal Division of the IRB (Citizenship and Immigration Canada, 2016).

Canada adheres to the "safe-third-country" principle, which prevents individuals from making a refugee claim in Canada if they have already found a safe haven in another country. So far, Canada considers only the United States as a safe third country. This principle is intended to deter "asylum shopping"—situations in which individuals seek refugee status in one country even though they may have already secured a safe haven elsewhere. However, critics argue that by agreeing to this principle, Canada is turning its back on some genuine refugees and indirectly sending them back to strife-torn situations where their lives are in danger. For example, through the in-Canada refugee protection process, Canada accepts a significant portion of refugee claims from individuals coming from Colombia. The United States government, however, generally does not accept refugee claims made by individuals from Colombia. Difficulties and double standards arise when some Colombians manage to enter the United States but subsequently try to gain entry to Canada in order to claim refugee status here. Because they are in a safe third country—the United States—they are either turned back at the Canada-US border or not allowed to make a refugee claim in Canada and are returned to the US. They are told that if they have to make a refugee claim, they should do it in the United States—their safe third country. Even though these refugee claimants might temporarily have a safe haven in the United States, there is no guarantee that the US will accept their refugee claims and not return them to a dangerous situation in Colombia. Critics point out that had such refugee claimants managed to arrive directly in Canada, their cases may have been adjudicated differently and they would have had a better chance of staying.

The introduction of the designated countries of origin policy and the safe-third-country agreement reflect the former Conservative government's belief that the in-Canada refugee protection process was too lax, and encouraged individuals to make unfounded refugee claims. Writing about the refugee determination system before these changes were introduced, Stoffman (2002: 154) argued that "most of those making refugee claims in Canada are not refugees but immigrants using the refugee system to cut to the front of the immigration line." Critics of these policies, including the Canadian Council for Refugees, Amnesty International, the Canadian Association of Refugee Lawyers, and the Canadian Civil Liberties Association suggest that these changes are unfair and put legitimate refugees at risk.

Economic Immigrants

The largest category of immigrants to Canada is made up of economic immigrants. As noted in Table 4.2, the 165,088 economic immigrants and their families admitted to Canada in 2014 made up 65.7 per cent of the 260,404 immigrants admitted to the country that year. There are several subcategories of economic immigrant, and each of these entails different rules for selection and admission. The main categories are skilled workers, self-employed, live-in caregivers, and provincial/territorial nominees.

Skilled workers

Skilled workers must meet a number of criteria in order to be admitted. To be considered as a skilled worker under the newly introduced express entry system, individuals need to fill out an online profile that outlines their English- and/or French-language skills, level of education, and work experience. Applicants are then ranked against others in a pool, and those who are highly ranked are then invited to apply for permanent residence in Canada. Under this new system, the federal immigration department commits to review and process applications in six months or less. This change was introduced because under the previous skilled-worker selection system, the number of applications was unlimited and applications were processed on a first-come-first-served basis, which meant that some applicants had to wait several years before their applications were processed by a visa officer (Fleras, 2015; Satzewich, 2015). In addition, applicants must meet certain minimum financial requirements if they do not have arranged employment in Canada. Skilled workers who bring four family members to Canada must have a minimum of $22,603 in their possession to show that they can support themselves after they arrive in Canada.

The ranking of applicants in the express entry system is based, in part, on the points system. The system originated in 1967 and since then has been modified a number of times. Currently, there are four selection factors, each carrying a different weight: core/human capital, spouse or common-law partner, skill transferability, and arranged employment or provincial nomination. Within these broad factors, age, level of education, official language proficiency, and Canadian work experience of the applicant and their spouse are assessed on a scale with a maximum of 1,200 points (see Table 4.3).

Interviews with applicants are now conducted infrequently, but immigration officers can exercise both "positive" and "negative" discretion. Positive discretion occurs in cases in which individuals who do not earn the requisite number of points for immigration to Canada may still be granted permanent residence status because an immigration officer believes that they are likely to be "good" for Canada. Negative discretion occurs in cases in which an immigration officer denies an application for permanent residence even though the applicant may have earned the minimum number of points (Bouchard and Wake Carroll, 2002; Satzewich, 2015).

The exercise of discretion by immigration officers is a controversial aspect of Canada's immigration system. In previous versions of the points system, immigration officers could allocate discretionary points for what was termed "personal suitability": they could use their discretion and award points based on their

Table 4.3 Summary of Points per Factor for Express-Entry Candidates

A. Core / human capital factors

Factors	Points per factor - With a spouse or common-law partner	Points per factor - Without a spouse or common-law partner
Age	100	110
Level of education	140	150
Official languages proficiency	150	160
Canadian work experience	70	80

B. Spouse or common-law partner factors

Factors	Points per factor (Maximum 40 points)
Level of education	10
Official languages proficiency	20
Canadian work experience	10

A. Core/human capital + B. Spouse or common-law partner factors = Maximum 500 points (with OR without a spouse or common-law partner)

C. Skill transferability factors (Maximum 100 points)

Education	Points per factor (Maximum 50 points)
With good/strong official languages proficiency and a post-secondary degree	50
With Canadian work experience and a post-secondary degree	50

Foreign work experience	Points per factor (Maximum 50 points)
With good/strong official languages proficiency (Canadian Language Benchmark [CLB] level 7 or higher) and foreign work experience	50
With Canadian work experience and foreign work experience	50

Certificate of qualification (for people in trade occupations)	Points per factor (Maximum 50 points)
With good/strong official languages proficiency and a certificate of qualification	50

A. Core/human capital + B. Spouse or common-law partner + C. Transferability factors = Maximum 600 points

D. Additional points (Maximum 600 points)

Factor	Points per factor
Arranged employment (positive Labour Market Impact Assessment required)	600
Provincial/territorial nomination	600

A. Core/human capital + B. Spouse or common-law partner factors + C. Transferability factors + D. Additional points = Grand total – Maximum 1,200 points

Source: Citizenship and Immigration Canada. 2015.

perception of the applicant's adaptability, motivation, initiative, and resource-fulness (Jakubowski, 1997: 20). Discretion is controversial because some analysts believe that it is one of the ways that racial discrimination can creep into the immigrant selection system (Pratt, 2005). Critics argue that under previous versions of the points system, it was harder for visible minority immigrants to earn discretionary points for personal suitability. In the 1980s, Anderson and Frideres argued that

> depending on the selection officer's bias (or views about racial groups), the applicant can receive zero points in this category, thus lessening the applicant's chance of entering Canada. As the saying goes, "If you're White, you're right, if you're Brown, stick around and if you're Black, stand back." (1980: 227)

The Canadian Race Relations Foundation (2001), Evelyn Kallen (2003: 112), and Henry and Tator (2010: 68) all claim that the exercise of discretion in the current immigration system continues to put visible minority immigrant applicants at a disadvantage.

While intriguing, the allegation that racism informs the exercise of discretion should be considered more of a hypothesis than a statement of fact. Even though immigration officers may use their discretion to assess applicants for permanent resident status, there is no empirical evidence available to substantiate the allegation that immigration officers systematically awarded visible minority applicants fewer points for personal suitability under the old points system or that they are now more likely to subject visible minority applicants to more negative and less positive discretion than they do white applicants (Satzewich, 2015).

Another way that discrimination is said to continue to affect the selection and admission of skilled immigrants has to do with the distribution of immigration visa offices abroad. Currently, there are 42 immigration offices variously located in Canadian embassies, High Commissions, and consulates abroad. Decisions about where these offices are located and decisions on the number of staff allocated to each office are arguably two of the ways that the federal government informally controls immigration from certain countries and regions of the world. While overt racism has admittedly been removed from the immigration system, Jakubowski (1997: 21) argues that "in less obvious ways, immigration law is still racist. The number and location of immigration offices outside of Canada and the discretion awarded to immigration officers in determining adaptability suggests that immigration, to some degree, is still being 'controlled.'"

Government resources are limited, of course, and it would be unrealistic to expect that every immigration office be provided with unlimited resources for processing applications for admission to Canada. The existing transportation and communication infrastructure in different countries may affect processing times as, no doubt, do security and identity considerations. Further, immigration officials claim that overseas staffing resources are allocated on the basis of where they will do the most good: not all countries in the world are defined as containing enough potential immigrants with the educational, occupational, and language skills that Canada is looking for. As a result, offices and resources are allocated on the basis of where they are likely to net the most in terms of what Canada defines as desirable immigrants (Simmons, 1998: 103).

Business class

Canada's Business Immigration Program is designed to admit individuals who can invest in or start businesses in the country. There are two categories of business immigrants: investors and self-employed. Individuals applying under the Immigrant Investor Venture Capital Pilot Program must have certain English- and/or French-language skills, have completed one year of post-secondary education, and have a personal net worth of $10 million or more in order to be eligible. Individuals who are worth over $50 million have the educational factor relaxed. Investors approved under the program are required to invest a minimum of $2 million in an Immigrant Investor Capital Fund. The current rules allow for the department's acceptance of 60 applications per year. Those applying in the self-employed category must have relevant experience in cultural activities, athletics, or farm management. They must have the intention and ability to establish a business that at minimum will create employment for themselves. They must also qualify under a revised points system, but the bar for self-employed is set much lower than that for skilled workers.

Business immigrants represent a significant, though declining, proportion of all immigrants admitted to Canada (Fleras, 2015). In 1994, the 27,404 business immigrants who came to Canada represented 12.4 per cent of all immigrants admitted that year. By 2014, however, the 8,351 business immigrants and accompanying family members represented just 3.3 per cent of all immigrants admitted. The relatively large number of business immigrants recruited from the late 1980s to the mid-1990s was in part the result of the British government's announcement that it would transfer authority over Hong Kong to China in 1997. Many wealthy business people and entrepreneurs feared the impending takeover. Concerned that the Chinese government would undermine the free-enterprise environment that characterized Hong Kong, many sought to find a safe haven for themselves, their families, and their capital in Canada. Canada was more than willing to oblige and so ramped up the Business Immigration Program to capitalize on the fears and anxieties of Hong Kong residents.

A number of other countries are also keen to recruit business immigrants. The United States, Australia, Britain, and New Zealand, for example, all have business immigration programs aimed at recruiting wealthy individuals eager to gain permanent residence status by expressing an intention to invest at least part of their wealth in the country (Borowski and Nash, 1994: 228; Wong and Netting, 1992: 95).

Information collected by Citizenship and Immigration Canada indicates that between 1986 and 2002, immigrant investors collectively invested $6.6 billion in the country and that in 2002 alone immigrant entrepreneurs invested $122,615,713 and created 1,108 full-time and 753 part-time jobs in Canada (2002). But despite what appear to be obvious economic benefits associated with business-related immigration programs, not everyone is in favour of these kinds of programs and arrangements.

First, some critics have raised ethical issues associated with what amounts to the sale of permanent residence status and, eventually, a Canadian passport. Putting permanent residence status and citizenship up for sale to wealthy business people and investors is consistent with a wider neo-liberal project: "these class advantaged people embody the very spirit of neo-liberalism—they are independent, self-reliant, active, and entrepreneurial" (Abu-Laban and Gabriel, 2002: 173). Prioritizing the recruitment of business immigrants, in Abu-Laban and Gabriel's view, reflects a growing emphasis on seeing the economic contributions of a person as indicative of the sum worth of a person, which is a particularly "superficial and narrow reading of diversity" (173).

Second, business immigrants can be characterized as "transnationals"—individuals whose business interests as well as their identities and social and personal lives straddle more than one country (Wong and Satzewich, 2006). Many business immigrants maintain homes, social networks, and business interests both in Canada and in their country of origin. They travel relatively unencumbered by national borders and move easily around the globe. Critics of some business and other well-off transnational immigrants have called them "astronauts": individuals who settle their families in Canada, Australia, or the United States but continue to conduct their businesses in their home country and occasionally fly back to Canada to maintain their permanent residence status (Borowski and Nash, 1994: 247). These business immigrants and other upper-middle-class immigrants have been the targets of hostility for their real and imagined transnational behaviours. Further, when the children of these astronaut families occasionally get into trouble with the law or display their wealth ostentatiously, they are often the subject of media attacks and criticism. At the extreme, questions are raised about their political loyalties and how committed they are to Canada.

Finally, some analysts argue that the Business Immigration Program has helped to create a "race relations" problem in places like Vancouver, a city that is a major destination for visible minority business immigrants. In the late 1980s and early 1990s, Vancouver was at the centre of a number of controversies about the apparently negative social, cultural, and economic consequences of large-scale business immigration. According to Wong and Netting (1992), white residents of Vancouver blamed immigrants for driving up housing prices in the city and destroying the character of certain neighbourhoods by erecting "monster houses" and by cutting down stately trees on their properties because they interfered with the feng shui of the location. Some residents defined wealthy immigrants as being driven only by greed and suggested they were responsible for bringing organized crime from Hong Kong to Canada. Wong and Netting also argue, however, that class conflict underscored some of these racist attitudes in important ways. They argue that while white working-class British Columbians expressed alarm and resentment over the skyrocketing price of housing in the city, middle- and upper-class white Canadians were concerned that their neighbourhoods, their schools, and their clubs were also being negatively affected by seemingly large-scale migration and settlement of wealthy Chinese business immigrants (Wong and Netting, 1992: 119; see also Mitchell, 2004).

Live-in caregivers

In 2014, 11,693 live-in caregivers, along with 5,999 of their dependants, were admitted to Canada as permanent residents. Today, there are three streams within the Caregiver Program: (1) the Caring for Children Pathway, (2) the Caring for People with High Medical Needs Pathway, and (3) the Live-in Caregiver Program. The first two pathways are relatively new and provide avenues for permanent residence in Canada. The third pathway is in the process of being phased out.

Historically, live-in caregivers have been mainly women, and most have come from the Philippines or the Caribbean. Caregivers used to have to live in the private home of their employers and they could not work for more than one employer at a time. Under the current system, caregivers who provide services for families with children are not required to live in the homes of their employers. Those applying under the Caring for People with High Medical Needs Pathway are nurses, nurse aides, and home support workers for both individual families and larger care institutions. Under the previous system, phased out in 2014, live-in caregivers had a more or less automatic pathway to permanent residence in Canada. Under the new system, the pathways tend to involve only two-year work permits (which can be renewed for two more years), and only those with one year of post-secondary education in Canada (or its overseas equivalent) are allowed to apply for permanent residence status.

Many Canadians no doubt first heard of the Live-in Caregiver Program in the spring of 2009 when Ruby Dhalla, Liberal MP for Brampton East, was accused of mistreating two Filipina live-in caregivers in her family's employ. Though it did serve to raise the issue of the plight of live-in caregivers, one of the unfortunate and unintended consequences of the sensational nature of the coverage of the Dhalla case was that it seemed to personalize the problem of exploitation and harsh treatment of live-in caregivers: caregivers are poorly treated because certain employers are just nasty people (see Case Study Box 4.1).

While there are undoubtedly good and bad employers, despite various changes introduced over the years, the system that brings these women to Canada is exploitative by its very nature. Since caregivers are highly dependent on their employers, it is hard for caregivers to say no to employers when asked to do unreasonable jobs and to work longer hours than outlined in their contracts. Further, caregivers come from countries where there are few options for women to make a living and support their families, and many use caregiving in Canada and other places around the world to send remittances back to relatives in their countries of origin. Stasiulis and Bakan's (2005: 98) research showed that under the Live-in Caregiver Program in place in the early 2000s, many caregivers worked 50-hour weeks and only some received overtime pay for work in excess of 44 hours. The current system continues to leave people admitted under this program vulnerable to exploitation because they are dependent on their employers to help them fulfill the two-year employment rule to acquire permanent residence. If they quit, they may not be able to get another job, thus putting the condition for continuous

Case Study Box 4.1 As the Controversy Continues, the Live-in Caregiver Program Remains Unreviewed

Filipino advocacy groups strengthen their call to abolish the Live-in Caregiver Program (LCP) as the experiences of Filipina domestic workers once again make it onto the front page of the *Toronto Star*. The groups identify the abuses suffered by the live-in caregivers in the home of Liberal MP Ruby Dhalla as a testament to the state-sanctioned modern-day slavery in Canada.

While the general public is busy condemning our provincial and federal parliamentarians in their complicity to this ongoing violence, SIKLAB-Ontario, a local migrant workers' organization, and the National Alliance of Philippine Women in Canada (NAPWC) remind Canadians that the "Dhalla case" is beyond the isolated incidences of abusive high-profile employers. Rather, they encourage media and the public to interrogate the federal program itself, and investigate why the stories of Magdalene Gordo and Richelyn Tongson are common to all domestic workers employed through the LCP.

While both Gordo and Tongson were originally hired to care for the MP's mother, the Dhalla family had allegedly "seized their passports" and "forced them to do non-nanny jobs such as washing cars, shining shoes and cleaning family-owned chiropractic clinics." As more and more stories of "nanny abuse" cross the pages of mainstream print media, the Canadian public should examine the broader issues inherent within an anti-woman and racist program that is the LCP.

Kelly Botengan, spokesperson for SIKLAB and a former live-in caregiver, comments on the emerging uproar on the mistreatment of domestic workers in their employers' homes. She states that narrowing the blame on particular individuals leaves the LCP unquestioned. "Working with precarious status, being a live-in caregiver is literally like holding onto a knife's edge," says Botengan. "The mechanisms within the program leaves us women so vulnerable to abuse."

employment in jeopardy. As Stasiulis and Bakan explain, "the sharp demarcation in class and citizenship status between employers and migrant employees, supported by systemic factors in Canada and the world system . . . fundamentally shape the relations of paid domestic labour" (Stasiulis and Bakan, 2005: 106).

Provincial nominees

The final category admitted under the broad "economic class" of permanent resident is provincial nominees. There has been a dramatic growth in the use of the Provincial Nominee Program (PNP) since 477 workers were admitted when the program first started in 1999. The program was meant to allow employers to quickly fill labour shortages in specific niches. Now every Canadian province and territory has a Provincial Nominee Program. In 2014, 21,003 individuals along with 26,625 of their dependants were admitted as provincial nominees. The program seems to be increasingly used as a mechanism by employers to bypass the cumbersome

The LCP is one stream within the Temporary Foreign Workers Program that imports foreign labour in order to provide cheap private childcare, eldercare and care for people with disabilities. SIKLAB and NAPWC maintain the position in denouncing the LCP as Canada's "de facto" national childcare program, which, as a labour indentureship policy, is also essential to the further privatization of health care in Canada.

"The hiring of two caregivers to attend to Dhalla's elderly mother speaks of the inadequacy of the current health care system, as these women perform unregulated nursing duties with reduced wages," states Botengan. "Worse, the program has allowed employers like Dhalla to fully take advantage of these women, violating their most basic human rights."

From being trafficked through unscrupulous agencies, being forced to work outside the contract, to the sexual, physical, and emotional abuses—the groups hold the Canadian government accountable to the documented human rights violations maintained and perpetuated through state policies.

"The story of Magdalene Gordo and Richelyn Tongson is the story of our community," says Qara Clemente, a member of the Filipino Canadian Youth Alliance. "Not only are our women struggling from systemic violence and stalled economic mobility, but the marginalization of these women are also being passed on—one generation after the other."

Clemente also expresses how entire families going through such an experience unfortunately pass on these burdens even to the youth. "Majority of the children of former domestic workers are expected to supplement the family income instead of pursuing an education. While exploitative programs like the LCP continue to exist, the cycle of poverty and violence persist largely unexamined."

As the controversy surrounding the "Dhalla case" escalates, SIKLAB and NAPWC reinforce their position to scrap the Live-in Caregiver Program, demanding an end to the violence and exploitation of women and migrant workers in Canada.

Source: "As the Controversy Continues, the Live-in Caregiver Program Remains Unreviewed," *Filipino Journal*, 20 May–5 June 2009, vol. 23 (10). http://filipinojournal.com/v2/index.php?pagetype=read&article_num=05262009212040&latest_issue=V23-N10.

skilled-worker selection system, which under the previous system was slow, and which does not respond very well to specific employer needs and does not admit immigrants with low levels of skill or education.

The overall principle underlying the Provincial Nominee Program is that it helps employers fill jobs for which there are no workers in Canada. The specific jobs for which individuals qualify for entry to Canada vary by province, but basically the PNP allows provinces to develop their own **selection criteria** for immigrants. Individuals selected under these programs must have the "skills, language abilities, education, and work experience needed to make an immediate economic contribution to the province or territory that nominates them" (Kukushkin, 2009). The provinces are not bound to use the federal points system to identify qualified individuals. The nominee programs are essentially employer driven (Kukushkin, 2009: 17); employers can request that certain workers be fast-tracked in the immigration process so that job vacancies can be filled more quickly. The federal government has in turn agreed to prioritize provincial nominee requests, thus pushing other applications farther back in the processing cue.

Family Class

In 2014, the 66,661 family class immigrants admitted to Canada made up 25.6 per cent of the total number of immigrants. However, over the past two decades family class immigration has been diminishing in importance in Canada's overall immigration system.

For example, in 1994, the 94,185 family class immigrants admitted to Canada represented about 38 per cent of the total number of immigrants admitted to Canada. The reasons for the decline in the size of the family class are rooted in part in government perceptions that family class immigrants make fewer positive economic contributions to Canada than other categories of permanent resident.

Canadian citizens and permanent residents living in Canada may sponsor certain close relatives or family members who want to move to Canada. Individuals can sponsor spouses, parents and grandparents, dependent children (including adopted children), and children who they intend to adopt, as well as orphaned brothers, sisters, nephews, nieces, or grandchildren if they are under 18 and do not have a spouse. Federal immigration authorities recognized the validity of same-sex marriages even before federal legislation on this matter was passed in the summer of 2005. As a result, Canadian citizens and permanent residents may sponsor their same-sex partners under the family class. Sponsors must agree to financially support their family members for between 3 and 10 years so that they will not need to apply for social assistance. The length of time of the family support provisions depends on the age of the person sponsored and the nature of the relationship to the sponsor. For example, spouses (including common-law spouses) must provide financial support for 3 years from the date that the person becomes a permanent resident in Canada; sons and daughters, on the other hand, must provide 10 years of financial support to their parents and grandparents (Citizenship and Immigration Canada, 2016). Individuals who do not live up to these sponsorship conditions may not be eligible to sponsor further family members. With the exception of the elderly, individuals sponsored under the family class must sign an undertaking in which they agree to make every effort to become self-supporting in Canada.

Family class immigration is probably the most politicized of all immigration categories. The family class category is popular within many communities because it is a vehicle by which immigrants become reunited with their families. Immigrants in the family class do not face the same stringent selection criteria as skilled workers, and thus it is easier for individuals falling within one of the admissible groups to come and settle in Canada. The family class is particularly popular in urban ridings in Toronto, Vancouver, and Montreal that already have relatively large numbers of recent immigrants. As a result, members of Parliament representing large urban ridings are reluctant to support proposals that call for narrowing of the kinds of relatives eligible for family class immigration, reducing the overall size of the movement, or placing yearly caps on the number admitted in this category. One estimate suggests that for federal MPs in Toronto, Montreal, and Vancouver, immigration-related issues constitute between 60 and 80 per cent of all constituency casework, and that these MPs annually handle up to 40,000 immigration-related inquiries from their constituents (Malloy, 2003: 48). Immigration clearly matters to federal MPs in Canada's big cities, and they would be foolish not to court this segment of the electorate.

At the same time, however, the government is concerned that too many spousal applicants in the family class are not in "real" relationships. That is, the government alleges that many individuals enter into "fake" relationships, or "relationships of convenience," as a way to get into Canada. The allegation is that individuals who have no intention of living in a relationship with their partner are using the family reunification system as a way of bypassing regular immigration channels (Satzewich, 2015). Though there is no empirical evidence to show that the number of fake relationships is increasing, the immigration department nonetheless has introduced more stringent rules for spouses who come to Canada, and those include a requirement that they live together with their spouse for two years. If they do not, their permanent residence status can be revoked. Further, individuals who are sponsored must wait a minimum of five years before they can sponsor a new spouse or partner if their previous relationship broke down.

Controversies have also arisen over the economic performance of family class immigrants and whether they are a net drain on the Canadian economy (Francis, 2002; Borjas, 1999). Because they are not selected under the points system, family class immigrants are purportedly of poorer "quality" in the sense that they bring less human capital to Canada than skilled-worker immigrants, investors, and entrepreneurs. Critics of the family class argue that because they are less skilled, they do not do as well as skilled immigrants in the labour market, they are more likely to rely on social assistance than other immigrants, and they are a net drain on the Canadian economy (Stoffman, 2002).

Empirical evidence challenges the claim that recent family class immigrants are declining in "quality." Li (2003: 93–4) shows, for example, that among family class immigrants who landed in Canada in 1996, only 0.5 per cent can be expected never to reach the earnings level of the Canadian-born. Another 0.5 per cent catch up to Canadian-born earnings in one year's time, and the average time required to reach earnings parity with average Canadian earnings is 6.8 years for men and 5.8 years for women. In fact, the average time it takes for family class men and women to reach earnings parity has improved over the past decade. For instance, among family class immigrants who landed in Canada in 1986, it took men an average of 16.6 years to catch up to the average earnings of Canadian males and 14.8 years for women to reach parity with average female employment earnings.

Case Study Box 4.2 How Do Immigration Officials Try to Determine if Relationships Are "Real"?

Canadian visa officers must try to figure out if relationships are "real" in cases where someone in Canada wants to sponsor their spouse or partner who is not a Canadian. But genuine spousal and partner relationships take many different forms. How people fall in love, and indeed the place that love occupies in relationship formation, are culturally variable, as are the different ways that spouses and partners live with and relate to each other. As part of their immigration application, couples must tell the story of their relationship and submit things like photographs, letters, emails, bank statements, birthday cards, and telephone bills in order to corroborate that story. Sometimes, visa officers also conduct face-to-face interviews with applicants to try to clarify ambiguities in the story of a couple's relationship. Visa officers must assess this information and decide whether the couple is in a genuine relationship and whether they can live together in Canada "happily ever after."

How visa officers come to these conclusions is the subject of Vic Satzewich's research in *Points of Entry: How Canada's Visa Officers Decide Who Gets In*. He shows that visa officers have general understandings of types of relationships and use various indicators of "normality" to decide whether relationships are genuine. For example, they scrutinize photographs to see who attended a wedding ceremony and their demeanour. As the following quotation from his research shows, the fact that people are not smiling in photographs leads the visa officer to suspect that the ceremony has been staged.

Nobody in the photos is smiling. They have done the ceremony. It's a Sikh temple, so it's a serious occasion, but nobody is smiling. Nobody seems happy. This is a concern. . . . People are dancing, but still, nobody is smiling. There are no photos of private moments between the couple (Satzewich, 2015: 160).

When Satzewich asked a visa officer how she tries to figure out whether certain scenes in photographs are staged for the purposes of immigration and trying to get a non-Canadian into Canada, the visa officer explained:

> That's kind of hard to say. Are they making out in the pictures if it is the first time they actually met? Are they being too affectionate? The pictures taken in the bedroom on the wedding night–they are half naked. I am thinking, "Is this a natural position?" How many people take pictures in the bedroom on the wedding night? Sometimes you get too many wedding night pictures. (Satzewich, 2015: 159)

Source: Vic Satzewich. 2015. *Points of Entry: How Canada's Visa Officers Decide Who Gets In*. Vancouver: University of British Columbia Press.

Furthermore, data for Toronto indicate that in 1995, both economic class (skilled workers and business immigrants) and family class immigrants were net contributors to the tax base. On average, for every $1.60 that family class immigrants paid in income tax, they collected only $1.00 in welfare and employment insurance benefits. Economic class immigrants did even better: for every $3.50 that they paid in income tax, they received $1.00 in social assistance and employment insurance benefits (Preston, Lo, and Wang, 2003: 197–9).

Some critics suggest that the support conditions attached to sponsored immigrants are in fact a double-edged sword. While it may make economic sense for the Canadian government to want to limit its potential welfare liabilities for family class immigrants, the support provisions of the legislation can create economic dependency on the sponsor. This dependency is problematic and puts family class immigrants in possible jeopardy if they happen to be in an abusive relationship with their sponsor. Some sponsored immigrant women may be unwilling to leave abusive husbands out of fear that they will be violating their initial agreement with the federal government and hence jeopardize their permanent residence status in Canada. Though Canada and other countries have provisions that relax the support provisions in cases of abusive relationships, these provisions are not well known. Furthermore, for women in abusive relationships, there is no certainty that these provisions will be applied in their specific case.

Even though it is clear that critics of the family class immigration category exaggerate the negative economic consequences of this kind of immigration, there are other reasons that such criticisms are misplaced. Evaluating family class immigration solely on the basis of economic logic is a one-sided benchmark that downplays the social benefits that accrue to other immigrants and to Canada more generally from family class immigration. A number of commentators have argued that social capital is an increasingly important aspect of immigrant integration in Canada. Social capital refers to the social relations and social networks that may provide access to resources and support (Voyer, 2004). The relationship between immigrant economic success and the presence of family and ethnic networks is complex. While some argue that these networks may function in ways that reduce contact with "mainstream" society and dominant groups and hence reduce social capital (Ooka and Wellman, 2000), the presence of family members and other co-ethnics may strengthen the networks of social relations that provide support for immigrants, which may assist in the long-term integration of immigrants. In addition, efforts to quantify the economic contributions that family class immigrants make to Canadian society discount the social and mental health benefits associated with family reunification. Research suggests that there are long-term mental health benefits associated with having ethnic and family support (Noh and Kaspar, 2003: 342).

Migrants on the Margins

Any discussion of Canadian immigration policy is incomplete if it does not look at individuals on the margins. Although much of Canada's immigration program is oriented toward the admission of individuals as permanent residents, other aspects of the program are devoted to the admission of temporary workers. Moreover, discussions of immigration always raise the issue of non-status or illegal immigration. Both of these cases of migrants on the margins of Canadian society—temporary workers and "illegals"—raise implications for patterns of "race" and ethnic relations.

Temporary Workers

The fact that Canada admits a relatively large number of individuals as immigrants should not blind us to the fact that Canada also admits a relatively large number of individuals as *temporary workers*. They are different from immigrants in that they do not have the right to permanent residence, and they are admitted to Canada to do specific jobs for specific lengths of time (Sharma, 2006). If they are high-skilled temporary workers, they may apply for permanent residence in Canada; if they are low skilled they cannot apply for permanent residence and must return to their country of origin when their temporary work visas expire. While in Canada, they cannot quit or change their jobs without the permission of the federal government. If they do quit or change jobs without government permission, they are subject to deportation. Sometimes referred to as "guest workers" or "unfree migrant workers" (Satzewich, 1991; Sharma, 2001), they are a growing part of Canada's intake of foreign workers.

Canada allows individuals to work in the country on a temporary basis through the Temporary Foreign Worker Program. While Canada started to give temporary employment visas for farm workers in the late 1960s, and progressively expanded those provisions to other occupations in the 1980s and 1990s through the then Non-Immigrant Employment Authorization Program (NIEAP) (Sharma, 2001), the federal government has recently started to make it easier for other employers to hire foreign workers temporarily. Also included in the category of Temporary Foreign Worker are international students who come to Canada to study in provincially recognized educational institutions. The government has made it easier for these students to remain in Canada after they have completed their courses of study.

Sharma (2001) and Alboim (2009) argue that Canada is undergoing a relatively rapid transformation from an *immigrant-receiving* to a *migrant-receiving* nation. They worry that Canada is becoming a country that increasingly relies on migrant workers rather than permanent immigrants. In 2013, Canada admitted 194,075 international students and 118,024 temporary foreign workers, for a total of 312,099 temporary entry visas. As a result, the number of temporary entry visas is nearly double the number of permanent residence visas issued.

Talking about NIEAP, the previous incarnation of the Temporary Foreign Worker Program, Sharma argues that

> the operation of the migrant worker category can substantially enhance the ability of the Canadian government to attract and/or retain capital investment in its territory by giving employers in the country . . . access to a "cheap labour strategy"

of global competition. . . . The operation of the NIEAP enables those in the Canadian government to produce a group of non-citizens who, because of their classification as "non-immigrants," can legally be exempted from laws on minimum employment standards, collective bargaining, and the provision of social services and programs such as unemployment insurance, social assistance, old-age pensions, etc. (2001: 426)

Care needs to be taken in the interpretation of the meaning of the Temporary Foreign Worker Program as a traditional migrant worker program designed to recruit cheap, low-skilled labour. Many highly skilled temporary foreign workers and international students can use this as either a temporary or permanent entryway to Canada. Thus, in 2013, nearly 50 per cent of those admitted to Canada as temporary workers were in managerial or professional occupations or skilled trades. These workers might include an engineer from Japan who is working in Canada to help set up a new piece of technology and who has no interest in staying in Canada permanently. They would also include an American operations manager who, while working temporarily in Canada to help a major hotel set up a supply chain, likes what she sees in the country and eventually wants to bring her family and become a permanent resident. Also included would be young people from places like Australia or England who are taking a year off from school to work for a season at a ski resort in the Rockies and who have no intention of staying in Canada permanently.

However, an increasing number of workers are being admitted through this program for low-skilled work. During the Alberta oil boom of the early 2000s, for example, many temporary foreign workers were recruited from Third World countries to work in hotels as chambermaids, or in the fast-food industry flipping burgers or making pizzas. Canada's rules for these workers are different insofar as they cannot apply for permanent residence through this pathway. These low-skilled workers are the traditional migrant workers, and they are the ones who are particularly vulnerable to exploitation. The drop in world oil prices in 2014 resulted in significant cutbacks in the number of temporary foreign workers in the oil patch, and in the province more generally.

Workers coming to Canada through the Seasonal Agricultural Workers Program are one of the single largest categories for temporary foreign workers. Beginning in 1966 as a small experimental movement of 264 Jamaican workers to Ontario, the program now involves over 24,000 workers from various Caribbean countries and Mexico admitted on a yearly basis to work on farms in every province of Canada except Newfoundland and Labrador (Hennebry, 2012). Many work in Ontario in greenhouses or in fields picking tender fruit, vegetables, and tobacco. Some also work in food-processing plants.

As migrant workers, they come to Canada under labour contracts that stipulate that they can remain in Canada for between six weeks and eight months and that they must return to their country of origin when their contract expires. The cost of transportation to Canada is paid for by the farmers, but they can recover up to $550 from the workers from Mexico and $536 from workers from the Caribbean. Employers must provide workers with accommodation without charge.

Part of the reason that workers from the Caribbean and Mexico are so attractive to a seemingly increasing number of employers across Canada stems from their condition of unfreedom. Since they come from countries with high levels of unemployment and poor economic conditions, the wages offered in Canada can be quite attractive compared to the alternatives in their country of origin. Given this economic dependency on Canadian wages, workers are reluctant to do anything that would jeopardize their employment situation here. As a result, migrant workers are relatively compliant workers, reluctant to complain about their living and working conditions or possible health and safety violations in the workplace. They fear that they will be sent home before their contract expires or not be invited back by immigration authorities the next year. According to Basok's analysis,

> the growers realize, of course, that what makes Mexican (and Caribbean) labour so valuable is that the workers are not free to quit. If Mexican workers were to come as permanent residents, this advantage would be lost, as one grower points out: "The disadvantage of legalizing Mexicans would be that they would be free to leave the greenhouses and go to work cutting mushrooms, for instance. Mushrooms are "hi tech" now. They are air conditioned—sixty degrees. You'll get workers there. They will be there before they'll be here.. (2002: 126)

Migrant worker vulnerability is further aggravated by the fact that in Ontario, they are not protected by provincial labour standards legislation. As agricultural labourers, they are able to form "associations" but only in 2009 gained the right to bargain collectively with employers to improve wages or working conditions. Nor are they able to vote, which limits their political power and ability to lobby government representatives to change such policies.

Non-status Immigrants

Even though there is less research on non-status (or what is known colloquially as "illegal") immigration in Canada than there is in the United States, political elites and members of the general public in this country do occasionally become concerned about the issue. In the summer of 1999, the arrival of four ships containing 600 undocumented migrants from the province of Fujian, China, raised alarm bells that Canada was about to be swamped by hordes of illegal immigrants who would use the in-Canada refugee determination system to gain a foothold in Canada. The feeling was that these arrivals were just the tip of a much larger iceberg of illegal immigration from China to Canada. It was feared that many more "ghost" ships were lurking in the waters off British Columbia, waiting to disembark their human cargo in isolated bays, coves, and inlets along the coast.

Hier and Greenberg (2002: 161) argue that the Canadian media blew this incident out of proportion and succeeded in creating a moral panic about illegal immigration from China. They argue that the ensuing public debate eventually led to a "hardening of attitudes and policies related to undocumented migratory populations."

Even though Hier and Greenberg (2002) downplay the size of the movement and suggest that the fears about Canada being swamped with illegal immigrants were overblown, there is evidence to suggest that non-status immigrants are, in fact, a significant part of the social fabric of this country and that they are arguably an increasingly important element of certain sectors of the Canadian economy. One estimate suggests that there are between 50,000 and 100,000 non-status immigrants in Canada. Yet, contrary to Hier and Greenberg (2002), Canadians appear to have turned a blind eye to this kind of migration. It is common knowledge, for example, that the Ontario construction industry is heavily reliant on the labour of illegal immigrants, with as many as 76,000 working in that industry alone in 2003. In Toronto, there are reportedly certain parking lots and street corners where contractors and other construction industry employers know they can go to hire non-status immigrants on a day-labour basis. Other non-status immigrants are hired on more permanent arrangements to work in factories and restaurants and on farms. Thus, rather than leading to a stiffening of public attitudes and the implementation of stricter policies related to illegal immigration, the 1999 incident and its aftermath seems to be a distant memory in both policy-maker and public minds. It is probably more accurate to say that Canada and the United States appear to be more concerned about the initial interdiction of non-status immigrants at the border. If and when they get through the border, they are subject to a less stringent enforcement regime.

Non-status immigration is actually a catch-all term used to describe individuals in three different circumstances. First, some people enter Canada without official authorization. Often, these individuals come to Canada through human smuggling operations, and their final destination is the United States (Jiminez, 2005). The global traffic in human beings is estimated to be a five-to-seven-billion-dollar-per-year industry. It can, for example, cost individuals from China and other Asian countries between $30,000 and $40,000 (USD) to be smuggled into the United States through Mexico (Spener, 2001: 154). Human smuggling chains are often difficult to police because traffickers use sophisticated techniques to create false documents and hiding places and because they have complex networks that can be shut down or established on very short notice.

Second, some people are visa over-stayers. They enter the country legally on one particular kind of visa (a temporary work, student, or visitor visa) but stay beyond the time frame allowed in their original entry visa. Although Canada's visa-granting system is designed to prevent the arrival of individuals who mask their true intentions for wanting to come, Canada exercises very little control over people once they are legally admitted to Canada (Cox and Glenn, 1994). Visa over-stayers are difficult to police because Canada does not have a mechanism to track whether individuals given the right of temporary entry ever actually leave when their visas expire.

The third stream of non-status immigration in Canada is composed of failed refugee claimants. Indeed, as in other countries, there is sometimes a blurring of the distinction between illegal immigrants and legitimate refugees. One estimate suggests that in 1994, between 60,000 and 120,000 asylum-seekers were smuggled into Europe by migrant traffickers (Koser, 2001: 58). Individuals whose in-Canada applications for refugee status were denied but who have not left or have not been deported may become illegal immigrants in Canada. Some individuals use the in-Canada refugee determination system to get a foot in the door and to buy time in order to go underground. It is relatively easy for individuals to disappear from the system if their intention is simply to gain access to Canadian soil and better themselves economically. Furthermore, even though the fear that terrorists are using refugee systems to gain entry to places like Canada, the United States, and Europe is probably overblown, there may very well be a small number of individuals who use the refugee determination system as a way of gaining entry for more sinister reasons associated with participation in terrorist or other criminal activities.

While it is difficult to determine which of these three streams contributes the most to the total population of non-status residents in Canada, experts suggests that the latter two streams likely produce the largest numbers of non-status immigrants in Canada.

Non-status immigrants are in an even more precarious social position than migrant workers. With few rights and in constant fear of being apprehended, non-status immigrants in many ways constitute an ideal workforce for employers chronically short of labour whose profit margins are tight. Commenting about the United States but with no less relevance to Canada, Gimpel and Edwards argue that "the practice of employing low wage workers in squalid sweatshop conditions is surprisingly common in certain low-profit-margin businesses. The illegitimate employers routinely dodge wage and labor laws because they know the illegal workers they employ will not go to the authorities out of fear of being discovered and deported" (1999: 85). In addition, non-status immigrants may deprive themselves and their family members of important services, such as health care or police services when they need them, for fear of apprehension (Cox and Glenn, 1994: 284).

Canada and the United States have both undertaken measures to control non-status immigration. These measures range from border controls, to imposing visa regulations on certain countries deemed to produce illegal immigrants, to laws that prohibit persons from knowingly employing non-status immigrants. For example, the 1986 US Immigration Reform and Control Act states that employers who knowingly hire illegal aliens can be fined between $3,000 and $10,000 (USD) per worker or face terms of imprisonment for repeated infractions. In Canada, employers who do not carry out due diligence in determining whether an individual is legally entitled to work in Canada are subject to fines of up to $50,000 and/or two years' imprisonment. Workers found to be working illegally in Canada are subject to deportation, although if they make a claim for refugee status, they must receive a hearing before their case is disposed of. Canada also has carrier sanctions in place to help stem the flow of illegal immigrants. Airlines that board individuals without proper documentation on flights destined for Canada face "administrative" fees of up to $3,200 and must cover the cost of the individual's return to their place of origin (Cox and Glenn, 1994, 286; Canada, Department of Justice, 2002).

Summary

This chapter shows that the Canadian immigration system is complex and undergoing rapid change. There are a number of economic, political, and demographic factors shaping the contemporary immigration system. Though "race" was removed from immigration processes more than 30 years ago, critics continue to allege that there are racist overtones to many aspects of the ways that immigrants are allowed to come to Canada and in how Canadian society responds to the presence of immigrants. Some of these allegations are based on more solid empirical foundations than others.

Canada admits individuals from around the world under a variety of different categories: refugees, skilled immigrants, live-in caregivers, provincial nominees, family class immigrants, business immigrants, and migrant workers. Each of these forms of migration carries certain controversies: safe-third-country provisions for refugees are said to put some legitimate refugees at risk, skilled immigrants are said to be declining in quality, family class immigrants are accused of being a drain on the economy, and business immigrants are said to be responsible for skyrocketing housing costs in places like Vancouver. Many of these accusations are without strong empirical foundation.

Even though Canada admits about a quarter of a million immigrants per year, it also admits large numbers of migrant workers. The admittance of migrant workers raises hard questions about the unequal access to citizenship rights in this country.

Questions for Critical Thought

1. To what extent does racism continue to inform the contemporary Canadian immigration system?
2. Does Canada's adherence to "safe-third-country" principles actually put legitimate refugees at risk?
3. Why does Canada admit immigrants?
4. Canada is a country of immigrants, yet it also admits thousands of migrant workers to work on only a temporary basis. How can this apparent anomaly be explained?
5. Are family class immigrants a drain on the Canadian economy? What evidence supports this claim, and what evidence questions it?

Debate Questions

1. Canada competes with other countries (the United States, Australia, New Zealand, etc.) for attracting skilled workers. If we were to accept larger numbers of skilled workers, how should immigration policy change in order to facilitate this process?

2. Often in the past, during times of economic hardship, Canadian immigration policy restricted the numbers of immigrants allowed in the country. What should the government do today, when unemployment is rising? Should they restrict immigration numbers? Would this affect employment opportunities for other workers in the country? What jobs do recent immigrants usually get?

3. Should migrant workers, if they have been working in Canada for, say, five consecutive years, get permanent residence status? Why or why not?

4. Some countries introduce "amnesties" for those living there without legal status. Do such amnesties end up encouraging more people to try to migrate without legal status in the hope that they too might achieve legal status through an amnesty?

Annotated Additional Readings

Fleras, Augie. 2015. *Immigration Canada: Evolving Realities and Emerging Challenges in a Postnational World*. Vancouver: UBC Press. A thorough, up-to-date, and balanced examination of the current Canadian immigration system.

Hennebry, Jenna. 2012. *Permanently Temporary? Agricultural Migrant Workers and Their Integration in Canada*. Montreal: Institute for Research on Public Policy. A hard-hitting analysis of the experiences of migrant agricultural workers in Canada focusing on the contradictions associated with admitting people who are good enough to work in Canada but not good enough to stay permanently.

Satzewich, Vic. 2015. *Points of Entry: How Canada's Visa Officers Decide Who Gets In*. Vancouver: UBC Press. Based on unprecedented access to overseas visa officers, the book examines how visa officers make decisions about who ought to be given a visa to live in, or visit, Canada.

Simmons, Alan. 2010. *Immigration and Canada: Global and Transnational Perspectives*. Toronto: Canadian Scholars Press. A theoretically sophisticated and empirically rich analysis of immigration to Canada, this book focuses on the dynamics of international migration and immigrant integration into Canadian society.

Related Websites

Immigration, Refugees, and Citizenship Canada
www.cic.gc.ca/english/department/index.asp
Official Government of Canada website for Citizenship and Immigration Canada, the government department responsible for administering Canadian immigration policy.

International Organization for Migration
www.iom.int
This inter-governmental organization in the field of migration works closely with governmental, intergovernmental, and non-governmental partners to deal with a variety of migration-related issues.

Justicia for Migrant Workers—J4MW
www.justicia4migrantworkers.org
Justicia for Migrant Workers is an advocacy group organized around securing social justice for migrant workers.

Metropolis Project—An International Forum for Research and Policy on Migration and Cities
http://canada.metropolis.net
This site hosts a research network of scholars and policy-makers in Canada and around the world interested in immigration and settlement issues.

5

Understanding Social Inequality
The Intersections of Ethnicity, Gender, and Class

Learning Objectives

In this chapter, you will learn that

- John Porter's work, *The Vertical Mosaic*, has provided the groundwork for much of the current debate about social inequality in Canada.
- when taking occupational attainment and earnings into account, there has been a trend toward convergence among Canadian-born members of ethnic groups in relation to their socio-economic status.
- some sociologists argue that despite this convergence, the vertical mosaic metaphor continues to be relevant to Canadian society.
- some sociologists argue that there is a new colour-coded vertical mosaic in Canada.
- immigrant educational credentials are devalued in Canada, and this accounts for at least some of the inequalities between immigrants and the Canadian-born and between visible minority and non–visible minority immigrants.
- social class still is an important dividing line in Canadian society. Ethnic groups are not exclusively concentrated in one particular social class but are distributed across the range of class sites in Canada.
- gender and nativity (place of birth), along with class, constitute bases of inequality in earnings not only among but also within ethnic and visible minorities.

Introduction

It is clear that some people in Canada do better economically than others. Some people earn high incomes, are well-respected professionals, or own successful businesses or large corporations. People with what are perceived to be "really good jobs" live in big houses, drive nice cars, have summer cottages, and do not have to temporarily do without in order to afford a winter vacation. At the other extreme, some Canadians are homeless and sleep under bridges, rely on food banks, and live in grinding poverty. In between the extremes, there is the ill-defined "middle class" whose votes so many politicians want to court.

How do immigrants and members of racialized communities fit into this general picture of Canada? Are immigrants and members of visible minority communities concentrated at the bottom of the **socio-economic hierarchy**? Do they do the "dirty work" of Canadian society, characterized by low pay and poor and unsafe working conditions? Conversely, are white Canadians and the historically preferred European ethnic groups that we talked about in Chapter 3 concentrated at the middle and top of the rank? Do they have a monopoly over the good jobs characterized by status, prestige, and high income? Are the **labour market** experiences and socio-economic positions of men and women within immigrant, ethnic, and racialized communities the same, or are they different? Is it possible that at the same time that Canadian society restricts opportunities for mobility and economic advancement for some immigrants and members of ethnic and racialized communities, other members of the same communities do very well for themselves and find that this country truly is a land of opportunity?

These are complex questions, and they point to a complex reality. It is tempting to look for individual or cultural explanations for why some individuals and groups are better off economically than others. Some people think that things like hard work, talent, and education are the keys to explaining economic success. Others think that culturally determined values explain why some groups do better than others. American academics Amy Chua and Jed Rubenfeld argue that some ethnic, cultural, and religious groups (such as Cubans, Nigerians, Indians, Chinese, and Mormons) do better than others because they have the "triple package": (1) feelings of group superiority or exceptionality, (2) impulse control, and (3) feelings of insecurity (Chua and Rubenfeld, 2014). They argue that all of the successful ethnic groups in the US believe they are superior in some way, feel they have to prove themselves to others, and have cultivated a heightened sense of discipline and impulse control. In their terms, this "rare and potent cultural constellation" gives some groups a leg up over others and explains why they do better economically. Though they talk mostly about the United States, some think the argument is relevant in Canada as well. These variables, while arguably important, do not tell the full story about social inequality, either for immigrants, for the Canadian-born, for racialized communities, or for white, so-called non–visible minorities. As we noted in Chapter 2, it is hard to understand social inequality in this country without understanding the interrelationship between ethnicity, "race," class, gender, and place of birth.

This chapter has three objectives. First, it summarizes what John Porter meant when he characterized Canada in the 1960s as a **vertical mosaic**. Second, it provides an assessment of the debates surrounding the continued relevance of the vertical mosaic metaphor for Canadian society. In doing so, it considers debates about the declining significance of ethnic origin in the vertical mosaic. It also considers the continuing significance of visible minority status—or "race"—and immigration status in shaping the occupational distribution and incomes of individuals in Canada. In other words, it asks whether Canada is now characterized by a racialized or **colour-coded vertical mosaic**. Finally, the chapter provides an alternative perspective on the earnings inequalities of selected ethnic groups in Canada. In particular, we focus on the class divisions within ethnic groups. A different picture of social inequality emerges when we start from a different analytical lens.

The Vertical Mosaic: Porter's Legacy

Over the years, much of the research on social inequality in Canada has focused on the socio-economic performance of ethnic groups in order to demonstrate that Canadian society is hierarchically structured (Agocs and Boyd, 1993: 337). John Meisel, in his foreword to John Porter's *The Vertical Mosaic: An Analysis of Social Class and Power in Canada* (2015 [1965]), welcomes the timing of the publication as fortunate because it appeared "at the very moment when our national attention and preoccupation centre *on ethnic, rather than on class differences*" (Porter, 2015 [1965]: ix; emphasis added). Arguably, as we demonstrate at the end of this chapter, the call for bringing **social class** back into the analysis of social inequality in Canada is as current today as it was in 1965.

Porter sees his book as "an attempt to examine the hitherto unexplored subjects of social class and power in Canadian society" (2015 [1965]: x). He suggests that in multicultural societies, there was a relationship between membership in a cultural group and class position (and, consequently, power) (2015 [1965]: xii). The title *Vertical Mosaic* was originally assigned to the chapter that examines the relationship between ethnicity and social class in order to demonstrate the ethnic component of the structure of class hierarchy in Canada (2015 [1965]: xiii). Porter argues that immigration and ethnic affiliation were important factors in the process of social class formation in Canada, especially at the bottom and elite layers of the stratification system (2015 [1965]: 73).

His argument is based on an analysis of census data from 1931, 1951, and 1961. Porter argues that Canadian society, understood as an ethnic mosaic, is hierarchically structured in terms of the differential distributions of wealth and power among its constituent ethnic groups. Examining the Canadian labour market from a Weberian perspective, Porter found that ethnic groups were unequally represented in the occupational structure. Four of his findings are noteworthy. First, the **charter groups** (British and French) had appropriated higher positions of power and advantage in the social, economic, and political realms and had designated the "entrance status" groups to lower, less preferred positions. Over time, reinforced by stereotypes and social images, these divisions in status were hardened and perpetuated.

Second, "less preferred" groups that arrived in Canada later than the charter groups were relegated to an **entrance group** status. That is, they were employed in lower-status occupations and were subject to the assimilation processes laid down by the charter groups (Porter, 2015 [1965] 63–4). Third, ethnic affiliation implied **blocked social mobility**. Upward mobility of ethnic groups depended on the culture of the ethnic group in question and the degree to which it conformed to the rules of assimilation set by the charter groups. The improvement in the position of entrance status groups over time could be determined by their "assimilability" or their behavioural and structural assimilation (Porter 2015 [1965]: 67–73).

In terms of the relative hierarchical position of ethnic groups in the occupational structure, which he regarded as a crude substitute for class, Porter found that a pattern of ethnic inequality persisted. Canadians of Jewish and British origin were at the top. They were persistently overrepresented in the professional and financial occupations (higher status and income) and underrepresented in agricultural and unskilled jobs (lower status and income). The Germans, Scandinavians, and Dutch were closest to the British. Italians, Poles, and Ukrainians were next, with other southern Europeans (Greek and Portuguese) near the lower end of the spectrum (Porter 2015 [1965]: 90). The French, located between the northern and southern Europeans, were underrepresented in professional and financial occupations and overrepresented in agricultural and unskilled jobs. Aboriginal peoples were at the bottom of the hierarchy (2015 [1965]: 73–103).

Fourth, as far as the charter groups were concerned, the British were more pow-erful than the French (2015 [1965]: 91–8). In fact, despite the considerable influence exerted on the political system by French Canadians, not only in Quebec but also at the federal level (2015 [1965]: 417–56), and their access to high-status political positions and the media, it was the British who dominated Canada's economic life and were overrepresented in elite positions (2015 [1965]: 201–308, 337–416, 520–59).

Porter's work has been characterized as the most important book in Canadian sociology (Forcese, 1997: 83), and it set the stage for much of the debate on social inequality in Canada (Brym and Fox, 1989: 92; Ogmundson, 1993; McAll, 1990: 173; Li, 1988: 3; Jedwab and Satzewich, 2015).

Evidence for Ethnic Convergence?

Since the mid-1960s, sociologists have paid attention to the relationship between ethnic origin and class in Canadian society, and a number of significant ques-tions have arisen regarding Porter's findings and treatment of the data. Subsequent analyses of Porter's data and methods have shown that his claims might have been exaggerated on both mass and elite mobility levels (see Brym and Fox, 1989: 93–9, 103–19). Ascription, or the characteristics that you are born with, argue Cuneo and Curtis (1975), is not more important in determining status in Canada than it is in the US. Canada is not an ascriptive but an achievement society (Goyder and Curtis, 1979: 229). A detailed account of Porter critiques is not our aim here (see Brym and Fox, 1989; Ogmundson, 1991, 1993; Ogmundson and McLaughlin, 1992). However, it is necessary to place some of these criticisms in the wider context of the social inequality debate. Research on social inequality and on the lack of mass and elite mobility has been basically concerned with either supporting or refuting Porter's work. Here we examine only issues associated with mass mobility.[1]

Occupational Attainment and the Economy

Canada's economy rests upon capitalist principles (Clement and Myles, 1994). The production, distribution, and exchange of goods and services are done primarily for profit. Ownership of most profit-producing means (i.e., small and large enterprises, industries, buildings, stores, banks, mass media, ad agencies, etc.) is private. The labour market is a constituent part of the capitalist economy. It is a competitive arena in which the ability to work (labour power) is exchanged for wages and sala-ries. It constitutes the primary mechanism by which individuals engage in the pro-cess of work, either as sellers of their skills (workers), or as buyers (employers). It is the place where we get jobs. In such an arena there exist good and bad jobs. Usually, good jobs require workers with high levels of human capital (i.e., higher education and high technical skill levels). Good jobs pay high wages, have good benefits, enjoy job security, are mostly full-time, provide opportunities for advancement within the company, and are often unionized. They are prestigious, usually found in larger corporations and the public sector, and constitute what we call the primary labour market. They are the jobs many of us want. As you have probably experienced yourselves, not all jobs are good. If you have ever worked in a restaurant, in a small retail store, or at a gas station, where little human capital is required, you know what we mean. Jobs in the so-called secondary labour market do not require higher education or skills, do not pay high wages, do not provide benefits or opportunities for advancement, and are mostly part-time, highly susceptible to unemployment, and not unionized. They are the jobs we want to avoid, at least in the long term. Employment in the secondary labour market is usually "just a job," whereas employment in the primary labour market is a career. Part of the reason you are studying at university or college is because you want a career, not just a "survival job."

Employment (and unemployment) and the price of labour (wages and salaries) largely depend upon the general economic conditions that determine the supply and demand for certain occupations with specific educational and skill requirements in certain sectors of the economy. At present, for example, given the crisis in the auto industry, there are few jobs available in a sector traditionally thought to provide workers with decent salaries, a lot of overtime, and extended benefits. In fact, there are huge layoffs globally, and the Trans-Pacific Partnership, a free trade agreement negotiated in 2015 by the previous Conservative government, is expected to result in further declines in this sector of the Canadian economy (Keenan, 2015). In general, under conditions of capitalist competition, there are always more people seeking good jobs than are available. This keeps the cost of labour low for employers. Workers compete for all jobs, but there is greater competition for good jobs; not everyone can get one. It is not easy being employed, let alone having a career, especially under the current conditions of economic uncertainty. The labour market is a mechanism that produces inequalities (in earnings, benefits, etc.) and reproduces them over long periods of time. It creates structures of inequality.

Large numbers of women, young people, single parents, Aboriginals, recent immigrants, members of ethnic and "visible" groups, and, increasingly, the elderly, work in the secondary labour market, in substandard employment (Krahn et al., 2007). Even though employment opportunities for visible minorities have opened up over the years, there are still causes for concern even at the top end of the labour market. Howard Ramos (2012) shows that even though visible minorities earn doctoral degrees at rates above the national average, they are underrepresented in the ranks of university professors. And, of even more concern, their underrepresentation among university professors seems to be increasing even though employment equity policies introduced 30 years ago were meant, in part, to improve the representativeness of visible minorities at the upper ends of the occupational structure.

As we mentioned in Chapter 4, Canada recruits immigrants partly because it wants to keep the cost of labour down. Why are they underrepresented in good occupations? Is this accidental? Is it because they do not have the qualifications required for higher-level occupations (high skills and/or higher education)? Alternatively, could it be because discrimination exists in the labour market?

Since the 1960s, a number of researchers have maintained that differential occupational attainment among ethnic groups is substantial and an enduring feature of the labour market. Historically in Canada, the British have continued to enjoy higher occupational status than the French (Royal Commission on Bilingualism and Biculturalism, 1969; Breton and Roseborough, 1971; Boyd et al., 1981). Other ethnic groups, such as the Jews and northern and western Europeans, have been in advantaged positions. Southern Europeans, visible minorities, and Aboriginal peoples have been found at the bottom of the occupational hierarchy (Porter, 1985; Li, 1988; Lautard and Guppy, 1990; Reitz, 1990). Despite a decline since the 1960s, ethnic disparities in occupational status have been seen as persistent. Lautard and Guppy (2007), for example, argue that ethnic **occupational dissimilarity** is still substantial enough to justify the vertical mosaic image of Canada today.

But does occupational dissimilarity necessarily imply social inequality? Some have re-examined Porter's thesis and have argued that ethnicity does not play a significant role in occupational attainment or, more generally, in social mobility. Darroch (1979: 1–25) re-examined Porter's data and argues that Porter paid too much attention to the actual order of the ethnic hierarchy in occupational status and failed to notice the decreasing strength of the association between ethnicity and occupational level over time. In 1961, for example, ethnic occupational over-representation and underrepresentation was lower than in 1931. In 1931, occupational dissimilarity was great among all non-charter groups, but by 1961, the differences had almost disappeared for Germans and eastern and other Europeans and had declined significantly for every other group except Aboriginal peoples. The blocked ethnic mobility thesis, then, has no factual foundation, and Darroch suggests that we should be "skeptical of the idea that ethnic affiliations are a basic factor in generally limiting mobility opportunities in Canada" (1979: 16). Porter's mobility trap hypothesis, according to Darroch, is "an exaggeration" (1979: 22).

The success of visible minority candidates in the 2015 federal election seems to support those who question the validity of the blocked mobility thesis. At least 46 visible minority members of Parliament were elected in the October 2015 election and they represented 13.6 per cent of all MPs who were elected. Though visible minorities represent about 19 per cent of the population of the country, this was up from 28 visible minority MPs in the 2011 election, where they represented just 9.1 per cent of elected members of Parliament. Though holding political office is only one measure of power in Canadian society, it is nonetheless an indication that those with white skin or a European ancestry do not necessarily have a monopoly over political decisions about how the country ought to be run.

Earnings Inequalities

Along the same lines as the debate about occupation, some researchers suggest that there has been earnings equalization among ethnic groups, whereas others argue that ethnic inequalities persist in that area. Ornstein (1981, 1983) shows that ethnicity alone does not explain much of the variation in earnings. He argues that much of what appears to be ethnic differences in earnings may be attributed to place of birth, place of education, and language. He also demonstrates that class and gender, along with labour market variables, are more important determinants of earnings than ethnicity. Weinfeld (1988), examining 1971 and 1981 census data, argues that in that 10-year period there had been a reduction in income inequalities among ethnic groups. When sex, nativity, occupation, age, education, and number of weeks worked are statistically controlled, non-visible minority groups had almost the same income, whereas the earnings gap of visible minorities had become narrower. What matters, according to Weinfeld, is the percentage of the foreign-born within visible minorities and their amount and type of educational attainment (Weinfeld 1988, 603–5).

Winn (1988), using 1981 census data, argues that there is no necessary correspondence between low income[2] or low prestige and "visibility." Some non-visible groups, who presumably might have enjoyed higher prestige because of their "whiteness," had lower incomes than visible groups. In 1981, the Japanese were the third-highest income group. Indo-Pakistanis and Koreans were found in the second quintile of earnings (1988: 197, Table 17.2). Looking back at 1971 data, Winn argues that Asians were the second-highest income group (1988: 196, Table 17.1). The British in 1971 had lower incomes than lower-status groups such as the Jewish, Italians, other eastern Europeans, and other southern Europeans. Some higher-prestige groups, such as Scandinavians, Germans, and the Dutch, had incomes either below or around the national average (1988: 196–8). Therefore, argues Winn, it is plausible to suggest that there has been considerable ethnic mobility in earnings, especially as far as visible minority and lower-status groups are concerned. Winn suggests that upward mobility was experienced mostly by visible groups and downward mobility by higher-status, non-visible groups (1988: 198–200). In fact, Winn goes even further, suggesting that employment equity policies were unnecessary[3] since visible minorities and low-prestige groups had made considerable economic progress.

The New Colour-Coded Vertical Mosaic?

Even though questions have been raised about the persistence of the vertical mosaic when European ethnic groups are considered, some suggest that the vertical mosaic persists in a racialized form and that Canada is characterized by a *colour-coded vertical mosaic* (Galabuzi, 2006: 7; Fleras, 2012).

In 1984, the Royal Commission on Equality in Employment, using 1981 census data, found that among men, Aboriginal peoples, and visible minorities such as the Indo-Chinese (those from Vietnam, Laos, and Cambodia), Central and South Americans, and blacks had incomes below the national average and were at the bottom of the income hierarchy. Among women, Aboriginal peoples, Central and South Americans, the Indo-Chinese, and Koreans had the lowest incomes (Royal Commission on Equality in Employment, 1984: 84–5). These income disparities were attributed to systemic discrimination in the workplace. Visible minorities were often denied access to employment because of unfair recruitment procedures and were more likely to be unemployed. Their educational credentials, acquired outside Canada, were not recognized in the labour market or by governments. Sometimes, Canadian experience was required unduly (1984: 46–51). For Aboriginal peoples, the situation was even worse. Aboriginal men earned 60 per cent of the earnings of non-native men; Aboriginal women earned 72 per cent as much as non-Aboriginal women (1984: 33). Educational opportunities and training were seen as inadequate responses to the problem of inequality (1984: 34–5). Aboriginal people were more likely to be found in part-time or seasonal employment and less likely to move up the promotional ladder (1984: 37).

In response to Winn's argument that employment equity policies are unnecessary, Boyd (1992) demonstrated that visible minorities receive lower monetary rewards than their non–visible minority counterparts for similar qualifications. Using 1986 data, she showed that after controlling for age, region, place of residence, marital status, education, occupation, and employment status, the adjusted wages and salaries of visible minority men and women were lower than those of non–visible minority men and women (1992: 305–6, Table 5).

In the case of women (with the exception of the Chinese, who earned on average $237 more per year than other Canadian women), all visible minorities earned less than their non–visible minority female counterparts. West Asian women made $1,928 less than the average of $15,144 annually, and other visible minority women made between $491 and $233 less. French women earned the highest average income, $1,245 above the average for all women. However, non–visible minority women of Greek, Italian, Portuguese, other European, and Dutch descent made less than the average.

In the case of men, all visible minorities earned substantially less than the average of $28,074 per year. However, Greek men earned $3,344 less than the average (the second-lowest earnings, ranking only above Filipino men), eastern Europeans $669 less, Germans $326 less, Portuguese $300 less, and other Europeans $194 less. The British earned the highest average income among men—$3,306 more than the average for all men.

Lian and Matthews (1998) examined 1991 census data and analyzed ethnic inequalities in earnings, studying the relationship between ethnicity and education and between education and income. They argue that "race" is now the fundamental basis of income inequality in Canada. The French now earn more than the British, and there is a general trend of convergence of earnings among the European groups. Visible minorities, however, at all educational levels receive lower rewards, substantially below the national average (1998: 471, 475). Controlling for a number of variables, such as gender, age, marital status, province and place of residence, and year of immigration, Lian and Matthews suggest that in most of the 10 categories of educational level they examined, visible minorities make less than non–visible minorities (1998: 473, Table 5). These findings led them to conclude that the old ethnic vertical mosaic may be disappearing, but it is being replaced by a strong "coloured mosaic" (1998: 476; see also Pendakur and Pendakur, 1996).

In a hard-hitting analysis titled *Canada's Economic Apartheid: The Social Exclusion of Racialized Groups in the New Century*, Grace-Edward Galabuzi (2006) argues that there is substantial evidence, based on the 2000 census, to support the claim that there is a new colour-coded vertical mosaic. More current data lends further weight to this thesis. In a report prepared for the Canadian Centre for Policy Alternatives, Sheila Block (2010) finds that when looking at employment income, racialized men and women earn 73.6 per cent and 84.7 per cent respectively of the income of their non-racialized counterparts (see Table 5.1). Though these differences diminish somewhat when generational and educational differences are included, significant differences in income still remain. Table 5.2 shows, for example, that even when individuals are born in Canada and have university-level education, racialized men earn 73.6 per cent of what non-racialized men earn, while racialized women earn 89.3 per cent of what non-racialized women earn. Keep these differences in mind and compare them with

Table 5.1 Average Employment Income, Ontario, 2005

	Racialized	Non-racialized	Differential (%)
Men	37,010	50,255	73.6
Women	26,840	31,682	84.7
Total	32,042	41,355	77.5

Source: Sheila Block, 2010. *Ontario's Growing Gap: The Role of Race and Gender*. Ottawa: Canadian Centre for Policy Alternatives, p. 7; and Statistics Canada, 2006 Census, Catalogue number 97-563-XCB2006060.

Table 5.2 Average Employment Income, Ontario, 2005, by Generation, 25–44, with University Education

	Racialized		Non-racialized		Differential (%)	
	Men	Women	Men	Women	Men	Women
1st generation	48,057	34,337	72,732	42,675	66.1	80.5
2nd generation	60,066	44,472	81,581	49,805	73.6	89.3
3rd or more generation	73,351	47,005	81,993	49,289	89.5	95.4

Source: Sheila Block, 2010. *Ontario's Growing Gap: The Role of Race and Gender*. Ottawa: Canadian Centre for Policy Alternatives, p. 8; and Statistics Canada, 2006 Census, Catalogue Number 97-563-XCB2006060.

the after-tax income differences *within* ethnic and racialized groups, found at the end of this chapter.

Using 2006 data, Peter Li (2012) shows that there are significant differences in the earnings of university professors in Canada, and that visible minority professors, both men and women, tend to earn less than their white counterparts. He shows that when variations in earnings due to field of study, immigration status, province of residence, and holding a PhD degree are statistically controlled for, white male professors have the highest earnings. Male visible minority Latin American professors earned about $12,000 less than the average for all groups, while visible minority South Asian women earned about $19,000 less than the average for all groups. With one or two exceptions, every visible minority group earned less than white male university professors (Li, 2012). Even though Li is not able to statistically control for variations in earnings because of potential productivity differences among university professors, his findings are nonetheless disturbing to the extent that universities should be places where merit trumps factors like sex and "race" in determining the rewards received for the work that is done.

We will return to the colour-coded mosaic thesis later in this chapter. But before offering a critical perspective on it, we want to consider one more dimension of inequality that has been the subject of considerable research in Canada: inequalities between immigrants and non-immigrants.

Immigrants and the Vertical Mosaic

Another focus of sociological research on inequality examines what happens specifically to immigrants when they arrive in Canada. In other words, how do immigrants fare in the Canadian labour market once they are here, and is there evidence that they are treated fairly by employers and licensing bodies that regulate entry to various professions? These are not, as you might expect, simply academic questions. Policy-makers, immigrant advocates, and immigrants themselves are profoundly concerned about how immigrants, particularly those with valuable skills, education, and experience, are treated in Canada. After all, as we noted in Chapter 4, Canada needs, wants, and recruits skilled immigrants, but it is not clear whether the Canadian labour market fairly rewards all immigrants for the training and the talent that they bring to the country.

We examine two specific issues in this section. First, to what extent do immigrants earn the same income as native-born Canadians, even when other relevant background variables are taken into consideration? Second, what evidence is there that immigrant credentials are evaluated fairly in Canada? In other words, are immigrants who bring certain skills and educational credentials to this country fairly rewarded?

One way to assess the inequalities between different groups of immigrants and the Canadian-born is to compare data on earnings differences among them. Table 5.3 contains data from the 2006 Canadian Census[4] and shows median earnings

Table 5.3 Median[a] Earnings of Recent Immigrants and Canadian-born Earners, Both Sexes, Aged 25 to 54, with or without University Degree, 2005, for Canada, Provinces and Territories—20 per cent Sample Data

	Canadian-born		Immigrant population		Recent immigrants	
	With university degree	Without university degree	With university degree	Without university degree	With university degree	Without university degree
Canada	$51,656	$32,499	$36,451	$27,698	$24,636	$18,572
Newfoundland and Labrador	$50,117	$21,188	$58,155	$23,582	$50,087	*
Prince Edward Island	$44,012	$23,719	$40,580	$17,447	*	*
Nova Scotia	$45,367	$26,561	$38,317	$24,322	$23,874	$18,263
New Brunswick	$48,984	$25,037	$42,316	$25,101	$28,790	$17,379
Quebec	$48,987	$30,041	$29,695	$20,952	$20,081	$16,053
Ontario	$55,992	$36,532	$38,976	$30,027	$26,330	$19,335
Manitoba	$48,045	$29,968	$34,470	$26,223	$23,442	$20,124
Saskatchewan	$49,017	$29,493	$39,140	$24,828	$25,572	$16,142
Alberta	$54,953	$36,832	$38,982	$29,532	$27,432	$21,415
British Columbia	$47,279	$33,840	$33,512	$25,703	$22,920	$17,786
Yukon Territory	$55,622	$35,710	$40,110	$30,673	*	*
Northwest Territories	$73,176	$44,941	$64,019	$35,057	*	*
Nunavut	$80,316	$29,998	*	*	*	*

Notes:
a. Medians are not available for counts less than 250. Earnings are in 2005 constant dollars.
b. Recent immigrants for 2005 is defined as immigrants who immigrated between 2000 and 2004.
* Data is too unreliable to be published by Statistics Canada
Source: Adapted from Statistics Canada publication Income and Earnings, 2006 Census, Catalogue 97-563-XWE2006002

differentials among the Canadian-born, all immigrants, and recent immigrants. In addition, it portrays regional variations. Three patterns are clear. First, immigrants, as a group, make less than Canadian-born individuals in every Canadian province and territory. Second, these differences are greater among those with university education. For example, the median earnings of the Canadian-born with a university degree was $51,656 whereas those of immigrants with a university degree was only $36,451, a difference of $15,205. For those without a university degree, the difference was only $4,801 ($32,499–$27,698). It appears that immigrants with higher education, although they make more than other immigrants without university education, make a lot less than their Canadian-born counterparts. Third, the earnings of recent immigrants, that is, those who immigrated to Canada between 2000 and 2004, are a great deal lower than the earnings of both immigrants who have been in Canada longer than five years and the Canadian-born. For example, when compared with the Canadian-born with a university degree, recent immigrants with a university degree earn $27,020 less ($51,656–$24,636). Recent immigrants without a university degree make $13,927 less than their Canadian-born counterparts ($32,499–$18,572).

A closer look at the general trends of earnings of recent immigrants since the 1980s points to a steady decline in their earnings, compared with Canadian-born earners. Table 5.4 shows median earnings differences among male and female recent immigrants with and without a university degree from 1980 to 2005. Whereas in 1980 recent immigrant males with a university degree made 77 cents for every dollar their Canadian-born counterparts made, in 1990 they made 63 cents, in 2000 they made 58 cents, and in 2005, only 48 cents. Female recent immigrants with a university degree made 59 cents for every dollar their Canadian-born counterparts made in 1980, 63 cents in 1990, 52 cents in 2000, and only 43 cents in 2005.

Male recent immigrants without a university degree in 1980 made 84 cents for every dollar their Canadian-born counterparts made. In 1990 they made 67 cents; in 2000, 65 cents; and in 2005, only 61 cents. Female recent immigrants without a university degree in 1980 made 86 cents for every dollar their Canadian-born counterparts made. In 1990 they made 77 cents; in 2000, 66 cents; and in 2005, only 51 cents. In short, there has been a steady deterioration of recent immigrant earnings, irrespective of gender and university education. This is a troubling trend, given that today most recent immigrants have more educational credentials than those who immigrated to Canada in the 1980s.

Although there are individual variations (knowledge of official languages and foreign education play important roles in influencing immigrant earnings), in general, immigrant status has a strong, negative impact on earnings. As we have shown above, more recent immigrants experience higher levels of earnings inequality. They are more likely to work part-time than full-time, more likely to face unemployment, and less likely to move up the occupational hierarchy. They earn less than Canadian-born workers. Ostrovsky (2008: 24) argues that they also face earnings volatility or instability. Those initial earnings differences tend to persist in later years, especially during times of economic recession as we experienced in the 1990s

Table 5.4 Median Earnings, in 2005 Constant Dollars, of Male and Female Recent Immigrant Earners and Canadian-Born Earners Aged 25 to 54, with or without a University Degree, Canada, 1980 to 2005

Year	Recent immigrant earners[a]				Canadian-born earners[a]				Recent immigrant to Canadian-born earnings ratio			
	With a university degree		With no university degree		With a university degree		With no university degree		With a university degree		With no university degree	
	males	females	males	females	males	females	males	females	males	females	males	females
	2005 constant dollars								ratio			
1980	24,541	24,317	36,467	18,548	63,040	41,241	43,641	24,463	0.77	0.59	0.84	0.86
1990	38,351	25,959	27,301	17,931	61,332	41,245	40,757	23,267	0.63	0.63	0.67	0.77
2000	35,816	22,511	25,951	16,794	61,505	43,637	39,902	25,622	0.58	0.52	0.65	0.66
2005	30,332	18,969	24,470	14,233	62,566	44,545	40,235	25,590	0.48	0.43	0.61	0.56

Notes:
a. The numbers refer to all earners, whether or not they worked on a full-time basis for a full year. Individuals with self-employment income are included while those living in institutions are excluded.
Source: Adapted from Statistics Canada. 2006. Income and Earnings, 2006 Census, Catalogue 97-563-XWE2006002, Table 8.

(2008: 24–5). The impact of the recent recession is likely to have negative effects on the earnings of all Canadian workers, and especially on recent immigrants. Moreover, Nakhaie (2015) shows that immigrant status tends to have a negative effect on self-employment income. Among many immigrant groups, self-employment does not result in higher incomes than those derived from wage and salary employment, although self-employment in white-collar occupations in particular may be the exception.

How do sociologists explain these kinds of findings? Among other things, the patterns point to the devaluation of immigrant credentials as an important part of the explanation of social inequalities between immigrants and the Canadian-born. Devaluation of immigrant credentials refers to the lack of recognition of educational qualifications earned outside of Canada (Li, 2003: 113). There is evidence that shows that many immigrant teachers, doctors, nurses, and engineers find that their non-Western-university degrees and diplomas are of little value in Canada (Henry and Tator, 2010; Basran and Zong, 1998; Foster, 2009).

For many of these professionals, the choices they face are rather stark: (1) some simply give up trying to practise their professions in Canada and face a lifetime of underemployment and status dislocation; (2) some start from scratch and get a Canadian degree in the field that they have already been trained in, even though they already have the skills and knowledge required to practise their craft; (3) some take on lengthy and expensive battles with professional licensing bodies to have their credentials recognized as equivalent to a Canadian degree; and (4) some simply give up on Canada and either return to their country of origin or move to another country perceived to evaluate immigrant educational credentials more fairly. Although it no longer exists, a website called notcanada.com—purportedly run by disillusioned immigrants who have left Canada—explicitly warned individuals against moving to Canada because of the way it treats immigrants with high levels of educational credentials.

Jeffrey Reitz (2001) argues that in 1996 alone, the combination of immigrant skill underutilization and pay inequities between immigrants and non-immigrants resulted in a $55.5 billion earnings deficit for immigrants. Reitz (2008) has pointed out the need for institutional innovations for a new Canadian immigration model that will improve the labour market conditions for recent immigrants. For example, more information about the Canadian labour market and the economy should be available to prospective immigrants prior to their arrival in Canada. Bridge training programs should be introduced for recent immigrants to improve their skills, and subsidized internship or mentoring programs could add valuable Canadian experience. Such programs could assist recent immigrants not only in getting jobs that match their educational credentials and skills but also in enjoying the economic rewards that accrue from a better place in the occupational structure of the Canadian labour market.

Case Study Box 5.1 An Immigrant Success Story: Isa and Amina Odidi Are Successful Pharmaceutical Entrepreneurs

Nigerian-born Isa and Amina Odidi have changed the face of the pharmaceutical industry in Canada.

Isa Odidi belongs to Nigerian royalty, holding the title of Sardaun. Yet in a bid to see the Western world while garnering higher education in pharmaceutics, he left behind the stately life and went to the United Kingdom along with his wife, Amina. A few years later, in 1995, they came to Canada as research doctors with their children.

Isa was here on a two-year contract to help Canada's largest pharmaceutical firm, Biovail Corporation, set up its R&D department. "It wasn't our intention to come and live in Canada," remembers Isa. "It was supposed to be for only two years. But then the company became so successful with our presence—we made a lot of products for them and stock price went high and everyone became rich, so to speak—so two years became extended for more years."

Meanwhile, the Odidis fell in love with the country and decided to settle here permanently. The couple has flourished ever since, finding personal success and integrating into Canadian society.

"Immigrants need to engage on a political level, economic level, and social level," says Isa, noting that he is contemplating entering politics in the coming year. "If you are in politics you are in a position to take control in the decision-making process. If you are engaged socially, then you also have some sort of influence on what kind of decisions are going to be taken politically and economically. And, of course, if you are engaged economically and successful, you'll have the ability to make things happen."

In their case, the Odidis are engaged in several community-related activities and charities, such as support for sickle-cell disease awareness among African-born immigrants. They also support charities that raise funds for portable water wells, drugs for HIV/AIDS and malaria prevention, and eyeglasses for African countries. Amina is also involved in women's education and empowerment initiatives in Nigeria.

A Critical Assessment of Ethnic/ "Racial" Inequality Research

The research discussed above has made valuable contributions to the study of social inequality in Canada. In this section, we want to highlight a number of problematic aspects of this research. In some ways, the difficulties with this approach are summarized in Case Studies 5.1 and 5.2, which provide contrasting stories, one from Toronto, Ontario, and another from British Columbia, of how newcomers do in the Canadian economy.

First, there has arguably been an overemphasis on the ethnic/racial dimension of social inequality in Canada; the ethnic/racial approach now constitutes a

According to Isa, it takes a special kind of person to do business and be socially involved at the same time. "You have to be a Type A individual—somebody who can multi-task and days are more than 24 hours. You got to juggle all the activities."

The couple shows how it's done. They have managed to give back while building their careers with Biovail, and raise five wonderful children. Today they are also an entrepreneurial force in Canada's pharmaceutical industry, thanks to their sixth baby—Intellipharmaceutics International.

"Yes, it is like a child to us," says Amina, who holds a PHD in biopharmaceutics. She speaks excitedly about their drug research firm, which is now traded on both Toronto Stock Exchange and the US exchange NASDAQ.

The company, which was recently recognized by a Harry Jerome Award for Science and Technology, is definitely successful. Today, it works in profit-splitting deals with many pharmaceutical giants, offering patented drug formulas on a royalty basis. "When we were a smaller company, we used to sell our patents. But now we only license them to use our patent," Isa explains. The company holds 30 issued patents and patent applications.

They have in the pipeline about 15 products, including drugs for three chronic conditions—depression, peptic ulcers, and attention deficit hyperactivity disorder. Also coming is an advanced product for congestive heart failure that the couple hopes to file for approval soon.

At the centre of it all is the company's proprietary Hypermatrix technology, which facilitates controlled-release delivery of drugs. They apply the technology to the development of both existing and new pharmaceuticals.

Despite the time and effort they give to making their company successful, the Odidis never forget their philosophy of being socially engaged. One of the company's newest controlled-release drug innovations is Rexista, which is designed to overcome the well-documented abuses associated with oxycodone. "It's not just another profit-making drug, but a socially responsible innovation," Isa says, extremely proud of the product. "Because this controlled-release oral oxycodone formulation prevents addiction and drug abuse, and it's alcohol resistant!"

Socially conscious scientists indeed.

Source: Gloria Elayadathusseril, 29 May 2011. http://canadianimmigrant.ca/immigrant-stories/leaving-a-life-of-nigerian-royalty-behind-isa-and-amina-odidi-have-become-successful-pharmaceutical-entrepreneurs-in-canada.

dominant research tradition. Pluralist conceptions tend to reduce Canada to an amalgamation of ethnic groups (Driedger, 1996): Canada, a country of immigrants, is thought to be composed of ethnic/racial groups only. Our history of nation building, our present demographic reality, and the official policy of multiculturalism, among other things, tend to lend ideological credence to this argument. In response to the question of what is Canada, the usual rejoinder is that it is an ethnic/racial mosaic, an amalgamation of cultural/ethnic groups. When the question of social inequality arises, ethnicity becomes the main or the only dimension of analysis: some ethnic groups are doing better than others, and that is assumed to be the end of the story of social inequality.

Case Study Box 5.2 Allegations of Discrimination at Tim Hortons

In a November 2015 ruling, the British Columbia Human Rights Tribunal ordered that complaints lodged by five temporary foreign workers from Mexico against a Tim Hortons franchise in northern British Columbia go forward for a hearing. According to the complaint filed on behalf of the workers by the British Columbia Public Interest and Advocacy Centre, the workers experienced racist and derogatory comments at work, were forced to live in poor-quality housing by the franchise operator, and faced various types of discrimination at work. The complainants made a number of specific allegations about the franchise owner:

- They had no choice but to rent rooms in a house owned by the franchise owner.
- The house was overcrowded, with ten men living in a five-bedroom house with two bathrooms.
- The franchise owner would fire them if they tried to find alternative accommodation.
- Though the official rent was only $200 per month, they had to pay the owner an additional $200 per month as a "tip."
- They were required to perform work not performed by Canadian workers.
- The workers were given shifts that ended at midnight and new shifts that started at 5 or 6 a.m. the same morning.
- They were berated publicly by the owner when they made mistakes.
- They were not allowed to speak in Spanish to their co-workers.
- They heard numerous negative references made by the owner to Mexicans and Mexico, including statements that they were "idiots," "lazy," and "drug traffickers."

These allegations have yet to be proven but in some ways they are similar to allegations brought against another Tim Hortons franchise owner in Fernie, British Columbia, by a group of Filipino workers. Though Tim Hortons claimed that it was not responsible for the day-to-day operations of the franchises, the BC Human Rights Tribunal dismissed this argument and ruled that the company had to respond to the allegations along with the franchise owners. The Tribunal is encouraging the parties to engage in mediation to resolve the disputes.

Source: Complaint filed by the British Columbia Public Interest and Advocacy Centre, http://bcpiac.com/wp-content/uploads/2015/11/05-22-2013-Form-1E-Amending-Section-E1-Final.pdf. The Tyee, "Human Rights Complaint against Tim Hortons Moves Ahead," 7 November 2015. http://thetyee.ca/News/2015/11/07/Complaint-Tim-Hortons-Moves-Ahead/.

Ethnicity, no doubt, is a social reality. But it is not the only social reality. Demographic profiles and policies of official multiculturalism provide the empirical and ideological evidence that justifies the portrayal of Canada as being only multi-ethnic. But this is, of course, a one-dimensional and reductionist portrayal of the structure of the country, especially as far as social inequality is concerned.

Canada, it is important to remember, is also a capitalist and a patriarchal society, and it is necessary to incorporate these dimensions into the analysis of social inequality.

Second, with some exceptions (Li, 1988, 1992; Nakhaie, 1999, 2000), the class dimension of social inequality in Canada is not adequately examined. Porter himself argued that ethnic groups have internal hierarchies and are themselves stratified (Porter, 2015 [1965]: 73). They are not homogeneous: they are differentiated by religion and by whether they are recent or earlier arrivals (Porter, 2015 [1965]: 72), and by class (Li, 1988, 1992; Liodakis, 1998, 2002). As mentioned earlier, it is ironic that Porter's work, which was an effort to bring class back into the analysis of social inequality in Canada, has been interpreted by some social scientists as asserting the analytical dominance of ethnicity (Liodakis, 2002). Class and ethnicity are important dimensions of social inequality in Canada. They may also be viewed as competing theoretical approaches to the analysis of social inequality (McAll, 1990). Even if we accept that there was a period in the history of Canada during which ethnicity overlapped with class, there was never a one-to-one correspondence.

The vertical mosaic thesis should be questioned, not because we now have more ethnic equality but arguably because inequality in Canada is still very much based on social class, and ethnicity and "race" serve as sources of division within the broader class structure (Li, 1992). Ethnic inequality cannot be analyzed outside the class context (Li, 1988: 141). For example, Nakhaie (1999, 2000), using data from the 1973 Canadian Mobility Survey and the 1989 General Social Survey, has demonstrated that there were significant changes to the class composition of ethnic groups between 1973 and 1989 for both men and women. During this period, the English were not overrepresented in the ownership class categories (bourgeoisie, petty bourgeoisie, self-employed) compared to other ethnic groups. Ethnic differences in the managerial classes declined, especially for the French. The British, however, still dominated the business elite and were overrepresented in the managerial classes. The French and Italians were persistently overrepresented in the working class (Nakhaie, 2000: 168, Table 11.4 and 2000: 170, Table 11.5). Nakhaie (2000: 174) concluded that the effect of ethnicity in determining class position has declined. The relationship between ethnicity and class is in flux, and no ethnic group dominates the top of the Canadian class structure, as Table 5.5 shows below. But his analysis also shows that ethnic groups are not homogeneous. They are internally stratified in terms of class, and they are also stratified in terms of gender and place of birth. We are not suggesting that the choice is between class or ethnic analyses. Rather, we encourage the use of a multi-dimensional model in which the internal differences of ethnic groups are taken into account.

A third problematic issue in the analysis of social inequality in Canada is that there is sometimes a lack of definitional parsimony in the colour-coded mosaic thesis. As mentioned above, many researchers argue that there is a clear-cut division in Canadian society along racial lines. More often than not, the groups under examination, ethnic or racial, are defined in terms of Statistics Canada census categories. Categories such as "visible minorities," "racialized groups," "non-racialized groups," or even "whites" do not always have a clear social referent. Increased rates of exogamy among groups who immigrated to Canada before the 1980s have led to a decrease in the number of census respondents who report single ethnic origins. In addition, since the 1980s the number of visible minority immigrants has increased. These two trends make it increasingly difficult to compare single-origin, multiple-origin, and visible minority respondents when analyzing census data. There is, for example, evidence to suggest that "multiple-origin visible minorities whose origins are partly European face markedly smaller differentials in labour market performance than single-origin visible minorities" (Pendakur, 2005: 7). Moreover, many classifications used by Statistics Canada in the census tend to lump together groups from different ethnic backgrounds, often based on racial markers like skin colour. This makes it easier to statistically construct a dichotomy between visible and non-visible groups by adding their constituent parts together irrespective of their ethnic or cultural differences.

But what is statistically easy becomes theoretically and methodologically problematic. This taxonomy creates categories so broadly defined that the considerable internal socio-economic heterogeneity within groups is concealed (Boyd, 1992: 281; Liodakis, 2002; Nakhaie, 2015). The term *visible minority* emerged in the 1970s in response to the use of pejorative terms such as *coloured* or *non-white* and was used by activists and scholars who were fighting social inequality. The term is now embedded not only in census questions but also in state policies of employment equity and multiculturalism (Synnott and Howes, 1996: 137) and by extension in the language of social scientists and non-academics. A person is officially a member of a visible minority group if she or he is "non-white" in colour or "non-Caucasian" in "race," other than Aboriginal. The problem with this social construction of the concept of "visible minority," according to Synnott and Howes, is that when attempts are made to refer this concept back to the social reality it is supposed to describe, "it falls apart" (1996: 138). It does not have a social referent. It tends to homogenize and racialize diverse groups of people. As we noted in Chapter 3, census taking is not an innocent exercise of simply counting people. Melissa Nobles (2000) argues that censuses help to shape and reproduce a racial discourse that in turn affects public policies that either restrict or protect the rights, the privileges, and the experiences we commonly associate with citizenship. Statistics Canada is not necessarily a politically neutral institution that simply "counts" Canadians in an objective sort of way. It creates the conditions under which people will identify themselves so that Statistics Canada can count them afterwards. The terms *ethnicity, visible minority, whites/non-whites* are, to paraphrase Goldberg, "irreducibly political categories" that construct racial and ethnic groups (Nobles, 2000). The United Nations Committee to Eliminate Racial Discrimination recently suggested that the term *visible minority* may in itself be discriminatory.

The term also homogenizes the so-called non-visible minority category. Synnott and Howes argue that visible minorities are diverse in terms of their place of birth and place of residence as well as their length of residence in Canada, not to mention their age, class, and gender composition. This is also true, of course, of non–visible minorities. Such divisions, however, have important implications for their employment and level and type of education as well as earnings. For example, there are different unemployment rates within the category of visible minority. In 2005, the unemployment rate of non–visible minorities was 6.2 per cent and 6.6 per cent for visible minorities, but there was great variation within the category visible minorities: Filipinos averaged only 5 per cent and the Japanese only 5.1 per cent, below the national average of 6.8 per cent, whereas Arabs averaged 13 per cent, blacks 10.6 per cent, and west Asians 10.7 per cent (Statistics Canada, 2006).

There are also important differences in types and levels of education. If we aggregate members of diverse groups under the category "visible minorities," their internal differences are often concealed. For example, Davies and Guppy (1998) have shown that, as a group, visible minorities are better educated than non–visible minorities. And some members of the visible minority category are better educated overall than others. Filipinos, Koreans, Japanese, west Asians, and Arabs are more likely to have completed university than blacks, Southeast Asians, and Latin Americans. The former groups are also more likely than the latter to be found in managerial and professional occupations (Kelly, 1995: 5–7). As some of the studies reviewed above have shown, the broadly defined categories have different earnings as well. Nakhaie (2015) also points out that there are considerable variations in self-employment income among various visible minority groups in Canada and that these differences are masked when they are lumped into the same analytical category. In addition, not all members of the above-mentioned groups are visible or equally visible. Combining them in order to produce statistics on employment, educational attainment, or earnings is problematic. In other words, who is the "average" South Asian, black, or Filipino person? Who is the average southern European? In fact, Synnott and Howes argue that it is better to separate the various groups from one another and analyze their socio-economic conditions separately than it is to treat them all as "manifestations of a single (spurious) category" (1996: 142–3). Yet researchers who subscribe to the "visibility" thesis include them all in the dichotomy of statistical categories (see Li, 1998b; Lian and Matthews, 1998; Hou and Balakrishnan, 1999). In terms of the analysis of stratification, when we use racializing, homogenizing terms like *visible/non-visible minority* or *white/non-white*, we tend to conceal their internal differences along class, gender, and nativity lines as well as the cultural and ethnic differences among them.

Fourth, the colour-coded vertical mosaic thesis[5] overlooks anomalies that undermine its arguments. In much of the literature on social inequality (see, for example, Li, 1988) southern European groups—the Greeks, the Portuguese, and, to a lesser extent, the Italians—are not as well educated as the rest of the European groups and do not earn as much; in some studies, they have been identified as not as educated and as earning less than some visible minorities (Li, 1988: 76, Table 5.1; 78, Table 5.2; 82, Table 5.3; 84, Table 5.4; 88, Table 5.5). In Boyd's (1992) research, it was also evident that Greek, Italian, Portuguese, other European, and Dutch women made less than the average earnings of all women. In fact, in terms of earnings ranking, Greek and Italian women ranked lower than Chinese women. Portuguese women ranked lower than Chinese, Filipino, Southeast Asian, and black women. And Dutch and Eastern European women ranked lower than most visible minority women (Boyd, 1992: Table 5, 305-6). In the case of men, Greeks ranked lower than visible minority people of British descent, west Asians, South Asians, the Chinese, Southeast Asians, and blacks. Greek men had the second-lowest level of average earnings among all men (1992: Table 5, 305–6).

Lian and Matthews (1998) also found that individuals of Greek, Portuguese, Italian, and Spanish background do not receive rewards for their educational levels equal to other groups. They are, in fact, also disadvantaged and may be more disadvantaged than some visible minorities at most educational levels. For example, Greeks make less at all educational levels except in the category of "trades certificate." In the "degree in medicine" category, they make 50 per cent less than the British base group. This is the lowest percentage among all groups, visible and non-visible. In the category "earned doctorate," Greek-origin individuals make 26 per cent less, which is lower than west and South Asians, the Vietnamese, blacks, and other east and Southeast Asians. Similar patterns hold for other southern European groups. In short, the poor socio-economic performance of southern European groups raises hard questions about the validity of the new racialized vertical mosaic image of Canada.

More recent evidence suggests that there are large gender and racial group variations within the grand statistical category of "visible" minorities. Hum and Simpson (2007) have compared wages between "visible" and "non-visible" groups by analyzing the 2002 Survey of Labour and Income Dynamics (SLID) and examining gender. Overall, in 2002, Canadian-born visible minority women made 0.8 per cent more than their non–visible minority Canadian-born counterparts. In the Canadian-born category, Indo-Pakistani women made 26.7 per cent more, Arab women made 22.5 per cent more, and Latin American women made 11 per cent more. Although there is, indeed, a wage differential between the immigrant component of visible minority groups and the Canadian-born, there is no significant wage gap between visible and non–visible minority Canadian-born workers, with the exception of black and Latin American men (2007: 96, Table 5.3). There is no clear visible/non-visible division in earnings inequality. Indeed, the examples cited above may render the colour-coded vertical mosaic thesis as only partially accurate, if not misleading.

Bringing Class Back In

Central to the analysis of social inequality presented in this final section is the understanding that the production and reproduction of the conditions of people's existence is social. Individuals are interacting social subjects, situated in class, gender, and ethnic social locations (Satzewich and Wotherspoon, 2000: 13). In most advanced, liberal-democratic societies like ours, all social relations have class, gender, and "race"/ethnic elements. The class analysis in this section relies upon E.O. Wright's work on social class (1983). We do not claim that class is the only or the most important dimension of social inequality. We do claim, however, that along with gender, it accounts more for the earnings differentials among and within ethnic and racial groups than any of the other dimensions. Neither ethnicity nor visibility alone is a good "predictor" of earnings inequality in Canada (Li, 1988, 1992).

According to Wright (1983: 61–83, 76, Table 2.9), there are three main classes in capitalist societies—bourgeoisie, petty bourgeoisie, and proletariat—and three contradictory class locations between them. These classes are defined by

1. economic ownership of money capital (control over investments and resources);
2. control of the physical means of production; and
3. control of the labour power of others.

In this model, the bourgeoisie (big employers) has economic ownership and possession in all three areas: money capital, physical capital, and labour. The petty bourgeoisie does not have control of labour. The proletariat (workers) has no control of money or physical capital either but, unlike the petty bourgeoisie, must sell labour power in exchange for wages. Small employers, a contradictory location between the petty bourgeoisie and the bourgeoisie, have only minimal control over the labour power of others and not a lot of money and physical capital. Managers and supervisors occupy a contradictory location between the proletariat and the bourgeoisie since although they exchange labour power for wages, they do have a lot of control over physical capital, as well as over the labour power and process of workers, but less control over money capital than big employers do. Finally, semi-autonomous workers (often called professionals) occupy a contradictory location between the proletariat and the petty bourgeoisie because although they do not control the labour power of others and they sell theirs, they do have minimal control over money and physical capital and considerable control of their own labour process (Wright, 1983: 76). We do, however, recognize that this is a general analytical schema and in actual societies, these class locations contain sets of real people: men and women who come from different ethnic backgrounds and whose actual lives do not fit neatly into one exclusive category.

Whereas earlier traditions have tended to emphasize the "mosaic" dimension of inequality and to examine the earnings inequalities *among* ethnic groups, we emphasize the "vertical" dimension and examine the earnings inequalities both among and *within* these ethnic groups. Thus ethnic inequalities do not occur in a social vacuum but take place within a class society. The approach proposed here suggests that within each structural locational basis of inequality (ethnicity, gender, or class), the other two coexist. All classes have gender and ethnic segments.

Gender groups have class and ethnic segments. All ethnic groups are permeated by class and gender differences.

In the remainder of this chapter, we address two interrelated issues. First, we examine whether ethnic groups are homogeneous or heterogeneous in terms of class composition. Second, we examine the earnings differentials not only among but also within ethnic groups in terms of class, gender, and nativity.

Evidence of Ethnic Heterogeneity

The data used in this section come from the Public Use Microdata File on Individuals from the 2006 Canadian Census. The total number of people in the sample is 367,370. It includes persons of single ethnic origins from Ontario, Quebec, Saskatchewan, Manitoba, Alberta, and British Columbia, 25 to 59 years of age. The ethnic adjectives in the tables that appear in the following pages do not denote the subjective ethnic or cultural identity of the respondents but that of their ancestors and the categories used by Statistics Canada. They simply indicate ethnic or cultural origin.

To simplify our argument, we do not examine the class structure of every ethnic group in Canada. Instead, we selectively examine the social class composition of the following groups: Aboriginal, English, Caribbean, Chinese, Filipino, French, Greek, Italian, Jewish, Portuguese, and South Asian. These choices are based on the fact that the English and the French are the so-called charter groups, were part of the original vertical mosaic thesis, and feature prominently in all subsequent analyses of ethnicity. They have conventionally constituted the frame of reference for all comparisons. Jews, on the other hand, albeit accorded an "entrance status," have tended to outperform charter and all other groups in terms of educational attainment and earnings. They represent an anomalous case for proponents of the vertical mosaic thesis and/or its assimilationist versions. The three southern European groups—Greek, Italian, and Portuguese—are undoubtedly the least studied European groups. Some evidence indicates that Greeks may represent an anomalous case as well, which poses problems for the proponents of the racialized vertical mosaic argument (Liodakis, 2002). Often, because of their poor socio-economic performance, they do not very well fit the visible/non-visible dichotomy proposed by some (see Li, 1988; Hou and Balakrishnan, 1999; Lian and Matthews, 1998). The four visible groups we have chosen represent the most populous of all other single-origin visible groups in Canada.

As Porter argued (2015 [1965]), ethnic groups are not homogeneous; they differ in terms of their internal class structure. Table 5.5 provides further contemporary confirmation of this in that it presents the percentage distribution of the selected ethnic and racial groups among social classes.

If we look at social inequality from the perspective of class composition, it appears that in the case of the proletariat, there is no clear-cut visible/non-visible distinction. The Chinese, for example, are less proletarianized than the Portuguese,

Table 5.5 The Class Composition of Groups (per cent), 2005

Ethnic/racialized group	Workers	Semi-autonomous workers	Managers, supervisors	Petty bourgeoisie	Employers
Aboriginal	67.8	18.7	8.0	3.8	1.7
English	53.1	21.6	13.4	6.9	5.0
Caribbean*	64.9	20.4	8.6	4.1	2.0
Chinese	48.4	29.0	9.1	7.1	6.4
Filipino	70.5	20.3	5.6	2.1	1.5
French	51.1	26.8	10.7	7.2	4.2
Greek	48.5	21.5	14.3	7.5	8.2
Italian	50.4	22.3	14.6	5.8	6.9
Jewish	30.0	33.1	13.8	11.9	11.2
Portuguese	65.1	13.2	12.2	5.1	4.5
South Asian**	61.4	19.3	7.6	5.9	5.8
Canada	53.0	23.5	11.7	7.0	4.8

* Excluding Jamaican-origin responses
** Excluding East Indian–origin responses
Source: Calculated from Statistics Canada 2006 Census (Public Use Microdata File on Individuals).

the Italians, the Greeks, the English, and the French. The Portuguese are more proletarianized than the Chinese, Caribbean people, and the South Asians. Aboriginal Canadians are more likely to be found in the working class and less likely to be found in the other classes. Aboriginal, Caribbean, Filipino, French, and Portuguese individuals are underrepresented in the ranks of employers, while Chinese, Greek, French, and Jewish individuals are variously overrepresented among the ranks of the petty bourgeoisie. In the semi-autonomous worker category, the Chinese are well above the national average, second only to Jewish-descent respondents and above the Greeks, Italians, and Portuguese, who are not visible minorities but "whites." In the employer category, the Chinese and the South Asians are overrepresented, whereas other visible groups like Caribbean and Filipinos are underrepresented, along with the Portuguese, the French, and Aboriginals.

Despite these patterns of overrepresentation and underrepresentation, two important points stand out in Table 5.5. First, as one should expect, members of each of the 11 ethnic groups are variously distributed across the range of class sites. No single group is *exclusively* one class or another. Second, the dividing line is muddied between groups traditionally conceived as visible minorities and those traditionally conceived as non-visible minorities. In short, there are differences within ethnic and racialized groups in terms of their class compositions. There is no consistent pattern of distribution across class locations. There is considerable class heterogeneity both among and within the ethnic groups under examination. If analytical primacy is given to only one of the three dimensions we have examined, the important internal, within-group class divisions that affect their earnings are obfuscated.

In addition, ethnic groups have different gender and nativity compositions. For example, in terms of gender, the Caribbean and Filipino categories have more women than men in the labour market. In all visible groups, the percentage of foreign-born members exceeds 90 per cent, whereas in the non-visible category, the percentage is much lower (less than 50 per cent). These differences do affect their earnings but are concealed if we only look at them as homogeneous entities.

Earnings Inequalities among and within Ethnic Groups

If, as we have shown above, ethnic and racialized groups differ in their class composition, do they also differ in the rewards they receive from participating in the economy? In other words, is there variation in their earnings? And if so, are the differences among them greater than the differences within them? Table 5.6 shows that in Canada, there are considerable differences in the earnings of classes.

When we examine their after-tax income, it is clear that the petty bourgeois and the proletarians have mean after-tax incomes below the sample mean. The petty bourgeois make $11,245 less than the mean,[6] and the proletarians make $7,287 less. Employers make $15,085 more, semi-autonomous workers $7,319 more, and managers and supervisors $18,817 more. These results are consistent with the findings of similar research using 1986, 1991, 1996, and 2001 Canadian census data (Li, 1988, 1992; Liodakis, 2002). In percentage terms, the petty bourgeois make 30.1 per cent less and workers make 19.4 per cent less than the sample mean. On the other hand, employers make 40.2 per cent more than the mean; semi-autonomous workers, 19.5 per cent more; and managers and supervisors, 50.14 per cent more. The latter group represents the highest-paid class. These patterns also hold when we examine median earnings. Class differences are greater than differences between visible and non-visible groups. For example, in the same year, visible minorities made $8,670 less than non–visible minorities. Gender differences are also greater: women made $13,924 less than men, more than double the visibility difference. Foreign-born respondents made $4,602 less than the Canadian-born. In all ethnic groups, the class, gender, and nativity patterns of earnings inequalities hold.

If we understand ethnic groups as being fractured by class, gender, and nativity divisions, a more varied pattern of earnings inequality emerges. The overall class/gender/nativity income differentials within ethnic/racialized groups are greater than those among them, especially if we exclude the Jewish-origin respondents, who are the top earners ($56,536) and the Aboriginals, who are at the bottom ($21,160). Even within the top-earning ethnic category of Jewish-origin people, for example, male, native-born employers made $161,948, compared to female, foreign-born petty bourgeois members, who made only $25,803—a difference of $136,145. In the category of South Asian–origin respondents, the top group of male, native-born employers made $112,322, whereas foreign-born working-class women made only $12,833, for a difference of $99,489. In the group of Filipino-origin respondents, male, native-born petty bourgeois made $42,250, whereas the bottom group of female,

Table 5.6 After-Tax Income by Class, 2005

Class	N	Mean ($)	Std. deviation	Median ($)	± per cent of national average
Workers	194,539	$30,241	$22,508	$28,000	−19.41
Semi-autonomous workers	86,561	$44,847	$39,178	$41,000	+19.50
Managers/ supervisors	42,790	$56,345	$62,262	$44,000	+50.14
Petty bourgeoisie	25,669	$26,233	$40,869	$18,000	−30.10
Employers	17,811	$52,613	$80,282	$31,000	+40.20
Canada	367,370	$37,528	$40,157	$32,000	

Source: Calculated from Statistics Canada 2006 Census (Public Use Microdata File on Individuals).

native-born workers made only $13,277—a difference of $28,973. In the Greek-origin group, male, native-born employers made $68,647, which was $46,076 more than female, foreign-born workers, who made $22,571. In the case of Aboriginals, male managers and supervisors (their highest-paid segment) made $39,568, whereas female, petty bourgeois (their lowest-paid segment) made only $13,395, or $26,173 less.

Summary

In this chapter, we have reviewed whether the vertical mosaic thesis continues to be an accurate way of describing Canadian society. We began by discussing John Porter's conception of Canada as a vertical mosaic. We then reviewed occupational attainment and earnings data to assess whether the vertical mosaic metaphor continues to have relevance for Canada today. We argued that while there is a progressive convergence among ethnic groups, some differences continue to be important in discussions of social inequality.

In particular, we noted that some sociologists argue that skin colour has become the new dividing line such that there is now a new colour-coded vertical mosaic, with racialized minorities at the bottom of the socio-economic structure and non-racialized, white Canadians at the top. Some empirical evidence supports the colour-coded vertical mosaic hypothesis, yet other evidence calls this thesis into question. We also reviewed evidence for earnings differences between immigrants and the Canadian-born and suggested that part of the reason that some immigrants earn less than the Canadian-born, even when other possible sources of variation in earnings are accounted for, is that Canadian society devalues the educational credentials and job experience of non-Western-trained individuals.

Finally, the picture of social inequality that we presented in the last section of this chapter offers an alternative prism for the examination of social inequality. Canada may be a racially/ethnically stratified society, but it remains a capitalist, patriarchal society divided along class and gender lines. Taken on their own, social class inequalities are of a significantly larger magnitude in Canada than ethnic, racial, gender, and immigration status inequalities; at the same time, individuals do not occupy just one of these statuses, and it is important to understand how these dimensions intersect in order to understand the true complexity of social inequality in this country.

Questions for Critical Thought

1. What evidence is there to conclude that Canada is presently characterized by a colour-coded vertical mosaic? What are the problems with this kind of portrait of Canadian society?

2. Does a focus on social class offer a better picture of social inequality than a focus on ethnic/"racial" differences?

3. Does a focus on gender offer a better picture of social inequality than a focus on ethnic/"racial" differences?

4. How do you explain the earnings differences between immigrants and the Canadian-born and between visible minority and non-visible minority immigrants?

5. Assume that you are working for a telemarketing company and you are asked to place a call to people chosen randomly in order to guess their earnings. You are not allowed to ask them directly about their earnings. You can ask only three questions. What would those questions be?

Debate Questions

1. It appears that Canadian-born visible minority women make more on average than their non-visible minority counterparts. Can you explain why this is happening? When answering this question, consider that it is an anomaly for the colour-coded mosaic thesis.

2. Why has the median income of recent immigrants to Canada been deteriorating steadily since 1980, when compared to the income of non-immigrants?

3. Explain why the deterioration of recent immigrants' median income is worse for females than for males.

4. Galabuzi has shown that there was a 12.3 per cent difference in the average after-tax income between racialized and non-racialized groups in Canada in the year 2000. This translated to $2,895. Is this a big difference? Do you think that if we were to measure differences in wealth, the gap might have been greater? Why?

Annotated Additional Readings

Allahar, Anton. 2011. "The Political Economy of 'race' and class in Canada's Caribbean diaspora," *American Review of Political Economy* 8 (2): 54–86. A good, political-economy-based analysis of social inequality within the Caribbean community in Canada. Allahar questions the idea that there is a homogenous Caribbean diaspora and argues that there are significant class-based divisions that play a significant role in community dynamics.

Block, Sheila. 2010. *Ontario's Growing Gap: The Role of Race and Gender.* Ottawa: Canadian Centre for Policy Alternatives. Published by a prominent Canadian think tank, this study documents growing gender and racial inequality in the province of Ontario.

Galabuzi, Grace-Edward. 2006. *Canada's Economic Apartheid: The Social Exclusion of Racialized Groups in the New Century.* Toronto: Canadian Scholars Press. Galabuzi presents a powerful and controversial argument in support of the view that Canada is characterized by a new colour-coded vertical mosaic.

Porter, John. 2015 [1965]. *The Vertical Mosaic: An Analysis of Social Class and Power in Canada.* Toronto: University of Toronto Press. This book set the intellectual context for much of the discussion of social inequality in Canada over the past four decades. It was re-issued in 2015 on the fiftieth anniversary of its original publication.

Synnott, Anthony, and David Howes. 1996. "Canada's Visible Minorities: Identity and Representation," in V. Amit-Talai and C. Knowles, eds, *Re-situating Identities: The Politics of Race, Ethnicity and Culture.* Peterborough: Broadview Press. This is a thoughtful and thorough critique of the concept of *visible minority.* Synnott and Howes question whether it makes sense to lump together so many different groups, with different immigration histories and backgrounds, into a single analytical category.

Related Websites

Broadbent Institute
www.broadbentinstitute.ca
Founded by former New Democratic Party of Canada leader Ed Broadbent, the institute seeks to find ways to promote more social equality among Canadians.

Centre for Social Justice
www.socialjustice.org
This organization conducts research education and advocacy to address a variety of issues related to social inequality in Canada.

The Conference Board of Canada
www.conferenceboard.ca/hcp/aboutus.aspx
A not-for-profit organization that, in part, conducts research relating to the Canadian economy and society, including a focus on various patterns of social inequality.

The Maytree Foundation
www.maytree.com
The Maytree Foundation is a private Canadian foundation dedicated to the elimination of poverty.

Settlement.Org
www.settlement.org
Funded jointly by Citizenship and Immigration Canada and the Ontario provincial government, this organization seeks to provide various kinds of advice and assistance to newcomers as they navigate Canadian society.

Statistics Canada
www.statcan.gc.ca
This is the website of Canada's statistical data collection agency.

Notes

1. It should be mentioned that elite theorists of the Porter tradition have looked at the class composition of ethnic groups (Clement, 1975). However, they have looked only at their upper echelons, which comprise a very small group of people in elite positions. They have not examined the entire class structure of ethnic groups. See Nakhaie (2000) for an updated exchange between Nakhaie and Ogmundson and McLaughlin on the dominant position of the British in the Canadian elite.

2. Some researchers (e.g., Winn, 1988) use income when analyzing economic inequality. In our past work we have used earnings (Satzewich and Liodakis, 2007; 2010). In this work, we are using after-tax income, like Galabuzi (2006).

3. Thomas Sowell (1989) makes a similar and more theoretically informed argument against affirmative action programs in the United States and other countries.

4. At the time of writing, data on ethnicity and income from the National Household Survey were not available. Moreover, because of high non-response rates among less well-off segments of the population, some analysts consider data on income as unreliable.

5. It should be made clear that this chapter is not about racism in general or discrimination in the labour market. It is about earnings differentials and the internal stratification of ethnic groups in terms of their class, gender, and nativity dimensions. Unfortunately, there are not many studies or much preponderant evidence to support claims about discrimination in the Canadian labour market. See Henry and Ginzberg (1988) for a 1985 study of 201 job offers showing evidence of discrimination based on "race." See also an unpublished 1989 restudy of the Economic Council of Canada (1991), which claims that "no discrimination was discernable" (Henry, 1999: 233). Others, like de Silva (1992), argue that once immigrants are hired "there is no significant discrimination against immigrants in general. . . . More important, there is no detectable general tendency to discriminate against immigrants originating from the Third World" (1992: 37). Levitt (1994) puts forward the issue of relativity and the historical specificity of racism. He provides evidence that racism and discrimination are diminishing and argues that Canada today is not, in fact, a racist country, compared to earlier periods of time and other countries. This, of course, does not diminish the importance of combating racism. No "degree" of racism is acceptable.

6. This result should not be considered unusual. Consistently, across censuses from 1986 to 2001, the petty bourgeoisie has been the lowest-earning class and the proletariat the second lowest. Nikos Poulantzas has also claimed that the petty bourgeoisie shares an affinity with the working class (see Li, 1992). Marx might have been right after all.

Diversity, Multiculturalism, and Quebec Interculturalism

Learning Objectives

In this chapter you will learn that

- multiculturalism is part of pluralist ideology, a Canadian demographic reality, a set of government policies and programs, and an arena for ethnic competition for government funding and other resources—but also a controversial policy.

- the federal government claims that it assists in the development of cultural groups, in overcoming cultural barriers to their full participation in Canadian society, and in promoting creative encounters and exchanges among them in the interest of national unity.

- Canada's policy is subject to many different criticisms.

- evidence suggests that multicultural policies in Canada help to produce social integration rather than social division.

- Quebec has pursued a policy of interculturalism that promotes cultural interchanges and citizenship within the context of French unilingualism.

- Quebec is working toward reasonable accommodation, a pluralist notion that government policies and programs should not only tolerate but also accommodate the cultural differences of new immigrants and of minority groups.

- some critics argue that the policy is too effective; it promotes cultural relativism so that the Canadian identity is threatened.

- some see the policy as ineffective because it does not address the economic and political inequalities among and within dominant groups and minorities, undermines the special claims of Aboriginals and francophones, marginalizes ethnic and cultural issues, and hardens ethnic stereotypes.

Introduction

What do apples, bananas, coconuts, and Oreos have in common? Aside from being tasty snacks, these terms all speak to issues of ethnic and racial identity. In particular, they represent derogatory labels that have been applied by some members of visible minority communities to describe other members of the same group. An "apple" is an Aboriginal individual who is "red" on the outside but "white" on the inside; "coconuts" are South Asian–origin individuals who are "brown" on the outside but "white" on the inside; "bananas" are individuals of Chinese or Japanese origin who are "yellow" on the outside and "white" on the inside; and "Oreos" (if you have not figured it out by now) are individuals who are "black" on the outside but "white" on the inside.

What would make someone consider another person a banana, apple, Oreo, or coconut? It depends. Within Aboriginal communities, an "apple" can be a young person who goes on to university to achieve a higher education. In this case, the implication is that achieving a higher education is incompatible with an authentic Aboriginal identity. Among black youth, "Oreos" are sell-outs to white society; they "act white." Usually, these terms represent negative labels and identities that have been applied to minority individuals seen to have assimilated into the dominant white culture and who, through their attitudes and behaviour, have become less attached to their own communities.

These derogatory terms touch on a number of questions about the nature of ethnic and racial identity. For example, what does it mean to be South Asian, black, white, Ukrainian, Aboriginal, Afghani, or Palestinian in Canada today? Are ethnic and racial identities fixed and unchanging or are they flexible, situational, and negotiable? Can assimilation occur in multicultural Canada? Should it occur? Can individuals be integrated without assimilating? Can individuals have overlapping, multiple identities? As we have seen in previous chapters, answers to these questions are difficult. However, they lead to even broader questions about the role that government policies such as **multiculturalism** play in promoting certain kinds identities and ways of interacting with others. For example, what is the meaning of the federal government's policy of multiculturalism? What role does this policy play in helping groups sustain their identities and cultures? Are these policies divisive, or are they the glue that keeps us together? Do they discourage integration and assimilation?

These questions are more urgent given the seeming retreat from multiculturalism in other countries. In the 1990s, many other countries of immigration variously adopted ideologies and policies of multiculturalism. Now, however, they are turning their backs on their respective versions of multiculturalism. In a speech to the youth wing of her Christian Democratic Union party in 2010, German Chancellor Angela Merkel said, "at the start of the 60s we invited the guest-workers to Germany. We kidded ourselves for a while that they wouldn't stay, that one day they'd go home. That isn't what happened. And of course the tendency was to say: let's be 'multiculti' and live next to each other and enjoy being together, [but] this concept has failed, failed utterly" (cited in Connolly, 2010). In a 2012 speech at a security conference in Munich, Germany, British prime minister David Cameron echoed these sentiments. In an ominous warning to other countries that have adopted policies of multiculturalism, Cameron explained:

> What I am about to say is drawn from the British experience, but I believe there are general lessons for us all. In the UK, some young men find it hard to identify with the traditional Islam practiced at home by their parents, whose customs can seem staid when transplanted to modern Western countries. But these young men also find it hard to identify with Britain too, because we have allowed the weakening of our collective identity. Under the doctrine of state multiculturalism, we

have encouraged different cultures to live separate lives, apart from each other and apart from the mainstream. We've failed to provide a vision of society to which they feel they want to belong. We've even tolerated these segregated communities behaving in ways that run completely counter to our values. (Cameron, 2012)

As this chapter shows, many critics in Canada suggest that the multiculturalism policy in this country is also a failure, and for many of the same reasons that have been offered by Merkel and Cameron (see Kymlicka, 2010). The chapter begins with a discussion of the four interrelated dimensions and meanings of multiculturalism in Canada and an examination of the phases of the development of the policy of multiculturalism. We then turn to some of the more political debates associated with the efficacy of multiculturalism: some critics argue that the policy is a failure because it has not been effective in dealing with issues of racism, discrimination, and wider patterns of social inequality; other critics claim that the policy is a failure because it has been too effective in helping groups maintain their "old-world" identities, cultures, and attachments, and as a result has helped produce a lack of loyalty to Canada and Canadian identity. Finally, we examine Quebec's policy of "interculturalism."

Meanings of Federal Multiculturalism

As mentioned in Chapter 1, the processes and practices of ethnic enculturation that take place within ethnic institutions do not operate in a political, economic, or social vacuum. In Canada, an ethnically diverse liberal society, they operate within the context of multiculturalism. Multiculturalism, as we will see, encourages the maintenance of the ethnic and cultural identities of Canadians. Multiculturalism usually has four interrelated meanings: it is a demographic reality, it is part of pluralist ideology, it is a form of struggle among groups for access to economic and political resources, and it is a set of government policies and accompanying programs (Fleras, 2012; Fleras and Elliott, 1996: 325). It can be defined as an ideology, based on Canadian social reality, which gives rise to sets of economic, political, and social practices, which in turn define boundaries and set limits to ethnic and racial group relations in order either to maintain social order or to manage social change (Liodakis and Satzewich, 2003: 147).

First, when we say that multiculturalism is a fact in Canadian society, this means that demographically, the Canadian population comprises members of more than 100 ethnic groups. Canadian society has never been ethnically homogeneous, although historically it might have appeared as such because of the dominance of the British and the French. Canada was certainly a multicultural country long before the implementation of multiculturalism as policy. Simply put, until the introduction of the 1971 policy, Canada—although a multicultural society in terms of demography—was dominated by the hegemonic British and the French cultural norms, and the Canadian state actively promoted conformity to these norms by the rest of the population.

Second, as an ideology, multiculturalism includes normative descriptions about how Canadian society ought to be in terms of social organization based on ethnicity. The cornerstone of multiculturalism is the idea of pluralism. Pluralism, in its cultural interpretation, advocates tolerance of cultural diversity and, most importantly, promotes the idea that such diversity is compatible with national goals, especially those of national unity and socio-economic progress (Fleras and Elliott, 1996: 326). The basic principles of multiculturalism rest on the notion of cultural relativism. It prescribes tolerance and exalts diversity to achieve peaceful coexistence in ethnically heterogeneous societies. **Cultural relativism**, as opposed to ethnocentrism, holds that the evaluative criteria of culture should be drawn from within the culture in question and that no external standards are applicable. In other words, we should not judge any culture by our dominant norms. In short, if we recognize individuals' right to self-identification and promotion of their own culture, then, it is hoped, those individuals will extend the same courtesy to those who share different cultural norms and values. We should note, however, that **ethnocentrism** and prejudice are not synonymous: we can differentiate between enlightened and pernicious forms of ethnocentrism. The first seeks the self-interest of the in-group but respects the rights and interests of the out-group; the second seeks it at the expense of the out-group (Kallen, 1995: 43). Pernicious ethnocentrism is often called ethnic chauvinism, especially when it is associated with hostility toward other ethnic groups.

Third, multiculturalism is also a process of competition among and between ethnocultural groups for the acquisition of valuable economic and political resources. As sociologist Karl Peter has reminded us, multiculturalism "is first and foremost a political program with very defined political aims along with the means to accomplish these aims" (in Fleras and Elliott, 1996: 335). As such, it is a mechanism for conflict resolution. In Canada, it emerged out of social and demographic pressures and from the need to counterbalance western alienation and Quebec nationalism, as well as for the Liberals to acquire ethnic electoral support in urban centres (Fleras and Elliott, 1996: 335).

Fourth, multiculturalism refers to all government initiatives and programs that seek to realize multiculturalism as ideology and transform it into a concrete form of social intervention and organization. As policy, it is a relatively recent aspect of Canadian state activity, introduced by the Liberals under Pierre Elliott Trudeau in 1971. Ironically, it was not the historical legacy of racism, discrimination, and prejudice in Canada that multicultural policy initially aimed to address. In fact, these issues did not figure much into the initial framework for the development of multicultural policy. Instead, the policy was introduced in part as a response to Canada's "other" ethnic groups (non-English and non-French), who were dissatisfied with the terms of reference of the Royal Commission on Bilingualism and Biculturalism of the 1960s. Groups like Ukrainian Canadians were concerned that the federal government had failed to recognize that they too had made significant contributions to Canadian nation building. The policy was also an effort on the part of the Liberals to capture the increasingly large non-English and non-French vote in this country (Hawkins, 1989: 218) and a strategy on the part of Trudeau and the federal Liberal Party to undermine French Canada's claims for equality with English within the Canadian confederation (Abu-Laban and Stasiulis, 1992). In short, multiculturalism seeks to accommodate social cleavages, maintain the existing social order, and manage social change, all in the context of a culturally diverse society.

The Evolution of the Policy of Multiculturalism

Over the course of its 45-year history in Canada, four overlapping stages of multicultural policy have been identified by Augie Fleras (2012, 2015). These stages entail subtle shifts in emphasis and meaning associated with the policy. First, from roughly 1971 to 1980, emphasis was placed on ethnicity or folkloric multiculturalism, or on "celebrating our differences"—that is, on the idea that cultural diversity is the heart of Canadian identity. We no longer had an "official" culture. At that time, four principles guided federal multiculturalism:

1. The federal government would support all of Canada's cultures and seek to assist the development of those cultural groups that had demonstrated a desire and effort to continue developing a capacity to grow and contribute to Canada as well as a clear need for assistance.
2. The government would assist all cultural groups to overcome the cultural barriers to full participation in Canadian society.
3. The government would promote creative encounters and interchange among all Canadian cultural groups in the interest of national unity.
4. The government would continue to assist immigrants in acquiring at least one of Canada's two official languages in order that they would become full participants in Canadian society (Hawkins, 1989: 220).

In other words, the years of anglo-conformity had passed. All cultures were seen as equal. Culture had become an issue of personal choice, and there was no shortage in the Canadian ethnic supermarket. In this light, individuals were protected against discrimination stemming from their cultural choices and were strongly encouraged to cultivate and promote their cultures and to participate fully in all aspects of Canadian life.

The second phase of multicultural policy, which corresponds roughly with the 1980s, entailed a process of institutionalization, and focused, in part, on equity-related concerns. This phase was explicitly concerned with improving "race relations," and developing a more proactive anti-racist approach to understanding and critiquing how institutions worked. The upsurge in Quebec nationalism was countered by the repatriation of the Constitution (1982), including the adoption of the Charter of Rights and Freedoms; both were subject to interpretations consistent with the notion of multiculturalism as a fundamental characteristic of Canadian society. The Progressive Conservative government passed the Multiculturalism Act (1988), which essentially turned a de facto policy into a de jure, legal framework, thus elevating multiculturalism to a position of equality with the principle of bilingualism. And, finally, multiculturalism was increasingly cast in an economic dimension. Consistent with neo-conservative economic doctrine was the attempt to justify the 1988 Multiculturalism Act not only in terms of pluralist ideology but also in terms of potential economic benefits to the country. This involved a shift in emphasis away from a "culture for culture's sake" perspective toward a more instrumentalist view of the benefits of multicultural policy. One of the most obvious signals of this shift was the Multiculturalism Means Business Conference held in Toronto in 1986, which pointed to the beginning of a more market-driven approach to multiculturalism. In his opening address to the conference, Otto Jelinek, the Conservative minister of state for multiculturalism, told delegates that

> the competition is fierce; we need every edge we can get and one is knowledge of foreign languages.... The new mercantilism calls for a new type of corporate manager, a flexible cosmopolitan aware of cultural sensitivities ... who can cut costs and waste by knowing how culture affects behaviour, who can motivate workers with differing standards, read between the lines of reports from abroad, and pinpoint the pitfalls of overseas selling, what is or is not acceptable. (Jelinek, 1986: 5)

He went on to suggest that

> simply expressed, this government believes emphatically that multiculturalism can and does mean business. Increased business. More business. And from this newly tapped resource will flow a prosperity which will generate greater social mobility and open even more doors to opportunity in all avenues of endeavour. (Jelinek, 1986: 5)

Cultural pluralism, and the image of Canada as an equal, tolerant, and fair society, was therefore defined by the 1980s Progressive Conservative government as an asset within the emerging global economy (Moodley, 1983). In neo-liberal terms, the plethora of cultures and languages of Canadian society would lead to increased international trade and improve the comparative advantage of the country vis-à-vis our supposedly unilingual and monocultural competitors (Abu-Laban and Gabriel, 2002). What the Canadian government failed to recognize was that most countries in the world were by then multicultural in de facto if not in policy terms, so Canada's multicultural nature might not be so unique, or as much of an economic advantage as thought (see Harles, 2004).

In the 1990s, a new set of meanings and priorities was attached to multiculturalism. Fleras (2012: 311) calls this civic multiculturalism. It can be defined as a stage during which folkloric and institutional multiculturalism are coupled with citizenship, which temporarily assumed institutional expression in the Department of Multiculturalism and Citizenship, under the Canadian Heritage umbrella. One of the new foci of civic multiculturalism was society-building: fostering a common sense of identity and belonging that was considered essential for the participation and inclusion of all Canadians in national institutions (see Fleras, 2012: 311). Institutions needed to change to make themselves more reflective of the increasing diversity of Canadian society, but immigrant and ethnic groups also had to change by becoming fully involved in Canadian society.

Fleras (2012: 311–12) argues that we are currently in the fourth phase of multicultural policy, what he calls *integrative multiculturalism*. Building on the emphasis on greater civic engagement in the 1990s, this new phase of multiculturalism emphasizes the need to better integrate immigrants into Canadian society. Responding to wider concerns that too much diversity could be harmful for Canadian society, this new phase of the policy focuses on the "duty of immigrants and members of ethnic communities integrate into Canadian society and to adopt the values of liberal democracy. In other words, if immigrants and members of ethnic communities wish to retain elements of their cultures and values, this should not come at the expense of a commitment to share Canadian values and integrate into Canadian society.

Contesting Multiculturalism

Since its inception in the early 1970s, multicultural policy has been a contested terrain. There has never been agreement about the wisdom, desirability, or necessity of the federal government's multicultural policies and programs. Putting it in rather stark terms, some say that multiculturalism is what makes Canada a unique and great country, while others say that multiculturalism will lead to our eventual downfall. In the new millennium, particularly in the context of the attacks on the World Trade Center and the Pentagon on 11 September 2001; the 2006 arrest of 18 young Muslim Canadian men on the grounds that they were plotting terrorist attacks around the country; as well as events in Europe like the 2005 bombing of the London transit system, the January 2015 attack on the satirical magazine *Charlie Hebdo*, and the subsequent November 2015 and March 2016 bombings in Paris and Brussels, debates about multiculturalism have taken on renewed importance and a sense of political urgency. In this section, we want to review the two broad criticisms of multicultural policy. The first casts multiculturalism as an ineffective government policy; the second casts the policy as too effective.

Multiculturalism as Ineffective in Solving the "Real" Problems: Racism, Class Inequality, and Anglo-Dominance

One criticism of the policy of multiculturalism is that it is largely ineffective in dealing with the major sources and dimensions of social inequality in Canada. The early criticisms of the cultural emphasis within multiculturalism in the 1970s and early 1980s were that the policy only promoted those aspects of ethnic cultures that did not challenge Anglo-Saxon assumptions about the way society should be organized and that multiculturalism was an ideology (Roberts and Clifton, 1982; Lewycky, 1992). Critics suggested that there was too great an emphasis on depoliticized "song-and-dance" activities that were non-threatening to British economic, political, and cultural hegemony and that the policy mystified social reality by creating the appearance of change without actually changing the fundamental bases of ethnic and racial inequality within Canada (Bolaria and Li, 1988; Moodley, 1983). Furthermore, it was argued that identifying cultural barriers to full participation precluded a definition of the structural barriers that legitimize and indeed prioritize racism and discrimination (Bolaria and Li, 1988).

In addition to minimizing the role of racism in producing and reproducing social inequality, Rennie Warburton argues that "multiculturalism's silence on the issue of class is part of an ideological code that marginalizes analyses of class relations by defining them as radical, extreme or Marxist and, consequently, as not serious" (Warburton, 2007: 283). Multiculturalism is one of many ideological tools used by governments, media, and privileged social groups to invalidate class perspectives to reproduce individualistic, not communal, values and the inviolability of private property, which constitute the fundamental bases of capitalist class relations (Warburton, 2007: 285). As we showed in Chapter 5, not all ethnic and racial groups enjoy economic success in Canada. There exist great class, gender, and nativity earnings differentials among and within them. But in multicultural discourse only cultural differences exist; class, gender, or other socio-economic and political differences are absent or not worth discussing.

Along similar lines, Daiva Stasiulis (1980: 34) argues that in line with the state's role in legitimizing the existing social order, these interventions (multiculturalism, bilingualism) have a depoliticizing effect. By overemphasizing "cultural" and linguistic barriers to equality, they conceal other, perhaps more fundamental social inequalities based on people's property rights, position in the labour market, education, gender, and age. In fact, Canadian society is characterized by a clear ethnically based (and gender-based) class hierarchy and struggle, which, of course, is not addressed by multiculturalism because such struggle is challenging, if not threatening, to the existing social order. Multiculturalism obfuscates these antagonisms and shifts the struggle to the "cultural" realm.

Despite the shifts in emphasis of the policy, this line of criticism continues to be advanced. Bannerji (2000) argues that multiculturalism is a conceptual code used by governments and dominant social groups to maintain and reproduce hegemonic practices. As we mentioned above, multiculturalism defines boundaries and delimits ethnic and "race" relations in order to maintain the existing social, economic, and political order, and to manage social change. It purposefully ignores the structural contexts in which the Canadian society, economy, and polity have developed historically and operate currently. It has adopted a diversity discourse that portrays Canada as a horizontal—not as a vertical—socio-economic and political space (Bannerji, 2000: 50). It conceptualizes all cultural forms and differences in terms of a descriptive plurality, recognizing and asserting cultural essences, pointing to horizontal heterogeneity, not vertical hierarchy (Warburton, 2007: 283). Beneath the surface of multiculturalism operate mechanisms and relations of power among dominant and subordinate groups that serve, protect, and reproduce those relations. In other words, the policy continues to preserve the dominance of white, Anglo-Saxon men.

Often, minority communities use the multicultural framework to be recognized and be funded by government agencies in order to try to achieve anti-racist goals (Nadeau, 2005; Bonnett, 2000). But in doing so, there is a tension in organizations; they have to strike a balance between advancing their own understanding of problems and solutions with the way that the policy defines problems and solutions.

Srivastava (2007) argues that there was evidence of this tension in the 1980s when government-sponsored conferences were organized around issues facing immigrant and visible minority women. In order to receive funding, concepts and issues were framed in terms of dominant government multicultural discourses. The National Organization of Immigrant and Visible Minority Women (NOIVMW) and the Ontario Coalition of Visible Minority Women (OCVMW) were formed subsequently, partly with government direction and funding, to provide the political and institutional tools for addressing the issues confronting these groups. Srivastava (2007) suggests that the emergence of these organizations demonstrated how the multicultural framework recognizes certain types of differences by imposing particular labels and ignores others. The organizing principle of the NOIVMW and the OCVMW evolved around the categories *immigrant* and *visible minority women*, not around the term *women of colour*, which was used extensively by anti-racist feminist activists (Srivastava, 2007). The latter term is not neutral or empty of political meaning. It connotes a political identity, rooted in the anti-racist feminist movement and, importantly, it is not part of the multiculturalist discourse. The emphasis on immigrant and visible minority women directly influenced the nature of NOIVMW and OCVMW, their goals, their organizational structures, their practices, and their activism. Instead of addressing the real and pressing issues of racism, patriarchy, and class oppression, their actions tended to emphasize only the ethnic/racial dimension. They did not integrate analyses of racism, sexism, and classism into their agendas or activism, as pre-existing grassroots community organizations, such as the Cross-Cultural Communications Centre and several black and South Asian women's groups were doing before the establishment of the NOIVMW and the OCVMW (Srivastava, 2007: 296; 2007: 296–7). They tended to ignore the gender and class dimensions of social inequality. According to Srivastava (2007), they spent most of their time and funding dealing with drafting their constitutions, forming committees, often bypassing existing grassroots networks, and quarrelling over definitions of visible minorities. They were ineffective in addressing the concerns of their membership over issues such as reproductive technologies, employment, pay equity, education, and child care (Srivastava, 2007: 297).

Another example of the limits of multiculturalism is anti-racist education workshops. The premise of such educational activities is the so-called **contact hypothesis** discussed in Chapter 1. Consonant with the pronounced aims of multiculturalism, intercultural exchanges and interracial contact will, over time, reduce prejudice, discrimination, and racism; it will promote understanding, tolerance, and, for the optimists, even acceptance of difference and diversity. In many circles, such educational workshops represent a good strategy for combating discrimination and racism and promoting equity. In the 1990s, the NDP government of Ontario established the Ontario Anti-Racism Secretariat (OARS) whose mandate was, in part, to fund anti-racist education projects put together by various community organizations. Srivastava (2007) participated in several such workshops and even facilitated a few. She argues that although such initiatives do name racism as a social problem, they tend to limit the potential for anti-racist social change. They portray racism as individual ignorance that can be "cured" by education, not a systemic feature of Canadian society. They are based on the discussion of first-hand, personal, often emotional accounts of individual experiences of discrimination and racism. They represent a "let's talk" approach, run by professional facilitators who expect non-whites to share their experiences and feelings, while whites are expected to express their shock and show sympathy toward the victims. They do not question the systemic aspects of racism, but in the context of multiculturalism, emphasize individualistic, not political or organizational group responses to racism (Srivastava, 2007: 300 2007: 300–3). Although anti-racist workshops are a strategy for useful inter-group exchanges and do encourage public discussions of racism, they alone do not seem to be an effective tool in combating it. Although anti-racist workshops are a strategy for useful inter-group exchanges and do encourage public discussions of racism, they alone do not seem to be an effective tool in combating it. As Goldberg (1993) has observed, liberal multicultural analyses of racism rest on the idea that education alone has the capacity of eradicating racism. As with all radical social change, however, it requires collective social action (praxis).

Finally, in practical terms, many commentators were skeptical about how the relatively small amounts of money spent on multicultural policy by the federal government, an average of about $60 million allotted to multicultural programs annually, could possibly address the range of problems and issues involving such things as assistance to cultural groups in their quest to identify, preserve, and promote their cultural identities; cultural interchanges with other groups; official language(s) acquisition programs; and removal of the vaguely defined cultural barriers to social equality and full participation in Canadian society. Thus, early criticisms of multiculturalism focused around the policy's inherent inability to deliver the goods and solve the "real" problems of social inequality in Canada.

Multiculturalism as Too Effective

In the 1990s and 2000s, a bundle of new criticisms began to be levelled against multicultural policy by a combination of academics, social commentators, and political parties (Fleras, 2012; Fleras and Elliott, 1996: 348, Table 10.3; Banting and Kymlicka, 2010). These criticisms claim that multicultural policy helps to reproduce stereotypes of ethnic groups, undermines Canadian unity, ghettoizes minority issues, and takes away from the special claims that francophones and Aboriginal peoples have within Canadian society. More recently, commentators have defined multiculturalism as a recipe for intolerance and terrorism. These criticisms differ from earlier criticism in that the emphasis is now on the negative social consequences that multicultural policy has produced. It is implied that the "problem" with multiculturalism is that it is has been too successful as a social policy. A policy that had as one of its underlying intentions the improvement of inter-group relations is now defined as a policy that leads to deteriorating inter-group relations and is a threat to the coherence and stability of Canada. There are a number of variations of these criticisms.

The hardening of stereotypes

One criticism of multiculturalism as too effective is that it leads to the hardening of ethnic and racial stereotypes. In his 1994 book, *Selling Illusions: The Cult of Multiculturalism in Canada*, novelist Neil Bissoondath argues that multiculturalism reduces people to the lowest common denominator. By reinforcing stereotypes, it simplifies and thus devalues culture. This is a potent argument against folkloric multiculturalism. "Caravans," "folk fests," and other multicultural festivals do not promote serious cultural exchanges; instead, they are superficial and have the effect of commodifying and "Disneyfying" culture. According to Bissoondath (1994: 83), culture becomes "a thing that can be displayed, performed, admired, bought, sold, or forgotten." We have ended up, then, with no culture but theatre, no history but fantasy. Multiculturalism, therefore, is seen to encourage the devaluation of the very thing that it is intended to protect and promote. Manipulated to social and political utility, culture becomes folklore (Bissoondath, 1994: 83–4, 88). For Bissoondath,

> Multiculturalism, with all its festivals and its celebrations, has done, and can do, little to foster a factual and clear-minded vision of our neighbours. Depending on stereotype, ensuring that the ethnic groups will preserve their distinctiveness in a gentle and insidious form of cultural apartheid, multiculturalism has done little more than lead an already divided country down the path of social divisiveness. (1994: 89–90)

Moreover, by placing individuals into preconceived stereotypes (*what* people are, not *who* they are), multiculturalism diminishes the autonomy and role of the individual. We have become a nation of cultural hybrids, according to Bissoondath (1994: 224). "We are, as it were, of so many colours, that we are essentially colourless" (1994: 73).

On this point, Bissoondath is probably correct. There is no evidence to suggest that intercultural exchanges take place or have indeed assisted in the harmonization of racial and ethnic relations in Canada. Not only have the "problems" of minority relations not been defined, but also the little intercultural exchanges that do take place seem superficial and folkloric at best (Fleras and Elliott, 1996: 330–1). In fact, as Mullard argued in 1982, multiculturalism appears to focus on "saris, samosas, and steel-bands" in order to diffuse "resistance, rebellion and rejection" (in Henry and Tator, 1999: 98).

The promotion of cultural relativism

Another criticism of multiculturalism is that it promotes cultural relativism and hence undermines Canadian values and social cohesion. This criticism has been developed by Reg Bibby, a sociologist at the University of Lethbridge, and is echoed by Bissoondath, the old Reform Party of Canada in the 1990s, and even today in some sections of the Conservative Party of Canada. In *Mosaic Madness*, Bibby (1990) argued that one of the main social trends of our postmodern time is to increasingly value collective and individual freedom. While freedom is good in and of itself, Bibby argued that the consequence of this increasing emphasis on freedom is to promote individualism, pluralism, and relativism. Individualism, according to Bibby (1990: 1–2), leads to pluralism, and pluralism legitimizes diversity and in turn reinforces the values of both collective and individual freedom. Relativism, then, is the logical consequence of freedom, individualism, and pluralism. But what is relativism?

Bibby defines relativism in terms of the suspension of value judgments about how people live. He writes:

> Truth and best are not listed in the pluralism dictionary. The only truth is that everything is relative. "Cultural relativism" is accepted as a given; those who dare to assert that their culture is best are dubbed ethnocentric; those who dare to assert that they have the truth are labelled bigots. Truth has been replaced by personal viewpoint. (1990: 2)

Mosaic Madness suggests that pluralism does emancipate individuals and groups. Contrary to absolutist views about truth, which transcend cultures and individuals, cultural relativism argues that the truth is socially constructed and it thus "erases agreement on the norms that are essential to social life" (Bibby, 1990: 14). Cultural relativism, which is seen to be promoted by multicultural policy, leads to the undermining of social cohesion. We have enshrined into law our "good intentions" of bilingualism, multiculturalism, and anti-racism by institutionalizing appropriate policies. But in consequence, we have become a fractious nation that lacks a sense of community (Bibby, 1990: 15). Canada, in attempting to promote (peaceful) coexistence, is indeed promoting the breakdown of group life.

Bibby further argues that individual freedom coupled with pluralism leads to the construction of "mosaics within mosaics" (individuals and smaller groups within groups) (Bibby, 1990: 7–8). This, Bibby claims, is "too much of a good thing." Excessive individualism stresses individual rights over social rules. There is no "team spirit," no social spirit. We confuse choice with "the best" (1990: 98), and we give "everything an A" (1990: 176). Indeed, we are abandoning the "pursuit of the best" and slowly slipping into a state of multicultural mediocrity. Bibby does not suggest what "the best" is, who deserves an A, or who should decide these issues and how.

So, according to Bibby, Canadian society has changed as a result of multiculturalism but not in entirely positive ways. There appears to be a reversal of emphasis: whereas up to the 1950s, Canadians had placed emphasis on community, on the collectivity, since then we have been emphasizing the individual. Pluralism, although imperative for coexistence, does not offer a subsequent vision of the country, does not set national goals, and does not pursue a cause. According to Bibby (1990: 103: 103–4), we have ended up with a value system that contains nothing exclusively Canadian.

Bissoondath (1994: 71), in a similar vein, argues that multiculturalism has failed because it has eradicated the centre: "It has diminished all sense of Canadian values, of what is a Canadian." Most importantly, multiculturalism does not include an ultimate vision of the kind of society it wishes to create (1994: 42). Although Bissoondath does not advocate a return to the years of anglo-conformity, he argues that multiculturalism does not offer a vision of unity and encourages division by ghettoizing people into ethnic groups. It has imposed social controls and employs "divide and conquer" strategy and tactics. It is a myopic view of the present that ignores the future (Bissoondath, 1994: 44).

In the late 1980s and early 1990s, the Reform Party of Canada, a considerable conservative political force in those days that has found its way into today's Conservative Party of Canada, called repeatedly for the abolition of multicultural programs and the Department of Multiculturalism as a whole on the same kind of grounds expressed by both Bibby and Bissoondath. According to the party, cultural preservation is a matter of private choice, and the state has no place in promoting diversity. Instead, the government should be preserving and promoting our national culture and should encourage ethnic cultures to integrate into it (Reform Party of Canada, in Abu-Laban and Stasiulis, 1992: 373). Similarly, in Bissoondath's (1994: 219) terms, public policy has no place in personal culture and ethnicity. It has to be returned to individuals, who do not need to be defined culturally by Ottawa bureaucrats. Our ultimate goal should be a cohesive, effective society with cultural diversity. If our aim is reasonable diversity within rigorous unity, we must diminish the former to achieve the latter (Bissoondath, 1994: 224).

Influenced by the relative electoral appeal of Reform, the Progressive Conservative Party (which has now merged with Reform to form the Conservative Party of Canada) passed a number of resolutions at its 1991 annual convention that pointed clearly to a right-wing shift in its immigration and multicultural policies. With respect to multiculturalism, it was resolved that the party should abandon the policy and its department altogether and should instead "try to foster a common national identity for the people living together in harmony as equal citizens, loyal to the Canadian ideal" (cited in Abu-Laban and Stasiulis, 1992: 374). When this resolution was passed, the governing Conservatives were in an awkward position, having to defend a policy that their membership no longer supported. Gerry Weiner, then the minister of state for multiculturalism, defended the policy and argued that the convention's resolutions did not represent the majority of party members since there was not enough representation of ethnic and racial minorities in the body of delegates. This justification was an indirect admission that the Progressive Conservatives did not have an ethnic base and that those in government were trying hard to break into the ethnic vote. It is interesting that no one mentioned the lack of ethnic representation with respect to resolutions not related to multiculturalism (e.g., on the economy or on social programs).

What is common in criticism of this type is an appeal to the "national" character of Canada. The implication is that the current system is biased in favour of non-whites and non-Europeans and it should not be. In addition, people expressing such views are always silent or purposefully vague in describing what constitutes Canadian culture (most of the time they mean anglo-tradition) or defining what is Canadian or what Canadian values are. It is unclear exactly what ethnic subcultures or countercultures are to be integrated into.

The marginalization of ethnocultural issues

A third criticism of multiculturalism is that it promotes the ghettoization of ethnic issues. Ironically, this criticism was most forcefully developed within the ranks of the federal Liberal Party. The Liberals have historically been the party that has most identified with multiculturalism. The Liberal Party developed the non-discriminatory immigration policy, as well as the official policy of multiculturalism, and, during the 1970s and 1980s, was the party that was most rewarded by the "ethnic" vote. It too, however, harbours people opposed to the policy of multiculturalism. As Abu-Laban and Stasiulis write (1992: 375), a number of "ethnic" MPS were critical of multiculturalism's ghettoizing effects in the early 1990s. John Nunziata, then a Liberal MP, was the most vocal opponent of the policy, arguing that it no longer served a constructive purpose in Canadian society. When he ran and won as an Independent in the 1997 federal election, a number of his supporters raised the issue of the Liberals' grip on the Italian community in Canada, vowing to put an end to it.

One of Nunziata's criticisms is of particular interest: that the case of the internment and confiscation of property of Japanese Canadians during the Second World War was handled by the Department of Multiculturalism, not by the Ministry of Justice. These were justice issues, he argued, not ethnic ones (Abu-Laban and Stasiulis, 1992: 376). Subsequently, the Liberal Party, after reaffirming its support for multiculturalism at its 1992 convention, has proceeded to incorporate some of these criticisms into its platform. Specifically, it has recognized that multiculturalism may indeed have ghettoizing effects and that a single cultural policy may be a more appropriate course of action, accompanied by a single department of culture and communications. This was a clear shift toward society building—civic multiculturalism—which involved facilitating the inclusion and participation of all citizens by pursuing anti-racist policies and by promoting "citizenship" (Abu-Laban and Stasiulis, 1992: 376).

Sociologist Peter Li (1994a) takes this criticism a step further and focuses on the implications of multicultural policy on the world of the arts. He argues that the policy has inadvertently resulted in the marginalization of minority arts and cultural activities. There is, according to Li (1994a), a bifurcation of the arts world in Canada. On the one side is the formal arts world, derived largely from European and American influences and supported through mainstream institutions like the Canada Council for the Arts. On the other side is "ethnic" art that tends to be defined as the quaint forms of folkloric dance, music, and written expression that immigrants bring with them to Canada and which minorities are expected to perform at various festivals and multicultural events. According to Li,

> These two art worlds operate under separate infrastructures and rules and standards; and the source and magnitude of funding are different. The outlets for public display or performance of these art works also vary; and the art works of these two art worlds carry unequal market value and social status. As these two art worlds become increasingly institutionalized, the producers of minority art come to accept the rules and structure under which their works are to be produced, and their products reflect the public demand and expectations of what visible minority art ought to be. Hence, the multicultural world and the formal art world are distinguishable not only by the style and form of the works being produced, and by the unequal aesthetic and market value being attached to the products, but also by differences in social organization, operational rules and evaluation standards. {1994a: 387)

Multiculturalism and the undermining of special claims

Another criticism of multiculturalism as too effective is that it undermines the special claims that francophones and Aboriginal peoples have in Canadian society. As noted above, the inception of multicultural policy had an ulterior motive: namely, the undermining of the legitimacy of Quebec nationalism by reducing the Quebec factor to an ethnic phenomenon (Bissoondath, 1994: 40, 62). Initially, multiculturalism was seen as an attempt by the federal government to undermine the legitimate Quebec aspirations for "nationhood." "By severing culture from language, multiculturalism policy rejected the 'two nations' thesis about Canada's development, and reduced the status of French Canadians and/or the Québécois from that of 'founding people' to the same rank as the 'other ethnic groups'" (Abu-Laban and Stasiulis, 1992: 367).

This interpretation of multiculturalism was, of course, shared by René Lévesque and by many Quebec academics (Abu-Laban and Stasiulis, 1992: 367–8). Lévesque, for example, was dismissive of multiculturalism from the beginning because it obscured the Quebec issue (Bissoondath, 1994: 40). As Christian Dufour (1992) argued in *Le défi québécois*, multiculturalism was a mechanism to buy allophone votes and reduce the Quebec factor to an ethnic phenomenon; that is, reduce the francophone majority to just another ethnic group and undermine its historical claim to "nationhood." Harvey (1985, cited in Abu-Laban and Stasiulis, 1992) and Labelle (1990, cited in Abu-Laban and Stasiulis, 1992) argued that multiculturalism had an adverse effect on the Quebec collectivity by minoritizing it (similar to the process of racialization) (Bissoondath, 1994: 40). Quebec's assimilationist policies toward allophones (immigrants whose first language is neither French nor English) can be understood in this context.

Aboriginal people and organizations have expressed similar criticisms and have related reservations about multiculturalism. They argue that multiculturalism reduces them to "just another minority" and undermines their aspirations for self-government (Abu-Laban and Stasiulis, 1992: 376). They claim that they possess a distinct and unique set of rights that stem from being the first occupants of the land in Canada. Since Aboriginal people do not consider themselves part of a pluralist society but as distinct peoples, multiculturalism is seen as an actual threat to their survival. They prefer to negotiate their future in a binational framework (as the Québécois do) that recognizes their collective rights to special status and distinctiveness (Fleras and Elliott, 1996: 343).

Multiculturalism as a recipe for intolerance and terrorism

Finally, terrorist attacks in a number of countries around the world over the past few years have provided a context for renewed questions about and assaults on multi-culturalism policies in Canada and abroad; namely, that multiculturalism gives indirect support to the forces promoting violence and extremism (Banting and Kymlicka, 2010).

The two most trenchant post-9/11 criticisms of multiculturalism are that such policies encourage and tolerate the promotion of cultures and religions that are decidedly intolerant and that multiculturalism is a recipe for homegrown terrorism (Granatstein, 2007). Robert Fulford, in a *National Post* article, summarizes these two themes and describes the Canadian policy of multiculturalism as a "grave mistake." Following on an argument articulated in Britain in 2001 that the country was "sleepwalking to segregation," Fulford argued that

> multiculturalism has become a way of putting people in narrow categories. Some groups have decided to live in ghettos of their own making, apart from the rest of us. While living apart temporarily often is a necessary part of the immigration

process, if only because of language, those who see cultural isolation as a permanent way of life tend to cripple their own possibilities, limit their ability to contribute to Canada, and create impregnable communities in which they can nourish their imported grievances and generate hatred for democracy and the West. (2006: A19)

The view that multicultural policy leads to the creation of ethnic ghettoes is, at least in Canada, devoid of empirical support. It is a mistake to think that the visible non-English signage and concentration of businesses like restaurants, grocery stores, and other commercial enterprises and services in certain geographical areas necessarily indicate the existence of an ethnic ghetto or **ethnic enclave**. Places in Canadian cities that are described as Chinatown, Little Italy, Greektown, or Little India are more often than not constructed by tourism officials and marketed as exotic places to visit. Though they may be places where members of those communities first settled when they initially moved to Canada in earlier times, their existence today does not necessarily mean that many members of these communities actually live in them any more, or that co-ethnic members of these communities live their lives within the confines of the enclave and cultivate their grievances against Canadian society.

Assessing the critics

As a social policy, multiculturalism is one of Canada's favourite whipping boys. For some, the policy is too effective, while for others it is not effective enough. Even though the policy means different things in different places, other countries around the world are in the middle of even more contentious debates about multiculturalism. As discussed earlier in this chapter, there is something of a global backlash against multiculturalism, witnessed in part by various western European leaders who have declared the policy to be a failure because it contributes to segregation and, eventually, to terrorism. While we cannot offer a full-fledged defense of the policy here, we want to make two critical comments in support of multiculturalism, at least in its Canadian version.

First, critics of multiculturalism like Fulford and Granatstein go overboard when they claim that multiculturalism prevents immigrants from integrating into Canadian society and that multiculturalism promotes the formation of entire ethnic communities in Canada that are closed, insulated, and opposed to everything that Canada stands for. Howard-Hassmann (1999) has pointed to a basic fault in the criticisms advanced by those who claim that the policy prevents integration: they assume that Canadian multiculturalism calls for individuals to retain their ancestral identities. But the Canadian policy is *liberal*, not *illiberal*; that is, it does not impose the idea of maintaining ethnic differences, nor does it force individuals to identify with ancestral cultural groups. In Howard-Hassmann's view,

Multiculturalism "normalizes" a wide range of customs and makes the enjoyment of such customs part of what it means to be a Canadian. . . . Liberal multiculturalism acknowledges the social need for difference, for smaller, more close-knit communities separated from the Canadian mainstream. But it does not mandate such difference. (1999: 533)

She has also argued that far from promoting disloyalty to Canada and things Canadian, multicultural policy has the seemingly ironic consequences of integrating immigrants to the dominant society, promoting national unity, and encouraging "a sense of connection with other Canadians" (1999: 534). There are many indicators that immigrants and members of ethnic communities do, in fact, integrate into Canadian society even if they maintain some attachment to their ethnic identity and culture:

- Rates of ethnic and racial intermarriage are increasing. "Mixed-race" couples grew by 33 per cent between 2001 and 2006, more than five times the growth rate for all couples in Canada. Couples in mixed unions do better economically than couples not in mixed unions (www.statcan.gc.ca/pub/11-008-x/2010001/article/11143-eng.htm).
- In English-speaking Canada, the children and grandchildren of non-English-speaking immigrants do, in fact, learn English. Mother tongue transmission declines dramatically over the generations in Canada. For language groups as a whole, 41 per cent of the second generation and only 10 per cent of the third generation have knowledge of the first generation's mother tongue (www.statcan.gc.ca/pub/11-008-x/2011002/t/11453/tbl004-eng.htm).
- Immigrants in Canada do value Canadian citizenship. In 2006 in Canada, the citizenship acquisition rate was 79 per cent. In the US, the citizenship rate was only 46 per cent (Picot and Hou, 2011: 22).
- "Immigrants want to participate in Canada's democratic process, and the broader electorate is open to being represented by immigrants" (Kymlicka, 2010). In the federal election, 46 visible minority candidates were elected and they represented per cent of MPS in Parliament.
- In terms of educational achievement, the children of immigrants outperform the children of non-immigrant parents (Kymlicka, 2012).
- Attachment to a "Canadian" identity increases by generation in Canada. The Ethnic Diversity Survey shows that a Canadian or regional Canadian identity (e.g., Québécois, Acadian, or Newfoundlander) increases from 40 per cent for first-generation Canadians, to 78 per cent for second-generation, and 80 per cent for third-generation Canadians (Statistics Canada, 2003).

A second response to criticisms of multicultural policy is the argument that pluralism does not inevitably lead to relativism. Multiculturalism, as we experience it in our daily lives, does not encourage an "everything goes" mentality, although it does help to create some ambiguity about the lines between what is acceptable and what is not, lines that are usually contested in the courts and other public domain

Case Study Box 6.1 What Makes Canada Different from Other Countries and How Does Multiculturalism Help Produce Integration?

Even though many commentators in Canada have called into question the desirability and wisdom of the policy of multiculturalism, Canadians still seem committed to upholding its ideals. The 2015 federal election was highly contentious with some politicians and parties trying to play wedge politics that sought to scare and divide Canadians around issues like whether Muslim women ought to be able to wear their niqab at their citizenship ceremony and whether the country needed to take action against "barbaric cultural practices." Canadians seemed to firmly reject these efforts to stoke fears about multiculturalism. The interesting sociological questions are: (1) why has Canada not experienced the same retreat from multiculturalism as other Western countries?; and (2) how does multiculturalism actually produce social integration rather than social division?

Toronto-based writer Murtaza Hussain aptly describes the European situation in the following terms:

> A 2011 poll of European countries showed that 65 percent of Spaniards, Italians and Brits believed there were "too many immigrants in their country." The rising popularity of anti-immigration parties across the continent is a testament to the depth of this feeling, and even mainstream politicians like Angela Merkel and David Cameron have expressed similar sentiments.
>
> The flip side of this is the increasing Balkanisation of urban areas in many European cities. Immigrant quarters are sometimes considered no-go zones by locals, and the sense of separation between different races and ethnicities is perceptible to any observer. Minorities are often viewed as "the other" and they often come to view and define themselves that way as well.
>
> Even among second- and third-generation immigrants this feeling often persists, giving rise to a new class of people who do not feel truly at home in their place of birth nor in their place of ancestry. These are the new "globally homeless," and it is unsurprising to see the self-destructive expressions of anger, hopelessness, and even nihilism that this type of alienation can generate among some. As a French-Algerian friend once poignantly told me, "In France they call us foreigners and in Algeria they call us Frenchmen . . . home is on a plane." (2013)

In his view, a big part of the reason why Canada is different is that our policy does not force people to integration. That is, "'integration' tends to work on its own when it is not being forcibly compelled, and when it is not a zero-sum game where newcomers are expected to conform but not create."

Keith Banting and Will Kymlicka (2010), two of Canada's most thoughtful analysts of how multiculturalism actually works in Canada, explain how, seemingly counter-intuitively, the policy actually goes about producing integration both at the level of individual identity and the way that social institutions in Canada work. First, on the level of individual identity, they argue that the policy helps create a common focus for both native-born citizens and immigrants in Canada. They show that in

continued

many countries, those who are native born with a strong sense of national identity or pride tend to see immigrants as a threat to their identity.

> But the fact that Canada has officially defined itself as a multicultural nation means that immigrants are a constituent part of the nation that citizens feel pride in; multiculturalism serves as a link for native-born citizens from national identity to solidarity with immigrants. Conversely, multiculturalism provides a link by which immigrants come to identify with, and feel pride in Canada. (Banting and Kymlicka, 2010: 60)

As a result, for both the native-born and immigrants to Canada, multiculturalism provides a common point of identification with Canadian nationhood.

Second, Banting and Kymlicka argue that international comparative research shows that immigrants do best, both in terms of their own psychological well-being and socio-cultural outcomes, "when they are able to combine their ethnic identity with a new national identity. . . . Members of ethnic minorities will be more likely to identify with a new national identity if they feel their ethnic identity is publicly respected" (61).

They argue that multicultural policies also help to create more inclusive and equitable public institutions. For example, they suggest that multiculturalism gives Canada a comparative advantage because it helps immigrant students, and the children of immigrants, to succeed in school. School policies that prioritize issues of cultural and linguistic diversity help create the conditions for children to do well in school.

Multiculturalism also helps to make the political process more inclusive. They cite Irene Bloemraad's (2006) important comparative study of the integration experiences of Vietnamese refugees and Portuguese immigrants in Toronto and Boston. Even though Vietnamese immigrants in the two cities are demographically similar in terms of when they arrived, their level of education, work experience, and language fluency, Bloemraad (2006) shows that the Vietnamese in Toronto are more active participants in public life and have a stronger sense of Canadian citizenship than their counterparts in Boston. Multicultural policies

> encourage and enable the Vietnamese community to participate more quickly and effectively in mainstream Canadian institutions, by facilitating the self-organization of the community, by creating new cadres of community leaders who are familiar with Canadian institutions and practices, by creating new mechanisms of consultation and participation, and more generally by creating a more welcoming environment. (Banting and Kymlicka, 2010: 62)

According to Banting and Kymlicka (2010), taken together, these findings help to explain the actual mechanisms by which multiculturalism helps to produce social integration.

places of political struggle. According to Fleras and Elliott (1996: 354), multiculturalism operates within limits: "It rejects any customs that violate Canadian laws, interferes with the rights of others, offends the moral sensibilities of most Canadians, or disturbs central institutions or core values." For example, female circumcision is a cultural practice in parts of Africa and Asia and presumably part of the cultural heritage of some Canadians. In May 1997, an amendment to the Criminal Code of Canada outlawed female genital mutilation precisely because that practice violates the human rights of young women and offends notions of equality, human integrity, and other core values prevalent in Canada and internationally. This legislation was based in part on the United Nations Declaration on the Elimination of Violence against Women (1993) as well as the Declaration of the Beijing Conference on Women (1995). The Canadian legislation links the practice to criminal harassment and regards it as a threat to the life, liberty, and security of Canadian women. And, as the 2014 public reaction to the York University sociology professor who refused a Muslim male student's request to not participate in a group assignment for religious reasons shows, Canadians seem to strongly support the idea that gender-equality norms trump religious or cultural beliefs.

At the same time, questions about the relationship between multicultural policy and the role it plays in the preservation of ethnic cultures that are seemingly at odds with Canadian values need to be asked. Central to this debate is the question of whether liberal multicultural policies have an obligation to tolerate and encourage illiberal values and behaviours. It is probably fair to say that no country has arrived at an ideal solution to the issue of managing ethnic and racial diversity. Canada questions about approach to managing issues of diversity may not be perfect, but there are many far more problematic approaches to managing diversity that we should take pride in having avoided.

Quebec's Response: Interculturalism and Reasonable Accommodation

The Quebec government has pursued a policy of **interculturalism** (which is also prominent in Europe) instead of multiculturalism. Interculturalism recognizes cultural diversity within Quebec but does not reduce the "national question" in Quebec to an ethnic phenomenon; it discourages ethnic enclaves and promotes *linguistic assimilation* (Abu-Laban and Stasiulis, 1992: 368).

Interculturalism promotes cultural exchanges in the hope that as people of different cultures are exposed to various elements of other cultures, the ensuing dialogue may lead not only to tolerance but also to better understandings between various ethnic, religious, and cultural communities and the longer-settled francophone population of the province. That, in turn, should lead to a fusion of all *commonalities* of cultures within a francophone framework.

Historically, Quebec governments have been preoccupied with the protection of the French language, which has been the main tool for the preservation and development of Québécois identity and culture. The concern with language stems from two Quebec realities: first, the low birth rate in the province since the 1960s; second, the fact that allophone communities in Quebec tend to "gravitate linguistically towards the anglophone community" (Gagnon, 2004: 374). Immigration to Quebec and the integration of immigrants became the preoccupation of successive Quebec governments since the creation of the Quebec Ministry of Immigration in 1968. The Quebec Liberal government passed the Official Language Act (Bill 22) in 1974, making Quebec officially a unilingual French province. In 1977, with the Parti Québécois in power, René Lévesque introduced the Charter of the French Language, commonly known as Bill 101. Although ethnically diverse, Quebec pushed for the creation of a unilingual (political) community. In 1981, in response to the federal policy of multiculturalism, the Quebec Ministry of Communications launched an action plan in a document entitled *Autant de façons d'être québécois* (1981), or "the many ways of being Québécois," which spelled out the parameters within which immigration and immigrant integration should take place in Quebec. Unlike the federal government with its multiculturalism policy, Quebec would pursue a policy of "convergence" through interculturalism (Gagnon, 2004: 374–5).

Some researchers have argued that interculturalism is the most advanced form of pluralism today (Karmis, 2004: 79). They claim that it combines multiculturalism and multinationalism, with three interrelated features. First, it is more inclusive than either multiculturalism or multinationalism. It does not apply only to ethnic groups or nations but also applies to "lifestyle" cultures and world views associated with new social movements. For example, it is inclusive of cultural, gay, punk, ecologist, feminist, and other non-ethnically based identities. Thus, it includes nations, ethnocultural groups, and non-ethnic cultural groups. No cultural community is excluded from Québécois identity. Second, whereas multiculturalism is believed to undermine the national claims of peoples within Canada by juxtaposing communities composing the Canadian mosaic, interculturalism seeks to intertwine them. Third, interculturalism recognizes that most individuals do have multiple identities and that none of them is so dominant as to subordinate others (Karmis, 2004: 79–80).

In 1990, the Quebec *ministère des Communautés culturelles et de l'immigration* made the intent of its approach to interculturalism more explicit. Pushing for *citoyenneté québécoise* (Quebec citizenship), it spoke of a "moral contract" between the host society (Quebec) and immigrants in order to empower all citizens and create a "common public culture." The bases on which this moral contract is "signed" are (a) a recognition of French as the language of public life; (b) respect for liberal democratic values, including civil and political rights and equality of opportunity; and (c) respect for pluralism, including openness to and tolerance of others' differences (Kymlicka, 1998: 7).

In this setting, the French language would be the common language of public life and institutions. In such a society, the active participation of all is expected and encouraged. There exist not only rights but also reciprocal obligations among the participants in the "moral contract." Intercommunity exchanges are encouraged, but limits are imposed based on respect for principles of fundamental democratic rights (Gagnon, 2004: 375). As Carens has suggested,

> Immigrants can be full members of Quebec's society even if they look and act differently from the substantial segment of the population whose ancestors inhabited Quebec and even if they do not in any way alter their own customs and cultural patterns with respect to work and play, diet and dress, sleep and sex, celebration and mourning, so long as they act within the confines of the law. (2000: 131)

In this respect, then, it may appear that there is not much difference between federal multiculturalism and Quebec interculturalism.

The "centre of convergence" for different cultural groups in Quebec, however, is the "collective good" of the French language, which is seen as an indispensable condition for the creation of the *culture publique commune* (common public culture) and the cohesion of Quebec society. The French language needs to be protected and promoted. It constitutes the basis for the self-definition of Quebec as a political community—indeed, as a nation. Particular emphasis is thus placed on the educational system. As Stéphane Lévesque (1999: 4) has argued, "Common blood or ethnicity hardly creates social cohesion or nationhood, but an education system with a common language do make a 'homeland'. . . . It is language more than land and history, that provides the essential form of belonging." Federal multiculturalism promotes individualist approaches to culture, whereas interculturalism focuses on the collectivity. Former prime minister Pierre Elliott Trudeau had argued that there cannot be an official Canadian culture. Interculturalism stresses that the French language is crucial to the development of Québécois culture and citizenship and an instrument of democracy. Without the existence of a community of language, there cannot be democratic debate or decision making (Giroux, 1997: 137). Immigrants can maintain their language of origin, but at a minimum it is their obligation to learn French for use in public space and in order to exercise their citizenship rights. There are no clear "rules" on what constitutes public space, but common civic norms exist and they form the basis for social cohesion. The goal of interculturalism is "to achieve the largest possible consensus regarding the limits and possibilities of expressions of *collective* differences based on identity, weighed against the requirements of social cohesion and individual rights in a *common* public context" (Gagnon, 2004: 378, emphasis added).

In 1984, the National Assembly of Quebec established the Conseil des communautés culturelles et de l'immigration, a permanent and autonomous body that advises the minister on issues relevant to the integration of immigrants and on intercultural relations (Juteau, 2002). In 1996, following the 1995 referendum, the creation of the ministère des Relations avec les citoyens et de l'Immigration signalled a shift away from references to cultural communities, who were displaced to the margins, toward Québécois citizenship (Juteau, 2002: 447). The ministère de l'Immigration et des Communautés culturelles established the program *Québec interculturel*, which promotes the policy of Québécois citizenship by holding the annual *Semaine québécoise des rencontres interculturelles*, or a week of intercultural exchanges among Quebec's cultural communities. The theme in October 2006 was *Mille visages, notre avenir*, or "a thousand faces, our future." Despite the good intentions and efforts of successive Quebec governments, there is no evidence that immigrants in Quebec integrate better than immigrants in the rest of Canada. In addition, there is evidence that immigrants in Quebec were not yet imagined as true Québécois, and large segments have remained outside the Quebec community, as demonstrated by the controversy over the hijab (headscarf) that some Muslim women wear (Juteau, 2002: 444, 447). In Quebec, the position of Aboriginals—another "segment" with equally rightful claims to nationhood—abundantly demonstrates this. Quebec nationalism may still be more in tune with the "two founding nations" (British and French) image of Canada. Dualism has always been cherished in Quebec but usually resisted by anglophones (Stevenson, 2005). But dualism is no longer possible. Quebec has moved away from an ethnic definition of nation toward a cultural definition—away from the French-Canadian, Catholic "race" notion, toward a francophone common public culture and more recently Québécois citizenship (Juteau, 2002: 445).

In the spirit of Québécois citizenship, a new pluralist notion has emerged: that of **reasonable accommodation.** The term implies that Quebec government policies and programs should accommodate—not just tolerate—the cultural differences, the "otherness" of new immigrants and of minority groups. The Quebec government, in its efforts to open the debate, to get input, and hopefully to legitimize the policy, began public hearings in September 2007. Philosopher Charles Taylor and sociologist Gérard Bouchard co-chaired the *Consultation Commission on Accommodation Practices Related to Cultural Differences* (CCAPRCD). Consultations took place in 17 cities in the province and were concluded in June 2008. The CCAPRCD report, entitled *Building the Future: A Time for Reconciliation* (2008), exalted the virtues of and reaffirmed the need for interculturalism. It recognized

1. the underrepresentation of ethnic minorities in jobs in the public administration;
2. the urgent need to combat forms of multiple discrimination, **Islamophobia**, anti-Semitism, and the racism to which racialized groups, especially blacks, are subject;
3. that support must be offered to immigrant women;
4. the need to increase the resources of the Commission des droits de la personne et des droits de la jeunesse; and
5. the strengthening of economic and social rights in the Quebec Charter (Taylor and Bouchard 2008: 266).

Its proposed solutions included, among many things, the need for broader training among government employees in all public institutions, starting with the schools because of the role that they play in socialization, and the need to more extensively encourage community or intercommunity action projects and practices (Taylor and Bouchard 2008: 266).

Not all Quebecers, however, agreed with the need for interculturalism or the commission's proposals. There was a clear urban/rural split that reflected the socio-demographic realities of Quebec. Urban centres like Montreal have sizable immigrant populations and are more accepting of differences. Rural areas, on the other hand, are largely homogeneous and culturally conservative, and some would like to keep it that way. In January 2007, even before the commission began its hearings, Hérouxville, a small farming community of almost exclusively white, francophone, and nominally Catholic residents, gained national and international notoriety when its municipal council passed a resolution that set the terms under which new immigrants could live in their community. Specifically, the council resolution stated that immigrants who "cover their face," "carry weapons to school," "stone or burn alive women," or "perform female genital mutilation" were not welcome in their community. As André Drouin, a town councillor, put it, reasonable accommodation had reached a state of emergency in Quebec. The implication was clear: apparently, interculturalism and reasonable accommodation had gone too far, since, it is presumed, they "allow everything." The sentiments underlying the statement were clearly directed against Jews, Muslims, Sikhs, and other peoples from northern Africa, the Middle East, and Asia. Quebec premier Jean Charest suggested that Hérouxville's measures might be drastic and exaggerated, and not representative of Quebec society.

Hérouxville's publication of its life standards attracted widespread national and international media attention. The reaction of minority communities was swift. A delegation of women from the Canadian Islamic Congress visited Hérouxville and met with the town council and some local residents to discuss the issue, in the spirit of cultural understanding. After the exchange of niceties and gifts, the town resolution was watered down, but the controversy remained and sparked debates in other parts of the country among politicians, the media, students, professors, and many others.

Some commentators outside of Quebec used the Hérouxville affair as a way of beating up on the sovereignty movement in the province, implying that this proved that rural Quebecers were still committed to a form of exclusive ethnic nationalism rather than a more inclusive civic nationalism. The problem with this view, however, is that if one were to scratch the surface of small-town (and perhaps big-city) attitudes toward immigrants and diversity in the rest of Canada, it is not obvious that they would be significantly different from those reflected in the Hérouxville statement. When the Hérouxville statement was issued, conservative commentators in the rest of Canada and from around the globe seemed to congratulate the municipality for having said what silent majorities in their communities were thinking but did not have the courage to say out loud. In December 2011, the city of Gatineau, which is experiencing one of Canada's highest rates of growth in its immigrant population, published a "statement of values" that echoed the view that new immigrants need to understand "how things work" in the city: newcomers should be cautious about cooking smelly food, that it is wrong to try to bribe public officials, and that children should not be subject to forced labour (Peritz, 2011).

Like the issue of Quebec sovereignty, which for the rest of Canada will not go away despite the sagging fortunes of the Parti Québécois, the debate in Quebec about whether newcomers should integrate seems to not go away either. In the run-up to the 2014 provincial election in Quebec, the ruling PQ proposed Bill 60, otherwise known as the "Charter of Quebec Values." In the "Charter," members of immigrant, ethnic, and religious communities were expected to uphold the values of state-level secularism and religious neutrality, and of equality between men and women. The bill proposed that members of public bodies not wear "conspicuous" symbols of their faith, and that persons must have their faces uncovered when they either deliver or receive public services in the province. Quebec citizens protested the legislation on the grounds that it was discriminatory (see Figure 6.1).

The PQ lost the 2014 provincial election and so Bill 60 fell off the legislative agenda of the province. But the newly elected Liberal Party of Quebec introduced Bill 62 in June 2015, and it too reaffirms Quebec's commitment to secularism. Though not wanting to go back to regulating clothing of public employees as was proposed under Bill 60, it does propose that individuals must have their faces

Figure 6.1 Demonstrators Protesting the Proposed Legislation in Montreal, 2013

uncovered when they provide or receive public services. That bill was also introduced the same day as Bill 59, which introduced a series of measures to prevent, detect, and act against those considering committing acts of "ideological violence." According to Salam Elmenyawi, the head of the Muslim Council of Montreal, the fact that both pieces of legislation, which directly focused on Muslims, were introduced on the same day "stinks of discrimination and prejudice. . . . Every one of these debates makes life miserable for Muslims in Quebec" (Perreaux, 2015).

Summary

For historical reasons related to colonization, conquest, and immigration, Canada is, and will remain for the foreseeable future, a diverse society. In recent debates about multiculturalism, however, the social value of this diversity has been increasingly called into question. For some, multiculturalism and our accompanying diversity are what make our country both strong and unique. For others, to rephrase the immortal words of Jacques Parizeau, former leader of the Parti Québécois, our racial and ethnic diversity is like the toothache that just will not go away. As a policy, it has undergone significant change, from its earlier folkloric, song-and-dance dimension of celebrating our differences, to a civic, more progressive narrative, aspiring to integrate "Others" into mainstream institutions and combat racism. As discussed in this chapter, some see multiculturalism and the diversity that it claims to celebrate and promote as a deleterious social policy that has produced far more serious problems than it has resolved. Whereas some criticisms have assumed that the problem with multiculturalism is that it has been too successful in promoting difference and diversity and hence has led to an undermining of Canadian values, attitudes, and culture, other criticisms focused on its relative weakness in effecting social change. While some of the critics are probably correct in their assessment that multiculturalism fails to change the underlying structural conditions that produce inequality, racism, and discrimination, other criticisms attribute too much power and significance to an underfunded and beleaguered policy.

Questions for Critical Thought

1. Would you prefer to live in a country where there is no official policy of multiculturalism? What would be some of the advantages and disadvantages of living in a monocultural society?

2. Which is a better framework for accomplishing the full participation of Canada's minorities in the political, social, and economic institutions of the country? One based on the notion that Canada is constituted by two founding nations (British and French) or one that includes First Nations as well as other ethnic and cultural groups that migrated to Canada later? Why?

3.   Does multiculturalism undermine the special claims of Aboriginal peoples in Canada? Are they just another ethnic/cultural group? Can the policy and the programs associated with multiculturalism address social, economic, and political conditions of Aboriginal people in Canada?

4.   Should the Canadian policy of multiculturalism be adopted by other multi-ethnic countries? Why? Think of France, Belgium, Australia, and the US. What about countries that have been historically more culturally homogeneous, like Italy, Greece, Spain, or Ireland?

5.   Do you think that veiled women want to hide their identities? Or is veiling based on religious beliefs and/or cultural traditions? Canada is considered a tolerant society, it has an official policy of multiculturalism, and freedom of religion is protected by the Charter of Rights and Freedoms. So, should we allow veiled citizens to cast ballots? Before you grapple with this last question, you should know that both the Canadian Islamic Congress and the Canadian Council of Muslim Women agreed that veiled women should show their faces before voting. What do you think are the implications of this issue for the study of "race" and ethnicity in Canada? Who decides what is "reasonable" in reasonable accommodation? What are the criteria? What should they be?

Debate Questions

1.   Use your sociological imagination to describe what Canadian society would be like without an official policy of multiculturalism and its accompanying programs. Try to place yourself, your family, and your friends in such a Canada and explain how our political, economic, and education system would be different. Why would you be for or against such an alternative Canada? Would it be a better or worse place to live, and for whom?

2.   How should a society balance the principles of respect for religious freedom, cultural diversity, and equality rights for women? In cases where religious values are at odds with norms of gender equality, which should take precedence?

3.   Are you in favour of Canadian government initiatives to establish and fund anti-racist organizations? What are the arguments for and against such initiatives? Examine them thoroughly in light of the multicultural nature of the initiatives and their critics, and discuss possible alternative propositions and/or effective policies.

Annotated Additional Readings

Banting, Keith, and Will Kymlicka, 2010. "Canadian Multiculturalism: Global Anxieties and Local Debates,"*British Journal of Canadian Studies*, 23(1): 43–72. An insightful overview of the global backlash against multiculturalism and why Canada seems to be bucking the trend to retreat from the policy.

Bloemraad, Irene. 2006. *Becoming a Citizen: Incorporating Immigrants and Refugees in the United States and Canada*. Berkeley: University of California Press. A well-researched and well-argued analysis of how multiculturalism helps produce social integration among Vietnamese and Portuguese immigrants in Canada.

Bouchard, Gérard, and Charles Taylor. 2008. *Building the Future: A Time for Reconciliation*. Quebec: *Commission de consultation sur les pratiques d'accommodement reliées aux differences culturelles*. An in-depth investigation into the public discontent in Quebec about the issue of reasonable accommodation of ethnic and religious differences and recommendations for the provincial government.

James, Carl. 2010. *Seeing Ourselves: Exploring Race, Ethnicity and Culture*. Toronto: Thompson Educational. James uses personal accounts of students to examine what it means to participate in the ethnic mosaic of Canada.

Joppke, Christian. 2009. *Veil: Mirror of Identity*. Cambridge, UK: Polity Press. An outstanding introduction to the politics of the veil in Western societies. Joppke examines the multiple meanings of the Islamic headscarf, issues of Muslim integration, and the global backlash against multiculturalism.

Related Websites

Multiculturalism
www.cic.gc.ca/english/multiculturalism/index.asp
This site outlines the federal government's approach to multiculturalism.

Migrant Integration Policy Index
www.mipex.eu/about
An interactive website that collects data on immigrant integration in 31 countries around the world. On many indicators of immigrant integration, Canada is consistently at the top of the list of countries that integrate immigrants well.

Cross-Cultural Community Services Association
http://tccsa.on.ca/en
This association provides settlement services as well as education and language training to all cultural communities.

The Aga Khan Museum
www.agakhanmuseum.org
The aim of the Aga Khan Museum is to offer unique insights and new perspectives into Islamic civilizations and the cultural threads that weave through history binding all people together. The hope is that the museum will also be a centre of education and of learning, and will act as a catalyst for mutual understanding and tolerance.

The Canadian Institute for Identities and Migration
www.ciim.ca/en
An initiative of the Association for Canadian Studies, this website provides information about population movements and evolving identities in Canada and abroad.

7 Racism

Learning Objectives

In this chapter you will learn that

- scholars in Canada and in many other countries argue that racism has taken on new forms and new meanings.
- racism is not necessarily a "whites only" phenomenon.
- some suggest that Islamophobia is one of the new forms of racism that has emerged in many Western societies in the aftermath of the attacks in the United States on 11 September 2001.
- new forms of anti-Semitism have recently emerged in a number of countries.
- there are different ways that social scientists have tried to measure racism.
- institutional racism can take three forms.
- critics claim that zero tolerance polices in schools are racist.
- the spheres of sports and post-secondary education display elements of institutional racism.
- critics also claim that the over-policing and under-policing of minority communities further reflects the racist nature of Canadian society.
- the Internet and new communications technologies are making the articulation of racist ideas easier, and are arguably helping to make racism seem more commonplace.

Introduction

In January 2015, an article in *Maclean's* magazine described Winnipeg as the most racist city in Canada (Macdonald, 2015). Drawing on a mix of survey data, accounts Aboriginal people told of their experiences living in the city, social media posts, and the wider context of violence directed toward indigenous women in the city, the article painted a disturbing picture of the racialized antipathy that exists in Winnipeg, mainly toward Aboriginal people. The article began with the description of a Facebook post by a teacher at a local high school who said, "Oh Goddd how long are aboriginal people going to use what happened as a crutch to suck more money out of Canadians? They have contributed NOTHING to the development of Canada. Just standing with their hand out. Get to work, tear the treaties and shut the FK up already. Why am I on the hook for their cultural support." The teacher was suspended for about nine months, but is reportedly now back at work. Robert Falcon Ouellette, an Aboriginal man running for mayor, told of an encounter at a local mall, where upon learning who he was, a shopper said, "You're the guy running for mayor. You're an Indian. . . . I don't want to shake your hand. You Indians are the problem with the city. You're lazy. You're drunks. The social problems we have in the city are all related to you" (Macdonald, 2015). Though he came in third in the mayoralty race, later in 2015 he ended up winning a seat in Winnipeg for the Liberals in the October federal election. Though there was no data specifically on the city of Winnipeg, opinion poll data cited in the article lent support to the idea that Canadians' attitudes toward Aboriginal people and issues were most negative in the provinces of Manitoba and Saskatchewan.

Shortly after the *Maclean's* story hit the newsstands, Brian Bowman, the newly elected mayor of the city, reportedly fighting back tears, told a gathering at city hall, "We need to get real." Rather than downplay the story or deny that racism was as big a problem in the city as it was portrayed, the first Métis mayor of a major city in Canada told the audience, "It takes all of us working together, committed to inclusivity, equality, love, and compassion for everyone. And we're here today to call on all Winnipeggers and all Canadians to join us, to start this path to end racism right here at home and lead the nationa in tolerance for love for one another" (Luxen, 2015). He also announced that a race relations summit would be held in the new Canadian Museum for Human Rights in order to help the city move forward.

The subsequent fallout from the article around the city, and the rest of the country, was divided. Many Canadians thought that it was about time that a city mayor started to take the issue of racism seriously; they welcomed the visibility that the *Maclean's* article brought to the issue. Others questioned the journalist's interpretation and labelling of various events that were recounted in the story as "racist" and developed their own counter-explanations. Others noted how well other "races" were doing in the city and pointed out that the city had recently elected an Aboriginal mayor and that Winnipeggers had previously elected a Jewish mayor and Canada's first openly gay mayor. Critics claimed that this showed that Winnipeggers were not the racist monsters that they were made out to be in the article.

The debate that the *Maclean's* article generated is emblematic of the controversial and complex nature of racism in Canadian society. It revolves, in part, around the not insignificant issue of how racism ought to be defined, which we noted earlier in Chapter 2. But the debate also raises the issue of whether there are elements of truth to both positions. Is it possible that racism is a problem in Winnipeg at the same time that it is also a friendly, welcoming, and tolerant city? Racial antipathies in this country are often highly localized and unique to particular situations and contexts. In certain cities or regions, the presence of some groups do indeed evoke hostility and intolerance on the part of others, but in other cities or regions, the same groups might variously be welcomed, or go unnoticed and not be thought of in negative terms. The visible minority population, as we also noted in Chapter 6 is, diverse. As a result, some visible minority groups might face racist hostility in a city or region, but other groups in the same place might escape opprobrium. Moreover, it is possible that the overall class composition of a racialized group shapes how they are thought of by others. While some Winnipeggers may be hostile to Aboriginal people and issues, does this hostility stem exclusively from racism or does it stem from the negative perceptions of the overall low socio-economic status of Aboriginal people in the city? Does the fact that the current Métis mayor of the city is also a lawyer have anything to do with the electoral support he received? Is this a case of social class trumping "race" when it comes to how individuals are valued and socially evaluated? Is it possible that *racism* and *non-racism* are not necessarily zero-sum processes?

Chapter 1 introduced the concept of racism at the theoretical level. In this chapter, we want to extend the analysis by focusing on the ways in which racism is arguably manifested in Canadian society today.

Organized Racism

The concept of *new racism* that we introduced in Chapter 2 suggests that expressions of racism today are masked behind socially acceptable ideologies and language. Instead of explicitly referring to the inferiority of various "races," as we have seen in the discussion above, apparently "race"-neutral cultures, religious practices, and/or political positions become ways of expressing negative views about racialized groups of people without actually using the concept of "*race.*" It is important to remind ourselves, however, that not all forms of racism in Canada and around the world today are expressions of new racism. There is still plenty of *old racism* evident in Canada and in other parts of the world. This old-style racism is most often seen in the existence and activities of organized white supremacist hate groups, and occasions where explicitly racist violence occurs.

In Canada and the United States, groups like Stormfront, Aryan Nations, Blood and Honour, White Aryan Resistance, and Church of the Creator are all noted white supremacist groups. The Ku Klux Klan used to be quite active in parts of Canada in the 1920s and 1930s (Backhouse, 1999). Today, some of the former groups have a presence on the Internet where they offer up their ideology, accounts of their apparent strength, as well as sales of racist music, videos, clothing, flags, and other "memorabilia." Depending on the group in question, they explicitly rail against Jews, Aboriginal people, blacks, Muslims, and immigrants, as well as gays and lesbians, "political correctness," and "liberals." The targets of these groups are variously accused of undermining white civilization and the white race. Some explicitly praise the Nazis and Nazi Germany for its defense of the white race. Many of these groups make use of special symbols or codes from the Second World War Nazi era that help to sustain their identities. For example, "14/88" is a common code for white supremacist groups. The number 14 refers to the 14-word slogan: "We must secure the existence of our race and a future for white children." The number 88 refers to HH (*H* being the eighth number in the alphabet), which stands for Heil Hitler (Media Awareness Network, 2010). The group Blood and Honour draws its name from a slogan used by the Hitler Youth in Germany in the 1930s and 1940s.

Members of the various communities that are targeted by hate groups are accused of attacking the white race, causing war and conflict, and grabbing more than their fair share of public resources. In praising the white race, they also say that it and its accomplishments are under attack and threat. They preach the importance of maintaining white racial purity, defend the "honourable" historical accomplishments of the white "race," and promote the idea of racial segregation as a way of maintaining white superiority. As the Aryan Nations pithily puts it on its website: "Stop the hate—segregate" (www.aryan-nations.org).

It is hard to tell how influential these groups are and how many members they have. They tend to be secretive, and they also have an interest in exaggerating the size of their membership to make it appear that they have more supporters than is actually the case. But on occasion, members of these groups have crawled out from their basements and from the front of their computer screens to organize marches and protests. Blood and Honour attempted to organize rallies in Edmonton, Alberta, and London, Ontario, in the spring of 2012, but the reported 20 or so supporters in each city who showed up were overwhelmed by anti-racist protesters who got wind of their plans (Molotov, 2012).

Also, on occasion, members of these groups commit violence against members of racialized and minority individuals and communities. After the unsuccessful rally in Edmonton, two members of the group are alleged to have violently attacked two Sikh men (Humphreys, 2012). In 2011, two members of Blood and Honour in Vancouver were charged with lighting a Filipino-Canadian man on fire while he slept (Hutchinson, 2011).

The existence of these groups raises a number of sticky questions about what constitutes a hate crime, and where the line should be drawn between the principle of freedom of expression and hate speech. Hate crimes are defined in the Criminal Code of Canada as crimes committed to intimidate, harm, or terrify not only a person, but an entire group of people to which the victim belongs. It is also a criminal offense to incite hatred against a group of people based on their race, religion, colour, ethnic origin, or sexual orientation (CBC News, 2011). At the same time, the Canadian Constitution guarantees "freedom of thought, belief, opinion and expression, including freedom of the press and other media of communication."

In court proceedings regarding hate crimes, it is sometimes difficult to prove that a crime was committed to harm not just the immediate victim but an entire group or community. Further, where the line is between the principle of "freedom of expression" and "incitement of hatred" is a matter of debate. Some say that freedom of expression should be supported no matter how distasteful the comments; others argue that there must be limits on the kinds of things people can utter in public. Though he was not part of an organized hate group, the case of David Ahenakew, the former national chief of the Assembly of First Nations, brought some of these dilemmas to light. After speaking at an Aboriginal health conference in Saskatoon in 2002 where he alluded to Jews being responsible for starting the Second World War, Ahenakew was approached by a reporter asking him to elaborate on his views about

Jews. In the brief interview with the reporter that followed the speech, "Ahenakew praised Hitler for trying to 'clean up the world' when he 'fried' six million Jews in the Holocaust. He said Hitler's rise to power was a response to the 'disease' of Jewish world domination" (CBC News, 2003). Ahenakew was charged in 2003 under the Criminal Code with incitement of hatred for uttering those statements to the reporter. He was convicted in 2005 and fined $1,000. After his conviction he was stripped of his Order of Canada, which he received in 1978 in recognition for his service to Aboriginal and Métis people. He appealed his conviction and a new trial was granted. In his second in 2008, he was found not guilty, in part because the judge determined that the statements he uttered to the reporter were spontaneous and not an attempt to spread hatred of Jews. Though Ahenakew was eventually cleared of the charges, the case was all the more interesting because it highlighted the fact that a respected member of Canada's First Nations community, which had itself experienced a history of racism and discrimination at the hands of the Canadian federal government, had surprisingly little knowledge of the history of anti-Semitism, racism, and discrimination experienced by Jews. After the second trial, Ezra Levant, a noted right-wing commentator, argued that Ahenakew should never have been charged in the first place. Emphasizing the importance of the principle of freedom of speech, Levant argued that the insignificant ramblings of "a kooky old man" only served to "turn a bigoted nobody into a bigoted somebody" (Levant, 2008).

Racism, Surveys, and Public Opinion

One way that social scientists have attempted to measure the significance of racism in Canadian society is by collecting data through surveys. In this section, we briefly discuss two kinds of surveys: surveys that tap into an individual's sense of being a victim of racism; and social distance surveys that serve as proxy or indirect measures of racial prejudices.

Victimization surveys show that visible minority Canadians perceive that they have been discriminated against or have experienced unfair treatment because of their skin colour. For example, Parveen Nangia (2013) uses data from the 2009 General Social Survey to show that immigrants are much more likely to face discrimination in Canada than non-immigrants. The survey asked respondents a variety of questions about their experiences of discrimination and Nangia (2013) shows that 20 per cent of landed immigrants faced some form of discrimination in the five-year period leading up to the survey; 14 per cent of non-immigrants reported experiencing discrimination in the same period. Table 7.1 provides data on the different forms of discrimination faced by the two groups. The survey found that 12.6 per cent of immigrants said they faced discrimination because of their ethnicity or culture and that 10.6 per cent said they faced discrimination because of their "race" or colour. Moreover, 56.3 per cent of immigrants who reported experiencing discrimination faced it at work or when applying for a job or for a promotion. Nangia found that age and visible minority status were the two variables that had a significant effect on experiences of discrimination, with young and middle-aged

Table 7.1 Percentage of Population (15+ years) Who Experienced Discrimination in Canada, by Basis of Discrimination, 2009 (Table shows weighted percentage)

Basis of discrimination	Landed immigrants	Non-immigrants
Sex	4.3	4.8
Age	3.3	3.4
Race or colour	10.6	3.8
Ethnicity or culture	12.6	3.7
Language	7.2	2.0
Religion	3.9	2.1
Disability	0.7	1.3
Physical appearance	3.9	4.0
Sexual orientation	0.9	0.9
Other	0.8	0.6

Source: Statistics Canada. GSS, 2009

immigrants and visible minority immigrants more likely to face discrimination than others.

Other victimization survey research shows that Aboriginal people also report significant levels of discrimination. A health-related study conducted in Hamilton, Ontario, found that in their survey of 790 Aboriginal people in the city in 2009 and 2010, 40 per cent reported that they had been the victim of an ethnically or racially motivated verbal or physical attack at some point in their life. Fourteen per cent of respondents indicated that they had been the victim of a verbal attack in the previous 12 months, while 5 per cent reported being the victim of a physical attack in the previous 12 months (Smylie, et. al., 2011).

Victimization surveys provide valuable information, but they are not particularly good measures of the existence of racism in Canadian society. For one thing, individuals may experience discrimination but may not define it as such. For example, it is difficult for individuals to know the real reasons that they were not hired for a particular job or denied housing. The stated, non-racist reasons may be plausible, and an individual may accept those reasons as valid, but there may been deeper, racially based reasons for not hiring or providing housing to the person that never come to light. Institutional authorities sometimes dismiss the results of victimization surveys on the grounds that visible minorities are not objective, have "chips on their shoulders," and are too eager to identify racism as a problem in Canadian society (Henry and Tator, 2010: 80).

Another way that social scientists and others have tried to measure the existence of racism is through the use of social distance surveys. As noted above, being a racist is not a socially desirable character trait. As a result, individuals who hold negative attitudes about minority groups may be reluctant to admit to those feelings in surveys. Social distance surveys vary in terms of the kinds of questions they ask. Some ask how "happy" or how "concerned" respondents would be if a member of a specific minority group married their son or daughter, joined their social club, moved into their neighbourhood, and the like. Other surveys ask how "comfortable" individuals are "being around" different minority groups. For example, a 2000 survey asked individuals to indicate how they felt about someone from another country moving into their neighbourhood. The survey found that the individuals surveyed were more positive toward people from Britain and France than they were toward people from China, Jamaica, or Somalia (cited in Li, 2003: 175). A more recent 2014 poll conducted in collaboration with the CBC asked Canadians how "comfortable or uncomfortable" they were with a number of scenarios. As Table 7.2 shows, nearly 80 per cent of respondents indicated that they were "comfortable" or "very comfortable" with someone from a "different ethnic background" moving next door, working for someone of a "different ethnic background," and employing someone of a "different ethnic background." The comfort level decreased to 66 per cent when the question was related to being in a romantic relationship with someone of a different ethnic background. Respondents indicated slightly lower levels of comfort when the question was changed from "different ethnic background" to "Aboriginal" people (CBC, 2014). Depending on the question, between 5 and 13 per cent of respondents explicitly said they were either "uncomfortable" or "very uncomfortable" about the various scenarios relating to those with a different ethnic background.

Table 7.2 To What Extent Are You Comfortable or Uncomfortable with the Following Statements Regarding Immigration and Multiculturalism?

	Comfortable %	Uncomfortable %	Neither comfortable nor uncomfortable %	Don't know or no answer %
Someone with a different background moved next door to me	79	6	12	3
Working for someone of a different ethnic background	79	6	11	4
Employing someone of a different ethnic background	78	5	11	6
Someone of a different ethnic background married my best friend	78	6	12	4
Voting for someone of a different ethnic background	75	8	13	4
Someone of a different ethnic background married my child/brother/sister	71	9	14	6
Being in a romantic relationship with someone of a different ethnic background	66	13	15	6

Source: Adapted from *CBC News Poll on Discrimination*, November 2014, http://www.cbc.ca/news/canada/canadian-attitudes-toward-immigrants-conflicted-poll-says-1.2826022.

A 2015 EKOS poll suggests that Canadian attitudes may be becoming more unfavourable toward immigration in general, and toward visible minority immigration in particular. Their polling data shows that in response to the question, "In your opinion do you feel that there are too few, too many, or about the right number of immigrants coming to Canada?" 46 per cent of respondents indicated "too many." This was up from 25 per cent in 2005. Similarly, 41 per cent of respondents indicated that "too many" visible minority immigrants are being admitted to Canada, which was up from about 19 per cent in 2005. These attitudes varied significantly by various demographic factors. Generally, those with university-level education were less likely than those with high school education to indicate that there were "too many" immigrants, and "too many" visible minority immigrants in Canada. Interestingly enough, even though the number was lower than for those born in Canada, 36 per cent of respondents not born in Canada said there were "too many" immigrants coming to Canada (Graves, 2015).

Peter Li (2003: 172–6), in a stinging critique of survey research on anti-immigrant attitudes and racism, argues that this kind of research unwittingly lends legitimacy to racist ways of thinking. By asking Canadians to rank groups in terms of "comfort level" and "social distance" or by asking people to express preferences for white as opposed to "visible minority" immigrants, this research invites individuals to think about and problematize "race." Referring to the issue of survey research on attitudes toward immigrants, Li argues that

> the immigration discourse in Canada has a strong racial dimension, in part because of the changing racial composition of immigrants to Canada, but also in part because academic research has contributed to racializing immigrants and minority groups by encouraging the public to articulate their racial preferences and then legitimizing such preferences as harmless and democratic choices. (2003: 176)

Racism and New Media

The Internet has been described as the second-most important communication revolution in history (Meerman-Scott, 2012). The first revolution was sparked by Johannes Gutenberg's invention of movable type in printing in about 1440, which allowed for the mass production of relatively inexpensive books. His invention helped to make information available to ever-wider circles of the population. As with any revolutionary technology, human beings have been able to put this new technology to both socially beneficial and socially harmful uses. Obviously, books have been written to promote peace, harmony, and goodwill; they have also been written to promote intolerance and violence.

The invention and spread of the Internet and various new communications technologies are no different. The Internet has opened up the world to new information, and to new and better ways for human beings to communicate with each other. At the same time, there is a less prosaic side to this communication revolution. Some argue that the ease of electronic communication makes face-to-face communication less common, which has negative consequences for building relationships, mutual understanding, and the sense of community. The Internet also makes the communication of unsavoury and harmful ideas easier, and is arguably a new, more sinister vehicle for the promotion of hatred.

When the Internet first captured mass public attention and use in the mid-1990s, one of the concerns surrounding its use was the associated growth of hate-based groups on the Web. White supremacist and white nationalist organizations like the Ku Klux Klan and Stormfront initially embraced the Internet because it allowed them to spread their ideas to even wider audiences. For some of these organized hate groups, their embrace of Internet technology arguably has two main objectives: One is to give racists the impression that they are not alone and that there are many other like-minded people who believe in the same thing. The other is to "intimidate the targeted minority, leading them to question whether their dignity and social status is secure" (McElwee, 2013).

The relative anonymity of the Internet, however, has also created a space for racism and intolerance to flourish even among those who are not specifically affiliated with organized hate groups. Part of the reason why racism seems so vicious on the Internet is the relative anonymity of medium. Before the Internet, someone articulating racism either did it verbally, in writing on a printed page, or through physical violence. Though it was often possible to anonymously distribute printed racist material in the past in the form of graffiti, broadsheets, posters, newsletters, and the like, the Internet has created a space for racist ideas and images to spread more anonymously and relatively unencumbered by the physical limits of the printed word. The spread of hatred, and the use of racist language and images on the Internet and in new communications technologies has, in a way, made racism more banal and, in a way, lends it a degree of social acceptability. It is hard to not notice how some people use new communications technology to articulate racist ideas.

In 2015, six years into his presidency, US president Barack Obama sent his first tweet to the American public, and to the wider world. Obama's opening tweet was an upbeat, ironic post introducing himself to the American public: "Hello, Twitter! It's Barack. Really! Six years in, and they're finally giving me my own account." Within minutes, his account @POTUS (President of the United States) started to attract hate. Some replied hoping that he would kill himself or "get cancer." Others posted images of him with a noose around his neck with his earlier "HOPE" campaign poster doctored with the word "ROPE." Others addressed him as a monkey, and by a range of other racist slurs. According to the *New York Times*, "his advisors regard such hate speech as a relatively minor price to pay for the opportunity Twitter and other platforms provide to reach voters directly" (Hirschfeld Davis, 2015).

President Obama is, of course, not the only target of hate on the Internet, or on Twitter. Irfan Chaudhry (2015) analyzed racist tweets in six Canadian cities. He found that over a three-month period, there were 776 explicitly racist tweets in Toronto, Vancouver, Winnipeg, Calgary, Edmonton, and Montreal. In Toronto, Vancouver, and Montreal the term *nigger(s)* was the most frequently used racist term, while in Calgary, Edmonton, and Winnipeg, negative references to "native(s)" was most common. Examples of the content of those tweets include: "Your not much diff from natives when it comes to drinking . . . Except your clean," "Man these pakis need to leave the gym its starting to smell like stale Burger King in here," and "When my friends make me sit next to the nigger in the theater . . . #thanks-bitches" (Chaudhry, 2015). Though probably coming as no surprise, another Canadian study focused on Canadian students between grades 4 and 11 (Steeves, 2014). Among its many interesting findings, the report found that 48 per cent of students in grade 9, 50 per cent of students in grade 10, and 56 per cent of students in grade 11 see racist or sexist content online at least once a day or once a week. Seven in 10 students surveyed also indicated that "people say racist or sexist things online to pick on other people," while nearly 8 in 10 students said that "it is important to say something so people know that it is wrong." (Steeves, 2014).

The issue of racism on the Internet touches on a number of difficult questions about freedom of speech, what constitutes hate speech, and how to combat racism. In Brazil, a new anti-racism campaign undertaken by a local civil rights group is "taking racist comments posted on Twitter or Facebook, identifying the location of the commentator, and then buying billboard space near that person's home in order to display the comment in huge letters" (Boult, 2015). At the 5th Global Forum for Combating Anti-Semitism held in May 2015 in Jerusalem, an action plan calling for Internet censorship was developed as a way of combating anti-Semitism (Sokol, 2015). The conference ended by recommending the removal of Internet sites that deny the Holocaust, cancelling search results that advocate hatred, establishing a national body in every country to enforce legislation and require Internet providers to enforce their rules against hosting hate content, and adopting a unified global position of the Internet industry against hate speech and anti-Semitism (Israeli Ministry of Foreign Affairs, 2015). Though by no means uncontroversial, advocates of some form of censorship of hate speech on the Internet point out that Internet platforms have had both the will and the technology to take action against the spread of child pornography over the Internet, and they argue that similar techniques can be used to weed out and limit the spread of hatred. Anti-Semitic hate groups have taken notice of the conference recommendations and they use the recommendations to further the old racist allegation that Jews are in control of the world's media, and they now want to control the Internet.

Institutional Racism

Racism, as should be clear from the previous discussion, is not only about ideas and individual-level expressions of behaviour. Racism is also reflected in the ways that social institutions operate by denying groups of people fair and equitable treatment. Institutional racism can take three forms.

First, racist ideas and assumptions about the social capacities and incapacities of groups of people can explicitly inform the development of social policies, programs, or institutional practices. At present, there are few, if any, examples of this form of institutional racism in Canada. As noted in Chapter 4, many aspects of the pre-1967 Canadian immigration system were informed by racist assumptions about the relative capacities and capabilities of groups of people. The other two forms of institutional racism are far more relevant to contemporary Canadian society, although they are not entirely uncontested.

The second form of institutional racism occurs when ideas about the racial inferiority of groups of people inform the initial development of specific policies or programs but no longer sustain those policies and programs. In other words, certain policies and programs are racist in origin, and even though racism may no longer sustain them, the policies and practices continue to exist. The Indian Act is probably the best example of this form of institutional racism in Canada. The Act and its various nineteenth-century precursors explicitly assumed that Aboriginal people were inferior to Europeans and that Aboriginal needed the guiding hand of racially superior Europeans in order to have a future in Canada.

Another relevant example of this form of institutional racism is the Caribbean and Mexican Seasonal Agricultural Workers Program. In Chapter 4, we explained that the program originated because there was a shortage of labour to fill seasonal farm jobs in Ontario in the mid-1960s. Some government officials believed that black workers were racially suited for backbreaking labour under the hot sun and so justified the program in part on the basis of racist beliefs about the innate capacities of black people. Further, government officials thought that while black workers were useful as sources of temporary labour, they were not good as potential Canadian citizens because their presence in Canada would cause the emergence of a "race relations" problem (Satzewich, 1991; Basok, 2002). Although these racist ideas no longer explicitly sustain or justify the program, it is arguably a continuing example of institutional racism in Canada because it had its origins in racism.

The third form of institutional racism appears in certain policies or programs that may seem ethnically or racially neutral, but either intentionally or unintentionally put minority group members at a disadvantage. This form of institutional racism has generated the most heated debates in Canada because its existence is difficult to prove conclusively and there is ambiguity surrounding the true motives behind the policies and programs in question. In the remainder of this chapter, we consider four institutional spheres that have been the subject of controversies about institutional racism: **zero tolerance** policies in secondary schools, a diverse range of policies and practices in universities and in amateur and professional sports, and **racial profiling** by police.

Zero Tolerance Policies in Schools

A number of Canadian provinces have versions of so-called zero tolerance policies toward students who misbehave in schools. In Ontario the Safe Schools Act, introduced in 2001, incorporates provisions for zero tolerance (Henry and Tator, 2010: 211). When the policy was put into effect, it provided for the automatic suspension or expulsion of students who committed violent or aggressive acts, such as assault, drug trafficking, or selling or carrying weapons. Students who threatened to harm other students, engaged in vandalism, swore, or were in possession of or under the influence of drugs or alcohol also faced automatic suspension (Leslie, 2005).

Though initially designed to deal with apparently growing levels of violence and aggression in schools, zero tolerance provisions are often characterized as a reflection of institutional racism because either by design or by circumstance, they have resulted in the disproportionate targeting of black and other racialized youth. Critics argue that while the act appears to be ethnically and racially neutral, its weight disproportionately falls on black youth. According to one black youth, "something can't be right about a policy that winds up aimed at a single racial group" (Valpy, 2005: A1, A15).

Although it does not specifically examine zero tolerance policies, a recent Canadian study showed that perceptions of differential and discriminatory treatment by schools vary in part on the basis of the background of students. Ruck and Wortley (2002) argue that there is a skin-colour hierarchy when it comes to student perceptions of differential treatment within schools in Toronto. In their research, they studied perceptions of white, black, Asian, South Asian, and "other" (Aboriginal and Latin American) high school students about a range of issues surrounding teacher and police treatment at school, school suspensions, and the general school environment. According to Ruck and Wortley, student perceptions of differential treatment in schools vary, with

> black students generally being the most likely to perceive bias followed by South Asian students, students from "other" racial/ethnic backgrounds, Asian students, and finally White students. This is consistent with the view that the darker the skin colour the greater the social penalties that exist. (2002, 194)

Critics of zero tolerance policies argue that these perceptions are in fact a reflection of reality. Schools are obliged to follow certain procedures regardless of the reason for or context of misbehaviour. Because teachers and principals have little discretionary power, the policy comes down hardest on students who are the most disadvantaged and have the greatest need to stay in school. Some characterize zero tolerance policies as culturally insensitive because they are based on white models of appropriate behaviour that are at odds with black models of appropriate behaviour. As Jull argues,

> School discipline policies based on the principles of zero tolerance reinforce Anglo-Eurocentric sensibilities of right and wrong and the authoritative structures within public education. . . . To claim that social justice can be achieved

through the implementation of a so-called unbiased zero tolerance school discipline policy is to believe that discriminatory practice can be eradicated by
implementing policies that are blind to personal or individual and/or cultural
contexts.... Equal treatment in an unequal social and academic environment is
discriminatory. (2000: 4)

Finally, some critics also argue that zero tolerance policies help create a "school-
prison pipeline" for black youth (Solomon and Palmer, 2004). Former Ontario NDP
leader Howard Hampton argued that the Safe Schools Act should really be called a
"gang recruitment act" because the provisions end up putting youth who most need
to stay in school on the street. By kicking black youths out of school, school boards
are throwing them into the welcoming arms of gangs, who are more than happy to
recruit youth disaffected with school and "the system." As explained by the Ontario
Human Rights Commission in its report, *Disproportionate Impact of "Zero Tolerance" Discipline*, "Once kids are out of the mainline and expelled, then they are
on a different path. If you put anti-social kids together it escalates their anti-social
behaviour" (Ontario Human Rights Commission, 2005a).

In 2008, the Ontario government amended the provincial Education Act to
give principals more leeway about what to do in cases of certain violations of school
codes of conduct like possessing alcohol or illegal drugs in school, bullying, or
swearing at a teacher. Suspension may follow in such cases, but it does not have to.
Suspensions remain mandatory for things like possessing a weapon, sexual assault,
or committing a physical assault that causes bodily harm and requires attention of
a medical practitioner (Ontario Ministry of Education, 2016).

The controversy over zero tolerance policies raises complicated issues about
the appropriate balance between the exercise of discretion and the use of a strict,
rules-based approach to dealing with social problems or other kinds of issues. As
we saw in Chapter 4 on immigration, some critics claim that the exercise of discretionary power on the part of immigration officers is racially biased and puts
racialized minority individuals at a disadvantage in the immigration process. At
the other end of the spectrum, zero tolerance policies in schools, which are aimed
at curtailing the exercise of discretionary power by principals, vice-principals, and
the police, are criticized for being racially biased because they do not take into
consideration the social and personal contexts within which youth infractions of
rules take place in schools. In other words, critics suggest that the lack of discretion
is racist, and they call for a more sensitive and contextual approach to the problem
of dealing with youth misbehaviour in school. In short, one system is alleged to be
institutionally racist because it allows too much discretion, and another system is
alleged to be institutionally racist because it does not allow for discretion. Perhaps
the lesson to be learned is that there is no "one size fits all" approach to dealing
with allegations of institutional racism within Canadian society. This policy and
program dilemma is obviously not easily resolved.

Racism within University Settings

You might reasonably think that universities would be one of the last places on earth where you would find institutional racism. After all, universities are generally made up of pretty smart people. It takes at least 9 or 10 years of post-secondary education to get a full-time teaching job in a university, and writing a PhD dissertation is not that easy. Students have to study reasonably hard in high school to get the marks to get into university, and they have to work hard to keep those marks up once they are in. University chairs, deans, and presidents make their way through the ranks, and are chosen by committees of their peers because of their special combination of academic skills and leadership qualities. Universities pride themselves on being places of enlightenment, fairness, level-headedness, and free critical inquiry. Indeed, one of the central things that social science and humanities programs in universities claim to teach students is the ability to think critically. We like to think that we encourage students to question everything, and to not accept anything at face value. If racism is rooted in a lack of education or knowledge, one of the places you would not expect to find it is in the university.

But universities are not, according to some researchers, racist-free nirvanas. In fact, some claim they are the exact opposite (Henry and Tator, 2010). Social geographer Audrey Kobayashi (2009: 61) argues that "systemic racism is a normative aspect of Canadian ways of doing things, and deeply entrenched within university culture." Blatantly racist name-calling (of both students and of faculty) happens in universities, occasional incidents of racist graffiti appear in university dorms, and racialized students and faculty both report cases of outright discrimination. However, there are two broad aspects to the way that universities operate that some allege makes them racist as institutions. Systemic racism within university settings has standards and content-related dimensions.

Regarding standards, researchers suggest that the overall standards of university education are determined primarily by white academics and that these standards intentionally and unintentionally put racialized faculty members at a disadvantage. There are a number of ways university standards are said to do this (Kobayashi, 2009; Henry and Tator, 2010; Monture, 2009). Standards for tenure and promotion are said to put racialized faculty at a disadvantage because the nature of the work they do is different from that of the dominant white majority academics. Racialized faculty often have commitments to activism, and to their respective communities, that shape where they publish their research. Universities generally place higher value on peer-reviewed publications in academic journals. As a result, faculty who publish in places that are not peer reviewed or defined as sufficiently scholarly, such as magazines, newspapers, newsletters, community reports, and books meant for the general public, face greater difficulty gaining tenure and promotion. Haudenosaunee scholar Patricia Monture describes her orientation to research and publications and how this affects the experience of the tenure process at her institution in the following terms:

Most of the choices I have made in my professional life are grounded in a single value: what is "good" for "Indian" people. This means I saw (and continue to see) myself located in my community more than I saw myself located in the university. This is a consequence of university experiences that left me othered, as well as a personal choice to stand in my community. One example is my scholarship. I had never really considered that peer reviewed journal articles are an essential element of the phrase "publish or perish." I had not understood, until more recent decisions, that there is "the" journal in each discipline, and tenure is most easily secured if publication in these journals has been gained. But publication in these journals denies access to my work to many Aboriginal people as they have no access or knowledge of university libraries. Not only did I not consider this, but also no one shared this wisdom with me and certainly not in a timely fashion (such as shortly after hiring) that could have made a difference in tenure decisions. Without this information, I had chosen to publish in venues that are accessible to Aboriginal people, the people I write for (2009: 81).

Another dimension of the standards issue is that racialized faculty have excessive demands placed on their time to be role models to their students. They—formally and informally—become advisors and counsellors to racialized students, which detracts from the time they need to spend on their research and publications. Though "service" to the university, and sometimes to the community, are supposed to be taken into consideration in tenure and promotion decisions, providing good service rarely compensates for what is defined as inadequate quantity and quality of publications. Since white faculty members are ubiquitous in universities, white students do not place the same "extra" demands on their instructors that visible minority students do.

Another standards-related issue is that racialized faculty are underrepresented among faculty members and university administrators. Reza Nakhaie's (2004) research on university administrators shows, for example, even though visible minorities made up nearly 20 per cent of the population of Canada in 2001, there were no visible minority university presidents; only 3.6 per cent of university vice-presidents and 6.6 per cent of faculty deans were visible minorities. British-origin academics, however, were significantly overrepresented in the ranks of university administrators. Though there are now several visible minority university presidents in Canada, this overall pattern of underrepresentation "justifies various charges of racism directed at Canadian universities" (Nakhaie, 2004: 100). Related to this is the accusation that universities have a weak commitment to employment equity. Few universities have in place effective procedures to enforce equity-based hiring and to address the lack of representation of racialized faculty. Universities are also accused of having a weak commitment to on-campus human rights issues, and to addressing issues of racism and discrimination within their workplaces. According to Dua (2009: 183), university administrators are either unwilling to address issues of racism when they arise, or are defensive in their responses to allegations of racism within their institutions. In her research, university-based human rights and anti-discrimination officers report high levels of frustration at the lack of commitment on the part of university administrators to deal with racism.

Finally, regarding content, researchers argue that university education is determined primarily by white academics. University curricula are said to be full of Eurocentric assumptions about the world (Hernandez-Ramdwar, 2009: 114). White men have historically shaped course descriptions and content; the perspectives of racialized communities, and their types of valued knowledge, are generally lacking within courses. Patricia Monture argues, for example, that even within many courses that deal with First Nations issues, they operate according to traditional European conceptions of time and geography.

> The structure of many Native studies departments' curriculum reflects non-Indigenous ideologies and ideas about people. . . . Why is confederation considered an important historical marker in Indigenous history classes? What is the distinction between Canada and the United States and why is it relevant? After all, some of our nations, such as Mohawk, Blackfoot, and Mi'kmaq, straddle that border. (2009: 82)

This carries over into the relative silence within university curricula on issues of racism, diversity, and Aboriginal peoples. Some claim that even when these courses are offered, they are marginal to overall programs and pedagogy.

Racism and Sports

Like the university and educational systems, sports is another area of social life where it seems that racism should be absent. Sports are about talent, competition, and winning. Teams win by putting the best players on the field or the rink, and by working together. Talent and ability are critical to the success of sports teams. In theory, racism seems to run counter to the principles of competition and merit that sports are grounded in. If a good athlete is denied a place or a position on a sports team because of the colour of their skin, then this means that the team's chances of winning are reduced.

Both professional and amateur sports were not untouched by the wider racism in Canadian history that we discussed in earlier in chapters. There was a distinct colour line in teams in Canada, whether in baseball, hockey, or football. The first black player in the National Hockey League (NHL) was New Brunswick native Willie O'Ree, who played two games for the Boston Bruins in 1958 and then for most of the 1961 season. It was not until 1974 that a second black player, Mike Marson, made it to the NHL. Herb Carnegie almost made it to the NHL in 1938, but Conn Smythe, the owner of the Toronto Maple Leafs at the time, is reputed to have said, "I will give $10,000 to anyone who can turn Herbert Carnegie white" (Harris, 2003).

Though the colour bar in sports has been lifted, there is evidence of both individual-level and systemic racism in sports. It does not seem to matter whether it is on the soccer pitch, the hockey rink, the baseball diamond, or football field; cases where either fellow players, fans, or sports reporters racially abuse minority players are common enough to not simply dismiss them as aberrations. Former New York Knicks basketball phenomenon Jeremy Lin, whose parents migrated to the US from Taiwan in the 1970s, was the subject of a racial slur by a major sports network writer who titled one of his articles "Chink in the Armor" after Lin had a bad game. At a pre-season NHL game in London, Ontario, in September 2011, a fan threw a banana at Wayne Simmonds just as he was about to take a shot in an overtime shootout. Bananas are regularly thrown onto European soccer pitches, and monkey sounds are often made, when black players touch the ball. Many in the soccer world are nervously awaiting Russia's hosting of the World Cup in 2018, in part, because racism is so rampant in the game there, and by Russian soccer authorities' seemingly confused understanding of the problem. Flags bearing swastikas have been unfurled at soccer games in the country, as have banners endorsing white power (Borden, 2015). Black players are often jeered during games and regularly face racist taunts, even from supporters of the team they play for. Some team supporters lobby management to not hire black players, or to keep their numbers to a minimum. Emmanuel Frimpong, a Ghanaian-born player for Ufa in the Russian Premier league, was suspended for two games for raising his middle finger to a group of fans who were racially abusing him during a game. Team management told Frimpong that he should essentially "put up with it." Nothing happened to the racist fans. Ahead of the World Cup, Russian soccer authorities have recently created the position of "anti-racism inspector," but the mandate of the person hired to fill the position makes the appearance of doing something about racism in soccer in the country at the same time as downplaying its existence. According to a *New York Times* report, the newly appointed anti-racism inspector said, "We are of course concerned and find such incidents unacceptable . . . but one should not make a problem out of nothing" (Borden, 2015).

But racism in sports goes beyond individual-level taunting and abuse. In several sports and different leagues, racism is evident at the level of team and mascot names and player positions, as well as among the ranks of coaches and senior management. Professional and university sports teams in the US have been the focus of considerable controversy for their choices of team names and mascots (Morley Johnson, 2011). The Washington Redskins, the Atlanta Braves, and the Cleveland Indians have all been criticized for sticking with team names, and associated symbols, that reflect historical negative stereotypes about First Nations. Braves fans regularly use the "tomahawk chop" to celebrate when their team wins a game. The term *redskin* harkens back to America's racist past and evokes images of wild, savage Aboriginals preying on hard-working and well-meaning white settlers. The University of Illinois was embroiled in a two-decades-long controversy over its mascot, Chief Illiniwek, and his "war dance." After many complaints that the mascot and dance are racist, the National Collegiate Athletic Association (NCAA) eventually banned the mascot in 2005 because it was a "hostile and abusive American Indian nickname." Students and alumni of the university are undeterred by the criticism and the concern and are trying to bring the mascot, and the dance, back. They say that the mascot and the dance are in fact reflections of their deep respect for American-Indian culture. 2015 Grey Cup champions Edmonton Eskimos have been asked to change their name by Inuit leaders in Canada who argue that *Eskimo* is an offensive term that harkens back to Canada's colonial past. Some high schools in Canada have changed the racialized names of their sports teams to ones that are more neutral; Bedford Road Collegiate in Saskatoon, whose sports teams for the past 90 years were called The Redmen engaged in a heated debate about whether the name is racist and hurtful or whether the efforts to change the name reflects an attack on white Canadians (Johnson, 2011). After a debate that lasted for three years, the school changed its name in 2014 to the Redhawks in reference to the red-tailed hawk that is ubiquitous on the prairies.

The issue of the sports groups of people play, and excel at, and the positions within sports that certain athletes play, is also subject to debates about racism. Some have pointed out that in the National Football League (NFL), the most important leadership position is that of quarterback. Further, the position of quarterback is said to require the most intelligence on the field. In addition to being physically skilled, quarterbacks have to be able to read defenses, anticipate a variety of scenarios, choose among complex play options, change plans quickly, and communicate effectively with teammates. Even though black players make up about 60 per cent of team rosters, they are only about 15 per cent of starting quarterbacks. Commentators have argued that teams, either consciously or unconsciously, are reluctant to place an black in this critical leadership position and that this is one way that racism continues to infect professional sports. One study found that white coaches are more likely to start white quarterbacks, while black coaches are more likely to start black quarterbacks (Gains, 2011).

Carl James's work in Canada on high school student athletes adds another dimension to the argument about racial streaming in sports. He argues that

> beliefs about the types of athletic activities that best suit particular ethno-racial group members are part of the racist discourses and practices found in Canadian society in general and schools in particular. This sports discourse also tends to polarize and compare Whites and Blacks. Whites are represented as people whose skills in athletics come through learning, interest, motivation, talent (not "raw talent," a term that is often used with reference to Blacks), and exposure to particular sports: they "choose" to participate in sports, suggesting that they have alternative means of participation and paths to success in society. Blacks, on the other hand, are represented as people whose athletic skills, abilities, and interests are integral to who they are: they participate in sports because of their physicality/biology (2005: 63).

James argues that teachers, coaches, principles, and parents place subtle and not so subtle pressures on teenagers in high school to participate, and not participate, in certain kinds of sports. These pressures stem from stereotypes about the kinds of sports that different racialized groups are "naturally" good at. At times, the encouragement of black youth to participate in sports like basketball also reflect a sense that they are unable to achieve academically and that participation in sports is a substitute for academic shortfalls.

Finally, and related to the above, the ranks of coaching and management is another place where institutional racism is said to come into play. Within American football, as noted above, it is estimated that about two-thirds of the players are African American, but in 2015 there were only six head coaches of colour (five African Americans and one Latino) in the entire 32-team league (Lapchick and Robinson, 2015). The league instituted the "Rooney Rule" in 2003, which requires that teams interview minority candidates when a head coaching or senior operations job opens up. Though widely praised, the rule is not a quota, and simply interviewing a minority candidate does not necessarily mean they are offered an actual job. A recent European Union study of racism in sport argues that there is a "glass ceiling" within sports associations and individual clubs, and that this ceiling leads to "an underrepresentation of migrants and minorities at certain levels of sport. They also prevent sport from having a more positive impact on social cohesion and integration of European societies" (European Union, 2010: 45).

Racial Profiling and Policing

Arguably, the way that the justice system deals with minority groups captures the most headlines and generates the most concern in Canada when it comes to accusations of institutional racism. Police forces across the country have been accused of various acts of institutional racism, and allegations that the police engage in institutional racism are an almost weekly occurrence. Two of the most frequent accusations are that the police *under-police* minority communities when their members are the victims of crime and that they simultaneously *over-police* those communities when their members are suspected as the perpetrators of crime (Royal Commission on Aboriginal Peoples, 1996a/b: 37–9).

Regarding **under-policing**, it is alleged that the police do not take crimes as seriously or do not conduct thorough investigations when minorities are the victims of crime. The case of Robert Pickton (the Surrey, BC, pig farmer convicted of murdering several dozen women, many of whom were Aboriginal and working in the prostitution industry) raised concerns about under-policing. That is, the Vancouver Police Department was accused of institutional racism because it allegedly did not take the disappearance of these women from Vancouver streets as seriously as it would have had the missing women been white and middle class. Because they were members of marginalized racial and socio-economic groups, they were regarded as disposable people undeserving of full police protection. The Missing

Women Commission of Inquiry, which issued its five-volume report in November 2012, was directed to review the investigative procedures involved with the missing women cases (see www.missingwomeninquiry.ca/terms-of-reference/). Though families of the victims and police contested some of the evidence presented at the inquiry, the final report points to a number of faults with the way that the Vancouver Police Department handled and investigated reports that a woman had gone missing. Among the long list of "Critical Police Failures" were poor report taking, faulty risk analysis and risk assessment, lack of employment of an Aboriginal-specific investigative strategy, communication and collaboration problems across police jurisdictions, and lack of leadership on the part of police management on the issue. In seeking answers to *why* the investigations were faulty, former Attorney General of British Columbia and Inquiry Commissioner Wally Oppal concluded that "systemic bias against the women who sent missing . . . contributed to the critical police failures in the missing women investigations" (Oppal, 2012: 94). Careful to distinguish between individual and institutional bias, the Commissioner argued that "as a whole, the officers involved in the investigations were conscientious and fair minded people who would not consciously disfavour the interests of a class of people in the investigative process" (94). While pointing out that "the police did not consciously decide to under-investigate the missing women or deny protection to women in the DTES [Down Town East Side], . . . the effect of the policing strategies resulted in exactly those outcomes" (96). He found that systematic bias

- allowed faulty stereotyping of street-involved women in the DTES to negatively impact missing women investigations;
- resulted in the failure to take the lives of the women into account in the policing strategies, particularly in failing to recognize the duty to protect an endangered segment of our community; and
- contributed to a failure to prioritize and effectively investigate the missing women cases (Oppal, 2012: 96).

The other side of the policing coin—the **over-policing** of minority communities when members are suspected of perpetrating crime—has also raised allegations of racial profiling and institutional racism. Over-policing refers to situations in which police resources and energies are targeted against groups based on the stereotype that they are over-involved in criminal behaviour. There is an old adage in criminology circles that the police find crime where they look for crime. As a result, a group's overrepresentation in the justice system may be as much a reflection of over-policing as it is of real group differences in criminal behaviour.

In western Canada, Aboriginal people have been the main targets of over-policing. A number of inquiries and research reports have detailed over-policing issues related to Aboriginal people (see Royal Commission on Aboriginal Peoples, 1996a/b for a summary of these reports). Quigley describes the way that over-policing works and its consequences for Aboriginal people in the following terms:

Police use race as an indicator for patrols, arrests, detentions.... For instance, police in cities tend to patrol bars and streets where Aboriginal people congregate, rather than the private clubs frequented by white business people.... This does not necessarily indicate that the police are invariably racist (although some are) since there is some empirical basis for the police view that proportionately more Aboriginal people are involved in criminality. But to operate patrols or to allocate police on ... [this] basis ... can become a self-fulfilling prophecy: patrols in areas frequented by the groups that they believe are involved in crimes will undoubtedly discover some criminality; when more police are assigned to detachments where there is a high Aboriginal population, their added presence will most assuredly detect more criminality. (Quigley, 1994, cited in Royal Commission on Aboriginal Peoples, 1996a/b: 25–36)

In eastern Canada, the issue of over-policing has been framed by specific concerns about police engaging in racial profiling of the black community. Racial profiling in policing can be defined as

investigative or enforcement activity initiated by an individual officer based on his or her stereotypical, prejudicial or racist perceptions of who is likely to be involved in wrong doing or criminal activity. This conduct is systemically facilitated when there is ineffective policy, training, monitoring, and control mechanisms in the system. (Association of Black Law Enforcers, 2003: 2)

One of the main sources of evidence about racial profiling comes from personal accounts of minority group members who feel that they have been unfairly stereotyped and targeted by police. A number of task force reports, newspaper articles, and scholarly research studies contain the accounts of individuals who feel that they have been racially profiled by police or by other institutions in Canadian society. According to the Ontario Human Rights Commission, these reports have conclusively shown that racial profiling occurs in a wide variety of social institutions in Canada. In 2005, the commission published its own study of racial profiling in order to move the debate a step forward. In the study, the commission invited individuals to submit their experiences of racial profiling to highlight its negative social, economic, and community consequences. One person explained,

Even if I am standing in a MTHA [Metro Toronto Housing Authority] area with another university student and cops pass I always stop and look to make sure that I am not being challenged by the cops. It's a feeling of fear, and of being less than them as they are in an authoritative position. We shouldn't be afraid of people who are supposed to be protecting our rights. (Ontario Human Rights Commission, 2005b: 6).

The commission documented some of the negative social and individual consequences associated with the experience of being racially profiled. Among other things, the commission found that individuals felt alienated from police and other social institutions and had a diminished sense of citizenship and of being part of a community as a result of having been racially profiled. The commission also found that members of racialized communities described themselves as "living within a perpetual state of crisis due to the effects of racism." It suggested that the

> African Canadian community in particular stressed that racial profiling is having an overwhelming impact in their community. The sense of injustice that develops among individuals in these communities creates a state of psychological imbalance and inner conflict and reinforces their concern that racism exists and that they may be subjected to it at any time. (Ontario Human Rights Commission, 2005b: 12)

Part of the further unseen toll of racial profiling includes individuals changing their behaviour to avoid situations that might lead them to be stopped and profiled by police; individuals feeling ashamed of themselves and their backgrounds; individuals lacking trust in relationships; and individuals feeling helplessness, hopelessness, fear, and anxiety.

The report also argued that there are larger social costs associated with racial profiling. Individuals who felt that security personnel racially profiled them in stores and malls reported that one of their responses was to boycott the establishments. The morale of employees who work in organizations believed to engage in racial profiling is also damaged.

One of the limitations of reports based on personal experiences of racial profiling is that they rely on anecdotal evidence that does not present a full, accurate, and objective picture of the problem. As a result, efforts have been made to collect more systematic information, and a second kind of evidence about racial profiling has come from data collected by police. Some of the police data had been purposefully collected to shed light on the problem of racial profiling, but other data had been compiled from information that police routinely collect on stops and searches.

In 2002, the *Toronto Star* published a series of articles alleging that statistics collected by the Toronto Police Service confirmed what many black residents of Toronto had believed for many years: namely, that the Toronto police force practised racial profiling. The newspaper used the Ontario Freedom of Information and Protection of Privacy Act to gain access to Toronto police arrest data for the period 1996 to 2002. It analyzed data on 480,000 cases in which individuals were arrested or ticketed for an offence and 800,000 cases in which criminal charges were laid. The analysis showed that black people were overrepresented in certain charge categories, treated more harshly than whites after they were arrested, and much more likely to be held in custody for bail hearings than their white counterparts (Rankin et al., 2002). The findings of this study were widely contested in the press as well as by academics (Wortley and Tanner, 2003).

It was partly in response to allegations of racial profiling in his police service that William Closs, chief of police in Kingston, Ontario, committed the organization to transparency and agreed to undertake a study to examine whether racial profiling was being practised in Kingston. The chief felt that the debate about racial profiling needed to move beyond accusations and denials (Farmer, 2005). Concrete, purposefully collected data was needed in order to shed light on whether racial profiling was being practised by his force. Data collection for the project began in October 2003. Kingston police officers were required to complete "contact cards" every time they stopped and questioned a civilian in any manner. Between 1 October 2003 and 30 September 2004, officers recorded the age, gender, and "race" of the person stopped as well as the location of the stop, the reason for the stop, and the final disposition of the case (Wortley, 2005).

University of Toronto criminologist Scot Wortley analyzed the information on police stops, and a preliminary report was issued in the summer of 2005. Described as one of the first of its kind in Canada, the study found that even though black residents of Kingston represented only 0.6 per cent of the total population of the city, they experienced 2.1 per cent of all police stops during the study period. Aboriginal people were also over-policed in that they made up 1.6 per cent of the population of the city but experienced 2.4 per cent of all police stops during the study period (Wortley, 2005). When the results were announced, Chief Closs tearfully apologized to members of Kingston's black and Aboriginal communities. Since then, a number of other police jurisdictions have been accused of engaging in racial profiling. In Ontario in 2015, the Black Action Defence Committee launched a $200-million class action lawsuit against the Durham Regional Police Services Board "alleging that officers engaged in racial profiling" (Winsa, 2015). This followed on the committee's launch in 2013 of a similar lawsuit against the Peel Police Services Board. Both the British Columbia Civil Liberties Association (2010) and the Quebec Commission des droits de la personne et des droits de la jeunesse (2011) point to problems of racial profiling in their provinces.

The wider police community is, however, divided on its position on racial profiling. Many police officers and policing organizations make a distinction between racial profiling and criminal profiling. As Satzewich and Shaffir (2009) show, police admit that profiling is a critically important, and legitimate, aspect of the work that they do. But they argue that they engage in criminal profiling, not racial profiling. As one officer explained,

> As police officers, we are trained in certain ways, and then you build instincts. Because when we're out on the street, we rely on our instincts. We are trained investigators in the sense that we need to do profiling. And what kind of profiling is that? Criminal profiling. It has nothing to do with racial profiling. . . . We profile criminals. We do geographic profiling. It assists us to identify our problems and localize them and address them. When we go out . . . we do not target any specific culture or race. However, if we do come into a problematic area, and we start to ply our trade—policing—then if they happen to fall within those parameters, there's not much we can do (Satzewich and Shaffir, 2009: 210).

Another officer in the same study offered the following scenario of how "race" is but one of a variety of other contextual factors and variables that can factor into how they go about making their policing-related decisions.

> Some people seem to think that race is a dominating factor in the way the police do their job; that is, there's a black guy walking down the street. I'm going to stop him, maybe he's a drug dealer or something. [Right.] Whereas race is really one of several factors that the police will look at. Like, for instance, you might see a black guy walking down the street. He might be wearing a certain style of clothes, baggy clothes, hip-hop type clothes. [Right.] He might have a red bandana which is often worn by gang members. He might meet up with another guy. You might see them kind of make a hand slide to each other.... . You might see the one guy reach out, they quickly exchange something hand-to-hand. You look at all those factors. The conclusion the police officer is going to come to is a drug deal just went down. Looking at all those factors employed, the hand-to-hand, the hand slides, but when you approach that person, well [he will claim], they're just busting my ass cause I'm black (Satzewich and Shaffir, 2009: 211).

The Association of Black Law Enforcers (ABLE), in their *Official Position on Racial Profiling in Canada* (2003), also recognizes that a distinction needs to be made between legitimate "criminal profiling" and illegitimate "racial profiling." They argue that criminal profiling is a legitimate law enforcement tool and that there is a distinction between inductive and deductive criminal profiling. **Inductive criminal profiling** refers to generalizations about an individual criminal based on initial behavioural and demographic characteristics shared by other criminals who have been studied in the past. **Deductive criminal profiling** refers to the processes of interpreting evidence such as crime-scene photographs, autopsy reports, and other information to deduce specific offender characteristics. ABLE argues that legitimate criminal profiling may rely on "race" as a descriptor within a profile. However, legitimate criminal profiling turns into illegitimate racial profiling when "race" is construed as a factor leading to criminal behaviour. They explain the distinction in the following terms:

> ABLE is troubled by the connection being made between acts of violence being perpetrated by the criminal element within the Black community and racial profiling. We reject the notion of "Black on Black" crime in that the term is pejorative and appears only to be reserved for use when young Black men take the lives of other young Black men. Race-based terms are not used to describe violent crime that occurred in other racial or ethnic communities. For example when members of the Hells Angels and Rock Machine were killing each other in Quebec the situation was not referred to as "White on White" crime, it was called a "Biker War." (Association of Black Law Enforcers, 2003: 3)

The Kingston police chief's apology for racial profiling has not met with a great deal of enthusiasm from other police organizations or police boards. Indeed, other jurisdictions have been reluctant to embrace the allegation that racial profiling is routinely practised and widespread among the police in Canada. Like the Association of Black Law Enforcers, police forces make a distinction between legitimate criminal profiling and racial profiling. They argue that while criminal profiling is a necessary part of police work, racial profiling "does not exist" (Henry and Tator, 2010: 164).

The related issue of carding, or policing stopping, questioning, and documenting individuals who are not suspected of a crime, has generated a debate similar to that of the racial profiling debate. Inspired in part by police shootings of young black men in the United States and in Canada, groups like Black Lives Matter have focused their attention on how police interact with young black men. In Canada, they have been at the forefront of pressuring police organizations and the Ontario provincial government to put an end to carding, which they argue is a reflection of the systemic racism in the justice system in this country (Smith, 2015). In response to this pressure, the provincial government introduced regulations that severely curtail the powers of police to stop individuals and subject them to questions about who they are and their activities. Among the changes introduced, police must tell individuals why they are being stopped, that they do not have to provide information, and that they have the right to walk away. In addition, police must provide individuals with a written record of the interaction, including information about the officer and the police complaints system (Gillis, Rankin and Winsa, 2015).

New Racism and Religious Hatred: Islamophobia and Anti-Semitism

The discussion of new racism noted in Chapter 2 gives rise to debates about the relationship between racism and forms of religious hostility and hatred. In this final section, we briefly consider the issues of Islamophobia and anti-Semitism.

Islamophobia

The attacks on the World Trade Center in New York and the Pentagon in Washington on 11 September 2001 provided fodder for the emergence of yet another new form of hostility in Western societies—Islamophobia. Contemporary fears about Islam and its use by extremists to justify terrorist acts tend to transcend national boundaries, particularly in the developed Western world, and have added yet another layer of complexity to debates about forms of new racism. According to the British-based Runnymede Trust, Islamophobia is present when some of the following conditions are met:

- Islam is seen as a single monolithic bloc, static and unresponsive to new realities.
- Islam is seen as separate and other: (a) not having any aims or values in common with other cultures; (b) not affected by them; (c) not influencing them.

- Islam is seen as violent, aggressive, threatening, supportive of terrorism, engaged in a "clash of civilizations."
- Islam is seen as a political ideology, used for political or military advantage.
- Criticisms made by Islam of "the West" are rejected out of hand.
- Hostility toward Islam is used to justify discriminatory practices toward Muslims and exclusion of Muslims from mainstream society.
- Anti-Muslim hostility is accepted as natural and "normal" (cited in Miles and Brown, 2003: 164).

As we saw in Chapter 6, concrete manifestations of Islamophobia are legion and can be drawn from a variety of countries. In Britain in the fall of 2006, Labour MP Jack Straw provoked controversy when he wrote in a local newspaper that veils worn by Muslim women were barriers to good community relations in the country. British prime minister Tony Blair echoed this concern when he suggested that the *niqab* (a piece of cloth that covers the lower face, leaving the eyes exposed) worn by some Muslim women was a "mark of separation" that makes British non-Muslims "uncomfortable" (Valpy, 2006: A16). A Muslim teacher in the UK was required by law to remove her veil in the classroom, since, it was argued, "it hindered student learning." In April 2011, France banned the burka from all public displays in the country; some see it as a sign of female submission inherent in Islam that contradicts French values of equality and freedom. And former French president Nicolas Sarkozy openly mused about imposing DNA tests to "scientifically ascertain the blood relationship of parents and kids" from Muslim North Africa (ex-French colonies with mostly Muslim populations) before they are admitted to France as family members of legal immigrants.

Arab and Muslim Canadians reported that immediately after 11 September 2001, they faced various forms of harassment, intimidation, and violence (Arat-Koç, 2006: 220–1). Arat-Koç (2006: 227) argues that Islamophobia informs much of the new security agenda within Canada and the United States (and elsewhere), and as a result Muslim and Arab Canadians are increasingly concerned about how their travel patterns, their charitable donations, and their remittances to friends and family members overseas will be interpreted by other Canadians and by police and security forces. Further, the *niqab* has been the subject of various kinds of negative attention for nearly a decade in this country. In September 2007, three federal by-elections took place in Quebec. Marc Mayrand, Canada's chief electoral officer, was under pressure from politicians, the media, and "concerned citizens" to take a stance against allowing veiled Muslim women to vote unless they first showed their faces. Should women with their faces covered be allowed to vote? How could their identity be verified? He decided, in the spirit of being reasonable, that veiled Muslim women have the same rights as everyone else.

After this decision, Mayrand held a press conference in Ottawa to address some of the criticisms he had received. Allegedly, the chief electoral officer had "flouted the will of Parliament" by his loose interpretation of the Elections Act (*National*

Post, 10 September 2007). According to Mayrand, there is nothing in the current electoral law to prevent veiled people from voting. Moreover, the law allows citizens—for religious reasons—to vote with their face covered provided they show two pieces of valid ID and swear an oath. After all, said Mayrand, in the previous federal election, 80,000 people cast votes by mail (*Toronto Star*, 10 September 2007).

Prime Minister Stephen Harper and Official Opposition leader Stéphane Dion disagreed with this interpretation of the law, and argued that people must show their faces when voting to maintain integrity in the election process. Mayrand countered that if parliamentarians did not like his interpretation, they should have changed the law when they had the chance. On the other hand, John Ivison, a writer for the *National Post*, pointed out that neither has Parliament ruled "on voting by comic book characters but if Batman and Robin turned up in the polling booth, one hopes that Elections Canada staff would force them to reveal their secret identities" (*National Post*, 10 September 2007).

The debate about the *niqab* was resurrected during the 2015 federal election. This time, the context was the ruling Conservative government's effort to ban women who wear the *niqab* from the citizenship swearing-in ceremony. The Conservatives were arguably hoping to find a wedge issue that solidified the support of their traditional electoral base and so came out in support of the ban. Also during the election, they said that they would strengthen their just-passed Zero Tolerance for Barbaric Cultural Practices Act. During the election, they said that if re-elected, they would fund a "tip line" that would make it easier for Canadians to report to the Royal Canadian Mounted Police whether someone they knew was engaged in a barbaric cultural practice (Powers, 2015). Many of the practices deemed "barbaric" by the government seemed to come from Arab or broader Middle Eastern contexts, and so Islam was indirectly implicated in the promotion of practices like polygamy, getting married under the age of 16, and engaging in forced marriage. Though some Canadians, particularly in Quebec and parts of Ontario, seemingly supported the Conservative plan, the party ultimately lost the election largely because of the unpopularity of its leader, Stephen Harper, and his negative, divisive style of government. When Muslim women faced physical and verbal abuse in Canada after the terrorist attacks in Paris in November 2015, many commentators blamed the previous government and its anti-Muslim initiatives for giving other Canadians "permission to hate."

The question of whether Islamophobia is a new form of racism is a matter of debate. Arat-Koç argues that

> what has been new for Arab and Muslim Canadians since 11 September 2001 is not the experience of racism but its growing public legitimacy, spread, and mainstreaming in all major institutions, from the media to law and policy. (2006: 220)

In contrast to Arat-Koç, Miles and Brown (2003: 164) argue that since the "otherness" of Muslims tends to be constructed in religious rather than biological or physical terms, Islamophobia should not necessarily be regarded as an instance of racism. They do, however, recognize that this form of religious othering interacts with racism in that, in some cases, the negative evaluation of religious differences is accompanied by the negative evaluation of presumed physical differences. They also suggest that Islamophobia has many of the same consequences as racism, particularly in terms of social exclusion from jobs, border crossing difficulties, and conceptions of who constitutes a "good" Western citizen (Miles and Brown, 2003: 167).

Anti-Semitism

As we saw in Chapter 1, Nazi racist ideology that constructed Jews as both dangerous and inferior, and which justified the death of over 6 million Jews in Europe during the Second World War, led to postwar efforts to challenge racial theories and scientific forms of racism. Anti-Semitism, however, was not just a European phenomenon; Canada also has a long history of anti-Semitism. While some argue that anti-Semitism was most pronounced in the province of Quebec, it is clear that forms of anti-Semitism were present throughout Canadian society (Weinfeld, 2001). As in Europe, traditional forms of anti-Semitism in Canada reached their peak in the 1930s and 1940s, and took many different forms. They included name-calling, physical violence, the denial of opportunities for jobs, leisure, education, and housing, immigration restrictions, and defacing property and graveyards. To take only a few of many possible examples, Jews were denied entry to major universities like McGill and the University of Toronto in the 1930s, there were restrictive covenants that prevented property from being sold to Jews, fascist swastika clubs were formed, and there was an anti-Jewish riot at Christie Pits in Toronto. Signs outside of some swimming pools and beaches read "No Jews or Dogs Allowed." In 1939, a boatload of Jewish refugees from Nazi Germany was turned back to Europe by Canadian authorities on the grounds that there were already too many Jews in Canada (Weinfeld, 2001: 324–31).

These traditional forms of anti-Semitism, as with some of the current forms of Islamophobia, were based on a mix of religious and racialized intolerance. That is, for anti-Semites, Judaism as a religion, and Jews as a people, or "race," were simultaneously constructed and defined as the problem. According to Weinfeld, the wildly contradictory bundle of allegations about Jews—they were the killers of Christ and were inherently opposed to Christianity, a distinct "race" that had a natural inclination toward making money at other people's expense, the founders of communism, and secretly in control of the media, economics, and politics around the world—hung together by an overarching conspiracy theory. The idea was that Jews were out to dominate the world.

While some of these traditional forms and expressions of anti-Semitism in Canada appear to be declining, in other countries Jews continue to be targets of both verbal and physical attacks. In France, 50 per cent of the racist acts reported to the Interior Ministry in 2013 targeted Jews even though the approximately 500,000 Jews who live in the country represent less than 1 per cent of the population (Brenner, 2015). At a public rally in central Paris in July 2014 a group of demonstrators chanted "MORT AUX JUIFS! MORT AUX JUIFS!" (Death to Jews) and painted a swastika on the statue of Marianne, the goddess of French liberty (Brenner, 2015). Two days after the shootings at *Charlie Hebdo*, the satirical magazine that published cartoons and caricatures of the Prophet Muhammad, an armed gunman attacked a kosher supermarket and killed four people on the outskirts of Paris. In the face of these and other attacks, many Jews in France are actively considering leaving the country for the relative safety of Israel (Brenner, 2015).

Schoenfeld, Shaffir, and Weinfeld (2006: 291) argue that a new globalized form of anti-Semitism has emerged alongside its older forms (see Case Study Box 7.1). They argue that this new form of anti-Semitism tends to be politically framed in terms of opposition to Israeli government policy. As they explain, "It is often hard to tell when 'protests' against Israel are criticisms of policy, part of a campaign of delegitimation [of the existence of the state of Israel], or part of a war against 'the Jews.'" For some anti-Semites, opposing Israeli government policies (which became particularly sharp in the summer of 2006 in the context of the Israeli military response to Hezbollah rocket attacks staged from Lebanon) is a politically acceptable mask to cover their deeper anti-Jewish sentiments and actions.

Schoenfeld, Shaffir, and Weinfeld (2006) take care to suggest, however, that criticism of policies of the government of Israel should not always and automatically be equated with anti-Semitism. After all, many Jews in North America who see themselves as Zionists have themselves been critical of Israeli government policy (Schoenfeld, Shaffir, and Weinfeld, 2006: 293).

Case Study Box 7.1 US Department of State, "Report on Global Anti-Semitism," 2005

Global anti-Semitism in recent years has had four main sources:
- Traditional anti-Jewish prejudice that has pervaded Europe and some countries in other parts of the world for centuries. This includes ultranationalists and others who assert that the Jewish community controls governments, the media, international business, and the financial world.
- Strong anti-Israel sentiment that crosses the line between objective criticism of Israeli policies and anti-Semitism.
- Anti-Jewish sentiment expressed by some in Europe's growing Muslim population, based on longstanding antipathy toward both Israel and Jews, as well as Muslim opposition to developments in Israel and the occupied territories, and more recently in Iraq.
- Criticism of both the United States and globalization that spills over to Israel, and to Jews in general who are identified with both. . . .

Anti-Semitism in Europe has increased significantly in recent years. . . .

Beginning in 2000, verbal attacks directed against Jews increased while incidents of vandalism (e.g., graffiti, fire bombings of Jewish schools, desecration of synagogues and cemeteries) surged. Physical assaults including beatings, stabbings, and other violence against Jews in Europe increased markedly, in a number of cases resulting in serious injury and even death. Also troubling is a bias that spills over into anti-Semitism in some of the left-of-center press and among some intellectuals.

The disturbing rise of anti-Semitic intimidation and incidents is widespread throughout Europe. . . . European governments in most countries now view anti-Semitism as a serious problem for their societies and demonstrate a greater willingness to address the issue. The Vienna-based European Union Monitoring Center (EUMC), for 2002 and 2003, identified France, Germany, the United Kingdom, Belgium, and The Netherlands as EU member countries with notable increases in incidents. . . .

In Western Europe, traditional far-right groups still account for a significant proportion of the attacks against Jews and Jewish properties; disadvantaged and disaffected Muslim youths increasingly were responsible for most of the other incidents. This trend appears likely to persist as the number of Muslims in Europe continues to grow while their level of education and economic prospects remain limited.

In Eastern Europe, with a much smaller Muslim population, skinheads and other members of the radical political fringe were responsible for most anti-Semitic incidents. Anti-Semitism remained a serious problem in Russia and Belarus, and elsewhere in the former Soviet Union, with most incidents carried out by ultranationalist and other far-right elements. The stereotype of Jews as manipulators of the global economy continues to provide fertile ground for anti-Semitic aggression. . . .

At the end of 2003, and continuing into this year, some Jews, especially in Europe, faced the dilemma either of hiding their identity or facing harassment and sometimes even serious bodily injury and death. . . .

Source: US Department of State (2005). Available at www.state.gov/g/drl/rls/40258.htm.

Summary

Racism is both a sociological concept and an epithet. The fact that few people admit to being racist makes it particularly hard to study sociologically. The chapter reviewed some of the main lines of empirical evidence surrounding the existence of racism in Canada. It focused on the old forms of organized racism that still exist in Canada, but it also focused on how racism is measured in various types of surveys and public opinion polls. Victimization surveys and survey data on Canadians' attitudes toward immigrants and visible minorities were reviewed and critiqued in relation to their respective strengths and weaknesses. This chapter also provided a number of examples of what sociologists refer to as institutional racism. The chapter analyzed some of the major concerns about racism in professional sports, racism in Canadian schools as expressed in so-called zero tolerance policies and within universities, and racism in the justice system as expressed in the controversy over racial profiling and carding. The chapter also examined expressions of racism on the Internet and in new communications technologies such as Twitter. Racism seems ubiquitous on the Internet, in part because of the anonymity it provides. Racism also seems to be becoming a socially acceptable way that people describe and talk about each other and issues. Finally, the chapter examined two instances of new racism: the new anti-Semitism and Islamophobia.

Questions for Critical Thought

1. The police argue that there is a difference between racial profiling and criminal profiling. They admit that they practise criminal profiling but deny that they engage in racial profiling. To what extent is this a valid difference when it comes to the debate about the differential treatment of minority groups?

2. What are some of the appropriate methods and strategies for dealing with racism?

3. What are the forms of new racism? Historically speaking, is new racism all that new? Does the concept of *new racism* define racism too broadly?

4. How do seemingly neutral policies and procedures work to the disadvantage of some racialized groups? Are these forms of institutional racism?

5. What are the most effective ways that racism on the Internet can be combated?

Debate Questions

1. Can the policy of multiculturalism deal effectively with problems of racism? Why or why not? Read Chapter 5 again and try to suggest how the policy could change in order to combat racism more effectively.

2. After reading Chapter 5 a second time, attempt to compare the effectiveness of multiculturalism and interculturalism in combating racism in Canada. Which policy is more effective? Could either policy combat economic inequalities present in a capitalist society? How?

3. Is Islamophobia a form of racism?

4. Does it matter if Islamophobia and new anti-Semitism are characterized as forms of racism? What difference does it make it if they are defined as forms of racism?

5. Does government legislation with inflammatory titles like The Zero Tolerance for Barbaric Cultural Practices Act tacitly give permission to Canadians to express hatred toward other groups in Canadian society?

Annotated Additional Readings

Garner, Steve. 2010. *Racisms: An Introduction.* London: SAGE. A good analysis of the various forms and expressions of racism. There are fitting examples from around the world.

Henry, Frances, and Carol Tator. 2010. *The Colour of Democracy: Racism in Canada*, 4th edn. Toronto: Thomson Nelson. Frances and Tator have written a hard-hitting and unsettling discussion of the pervasiveness of racism in Canadian society.

Kazemipur, Abdolmohammad. 2014. *The Muslim Question in Canada: A Story of Segmented Integration*. Vancouver: UBC Press. An empirically rich analysis of the lives, attachments, and experiences of Muslims in Canada.

Miles, Robert, and Malcolm Brown. 2003. *Racism*, 2nd edn. London: Routledge. The authors present a comprehensive discussion and analysis of the concepts of "race" and racism. This book is essential reading on the topic.

Oppal, Wally. 2012. *Forsaken: The Report of the Missing Women Commission of Inquiry. Executive Summary.* British Columbia: Missing Women Commission of Inquiry. The results of the in-depth inquiry into the under-policing of women reported missing in Vancouver in the late 1990s and early 2000s.

Related Websites

Association of Black Law Enforcers
www.ablenet.ca
ABLE is an association of law enforcement professionals and associated community members who are committed to the betterment of the society in which they live and work.

B'nai Brith Canada
www.bnaibrith.ca
An organization representing the voice of the Jewish community in Canada. It is interested in, among other things, matters relating to anti-Semitism, racism, and human rights.

Canadian Race Relations Foundation
www.crrf-fcrr.ca/en
The Canadian Race Relations Foundation is Canada's leading agency dedicated to the elimination of racism in the country.

National Council of Canadian Muslims
www.nccm.ca
This is the Canadian chapter of an organization based in the United States. It was founded in 1994, in part to challenge misrepresentations of Islam and to present a more accurate understanding of Muslim communities in the two countries.

Missing Women Commission of Inquiry
www.missingwomeninquiry.ca/terms-of-reference
The website of the inquiry established in British Columbia to review and make recommendations about the missing women investigative process.

8 Aboriginal and Non-Aboriginal Relations

Learning Objectives

In this chapter you will learn that

- debates about Aboriginal identities are not simply matters of political correctness. They are important because these identities carry certain rights and because they try to express more authentic ways of being.

- there are four categories of Aboriginal peoples in Canada: Inuit, Métis, First Nations, and non-status Indians. These categories are based on a combination of self-definition and socio-legal definition.

- measures taken by the federal government in the 1980s to correct gender discrimination in the Indian Act have been controversial.

- some Aboriginal leaders claim that the federal government is continuing to pursue a policy of assimilation through the way that it defines *First Nations*.

- there are controversies within First Nations communities about how to define who is a band member.

- there are stubborn disparities between the health and socio-economic conditions of Aboriginal people and those of non-Aboriginal people.

- there are four main explanations for the disparities between Aboriginal and non-Aboriginal people: biological, cultural, structural, and historical.

- First Nations communities are not internally homogeneous. There are gender divisions and divisions between leaders and the led.

Introduction

What's in a name? What does it matter if someone is called an **Indian**, a *First Nation*, *indigenous*, or *Aboriginal*? Sometimes this kind of question is used as a way of trivializing issues of individual and collective identity. Sociologically speaking, however, the question of naming is far from trivial, and it is certainly not just a matter of political correctness. Ethnic and other identity labels can be externally imposed on groups of people, or they can be internally adopted. They can be sources of pride or terms of derision. They can also define social and political priorities as well as provide bases for political mobilization, rationales for social inclusion and exclusion, and the basis for claims to certain rights. As Kim Anderson (2000: 23) notes, "naming is politically and emotionally loaded" in the area of Aboriginal and non-Aboriginal relations (see also Alfred, 1999: 84–5).

This chapter is divided into three parts. First, it examines in more detail some of the current social and legal controversies about labels and identities of Aboriginal peoples in Canada. Second, it discusses inequalities between Aboriginal and non-Aboriginal people, and, third, it discusses inequalities within Aboriginal communities.

Labels, Identities, and Group Boundaries

In the spring of 1939, after a lengthy court battle involving the federal government and the government of Quebec, the Supreme Court of Canada ruled that **Eskimos** really were *Indians*, at least within the constitutional framework of the day (Backhouse, 1999: 18). In coming to this conclusion, the Supreme Court avoided the testimony of influential anthropologists who provided evidence about the cultural, religious, linguistic, and "racial" differences between *Eskimos* and *Indians*. Instead of taking this testimony into account, the Court based its decision on historical precedent. It argued that since the Fathers of Confederation thought that *Eskimos* were akin to *Indians* when the British North America Act came into force in 1867, then, from a legal perspective, *Eskimos* were *Indians*. At the time, the ruling was also significant for the way that it resolved a decades-old dispute about whether the provincial or federal government should be financially responsible for the provision of social support to the people indigenous to Canada's North. In defining *Eskimos* as *Indians*, the Supreme Court decided in favour of the province of Quebec and ruled that Eskimos were in fact a financial responsibility of the federal government (Backhouse, 1999: 53–5).

This case highlights some of the historical and contemporary complexities associated with defining Aboriginal peoples. The definitions of *Inuit*, *status Indians*, **non-status Indians**, **First Nations**, and **Métis**, and the formation of group boundaries around these identities, reflect a combination of self-definitions, externally imposed categories, historical precedent, and biological and cultural lines of descent (Siggner and Peters, 2014). In this section, we try to untangle some of the complexities associated with these definitions and also to draw out some of the social, legal, and political implications of the ways that group boundaries have been drawn around these categories.

One, albeit imperfect, way to begin to approach issues of naming and group boundaries is to start with the 1982 Constitution of Canada. The Constitution recognizes "the existing aboriginal and treaty rights of the aboriginal peoples of Canada." While the specific nature of these rights is subject to ongoing political and legal negotiation, the Constitution specifies that three groups fall within the general category of Aboriginal peoples: status Indians, Inuit, and Métis. One of the groups falling outside of those designated as Aboriginal peoples with Aboriginal rights is *non-status Indians*, although their position as a rights-claiming group is currently before the Supreme Court of Canada. The size of these groups is given in Table 8.1. How are they defined?

Table 8.1   Aboriginal Population of Canada, 2011

Status Indians	919,745 (2013)
Métis	451,795
Inuit	59,445
Non-status Indians	223,000 (estimate)

Source: "Registered Indian Population, by Residence and Gender, 2013," Indigenous and Northern Affairs Canada, https://www.aadnc-aandc.gc.ca/eng/1394032502014/1394032901691; "Aboriginal Peoples in Canada: First Nations People, Métis and Inuit", Statistics Canada, http://www12.statcan.gc.ca/nhs-enm/2011/as-sa/99-011-x/99-011-x2011001-eng.cfm.

Inuit

In 1941, the federal government conducted a special census in an effort to determine the exact number of Inuit in the country. Before then, trading-post managers, missionaries, and police officers carried out federal government enumerations of the Inuit population. These early efforts were problematic, in part because of the lack of a clear definition of who should be counted as Inuit. In conducting the 1941 census, the Royal Canadian Mounted Police allotted a "disc" number to each individual Inuk. Initially, these were four-digit numbers that were inscribed on thin discs the size of a Canadian quarter and were supposed to be worn around the neck. Later discs contained code numbers for family names and for the district of residence (Mitchell, 1996: 112).

Before disc numbers were discontinued in 1971, only those individuals with a government-provided identity number were officially defined as Inuit. Even though the institution of the disc number system implied that the government saw them as a distinct group of people, the 1939 Supreme Court decision (discussed earlier) ran counter to this approach when it ruled that for constitutional purposes, the Inuit should be considered *Indians*. Matters of defining the Inuit remain vitally important, particularly when it comes to the determination of who is eligible for the benefits associated with land claims settlements.

Politically, the Inuit of Canada continue to work to overcome the consequences of the 1939 Supreme Court decision that equated them with Indians and eventually brought them under the purview of the **Indian Act** and the federal Department of Indian Affairs. While the Inuit are no longer under the thumb of the Indian Act, the Inuit Tapiriit Kanatami, which is the main umbrella organization representing the Inuit of Canada, has argued for greater government recognition of their specific issues and concerns (Inuit Tapiriit Kanatami, 2004b). The organization claims that the Inuit are generally invisible and ignored within federal policy, and they lobbied to have the name of the former Department of Indian and Northern Affairs Development ment changed to its current Indigenous and Northern Affairs Canada. Furthermore, they argue that the government's "First Nations on-reserve" policy carries little relevance for them and that the amount spent on Inuit as opposed to First Nations or status Indian issues is grossly inadequate (Inuit Tapiriit Kanatami, 2004a: 3).

Métis

The term *Métis* is the French word for "half caste." In the sixteenth and seventeenth centuries, the term was used for the descendants of unions between French-Canadian fur traders and Indian women. Later, it was extended to the descendants of English fur traders and Indian women living in and around Hudson Bay. By the nineteenth century, the term came to be used more generally to refer to the "mixed blood" descendants of European (regardless of their specific origins) and Indian relationships who were living in western Canada in the vicinity of Hudson Bay and the Red River Valley in present-day Manitoba and in parts of Saskatchewan and Alberta.

At present, however, there are two approaches to the definition of *Métis* (Standing Senate Committee on Aboriginal Peoples, 2013). One is a fairly narrow and exclusive definition with relatively well-defined group boundaries. The other is a looser definition with more fluid and flexible boundaries. These competing definitions are reflected in the two main organizations that currently claim to represent the interests of Métis people in Canada: the Métis National Council (MNC) and the Congress of Aboriginal Peoples of Canada. In September 2002, The MNC became the first Métis organization in Canada to adopt a formal definition of *Métis*. In its rather narrow definition, "Métis means a person who self-identifies as Métis, is of historic Métis Nation Ancestry, is distinct from other Aboriginal Peoples, and is accepted by the Métis Nation." While self-definition is an important aspect of this approach (i.e., a person has to believe him- or herself to be a Métis person), a number of other important conditions apply. One of the key elements in this definition is the concept of "historic Métis Nation." This refers to people "known as Métis or Half-Breeds who resided in the Historic Métis Nation Homeland" in "west central North America." In effect, this provides for a definition of *Métis* that is limited to individuals recognized as descendants of "the original" Métis people who lived in northern Ontario, Manitoba, Saskatchewan, and Alberta (Métis National Council, 2014). The MNC adopted this narrow approach to the definition of its group boundaries in part because it felt that it had to have a distinct national content for rights recognized under the Constitution. In other words, the MNC wanted to present itself as a nation and not just an agglomeration of individuals united simply by their ancestors' choice of marriage partners (see Case Study Box 8.1).

On the other hand, the Congress of Aboriginal Peoples does not use a formal/legal definition of a Métis person. In the view of the Congress, *Métis* are more broadly defined as "mixed populations" who include but are not limited to the historic Métis as defined by the Métis National Council (Congress of Aboriginal Peoples, 2014). That is, for the Congress, Métis ancestral origins need not be rooted in the historic Métis homeland in western Canada, and the Métis can include, for example, the more recent descendants of "mixed" European/Aboriginal ancestry in places like Nova Scotia, British Columbia, and southern Ontario and who, over the

Case Study Box 8.1 The Métis Community of Saint Laurent

In 2012, the Standing Senate Committee on Aboriginal Affairs was tasked to examine and report on the evolving legal and political recognition of the collective identity rights of the Métis in Canada. In addition to making a number of recommendations, the report highlighted the diversity of Métis people and their communities in Canada. The following is a description of one particular Métis community.

Saint Laurent, Manitoba: Culture and Identity

The Saint Laurent area, located along the southern shore of Lake Manitoba, was first inhabited by Métis families who migrated north from the Pembina territory in the United States in the early 1820s. Other Métis in the area included those who migrated from the Red River Settlement, in and around present-day Winnipeg. The Métis who established semi-permanent settlements in the area were primarily fishers, traders with the fur company posts, and socio-economic intermediaries with the local Cree and Assiniboine populations.

The traditional economy in Saint Laurent continues to be based around the lake fishery: other traditional sources of livelihood include hunting, trapping, gardening, and farming. Recent legal and policy developments have supported Métis Aboriginal harvest rights in the area. In 2009, the Provincial Court of Manitoba, applying the *Powley* criteria, found that a historic Métis community and associated hunting rights existed across a large portion of southwestern Manitoba. Provincial government and conservation officials have since

generations, have constituted themselves as a distinct culture and group (Congress of Aboriginal Peoples, 2014).

Notwithstanding these debates about how to define *Métis*, recent court decisions have clearly established that Métis people, like status Indians, are a "rights-bearing group." They fall within federal jurisdiction for the purpose of policy-making and they have certain Aboriginal rights related to hunting for food. The latter was affirmed in the Supreme Court of Canada's decision in the 2003 *Powley* case, and many commentators believe that decision has far-reaching implications for the nature of other rights claimed by the Métis (Standing Senate Committee on Aboriginal Affairs, 2013).

First Nations

The term *First Nations* is now commonly used to describe "status" or "registered" Indians. It is not necessarily an ethnic identity, since many people use it instead of the concept of *status Indians*, and it can include individuals who have older linguistic and tribal identities. The term First Nations came into widespread worked with the Manitoba Métis Federation (MMF) to develop rules for recognizing Métis harvesting rights across southern Manitoba, culminating in the September 2012 harvesting agreement between the Province of Manitoba and the MMF.

The Michif language spoken in the area, generally a mixture of French and Cree, was historically a vital element in the development of Métis identity in Saint Laurent. The language, along with music, dress, harvesting activities and other aspects of material culture remain important to Métis identity and ways of life in the area. Indeed, Saint Laurent is featured in a permanent exhibition of contemporary Aboriginal life and identities at the Smithsonian's National Museum of the American Indian in Washington, DC.

The Michif language is an important aspect of Métis identity in Saint Laurent, despite a range of historic and contemporary challenges to its continued use and preservation. The old mission schools in the area, for example, actively discouraged previous generations from speaking the Michif language. Today, the influence of English is increasing as the community continues to grow and change demographically. Another challenge relates to the nature of the language itself: Michif is primarily a spoken language with many regional variations, which complicates efforts to compile written vocabulary or design education curricula.

In supporting the use and preservation of Michif, local educators told the committee that families are the best teachers of the language to the younger generations. Their pedagogical approach focuses on providing programs to support parents in transmitting the language and culture to their children, integrating lessons in Aboriginal culture into the existing provincial curriculum, and teaching values relating to personal and group identity, diversity and multiculturalism. As one educator noted, Métis students must recognize who they are before they can recognize the person in front of them.

Source: Senate Standing Committee on Aboriginal Affairs, 2013: 63–5.

use in the early 1980s with the transformation of the National Indian Brotherhood into the Assembly of First Nations (AFN). The term *First Nations*, leaders argued, better reflected their unique social and legal status in this country; namely, that they had special rights because they were the first occupants of the land. Despite the growing use and popularity of the term *First Nations*, the terms *Indian* or *status Indian* are still occasionally also used by organizations like the Saskatoon Indian and Métis Friendship Centre and the Hamilton Regional Indian Centre.

Historically, the federal government's need to define precisely who was an "Indian" stemmed in part from the way that powers between the federal and provincial governments were divided in the 1867 British North America Act. Within the act, many aspects of policy-making, such as matters pertaining to education, health care, and social services, were defined as responsibilities of provincial governments. However, "Indians and lands reserved for Indians" were defined as responsibilities of the federal government. In taking on this responsibility, the federal government was forced to figure out and define exactly whom the people were that they were responsible for (Satzewich and Wotherspoon, 2000).

As noted in Chapter 3, Indian policy was articulated in the Indian Act, which was the basic framework for the federal government's approach to dealing with Indian matters. A major preoccupation of the various incarnations of the Indian Act was therefore the question of whom the government defined as an *Indian* person.

The early historical definitions of who was an Indian were based on a mix of blood, line of descent, and community acceptance. While the definitions of *Indian* contained in the various incarnations of the Indian Act are complex and full of complex legal/bureaucratic jargon, in the Indian Act of 1876, an *Indian* basically was any male person of Indian blood reputed to belong to a particular band, any child of such person, and any woman who is or was lawfully married to such a person (Ponting and Gibbins, 1980: 9). This definition allowed the Department of Indian Affairs to create a "register" or list of individuals in Canada whom they considered to be Indians under Indian Act legislation. Hence, the term *registered*, or *status*, *Indian* came to be applied to people who were officially recognized as Indian persons by the federal government. Self-definition became less important than an externally imposed legal definition and social acceptance.

In defining who was an Indian, the Indian Act also defined how someone could lose his or her Indian status or stop being an Indian, at least from the perspective of the federal government. The concept of **enfranchisement** referred to the processes whereby individuals could forcibly lose or voluntarily give up their legal status as an Indian. For a time, Indians who earned a university degree, lived outside of the country for five years or more, or became lawyers, doctors, or Christian ministers were forced to give up their Indian status (Furi and Wherrett, 2003: 2). This policy essentially meant that being an Indian person was incompatible with being highly educated, a respected professional, or a member of the clergy. In fact, it created a disincentive for Indian persons to get a higher education, which they might need to improve their socio-economic status.

The other, more common way that individuals lost their status as Indians was through intermarriage (Frideres and Gadacz, 2012). Under the pre-1985 provisions of the Indian Act, Indian men who married non-Indian women were allowed to retain their Indian status; their children and their non-Indian spouses also acquired Indian status. On the other hand, Indian women who married non-Indian men lost their Indian status, as did their children. Non-Indian men who married Indian women were not granted Indian status.

Non-status Indians

These enfranchisement provisions led to the creation of the social category and political identity of "non-status" Indians. Generally, the term non-status Indian refers to individuals who lost their legal status as Indians through one of the enfranchisement provisions, which have since been eliminated from the Indian Act. The differences between non-status Indians and the Métis are sometimes difficult to untangle. Some individuals who lost their Indian status because their mother or grandmother married a non-Indian man define themselves and are socially accepted as Métis. Yet others reject the label of Métis or are not accepted as Métis by virtue of the more narrow definition of the Métis National Council and therefore define themselves as non-status Indians. Non-status Indians are different from other Aboriginal groups in that even though they define themselves as Indian or Aboriginal, they are not specifically included in the constitutional definition of Aboriginal peoples in Canada.

The blatantly obvious sexual discrimination built into the pre-1985 versions of the Indian Act became the object of political struggle in the 1960s and 1970s. In being forced to give up their Indian status, Indian women were no longer eligible for reserve-based benefits such as housing or support for higher education. Further, even if their marriages to their non-Indian male partners broke down, there were no provisions for women to regain their Indian status, return to their communities, and claim rights and resources as band members.

The momentum for change built up in the early 1970s as Jeannette Lavell and Yvonne Bédard challenged the sexual discrimination inherent in the enfranchisement provisions of the Indian Act. The Supreme Court of Canada ruled against Lavell and Bédard in 1973 on the grounds that the Indian Act was exempt from the equality protections of the Canadian Bill of Rights. However, further challenges to the law followed. In 1977, Sandra Lovelace filed a complaint against Canada with the United Nations Human Rights Committee in Geneva, and four years later the Canadian government was embarrassed by the committee's finding that the Indian Act was in breach of the International Covenant on Civil and Political Rights because it denied Lovelace and other women in the same circumstance the legal right to live in the communities of their birth (Silman, 1987: 176). After continued lobbying, the federal government amended the Indian Act in 1985 by passing **Bill C-31**.

The terms of the amendment to the Indian Act are complex, but at its simplest, Bill C-31 provided for

a. elimination of the "enfranchisement" provisions of the Indian Act and the reinstatement of certain individuals who had lost their Indian status as a result of the previous enfranchisement provisions;
b. elimination of patrilineal definitions of eligibility for Indian status;
c. the opportunity for bands to develop membership codes and to assume control over the definition of who was a band member;
d. the opportunity for bands to deny membership to certain individuals even though they had legal Indian status (Daniels, 2005: 1).

The Fallout from Bill C-31: A Case of "Abocide"?

The changes to the Indian Act introduced under Bill C-31 attempted to correct a legitimate historical injustice. However, as sometimes happens when governments try to correct historical wrongs, Bill C-31 resulted in the creation of further controversies and social divisions, and arguably laid the groundwork for future injustices.

First, in enabling individuals to regain their Indian status, the legislation has led to a significant increase in the status Indian population of Canada. As can be seen in Table 8.2, the number of status Indians in Canada has nearly doubled since it was introduced. In 1981, the status Indian population stood at 323,782 while in 2004 it was 637,227. While some of the recent increase in the Indian population is due to natural population growth among non–Bill C-31 Indians, much of the growth in the status Indian population in the late 1980s and early 1990s was the result of the reinstatement of individuals who had earlier lost their Indian status. Because many of the individuals who have had their status reinstated live in urban areas, there has also been a dramatic increase in the number of urban-based status Indians. In 2011, 51.7 per cent of status Indians lived off-reserve, compared to 19.5 per cent in 1966 (Frideres and Gadaacz, 2012: 62; Statistics Canada, 2011).

Second, some argue that **abocide** was in fact part of the hidden agenda in the government's 1985 solution to the problem of sexual discrimination in the Indian Act. In defining what he means by "abocide," Harry Daniels, former president of the Congress of Aboriginal Peoples, argues that the

> Bill not only continues but will actually accelerate the extermination policies—the integration of Canada's Indian population into mainstream society—that have always been at the heart of the federal Indian Act regime. So serious are the Bill's implications in this regard that, within a few generations, there may no longer be any status Indians left in Canada. (Daniels, 1998)

Table 8.2 Registered Indians and Indians Registered under Bill C-31, Average Annual Growth Rates, Canada, 1981–2004

	Registered Indians			Average Annual Growth (%)	
Year	Excluding Bill C-31	Bill C-31 Population	Total	Excluding Bill C-31	Including Bill C-31
1981	323,782	0	323,782	2.59	0.00
1985a	358,636	1,605	360,241	3.16	7.66
1989b	399,433	66,904	466,337	4.20	5.11
1991	429,178	92,282	521,460	3.55	4.23
1996	506,005	104,869	610,874	2.83	3.01
2001	517,226	105,675	622,901	2.16	1.93
2004	527,570	106,456	637,227	2.00	2.03

a. In 1985, the Indian Act was amended to allow, through Bill C-31, the restoration of Indian status to those who had lost it due to discriminatory clauses in the Indian Act.
b. The high annual growth rate between 1989 and 1991 is due in part to the upward adjustments of the Indian Register for the purposes of the projections and to the Department's estimate of 86,000 Bill C-31 registrants in 1990–91 plus the growth due to natural increase.

Source: Reproduced with the permission of Indigenous and Northern Affairs Canada.

Although Daniels may exaggerate the rate at which status Indians might drop off the political landscape of Canada, he does identify a legitimate long-range issue. While the new group membership rules are complex, essentially if two consecutive generations of status Indians marry non-Indians, the children of the second-generation relationships will no longer be eligible for Indian status. That is, to qualify for Indian status in the future, a grandchild of individuals who are currently status Indians has to have either both parents as status Indians or one parent as a status Indian, both of whose parents (the grandparents) were status Indians. Daniels argues that as time goes on, many individuals will not be able to meet this test, and he predicts that even though there has been a temporary increase in the size of the status Indian population and a temporary decline in the non-status Indian population, in 20 years' time the trend will reverse: there will be an explosion in the number of non-status Indians and a decrease in the number of status Indians.

While the Canadian government does not phrase it in quite the same way as Daniels, they also predict a decline in the rate of status Indian population increase, and an increase in the percentage of people living on-reserve that do not have registered status (including a significant increase in non-status descendants) in Canada's future (see Figure 8.1).

Because status Indians have special rights in the Constitution and non-status Indians do not, this potential trend is identified as yet another way that the federal government is trying to rid itself of the so-called "Indian problem" (Dyck, 1991). Indeed, Bonita Lawrence (2004: 67) suggests that "intermarriage now represents a 'ticking time bomb' in Native communities" because it will eventually reduce the size of the status Indian population that can claim special rights.

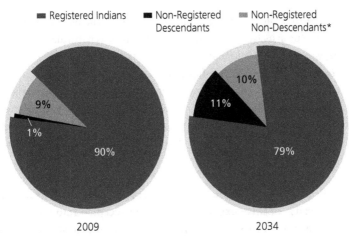

* Non-registered non-descendant population estimates are based on census of population data and may include individuals residing on leased reserve lands.

Figure 8.1 Projected Composition of the On-Reserve Population, Canada, 2009 and 2034

Source: Reproduced with the permission of Indigenous and Northern Affairs Canada.

Third, even though Bill C-31 made it possible for individuals to have their Indian status reinstated, this has not necessarily meant that people have been socially accepted as part of their former communities. In other words, legal definitions of identity continue to clash with self-definitions and community acceptance. As part of the amendments included under Bill C-31, bands were invited to develop rules that defined whom they considered a band member. Between 1985 and 1999, 236 of 610 First Nations had developed their own band membership codes. These codes are not necessarily the same as the rules that the federal government uses to determine Indian status (Furi and Wherrett, 2003: 10). This has created cases in which individuals have had their Indian status reinstated by the federal government but have not been reinstated as band members with the right to access band resources, participate in band elections, and live and own property on reserves.

According to some commentators, Bill C-31 has led to the creation of an increasingly complex "caste system" under the Indian Act (Daniels, 1998: 5). Research has begun to document some of the tensions in reserve communities surrounding the reinstatement of Bill C-31 Indians (Lawrence, 2004: 70–3). According to one study conducted in British Columbia, some women who have been reinstated report that they have been treated as second-class citizens in their communities and that bands are reluctant to share resources with those who are reinstated (Huntley and Blainey, 1999). In Alberta, Bill C-31 Indians have been characterized as "strangers who would bring conflict, stress, and problems" to reserves.

Alfred, in summarizing what needs to be done to address the conflicts and tensions surrounding the social consequences of Bill C-31, expresses a rather harsh assessment of those who have sought reinstatement as a result of the Bill:

> White society must do something to address the concerns of individuals who have been incorrectly associated with our nations. This issue is particularly relevant in Canada, where tens of thousands of self-identifying and minimal-blood persons who are excluded from membership in Indian communities are recognized as "Aboriginal" by Canadian governments, receiving benefits and legal entitlement to the resources of indigenous nations. It seems that white society feels some obligation to these people—probably because they are actually white, and therefore likely to cooperate with government efforts to eliminate indigenous nations as political forces. (1999: 86)

Although it is difficult to know how widespread such opinions and conflicts are, in part because positive experiences of being accepted into a community do not make the news, the existence of such tensions continues to speak to the continued importance of clashes between externally imposed definitions of identity, individual identity choices, and the social recognition of those identity choices. While many ethnic groups have formal and informal debates about group membership, who belongs and who does not belong, and what makes a particular individual "Hungarian" or "Yoruba," the political debate about who is an "authentic Indian" is more heated because in Canada the latter is a rights-bearing identity.

Fourth, there are controversies over the nature of membership codes that have been developed by some bands (see Clatworthy, 2013, for a summary of these codes). According to Furi and Wherrett, First Nations bands have developed four main types of membership codes:

1. one-parent descent rules whereby a person is eligible for membership based on the membership eligibility of one parent;
2. two-parent descent rules, which declare that for a person to become eligible, both of that person's parents must be members or eligible for membership;
3. blood quantum rules, which base eligibility on the amount of Indian blood a person possesses (typically 50 per cent);
4. Indian Act rules that base membership on sections of the Indian Act (Furi and Wherrett, 2003: 10).

Bands that have developed blood quantum rules have been the most criticized. Daniels argues that the federal government's new rules regarding the maintenance of Indian status through the generations will place pressure on bands to "maintain the 'racial purity' of their community and to discourage unions with Non-Status partners" (Daniels, 1998: 3). The Kahnawake Mohawk community's 1984 code is probably the most controversial, in part because it is the most high-profile community to have developed a blood quantum code. There were two basic elements to its 1984 code:

1. *Moratorium on mixed marriages*: Any Mohawk who married a non-Native after 22 May 1981 loses the right to residency, land holding, voting, and office holding in Kahnawake.
2. *Kahnawake Mohawk law*: As of 11 December 1984, a biological criterion for future registrations requires a "blood quantum" of 50 per cent or more Native blood (cited in Lawrence, 2004: 78).

Though the community's current membership code does not use the language of "blood," membership is nonetheless contingent, in part, on having four or more great-grandparents who were members of the community (Mohawk Council of Kanawà:ke, 2007).

Culture and individual identity are also factors in Mohawk identity, but they seem to be subordinate to descent. As Alfred notes, "Today there are many different ideas about what constitutes a Native person. We know what does not: pure self-identification and acting the part, however diligent the research or skilful the act" (1999: 85).

In this context, individuals in Kahnawake have lost jobs and have not been allowed to run for office because they have less than the requisite 50 per cent blood quantum. In 1995, efforts were made to bar children who were deemed to not have the requisite 50 per cent blood quantum from Kahnawake schools (Lawrence, 2004: 79).

Critics have argued that these kinds of membership codes are racist and in violation of basic human rights (Lawrence, 2004: 78; Hamilton, 2015). In defence of the code, Alfred (1995: 174–7) argues that in the absence of an easily operational set of cultural criteria to define what being a Mohawk means, "Indian communities in the modern era have been forced to accept race-based criteria" (Alfred, 1995: 174). This kind of racialized definition of group membership is "easy to police" because once the criteria are established, it is easy to measure "race." Alfred further argues that the use of these criteria is the natural by-product of living in a racialist society with a racialist history. Some have pointed out that critics use a double standard when they condemn the Mohawks for developing this kind of code. According to Lawrence (2004: 78), the Canadian government regularly uses blood quantum in its determination of who is eligible for resources in land claims settlements, yet it is rarely criticized for using racialized criteria in this context.

Alfred (1995) justifies the blood quantum codes on the grounds of the right to self-determination: what is the right to self-determination if it is not a right to define your own group boundaries? In Alfred's view, "To deny the Mohawks of Kahnawake the right to determine for themselves what the boundaries are between theirs and other communities is itself inherently colonial." "Membership," Alfred (1999: 85) says, "is a matter of blood and belonging determined through the institutions governing a community at a particular time." The problem, as we noted in Chapter 1, is that "race" is neither fixed nor obvious. In fact, it is very difficult to define "race" from a biological or blood quantum point of view, and any definition will inevitably draw arbitrary boundaries between those who belong and those who do not belong.

Comparing Collectivities: Between-Group Differences

A common way of trying to understand the position and experiences of Aboriginal people in Canada is to compare their social, health, educational, and economic conditions to those of non-Aboriginal people. In this section, most of the comparisons are between First Nations or status Indians living on reserves in Canada and the Canadian population as a whole. Generally, the differences between Canadians as a whole and First Nations living in urban areas or Métis people are less dramatic than the former (see Siggner and Peters, 2014, for data on non-status Indians). While most of the measures used to gauge socio-economic differences between reserve-based First Nations and other Canadians indicate that there is a declining gap between these two broad collectivities, these measures also tend to show that there are still stubborn disparities.

Even though Canada prides itself on its publically funded health care system, there are significant differences in the health status of First Nations and other

Canadians. According to the Assembly of First Nations (2011), tuberculosis among First Nations is 31 times the national average; one in five First Nations is diabetic (three to five times the national average); average life expectancy is five to seven years less for Aboriginal than non-Aboriginal people; and suicide rates among First Nations youth are five to seven times higher than other non-Aboriginal Canadians.

There has been a steady improvement over the years in some dimensions of housing. Though the federal government has invested in housing for reserve communities—in 1999–2000 alone it spent well over $250 million—the housing stock on reserve communities is still far from adequate. One estimate suggests that 16,000 new houses need to be built to keep pace with population growth in reserve communities (Frideres and Gadacz, 2012: 125). The overall quality of housing does not appear to be getting much better: in 1999–2000, for example, 56.9 per cent of on-reserve housing was considered "adequate" (defined as houses that do not require any minor or major renovations or replacement), but in 2011, this figure was virtually the same (Assembly of First Nations, 2011). Over 5,000 houses on reserves in Canada are without sewage services, and almost half of all reserve housing has mould contamination problems (Assembly of First Nations, 2011). Overcrowding remains an issue. The number of Aboriginal homes with more than one person per room is 200 to 300 times higher than that of the overall Canadian population (Frideres and Gadacz, 2012: 125). In Canada as a whole, the average number of persons per dwelling is fewer than 2, but the number of Aboriginal persons per dwelling is 3.5. The average Canadian dwelling has 7.2 rooms, but the average Aboriginal dwelling has 5.8 rooms (Frideres and Gadacz, 2012: 125). Overcrowding leads to deteriorating housing stock and to other social problems.

On top of these inadequacies is the problem of the quality of services available to reserve residents. The October 2005 mass evacuation of the Kashechewan reserve in northern Ontario because of water supply problems shows that decent water supplies are not available to all reserve communities; indeed, 98 other reserve communities were also under boil-water advisories (Curry, 2005). In 2006, 23 per cent of reserve communities had water services that were inadequate or lacking, and in 2011, 12 per cent of First Nations communities, impacting about 75,000 people, had to boil their drinking water (Friders and Gadacz, 2012: 127; Assembly of First Nations, 2011).

A variety of measures can be used to assess income differences, and it is not possible to provide complete documentation here. As with other measures of well-being (Cooke, Beavon and McHardy, 2004), evidence suggests that the economic gap between First Nations and other Canadians is slowly closing but that persistent differences remain (Pendakur and Pendakur, 2011). Government transfer payments constitute a greater proportion of Aboriginal people's total income than that of non-Aboriginal people. In 2012–13, 33.6 per cent of the on-reserve population received social assistance, compared to just over 5 per cent of the Canadian population as a whole. In 2005, among status Indian families, 33.3 per cent were low income, compared to 11.6 per cent of non-Aboriginal families (Frideres and Gadacz,

2012: 104). In 2005, average individual income for non-Aboriginal men was $37,365 and non-Aboriginal women was $25,955. Average income for on-reserve men was $14,907 and on-reserve women was $13,968 (Frideres and Gadacz, 2012: 105).

Differences in employment status are also evident. In 2011, the unemployment rate for all men in Canada was 7.8 per cent, but for on-reserve men it was 26 per cent. In the case of Canadian women, the overall unemployment rate was 7 per cent, but for on-reserve women it was 15 per cent (Aboriginal Affairs and Northern Development Canada, 2011). Unemployment rates on specific reserves are even higher and in some cases reach more than 50 per cent. Unemployment rates for non-status Indian and Métis men and women are considerably lower and are within 1 to 4 percentage points higher than the average for all Canadians. Labour force participation rates are correspondingly lower for status Indians than they are for non-Aboriginal people. When it comes to the kinds of jobs that people do, compared to other Canadian men, First Nations men are underrepresented in management, business, finance and administration, natural science, and related occupations, and overrepresented in the ranks of skilled, semi-skilled, and other manual occupations (Aboriginal and Northern Development Canada, 2011; see also Centre for the Study of Living Standards, 2012).

There are fewer variations between Aboriginal and non-Aboriginal women in Canada. Compared to Canadian women, Aboriginal women are overrepresented in service occupations and slightly underrepresented in clerical occupations. At the upper end of the occupational scale, Aboriginal women are distributed in roughly the same proportion as non-Aboriginal women (Frideres and Gadacz, 2012: 107).

Overall, the educational attainment of Aboriginal people is improving, but as with other dimensions, there remains a gap. For example, in 2011, 29 per cent of the Aboriginal population had less than a grade 9 education; for the non-Aboriginal population, the figure was 12 per cent. Conversely, while 65 per cent of non-Aboriginal Canadians had some form of post-secondary education, only 48 per cent of the Aboriginal population had similar educational achievements. Generally, when it comes to higher education, status Indian women do better than status Indian men; of the 26,900 status Indians with a university degree, 70 per cent were female (Aboriginal Affairs and Northern Development Canada, 2011).

Finally, as several commentators and research studies have noted for many years now (Royal Commission on Aboriginal Peoples, 1996a; Aboriginal Justice Inquiry of Manitoba, 1999), Aboriginal people are significantly overrepresented in federal and provincial prisons in Canada. According to the Office of the Correctional Investigator of Canada (2014), even though Aboriginal people make up about 4 per cent of the Canadian population, in 2013, for example, 23.2 per cent of the population of federal jails was Aboriginal. Of the approximately 3,400 Aboriginal offenders in federal penitentiaries, 71 per cent are First Nation, 24 per cent are Métis, and 5 per cent are Inuit. Among women, the rate is even higher: Aboriginal women represent 33.6 per cent of all federally sentenced women in the country. These figures are even more alarming when specific institutions are examined. At Stony

Mountain Institution in Manitoba, 389 of 596 inmates (65.3 per cent) were Aboriginal. The overall federal incarceration rate for Aboriginal adults in Canada is estimated to be 10 times higher than the rate for non-Aboriginal people (Office of the Correctional Investigator for Canada, 2014). Incarceration rates in provincial institutions, particularly in the Prairie provinces, are also significantly higher for Aboriginal people than non-Aboriginal people (Correctional Service Canada, 2013).

Explaining Aboriginal Conditions

How do social scientists try to explain the above-noted differences between Aboriginal and non-Aboriginal people? In this section, we review four kinds of explanations: socio-biological, cultural, structural, and historical. It should be noted that some explanations are invoked to explain more general differences while other explanations focus on specific issues.

Socio-biological Explanations

As noted in Chapter 2, socio-biological explanations of behaviour and of ethnic and racial relations have generally fallen out of favour in the social sciences. However, one area in which socio-biology explanations tend to remain both popular and influential is First Nations alcohol addiction. Thatcher (2004) argues that the predominant explanation for First Nations people's alcohol abuse problems, which he describes colloquially as the "firewater theory," is a form of the disease model of alcoholism. At its simplest, in this model individuals who develop the disease of alcoholism are predisposed to it because of chemical dysfunction in the brain. This dysfunction is reinforced and aggravated by extensive alcohol consumption. The disease is chronic, and those who suffer from it must manage the disease through complete avoidance of alcohol. Further, it is characterized by a complete loss of control during an alcohol consumption episode (Thatcher, 2004: 29–30). Thatcher argues that

> inherent in the firewater complex is the belief that aboriginal Canadians are constitutionally (genetically) incapable of moderation in the amount of alcohol they consume in drinking episodes. Drinking, moreover, is seen as a social activity, typically carried out in venues devoted wholly to group drinking. It also tends to be carried out through binges, rather than as persistent, ongoing, addictive drinking. The firewater complex also includes the popular belief that "Indian drinking" is inevitably associated with extreme impairment and irresponsible and antisocial behaviour. The assumption is that, once a drinking episode has begun, indigenous North Americans lose their capacity to regulate their drinking behaviour, the amount they drink, as well as other behaviours during the episode. Colloquially stated, Indian drinking tends to quickly get "out of control," a concept which is consistent with conventional notions of alcoholic behaviour described in the disease model of alcoholism. (2004: 130–1)

This approach to understanding Aboriginal alcohol problems is shared by many health professionals and is incorporated into treatment programs run by and for First Nations communities. Thatcher argues that the thinking behind the "fire-water complex" has been extended to explain many other social problems in reserve communities, including gambling, co-dependency, family violence, anxiety, depression, anger, and rage (2004: 139).

One of the problems with this explanation is that it is based on essentialist and primordial understanding of "race" differences. Assessing the evidence on the impact of biological factors on alcohol use, Thatcher (2004: 122) argues that there is "no convincing evidence" that Aboriginal people "are genetically prone to alcohol problems or that they are necessarily problem drinkers if they do drink." As an alternative explanation, Thatcher suggests that problem drinking among First Nations is the result of complex sociological and historical factors. These factors include the patterns of learning about drinking within First Nations communities; the federal government's historical encouragement of dependency on the part of First Nations; the breakdown of social controls within communities to regulate anti-social drinking; and the absence of "stakes in sobriety" for many First Nations people (Thatcher, 2004: 166–93).

Cultural Explanations

A second explanation for Aboriginal conditions is cultural and focuses on presumed value, attitudinal, and behavioural differences between Aboriginal and non-Aboriginal people. There are three versions of cultural theory: the first sees culture, cultural difference, and the unwillingness and/or inability to assimilate to "mainstream" society as the source of many of the socio-economic problems that First Nations face; the second, which tends to be articulated by some Aboriginal people themselves, uses cultural explanations as a justification for self-government, but it has implications for understanding existing inequalities; and the third, which has certain affinities with the theory of segmented assimilation as outlined in Chapter 2, suggests that many of the problems in Aboriginal communities stem from too much assimilation into "mainstream" culture.

According to the first version of cultural theory, Aboriginal people tend to be poor or in ill health because their culture is different from, or incompatible with, the dominant culture. The dominant culture values things like personal autonomy, private property, individual economic success, and individual well-being. Elements of this view are contained in volume 1 of the report of the Royal Commission on Aboriginal Peoples, *Looking Forward, Looking Back*. Quoting Clare Brant, a Mohawk psychiatrist, the report suggests that within Aboriginal communities, there is a "core ethic of non-interference," which is a "behavioural norm of North American Native tribes that promotes positive interpersonal relations by discouraging coercion of any kind, be it physical, verbal, or psychological" (Royal Commission on Aboriginal Peoples, 1996b: 9.1). Related to this core ethic are the ethics of non-competitiveness, emotional restraint, sharing, and a number of "less influential" ethics such as "a concept of time that emphasizes doing things 'when the time is right' rather than by the clock; shying away from public expressions of praise; ordering social relations by complex but unspoken rules; and teaching by modeling rather than shaping" (Royal Commission on Aboriginal Peoples, 1996b: 9.1). The report suggests that while these interrelated behaviours were required for survival in a small community in which a high degree of co-operation was required, a person could be put at a serious disadvantage if that person's environment changed and success and survival depended on competitive achievement (1996b: 9.1).

Economist John Richards explains the profound cultural dilemma that Aboriginal people in Canada face in the following terms:

> Personal success in an industrialized society requires that people restrict voluntary sharing of their personal income and wealth essentially to those in their (extended) family; it also requires that they invest in individual training and defer consumption via financial savings. Such activities are severely at odds with the values of most traditional cultures, and realizing a workable synthesis of the traditional and the modern is far from easy. (1995: 156)

Richards argues that historically, most ethnic and racial groups around the world have more or less successfully confronted the problem of the transition from traditional to modern culture. Aboriginal people in Canada are unique, not because their traditional cultures are substantially different from other traditional non-European cultures but rather because of the relatively recent timing of their transition. According to Richards,

> For those of European or Asian origin, the cultural journey from feudal agriculture to modern industrial society has been a long and tortuous one. In an anthropological sense, however, that journey has been shorter and more direct than the one to be undertaken by people who start from a pre-agricultural society. The cultural adjustments required of a Punjabi farmer who moves from rural India to urban Toronto may be huge, but they are less than those required of a reserve-based aboriginal who moves from northern Saskatchewan to Regina. (1995: 156)

Frances Widdowson and Albert Howard's (2008) controversial book *Disrobing the Aboriginal Industry: The Deception behind Indigenous Cultural Preservation* continues this line of thought. They say that because many Aboriginal people participate in modern society as consumers rather than producers, they remain stuck at an earlier, "Neolithic" stage of human development:

> Isolation from economic processes has meant that a number of Neolithic cultural features, including undisciplined work habits, tribal forms of political identification, animistic beliefs, and difficulties in developing abstract reasoning, persist despite hundreds of years of contact. (Widdowson and Howard, 2008: 13)

They argue that the cultural gap that exists between Aboriginal people and the rest of Canada prevents the integration of Aboriginal people and is responsible for many of the social problems and pathologies that exist within their communities.

In contrast to this version of cultural theory, a second version has tended to be put forward by some Aboriginal people themselves. Emphasis on the enduring cultural differences between Aboriginal and non-Aboriginal people is used by some as a justification for self-government and as an argument for the transfer of more decision-making powers to Aboriginal people. Whereas the first version of cultural theory tends to cast Aboriginal culture in a negative light insofar as it is the source of "the problem," the second is a positive portrayal of the values, beliefs, and attitudes of Aboriginal people and part of "the solution."

The latter version is reflected in the report of the Royal Commission on Aboriginal Peoples on the justice system, titled *Bridging the Cultural Divide* (1996a). While careful to place Aboriginal justice issues in the wider context of colonialism and economic disadvantage, the report also provided a powerful statement of the role that cultural differences play in the problem of and solution to Aboriginal people's overrepresentation in the justice system. One of the major findings of the commission was that "the Canadian criminal justice system has failed the Aboriginal peoples of Canada—First Nations, Inuit and Métis people, on-reserve and off-reserve, urban and rural—in all territorial and governmental jurisdictions." The commission's explanation "for this crushing failure is the fundamentally different world views of Aboriginal and non-Aboriginal people with respect to such elemental issues as the substantive content of justice and the process of achieving justice." (1996a: 309).

Part of the solution, the report went on to suggest, stems from the constitutional right of Aboriginal people to self-government. In the commission's (1996a: 310) view, "Aboriginal nations have the right to establish criminal justice systems that reflect and respect the cultural distinctiveness of their people pursuant to their inherent right to self-government."

The third take on the role of cultural differences between Aboriginal and non-Aboriginal people suggests that many of the social problems in Aboriginal communities do not stem from a lack of assimilation, or from cultural differences, but rather from the fact that too many Aboriginal people, particularly leaders of Aboriginal communities, have become too assimilated into some of the negative features of dominant Canadian society and have drifted too far away from their authentic Aboriginal roots. This explanation has certain affinities with the theory of segmented assimilation that we outlined in Chapter 2. Recall that this theory, initially developed in the United States, suggests that some immigrants to the US become integrated into the existing American underclass (Zhou, 1999). As a result, the economic problems that some immigrants face do not stem from their supposed lack of assimilation into American society but rather from their assimilation into the "wrong" segment of American society—an underclass subculture that rejects economic success. While not directly applicable to Canada, this theory does have similarities to the third version of cultural explanation for First Nations conditions in Canada in that problems are seen to be rooted in too much assimilation into "mainstream" culture. According to Alfred,

> The only way we can survive is to recover our strength, our wisdom, and our solidarity by honouring and revitalizing our traditional teachings. Only by heeding the voices of our ancestors can we restore our nations and put peace, power and righteousness back into the hearts and minds of our people. (1999: xii)

In this kind of formulation, "white society" and various "white man's diseases [and cultural patterns]" have persistently "eaten away at the purity of the First Nation person or culture" (Thatcher, 2004: 139).

What are we to make of cultural explanations for Aboriginal conditions? As the above discussion indicates, notions of "cultural difference" and "traditional culture" are rather flexible friends: cultural differences can variously be seen as both the problem with and the solution to Aboriginal conditions. On their own, cultural explanations are problematic for a number of reasons. First, some versions of cultural theory tend to portray Aboriginal people as cultural cripples and throwbacks who, despite centuries of contact with European society, have been unable or unwilling to make the transition to a dominant society that is fast-paced, competitive, and individualistic. Widdowson and Howard's (2008) analysis thrives on the view that after the decline of the fur trade, Aboriginal people became completely marginal to Canadian economic development and that currently they live in a world dominated exclusively by government transfers and welfare. Even though there are real disparities in income and labour force status between Aboriginal and non-Aboriginal people, 70 per cent of total income for status Indians both on- and off-reserve comes from employment income. The comparable figure for the non-Aboriginal population is 77 per cent (Williams, 2008). Since employment income is a sign that Aboriginal people are not just "consumers" but "producers," it is clear that many Aboriginal people are participating in the modern economy and society.

Second, within each of the approaches, the definition of what constitutes authentic Aboriginal culture is often vague and sometimes relies on unsubstantiated stereotypes. These explanations also make use of an uncritical essentialism that tends to portray both Aboriginal culture and the dominant "Euro-Canadian" culture as monolithic, all encompassing, and inherently ingrained. In other words, all individuals within these broad groups have or should have these particular world views if they are to be authentic group members. This is particularly evident in Alfred's (1999: 42) characterization of "Western" and "indigenous" understandings of justice. Furthermore, according to anthropologist Noel Dyck,

> The "culturalist" arguments advanced by Indian leaders in support of aboriginal claims, effective though these may be, run the risk of encapsulating Indians' political initiatives within . . . a straightjacket. The danger is that the honouring

of static images of Indian culture may run counter to development of critical support for the less culturally "colourful" but, nonetheless, pragmatic aspirations of
Indians. (1991: 151)

Third, cultural explanations tend to overgeneralize and assume that because
an individual has a certain background or origin, that individual must automatically believe in certain things (Crowley, 1995: 76). According to Crowley (1995: 76),
"one can assume nothing about how real flesh-and-blood individuals feel or what
they believe or the sort of life they want to live simply because they are aboriginal."
It is just as wrong to generalize about what white people think and believe as it is to
generalize about what Aboriginal people believe.

Fourth, some critics challenge the excessive assimilation into "white society"
thesis on the grounds that it is a form of "reverse racism." Thatcher argues that

a broad-brush stroke of blame is painted over both irresponsible corporate directors and unsympathetic politicians and those who are seriously and demonstra-
bly concerned about and victimized by the same influences as those which cause
great concern among aboriginal people. Ordinary, struggling workers and parents
of non-aboriginal ancestry are placed on the same plane as the big shareholders
and managers of corporations that produce and sell such potentially corrupting
products as violent Hollywood movies, fatty hamburgers, cigarettes, or alcohol.
(2004: 139)

As Thatcher notes, the idea that an undifferentiated "white society" is to blame
for Aboriginal conditions assumes that all white people, regardless of the amount
of power they have or do not have, are equally implicated in the problems facing
First Nations people.

Structural Explanations

Structural explanations locate the cause of Aboriginal people's poor socio-economic
conditions in racism, discrimination, and economic disparities within the wider
society. Structural explanations focus on the historical and contemporary obstacles
that are both deliberately and accidentally placed in the way of Aboriginal people.
As we saw in Chapter 3, there are many historical examples showing how social
and economic opportunities and basic human rights were denied to First Nations
(status Indians).

Some researchers focus on economic disadvantage as the source of Aboriginal people's over-involvement in certain aspects of the justice system (see Royal
Commission on Aboriginal Peoples, 1996a: 42–4, for a good summary). According to this approach, Aboriginal peoples are disproportionately impoverished, and
their overrepresentation in the justice system simply reflects the wider correlation between economic disadvantage and criminality. Relatedly, many Aboriginal

offenders end up in jail because they default on the payment of fines. As a number of inquiries into the operation of the justice system have noted, many Aboriginal males are currently serving time in jail simply because they cannot afford to pay fines. Thus, their over-incarceration is not due to any inherent cultural difference with the rest of Canadian society but rather a direct reflection of their poverty.

The Weight of History

The fourth explanation for Aboriginal socio-economic conditions is what we refer to here as the "weight of history" argument. There are two versions of this argument, one liberal and one conservative. Whereas liberal versions place blame on colonial oppression, conservative versions place the blame on the supposed generosity of the Canadian government.

Liberal versions of the "weight of history" argument are perhaps the most popular of the current explanations of Aboriginal conditions. The Truth and Reconciliation Commission (2015), in its June 2015 report on the Indian residential school system, lent further credibility to the argument that there are continuing impacts on First Nations people and communities of historical, colonial-driven policies. Generally, this perspective suggests that many of the particular maladies found within Aboriginal communities can be attributed to past government policies and practices (Waldram, Herring, and Young, 1995: 270). Colonialism, and its attendant ideologies, practices, policies, and controls, is the most frequently cited culprit. Noel Dyck, for example, argues that the cumulative weight of historical coercive tutelage has produced negative consequences both for First Nations people and their communities and for non-Aboriginal people. Dyck argues that coercive tutelage has been premised on the stated and unstated assumption that the personal and/or cultural deficiencies of Indians are the source of the Indian problem (Dyck, 1991: 107). According to Dyck,

> Although the difficulties that Indians, like all human beings, suffer are many and various, the "problem" that has dictated their lives for so long and with such sad consequences has resulted from the usually well-intentioned but, nonetheless, coercive and arbitrary rule to which they have been subjected. (1991: 162)

Colonialism is also blamed for the creation of complex psychological problems for Aboriginal people. In some formulations of this argument, First Nations are a group of people who have been profoundly damaged on a basic psychological level by the racism, discrimination, and disempowerment that has characterized Euro-Canadian/Aboriginal relations in Canada. According to Alfred,

> Long-term subjugation has a series of effects on both the mind and the soul. We must recognize and take seriously the effects of colonial oppression on both individual and collective levels. In many people's view, political and economic

problems are less urgent than the damage to our psychological health. As the psychologist Eduardo Duran has characterized the problem: "Once a group of people have been assaulted in a genocidal fashion, there are psychological ramifications. With the victim's complete loss of power comes despair, and the psyche reacts by internalizing what appears to be genuine power—the power of the oppressor. The internalizing process begins when Native American people internalize the oppressor, which is merely a caricature of the power actually taken from Native American people. At this point, the self-worth of the individual and/or group has sunk to a level of despair tantamount to self-hatred. This self-hatred can be either internalized or externalized." (1999: 34–5)

Alfred argues that "denied, medicated, rationalized, ignored, or hated, this is a reality that affects all indigenous people to one degree or another" (1999: 35).

Another frequently articulated version of the weight of history argument is that there is a "residential school" mentality or syndrome that continues to plague individual Aboriginal people and wider Aboriginal communities (Thatcher, 2004: 161; Truth and Reconciliation Commission, 2015). Even though residential schools began to be phased out in the 1950s, one of the long-term negative consequences of the system was that it did not allow for a normal family life. In this context, parents did not have the opportunity to raise their children independently of government intervention, and children did not learn normal parenting skills when they were being raised. According to Kim Anderson,

> For a full century, native children were removed from biological parents and placed in residential schools where they often learned negative behaviours related to sex, intimacy and love. Many learned their dysfunction in foster homes where they were abused. We are seeing the effects of history pass down through the generations. . . . Many of our families have no means to teach intimacy and love because they were not party to these lessons themselves. (2000: 200)

There are, however, conservative versions of the "weight of history" argument as well. According to John Richards (1995), one of the main reasons for the continuing high rate of Aboriginal poverty is the historical generosity that the Canadian welfare state has displayed toward Aboriginal people.

> Whatever the historical injustices [that Aboriginal people have experienced], the relative generosity of transfer programs available to aboriginals has become part of the explanation for—not the solution to—aboriginal poverty. . . . Whether they be aboriginals or not, the psychological effect on people from long-term dependence on transfer income is damaging. . . . Among men, particularly, long-term welfare induces a loss of self-respect, increased rates of depression, and a tendency towards self-destructive activities (such as substance abuse and family violence). (1995: 161)

Political scientist Thomas Flanagan argues that by providing what he sees as overly generous and virtually unlimited support through a variety of social assistance measures, the federal government is part of the problem. According to Flanagan, the "problem" is that Aboriginal people

> have little sense of real-world trade-offs because everything their governments do for them is paid for by other people. They never have to give up anything in order to get additional programs. If they had to make the same claims that other Canadians routinely make, they would, I predict, take the axe to many of the government programs proliferating luxuriantly in their communities. (2000: 197–8)

Whereas liberal versions of the weight of history argument see "compensation," more government intervention, and better policies and programs as the solution to many of the problems facing First Nations and Aboriginal communities (Thatcher, 2004: 134–7), conservative versions see the solution as lying in less government intervention and allowing market forces to solve problems.

Clearly, history matters. Historical conditions and past policies and practices, as we have seen in Chapter 3, have long-lasting consequences and shape current policies, practices, and institutions. At the same time, care needs to be taken in invoking "history" as the explanation for contemporary maladies and conditions. Some historical explanations lack specificity, and broad generalizations about historical policies are sometimes used as a substitute for concrete analysis of the specific connections between particular social behaviours and historical conditions. For example, while many individuals were undoubtedly damaged by the residential school system, at its zenith in the 1940s and 1950s, less than one half of school-age First Nations children were enrolled in residential schools; a larger number were enrolled in some type of day school run either by the federal government or a provincial school board. Furthermore, are people simply victims of history? Some individuals have succumbed to the weight of negativity stemming from historical forces and have internalized the prejudices of wider society by losing respect for themselves, their families, and their communities, yet others have overcome those forces (Anderson, 2000). According to Thatcher,

> The temptation of this metaphorical thinking is understandable, originating as it does in a knowledge of the actual historical record. However, in a fundamental way it also assumes and reinforces a sense of powerlessness and it can thus serve as a self-defeating prophecy. This singular blame attribution, however, completely ignores external and internal social class differences, treating all levels of reserve society in a unitary, blame-free fashion, and all levels of non-aboriginal society as being equally responsible for causing reserve problems. (2004: 135)

As Thatcher suggests, it is not enough to simply invoke abstract, metaphorical notions of "history" as the explanation for current social conditions and social relations. While "history" is without question highly relevant to the present, concrete connections need to be made between those historical conditions and individual biographies.

Stratification and Differences within Aboriginal Communities

One of the problems involved in comparing Aboriginal and non-Aboriginal people along traditional dimensions of income, education, and occupation, and then offering broad explanations of those differences is that such comparisons tend to homogenize both the category of "Aboriginal" and the category of "non-Aboriginal." That is, by focusing on differences in average rates of educational achievement, income, labour force participation, incarceration, health status, and other variables between Aboriginal and non-Aboriginal people, there is a tendency to blur differences within the Aboriginal population of Canada. This kind of statistical benchmarking (Li, 2003) can also unwittingly contribute to reinforcing outmoded stereotypes, which the comparisons are often meant to undermine. These comparisons are usually made with good intentions in that they are intended as a way of demonstrating how bad the situation is for Aboriginal people and asserting that it can improve through the provision of more resources, better policies, and better government treatment. However, the comparison and a constant focus on the negative aspects of Aboriginal people's lives and conditions tend to imply that Aboriginal people and communities rarely if ever do anything right, and that all Aboriginal people occupy the same decrepit positions in Canadian society.

An alternative way of looking at Aboriginal conditions is to look more closely at within-group differences. Aboriginal people represent another instance in which intersectional analysis of gender, "race," and class has the potential to be fruitful. Often, Aboriginal scholars are most aware of social, political, and economic differences and conflicts within Aboriginal communities and as a result are the most articulate advocates of intersectional analysis. A number of social divisions within Aboriginal communities have been identified (between urban and reserve-based First Nations; between different socio-legal categories of status Indian; between the interests of Métis, Inuit, and Indians), and we have already touched on some of these divisions in earlier sections of this chapter. In the remainder of the chapter, we want to focus on two main axes of difference: gender differences and differences between "leaders and led."

Gender

Aboriginal communities are no different from other minority and "mainstream" communities to the extent that gender divisions and politics are important lines of difference.

One of the first public manifestations of gender divisions within First Nations communities came in the 1970s in the context of Indian women challenging the sexually discriminatory nature of the enfranchisement provisions of the Indian Act. Ironically, some of the male leaders of the Assembly of First Nations and other Aboriginal organizations were originally against changing the Indian Act to address the issue of sexual discrimination. Some argue that their resistance was rooted in continuing sexist attitudes within a largely male leadership (Silman, 1987: 200). Others suggest that the AFN leaders opposed the changes because they were lobbying for a complete rewriting of the Indian Act and not just piecemeal changes. This issue, they argue, needed to be negotiated in the context of a wider re-evaluation of the Indian Act. Furthermore, the largely male leadership of the organization was also concerned about the financial implications of large numbers of individuals having their Indian status reinstated; without corresponding increases in funding, an already small pie would have to be cut into ever-smaller pieces. Whatever the explanation for the male leadership's opposition to reforming a clearly unjust situation, one of the long-term consequences of that opposition was the creation of a more politicized attitude among First Nations women and a recognition that the interests of male First Nations leaders were not necessarily the same as theirs.

The small number of female chiefs is, according to Anderson (2000: 218), "largely due to the imposed Euro-Canadian political system that only validates the voices of men by handing them exclusive authority over the governance of our nations." According to Anderson (2000: 239), the colonial system played a fundamental role not only in reorganizing gender relations within Aboriginal communities but also in distorting certain aspects of Aboriginal male existence and power. While elevating men politically, the system also disempowered and emasculated them:

> Native women acknowledge the suffering of Native men, interpreting those who engage in dysfunctional behaviour as products of colonization. Many Native women have been able to continue their traditional responsibilities of creation and nurturing, but many men's responsibilities have been greatly obscured by the colonial process. It is more difficult for men than it is for women to define their responsibilities in the contemporary setting and reclaim their dignity and sense of purpose. . . . Our communities moved away from the land where men could hunt and provide into a more urban, industrialized society where men had to "find jobs" to provide. And of course, racist barriers kept Native men out of jobs. The introduction of the social welfare system intensified dependency that Native men had never experienced before. These are the things that pushed the men further away from their roles. (Anderson, 2000: 239)

Cora Voyageur's (2008) groundbreaking study of female chiefs in Canada examines how they negotiate their multiple roles, and how they navigate issues of gender, "race," and politics. She documents how female chiefs advance the interests of their respective communities but at the same time overcome sexism within First Nations and wider Canadian society, racism from the wider society, and their own self-doubts. She argues that like other women in positions of political responsibility, they struggle with maintaining a balance between work, family, and personal life.

Leaders and Led

Aboriginal leadership has recently come under attack from a variety of quarters. Sadly, stories of alleged corruption and the mismanagement of band funds are common in the media. On occasion, band chiefs and council members are accused of corruption and not acting in the interest of their communities. At the same time, these sensational cases may be overblown and attract attention only because they play on already existing negative attitudes toward Aboriginal people. Communities that are run honestly, efficiently, and with the collective good in mind are simply not newsworthy.

Menno Boldt (1993) argues that the main division within Indian communities is between "elite" Indians who control Indian governments and the mass of Indians who are outside of the small circles that control political and economic resources on reserves.

Others cast the divisions between leaders and led within Aboriginal communities more in terms of the concept of social class. A number of versions of class-based theory have been used to understand the position of Aboriginal people in Canadian society.

Howard Adams (1999), a Métis academic, has put forward a two-class model. For Adams, there is an Aboriginal bourgeoisie and an Aboriginal underclass. Even though they face certain common issues and are both subject to the racism of the larger white society (Adams, 1999: 111), these two classes have complex relationships with each other and with elements of white society.

Adams further divides the Aboriginal bourgeoisie into three segments. The first is broadly defined as "elite leaders" of national Aboriginal organizations such as the Assembly of First Nations, the Métis National Council, and the Congress of Aboriginal Peoples. In a rather uncomplimentary manner, he describes them as "Uncle Tomahawks" because they collaborate with white society to maintain the larger structure of racial and class privilege. The second segment consists of Aboriginal professionals and intellectuals such as lawyers, academics, teachers, and social workers. And the third consists of small business owners, government administrators, and directors of various training programs. According to Adams (1999: 118–19), the common feature among these three segments of the Aboriginal bourgeoisie is that "driven by the need to establish social status, this group strives to achieve mastery of the colonizer's cultural practices and language, while appearing authentically Aboriginal."

The Aboriginal bourgeoisie, in Adams's view, stands in opposition to the rest of the Aboriginal population, who occupy an underclass position in Canada. Their underclass position stems from their relationship to the means of production; they are the people who "do the unskilled, menial work" within a capitalist society (Adams, 1999: 111). According to Adams, the classification of the majority of Aboriginal people as part of the underclass "has no relationship to intelligence, skill, or personal qualities, rather it has to do with race and oppression."

Within Aboriginal communities, the relationship between these two classes is characterized by a combination of economic exploitation of the underclass by the bourgeoisie and a colonized psychological relationship between the two. Adams argues that Aboriginal business owners and those who control the large development corporations that have arisen in the context of land claims settlements have increasingly injected Aboriginal communities with traditional class-based conflicts that many Marxists originally thought were only endemic to white society. Adams applies the notion of a "comprador capitalist" class to the situation of the Aboriginal bourgeoisie. This comprador class acts as a go-between for "white capitalists" and government and the larger mass of the Aboriginal underclass. They owe their positions to the power of white society, and their main role is to act as agents of social control on behalf of the larger capitalist structure. In Adams's view, "Aboriginal workers are kept in rigid control through the capitalist class structure. They are confined to the bottom of the occupational ladder; as a result, few are unionized. Within the last ten years, class divisions have developed within Native communities which have resulted in even greater exploitation and control" (Adams, 1999: 124–5).

In Adams's view, complex relations of psychological exploitation supplement this economic exploitation:

> Since the Indian/Métis bourgeoisie live largely in the white middle-class society of make-believe, the masks which they wear give them a sham life-style, and conceal the feelings of inferiority and hypocrisy that haunt their inner lives. Although they loudly proclaim their Indian heritage, they desperately attempt to escape from the Aboriginal under-class. . . . In attempting to evade identification with the Indian/Métis under-class they have developed self-hatred. These Aboriginal bourgeois try to shield themselves from racial discrimination and the contempt of the white people as they struggle for assimilation. (1999: 119)

Marybelle Mitchell's (1996) analysis of the class structure within the Inuit population is somewhat less hard on the Aboriginal bourgeoisie than Adams's. Mitchell argues that what is important about the definition of social class is not so much ownership of but rather control over the means of production. She argues that the economic development corporations that have arisen as a consequence of land claims settlements are vehicles by which capitalist class relations are creeping into Inuit and other Aboriginal communities in the North. Since 1973, when the comprehensive claims process was instituted, 15 comprehensive land claims agreements have been completed, with dozens of other communities currently involved in various stages of negotiation (Frideres and Gadacz, 2012). While land claims settlements are complicated, they generally involve the exchange of vast tracts of land in return for cash payments, control over smaller allocations of land, control over wildlife management, protection of the environment, and resource royalty-sharing arrangements.

Not unlike the land surrender treaties that were agreed to between Indians and the federal government 100 years ago, contemporary comprehensive land claims settlements are also mainly about clearing away political/legal obstacles to development and capitalist expansion. As the search for oil and gas, diamonds, gold, and other precious metals and minerals in the North intensifies, so too does the need to ensure that development takes place on a firm legal footing. As a result, since many Aboriginal communities, including the Inuit, have never formally ceded land to the Canadian state, the federal government has taken the lead in negotiating land claims settlements with Aboriginal peoples, including the Inuit, as a way of clearing away these potential political/legal obstacles to exploration and development.

Even though land claims settlements are meant, in theory, to benefit all Aboriginals who fall within the terms of reference of the settlement and are sometimes framed in terms of the need to preserve and maintain Aboriginal cultural identity and values, in practice the chief beneficiaries of the settlements are those in position to control the development corporations. Mitchell argues that patterns of ethnic relations overlap with class relations. The Inuit ruling class is a creation of the Canadian state. As a result, this ruling class lacks certain features of other capitalist classes that have more autonomy from the state. At the same time, they are also an ethnically subordinate ruling class:

> Inuit have many interests in common with the working class, and we can begin to talk about Inuit participation in the ruling class as one effect of the institution of development corporations. There is within the political structures available to Inuit and the development corporation an element or "class" that controls labour, means of production, allocation of resources, and investments *in alliance* with an outside ruling class; but to reiterate, *because* they are Inuit, it is an unequal alliance. All Inuit are shareholders in the development corporations, but a class of people is benefiting disproportionately. They do not own the corporations, but they control them. (Mitchell, 1996: 404)

This approach emphasizes the importance of historical conditions, but at the same time it does not portray Aboriginal people as victims of historical forces over which they have no control. Some have access to resources, power, and influence; some have different values, and so on. A focus on class and other inequalities within Aboriginal communities is not meant to foment divisions and discontent within these communities. Divisions and discontent already exist, and the tools to better understand those divisions are needed.

Summary

In this chapter, we have focused on three main issues. First, we sought to understand the complexity of Aboriginal identity and the interrelationship among externally imposed labels, internally adopted identities, and the social conflicts arising from different ways of understanding Aboriginal identity. Second, we provided documentation on some of the main socioeconomic differences between Aboriginal and non-Aboriginal people and critically reviewed some of the main explanations for those differences. Finally, we considered the problem of divisions within Aboriginal communities in Canada and focused on emergent gender and leadership-related concerns.

Questions for Critical Thought

1. What evidence is there that the federal government continues to pursue a policy of assimilation in relation to First Nations? Is it accurate to call Bill C-31 an "abocide" bill?

2. Why are debates about Aboriginal identity important? Are these debates simply matters of political correctness?

3. What are the strengths and weaknesses of the four explanations that have been offered to explain the socio-economic and health status differences between Aboriginal people and non-Aboriginal people?

4. What are some of the ways that First Nations communities are internally stratified? Are these differences less important than collective differences between First Nations and non-First Nations?

Debate Questions

1. Are cultural or structural explanations better in explaining the socio-economic differences between Aboriginal and non-Aboriginal people? Why? Could they both be right? In what respects?

2. Are cultural or structural explanations better in explaining the socio-economic differences that exist among Aboriginal groups? Why? Could they both be right? In what respects?

3. Are you convinced by socio-biological explanations of Aboriginal conditions? Justify your response.

4. Many Aboriginal groups advocate self-determination. Is this feasible? Think of the ways that this can be accomplished within the framework of Canadian federalism.

5. Is social inequality within Aboriginal people different than social inequalities within other groups in Canada? In what respects?

Annotated Additional Readings

Cannon, Martin, and Lina Sunseri, eds. 2011. *Racism, Colonialism, and Indigeneity*. Toronto: Oxford University Press. An edited collected of articles written primarily by Aboriginal scholars who explore the interrelationship between racism and colonialism and how these forces shaped the lives and experiences of indigenous people in Canada.

Truth and Reconciliation Commission of Canada. 2015. *Honouring the Truth, Reconciling for the Future: Summary of the Final Report of the Truth and Reconciliation Commission of Canada*. Ottawa: Truth and Reconciliation Commission of Canada. This is an in-depth report of the Commission's investigation into the experiences of Indian children and families of the residential school system. The numerous stories of abuse—physical, sexual, and emotional—that occurred in the schools makes for difficult but essential reading for all Canadians.

Voyageur, Cora. 2008. *Firekeepers of the Twenty-First Century: First Nations Women Chiefs*. Montreal and Kingston: McGill-Queen's University Press. An in-depth study of First Nations women as they increasingly take on formal leadership roles within their communities. The study examines how women negotiate the overlapping worlds of gender, "race," and reserve politics.

White, Jerry P., et al. 2006–2010. *Aboriginal Policy Research*. Toronto: Thompson Educational. This is a 10-volume series of publications that contains a wealth of data and analysis of various demographic, social, and policy-related issues concerning Aboriginal people in Canada.

Widdowson, Frances, and Albert Howard. 2008. *Disrobing the Aboriginal Industry: The Deception Behind Indigenous Cultural Preservation*. Montreal and Kingston: McGill-Queen's University Press. A highly controversial account of the way that land claims settlements and Aboriginal self-government arguably contribute to the reproduction of a variety of social problems in First Nations communities.

Related Websites

Assembly of First Nations
www.afn.ca
This is the website for the national organization representing status Indians/First Nations in Canada.

Indigenous and Northern Affairs Canada
www.aadnc-aandc.gc.ca
Previously known as known as Aboriginal Affairs and Northern Development Canada (AADNC), this is the federal government department responsible for administration of Indian policy in Canada.

Indian Residential Schools Settlement
www.residentialschoolsettlement.ca/english.html
This website outlines the mechanisms for the resolution of claims stemming from the residential school experience.

Métis National Council
www.metisnation.ca
The Métis National Council is the organization representing the interests of Métis people in Canada.

Truth and Reconciliation Commission of Canada
www.trc.ca
This is the website for the Truth and Reconciliation Commission of Canada, which investigated the experiences of First Nations people of the residential school system.

9

Transnationals or Diasporas?
Ethnicity and Identity in a Globalized Context

Learning Objectives

In this chapter you will learn that

- rationales have been offered to support the concepts of diaspora and transnationalism.
- definitions for the concepts of transnationalism and diaspora have developed over time.
- there is a Canadian diaspora.
- some of the rationales advanced in favour of the concepts of diaspora and transnationalism are problematic.
- transnationalism among immigrants is not historically new.
- legal distinctions between immigrants and migrant workers are still very important.
- there are numerous examples of transnational practices among immigrants and ethnic community members.

Introduction

In the summer of 2009, French president Nicolas Sarkozy, in his first state-of-the-nation address to both the National Assembly and the Senate, explained that in his view,

> The burka is not a religious problem, it's a question of liberty and women's dignity. It's not a religious symbol, but a sign of subservience and debasement. I want to say solemnly, the burka is not welcome in France. In our country, we can't accept women prisoners behind a screen, cut off from all social life, deprived of all identity. That is not our idea of freedom. (cited in Poirier, 2009)

According to one report, his statement about the burka won "rapturous applause and there is little doubt that an overwhelming majority of the French agreed with his every word" (Poirier, 2009). Earlier in the year, 60 members of the French National Assembly demanded that a debate be held about banning the burka and *niqab* in public; Sarkozy's speech lent unambiguous support for having a debate that would hopefully lead to a ban on wearing that particular form of Muslim women's attire. At the time, many commentators noted the difference in reaction such a legislative plan would garner in countries like Britain and Canada. Commentators noted that "similar debates are impossible in Britain," pointing out that three years earlier, Labour MP and former foreign secretary Jack Straw was criticized for his statement that the burka was a "visible statement of separation and difference" (Poirier, 2009). Many were further outraged when he explained that he had asked Muslim women to remove their veils when they came to visit his constituency office in Lancashire because the veil impeded communication. Canadian columnist Margaret Wente said, "No politician would dare say anything like that in Canada, where all diversity is supposed to be equally good. He'd be denounced for racism and intolerance" (Wente, 2009).

Fast-forward six years. During the 2015 federal election, the *niqab* (and burka) became the subject of considerable debate in Canada. In its bid to find a wedge issue to bolster its core supporters, the ruling Conservatives proposed to introduce an amendment to the Zero Tolerance for Barbaric Cultural Practices Act and establish a "tip line" so that Canadians could report such practices to the police (see Chapter 7). Though not without some support, the idea was widely condemned by Canadians as a thinly veiled form of race-baiting and as stoking fears about Muslim integration into Canadian society. The fact that many Canadians stood up and spoke out against such a proposal as racist is a good thing, and is a testament to the continued support for the values of multiculturalism in Canada.

Many other countries are currently in the throes of similar debates about the burka, the wider presence of Muslim communities, and their alleged disinterest in integrating and conforming to "Western" norms and values. As one British politician explained, "Muslims have become the new political black," implying that the previous waves of anti-immigrant hysteria in Europe that focused on black immigrants has now shifted to Muslims. The Netherlands, for example, has retreated from its past commitment to multiculturalism, and now emphasizes the importance of integrating immigrants. The retreat from multiculturalism in the Netherlands in the 1990s is widely attributed to the perception in that country that Muslim immigrants and their children were not integrating into Dutch society, and that steps needed to be taken to ensure that the Muslim newcomers and their descendants are buying into Dutch values and norms. As a result, its new integration policy requires that newcomers pass an exam that proves their Dutch language skills and their knowledge of Dutch culture and society before they arrive. Once they are admitted, newcomers have to attend civic integration courses (Bruquetas-Callejo, Gares-Mascarenas, Penninx, and Scholten, 2006).

Somewhat ironically, one of the places where wearing the burka is generally a non-issue is the United States (Joppke, 2009). One might think that as the country targeted by the 9/11 attacks, the November 2015 attack in San Bernardino, California, and the June 2016 mass shooting at an LGBT nightclub in Orlando, Florida, this would be one of the places leading the current charge against public displays of Islam that involve women wearing veils or burkas. Security certainly has been tightened at the US border; it is undoubtedly the case that Muslims are targeted at the border and by other security forces, and some right-wing commentators have raised concerns about the wisdom of admitting Muslims as immigrants to the country. Republican presidential candidate Donald Trump has called for a complete ban on Muslim immigration to the US "until our country's representatives can figure out what is going on," and many Americans seem to agree (Diamond, 2015). However, so far, there is little public debate in the country about what Muslim women and girls can and cannot wear in public in part because of the value Americans place on religious and other forms of liberty (Joppke, 2009).

Because of the attacks in Orlando and San Bernardino, Americans may be starting to worry more about Muslims (regardless of whether they are immigrants or born in the US) and whether Muslim women and girls wear a veil. But until 2015, they were far more worried about Mexican immigration and the negative consequences that both legal and illegal immigration from Mexico was having on the country than they were about Muslim immigration. Harvard University professor Samuel Huntington, famous for his "clash of civilizations" thesis in the 1990s, argued before his death in 2008 that the biggest threat the United States faces comes from Mexican and Latin American immigrants and their descendants. In his view, "The single most immediate and serious challenge to America's traditional identity comes from the immense and continuing immigration from Latin America, and especially from Mexico" (Huntington, 2004: 32). His concern about Latin American immigration was framed in a broader context where the Anglo-Protestant culture of the United States is under assault by

> the popularity in intellectual and political circles of the doctrines of multiculturalism and diversity; the rise of group identities based on race, ethnicity, and gender over national identity; the impact of transnational cultural **diasporas;** the expanding number of immigrants with dual nationalities and dual loyalties; and the growing salience for US intellectual, business and political elites of cosmopolitanism and transnational identities. The United States' national identity, like that of other nation-states, is challenged by the forces of globalization as well as the needs that globalization produces among people for smaller and more meaningful "blood and belief" identities. (Huntington, 2004: 32)

For Huntington, Mexican immigrants and their descendants, with their high birth rates and apparent disinterest in assimilating, constitute a kind of ticking time bomb; they represent the quintessential unassimilated dangerous immigrant that does not display full and complete loyalty to the US and is bent on changing America rather than changing to become American.

While the nature of anti-immigrant discourse varies from country to country, there is a similarity in the underlying concerns. The debates about burkas, veils, and the wider Muslim presence in Europe, and about Mexican and Latin American immigrants in the United States betray common fears about the apparent lack of assimilation or integration of certain newcomers, and the seeming new importance of dual political and ideological loyalties among these new waves of immigrants. In both of these contexts, previous waves of immigrants are portrayed as "good immigrants" because they seemingly assimilated and integrated, and left behind their "old world" identities, cultures, and political battles. The new immigrants, whether Muslim, Mexican, or black, are "bad immigrants" because they do not integrate, they retain too much of their "old world" culture and identity, and they are too preoccupied with events in their places of origin. Indeed, they may even harbour secret hatred for their countries of settlement. Within this context, state policies and practices of loosely defined "multiculturalism" have been implicated as enabling these seemingly negative developments. What is particularly galling to these commentators is that governments are encouraging these negative behaviours by their efforts to be multicultural either in policy or in practice. These seeming commonalities should lead us to think more broadly about issues of immigration, settlement, and identity formation.

In the first eight chapters of this book, we have offered a number of important conceptual distinctions and sociological perspectives in the field of "race" and ethnic relations. Some chapters have spoken of the differences between immigrants, migrants, refugees, and **illegal immigrants**. Other chapters have spoken of ethnicity, visible minorities, non-visible minorities, and "race" and racism. In much of our discussion, these concepts have overlapped.

Furthermore, even though we have touched on a number of concepts and theories in our discussion, our approach has still not covered all of the main theoretical and conceptual traditions in the field. In this final chapter, we want to broaden our discussion both conceptually and geographically. We want to consider how the recent concepts of **transnationalism** and diaspora can help to broaden our understanding of "race" and ethnic relations here in Canada, but also in other places around the world. The two concepts feature heavily in Huntington's assessment of the problem with historical patterns of Mexican immigration to the US; the new patterns and dynamics that they point to underlie many of the concerns about Muslim immigration to Europe.

This chapter aims to provide a critical appreciation of both concepts. First, we delineate some of the main similarities and differences between the concepts of *diaspora* and *transnationalism* and assess their relative strengths and weaknesses. Second, we try to offer a way of thinking about the links between the two concepts and approaches. We use instances and examples from Canada and from other countries around the world to highlight some of the main issues involved in looking at the world through these particular conceptual lenses.

The Genealogy of Diaspora and Transnationalism

Over the past 25 years, a number of social scientists have expressed dissatisfaction with the kinds of approaches to understanding ethnicity, "race," and immigration that we have outlined so far. Put simply, their argument is that in this new age of globalization, war, and seemingly intractable ethnic conflicts, we need new theories and new concepts in order to truly understand the complexities of migration, ethnic group formation, and identity maintenance and change. Some, like Andreas Wimmer and Nina Glick Schiller (2002), argue that social scientists need to move beyond what they call **methodological nationalism**, or the assumption that the things going on within the boundaries of nation-state are the natural units of analysis for research. As a result, the concepts of *diaspora* and *transnational* have become popular alternatives to many of the terms we have used so far to describe people who have moved abroad, their patterns of settlement, their identities, and their communities. Many scholars now talk about "transmigrants" (Basch et al., 1994), "transnational immigrants" (Glick Schiller, 1999), "transnational communities" (Van Hear, 1998), "ethno-national diasporas" (Sheffer, 2003), "ethnic diasporas" (Tatla, 1999), or "transnational ethnic diasporas." Some, like Huntington, regard the apparent growth of the new patterns of migration and settlement described by these concepts with alarm. For others, these new patterns are cause for celebration as they represent a breakdown of borders and barriers, and the opportunity for the creation of new, more cosmopolitan identities.

The perceived failures of so-called **ethnicity and "race" paradigms** include their primary focus on processes such as "assimilation, integration and accommodation or ethnic conflict and exclusion" within the nation-state (Anthias, 1998: 559). According to Anthias, "The terms 'ethnicity' and 'race' turn the analytical gaze to processes of inter-group relations within particular territorial boundaries" (1998: 559) rather than on the ways that inter-group relations are shaped by forces and conditions outside of particular national borders (see also Brubaker, 2005). In other words, Anthias would argue that in order to truly understand the structure and dynamics of groups like Croatians, Sikhs, or Muslims in Canada or in other countries of settlement, one needs to understand where they come from, how they maintain contact with their ancestral homelands, and how they relate to members of their respective communities in other countries of settlement.

In justifying the use of the concept of *transnationalism*, Basch et al. (1994) similarly argue that the traditional terms in the sociology of migration literature that are used to understand individuals who have moved abroad, which include *immigrant* and *migrant*, no longer capture a complex social reality. In their view,

> The word "immigrant" evokes images of permanent rupture, of the abandonment of old patterns of life and the painful learning of a new culture and often a new language. . . . The popular image of immigrant is one of people who have come to stay, having uprooted themselves from their old society in order to make for themselves a new home and adopt a new country to which they will pledge allegiance. Migrants, on the other hand, are conceived of as transients who have come only to work; their stay is temporary and eventually they will return home or move on. Yet it has become increasingly obvious that our present conceptions of "immigrant" and "migrant," anchored in the circumstances of earlier historical moments, no

longer suffice. Today, immigrants develop networks, activities, patterns of living, and ideologies that span their home and host society. (Basch et 1994: 3–4)

Clearly, the intellectual justifications for both the concept of *diaspora* and the concept of *transnationalism* point in the same direction. Both concepts, proponents argue, better capture the importance of real and imagined places of origin in immigrant and ethnic groups, lives, and identities as well as the complex interactions between "here" and "there" for individuals, families, and communities that have moved abroad.

A number of efforts have recently been made to define, operationalize, theorize, and critique the two concepts (Akenson, 1995; Brubaker, 2005; Cohen, 1995, 2008; Vertovec, 1999; Glick Schiller, 1999; Reis, 2004; Satzewich and Wong, 2006). However, there has been less interest in systematically analyzing the relationship between the concepts of *diaspora* and *transnationalism*. While Brubaker (2005: 6) notes in passing that there has been a fusing of the literature on transnationalism and diaspora in recent years, he does not systematically analyze this trend. Do these concepts describe the same social reality, or do they try to capture different aspects of social life? If there is a difference, then how should researchers conceptualize the relationship between the terms *diaspora* and *transnationalism*? What are some of the strengths and weaknesses of diaspora and transnational studies? And do these approaches really constitute effective alternatives to the approaches and concepts that we have outlined so far in this book?

Even though the two concepts emerged out of similar critiques, one major difference between them is the extent to which they have permeated popular consciousness and wider public discourse. The concept of diaspora has become so popular—and elastic—that groups outside of an immigrant or ethnic nexus have adopted the label or have been described as such (Brubaker, 2005). A search of the Internet will find references to, among others, a social networking website; a website devoted to diseases spread through airline travel; a *Battlestar Galactica* game; a "gay and lesbian diaspora"; a US "pro-war" biker diaspora; various diaspora hair salons, funeral parlours, and restaurants; and a "mountain biker diaspora" in White Plains, New York, that "wandered nomadically from shop to shop looking for good, friendly advice without attitude, fair prices without a bargain-basement atmosphere, and a fine selection of merchandise." Many immigrant and ethnic groups now define themselves as a diaspora (Brubaker, 2005). Furthermore, groups that once rejected the label now routinely use the term to describe their larger community of co-ethnics who have settled abroad. For example, in the 1970s, Ukrainians in North America generally avoided use of the term *diaspora*. At that time, the concept had negative connotations in that it was seen as a Soviet-inspired term meant to discredit Ukrainian and other émigré nationalists living abroad who were awaiting, and in some cases actively working toward, the overthrow of the Soviet Union. The same sentiment seemed to characterize the Ethiopian government's understanding of its diaspora in the early 1980s, which it saw as being made up of "unpatriotic" and disorganized opposition groups. As a result, it regarded with suspicion any overseas involvement in homeland issues (Addis Fortune, 2015). As an alternative, Ukrainians at the time tended to define themselves as being "in the emigration" rather than as a "diaspora." Now, however, the concept is embraced, and many Ukrainians and their organizations in North America wrap themselves in a diaspora label (Satzewich, 2002). Many governments around the world, Ukraine included, now have various policies and programs, and even departments and ministries, to help them manage relations with their respective diasporas.

In contrast, the concept of transnationalism has generally not filtered down into the vocabulary of the non-scholarly community or into immigrant and ethnic community organizations. Indeed, it is difficult to find any statements by leaders of ethnic or immigrant organizations or communities that describe their collectivity as "transnational."

This begs the question of why there is a difference in the way that the two concepts have filtered down into the individuals, communities, and organizations that academics study. In other words, why have ethnic, immigrant, and a range of other groups adopted the diaspora label to describe themselves, and, conversely, why does the transnational label seem to carry less political currency than the term *diaspora*?

There are a number of hypotheses. Robin Cohen (1997: x) provides one possibility, arguing that adoption of the label *diaspora* may be "functional" for groups in the sense that it allows for "a certain degree of social distance to displace a high degree of psychological alienation" that immigrants experience in their countries of settlement. In other words, groups like the Sikhs may define themselves as a diaspora community because they do not feel as though they are full and equal members of the countries in which they have settled.

A second possible reason why the concept of diaspora has been widely adopted by ethnic and immigrant groups is that it carries certain *positive* connotations that derive from the Jewish historical experience. As many have noted, Jews have been defined as the "classic" diaspora (Mandelbaum, 2000; Cohen, 2008). Despite the Jews' history of persecution and suffering, some ethnic elites outside of Jewish communities may perceive them as having cracked the problem of successfully maintaining group boundaries, ties to their ancestral homeland(s), and a relatively viable religious, educational, and community life in various countries of settlement. Arguably, for at least some leaders of ethnic communities, Jews are akin to a "model minority" whose real and apparent success in integrating into their respective societies and maintaining a Jewish identity and vibrant community life outside of Israel should be emulated (Weinfeld, 2001: 7).

Third, it may be that the concept of *diaspora*, with its emphasis on different forms of traumatic dispersal and the actual and potential victimization faced by earlier generations of co-ethnics, may play a role in helping contemporary community leaders and elites to try to maintain group boundaries and cultivate solidarity within the larger imagined community. That is, the promotion and cultivation of victim narratives, along with adopting the diaspora label itself, may be strategies that elites employ to develop and sustain community solidarity, collective identities, and group boundaries (Brubaker, 2005). Writing about Kurds in Sweden and France, Khalid Khayati argues,

> By maintaining that "we are all Kurd," "we belong all to an oppressed nation no matter where we live" and "we do not belong here because here is not our country," the advocates of the popular victim diaspora discourse, who can be found in all Kurdish political organizations and socio-cultural institutions and networks in Western societies, depict diasporan Kurds as members of a homogenous community, who carry out the social, cultural and political activities for the good of the Kurdish "homeland" in order to make it ready for the "reception of its returnees." (2008: 4)

In contrast, the concept of *transnationalism* does not have the same rhetorical value and is not saturated with the same deep historical and contemporary narratives about trauma, victimization, and survival despite the odds. Because of this, *transnationalism* may have less political resonance within immigrant and ethnic communities and wider publics, and this may account for its relative absence in the claims-making process.

The various efforts undertaken to define and theorize the two concepts have a number of nuances. The next section of this chapter will not review all of the subtleties of the different definitions and approaches (see, for example, Anthias, 1998; Vertovec, 1999; Smith, 1999). Instead, we focus on what we think are good representative definitions of each concept and provide relevant examples to highlight how the approaches and concepts are used to better understand the world.

Diasporas

Sociologist Robin Cohen (2008; see also Safran, 1991) offers one of the most comprehensive and influential definitions of *diaspora* and an extensive argument elaborating how and why the concept can be helpful in understanding immigrants and their descendants.

Cohen uses the cases of the Afro-Caribbean, British, Armenian, Chinese, Jewish, Lebanese, and Sikh communities to construct both an ideal type of diaspora and a typology of different kinds of diasporas. He suggests that diasporas "normally" exhibit several of the following features:

- dispersal from an original homeland, often traumatic;
- alternatively, expansion from a homeland in search of work, in pursuit of trade, or to further colonial ambitions;
- a collective memory and myth about the homeland;
- idealization of the supposed ancestral home;
- a return movement;
- strong ethnic group consciousness sustained over time;

- a troubled relationship with host societies;
- a sense of solidarity with co-ethnic members in other societies;
- the possibility of a distinctive creative, enriching life in tolerant host countries (Cohen, 2008: 161–2).

Though an important element in Cohen's (2008) definition is forcible and traumatic dispersal from an ancestral home, diasporas can also be made up of mass movements of people who move for economic reasons, such as a search for work or trading partners. Political persecution is therefore not the only precondition for diaspora formation.

According to Cohen, the type of diaspora a group becomes depends largely on their initial reasons for leaving. **Victim diasporas**, such as the Jews and Armenians, as well as the Vietnamese boatpeople who left after the war in Vietnam ended and Syrian refugees who have fled the ongoing conflict in their country, are formed as a result of the traumatic political or military events that occurred in their homeland and resulted in large-scale and widespread dispersal. **Imperial diasporas** are formed out of the colonial or military ambitions of world powers. Despite the cultural differences between the Scots, English, and Irish, Cohen argues that people from the United Kingdom who moved overseas to places like Canada formed a larger British imperial diaspora. Some say that there is an American diaspora (Croucher, 2012) that is between 5 and 7 million people strong and which is dispersed around the globe. Though most have not been deliberately sent abroad by their government, their presence in other countries may arguably help to further solidify American influence around the world. **Labour diasporas** consist of groups who move mainly in search of wage labour. They include the Turks who, after the Second World War, emigrated to a variety of countries in Europe, North America, and the Middle East. The thousands of people who have moved from Ukraine to European Union countries like Portugal and Spain over the past decade and one half are also arguably starting to constitute themselves as a labour diaspora. **Trade diasporas**, like those formed by the Chinese merchants who emigrated to southeast Asia in the nineteenth and early twentieth centuries, consist of people who left their homelands to pursue opportunities as movers of goods and services in the emerging system of international trade. Today, individuals from Otavalo, a small community in Ecuador, have been termed a *trade diaspora* for their role in marketing and organizing the availability of South American–style handicrafts (blankets, sweaters, tuques, mittens, music, and jewelry) around the world (Kyle, 1999). And, finally, Cohen develops the notion of a **cultural diaspora** to characterize the migration and settlement experiences of migrants of African descent from the Caribbean after the Second World War. Cohen (2008: 18) considers these migrants as the paradigmatic case of people who have developed a unique culture and identity out of the influences of Africa, the Caribbean, and their new countries of settlement.

One of the reasons that Cohen's delineation of an ideal type of diaspora is useful is that it provides social scientists with a conceptual framework to study ethnic communities in their totality. It is possible to use this approach to socio-logically analyze the extent to which communities conform to or deviate from the ideal type and to offer theoretical explanations for these patterns. This ultimately helps to illuminate and understand the dynamics of ethnic community life. As we discussed in the previous section, Jewish communities outside of Israel are often considered to be "classic" victim diasporas. Thus, it is not surprising that Cohen (2008) argues that Jews display many of the features of his ideal type. At the same time, many other diaspora communities share elements of the Jewish historical experience. Let us draw out some of the aspects of Cohen's ideal type.

Regarding the place of return movements within diasporas, Cohen suggests that they are the product of a complicated sense of attachment to ancestral home-lands and government incentives. Return movements can take many forms. In Canada, for example, the federal government launched the Canada Research Chairs Program in 2000 to help bolster the country's research capacity. The program appears to have been designed, in part, to entice prominent Canadian researchers who have established successful research careers outside of the country back to Canada (Innovation, Science and Economic Development Canada, 2014). The Israeli Law of Return provides that Jews from anywhere in the world have a right to move to Israel to live and work. Many Jews have taken advantage of this, particularly when incidents of anti-Semitism erupt in the countries where they live (Schoenfeld, Shaffir, and Weinfeld, 2006). Jews in Russia and other countries of the former Soviet Union have also taken advantage of the Law of Return to move to Israel; it is estimated that in the 1990s, some 800,000 Jews left countries in the former Soviet Union and moved to Israel. Many other Jews return to Israel to visit family and friends or to discover their roots. Organizations like Birthright encourage temporary returns to help individuals living in Canada, the United States, and elsewhere sustain a Jewish identity, learn about Jewish history, and maintain contacts with an ancestral homeland.

Other countries around the world have also encouraged members of their respective diasporas to return "home." Some countries, like India, encourage return because they value the business acumen and capital of individuals who have lived abroad (Bose, 2007). According to a 2000 strategy in the Indian state of Gujarat, "we would appeal to their [non-resident Indians] emotions and ask them to lend for development in the motherland" (Bose, 2007: 178). Sometimes, return is envisioned as only temporary and is simply meant to increase tourist revenue. At other times, states encourage skilled professionals like doctors and nurses who have emigrated abroad to return "home" to help staff hospitals and medical clinics temporarily.

In yet other cases some governments encourage the permanent return of co-ethnics who have settled abroad because their population growth rates are low and/or declining. The Scottish government has recently developed a "diaspora strategy," drawing insights and inspiration from the case of Ireland, which is seen to have successfully capitalized on its relationship with the Irish diaspora, and which, until the recent global economic troubles, saw a significant return movement of individuals with Irish ancestry to Ireland.

In his study of how the Sierra Leonean community in London, England, helped in the battle against the Ebola outbreak in that country in 2014, Rubyan-Ling (2015) shows that the diaspora helped provide financial and material support for various treatment strategies. Even more, through cell phones, computers, and communications applications like Facebook and WhatsApp, members of the diaspora were able to communicate with friends, relatives, and colleagues to challenge rumours about the disease and provide advice about ways to prevent its spread. He shows in particular how diaspora members of the Kono District Development Association (Kono is a district in eastern Sierra Leone) living in England were able to communicate with local leaders to help coordinate public health strategies. As explained by one member of the association,

> We spoke to the paramount chiefs—you see we have 14 chiefdoms in Kono and each of them have paramount chiefs, who are in charge of local administration, and oversee the welfare of the people. There is a council of paramount chiefs and so we saw this as a way of ensuring communication is passed on to others, because some of them we don't have the contact numbers.
>
> So we were able to contact the chairman of the council, and asked them to put 1 or 2 things in place, to monitor burial and to pass the information on.
>
> They were able to put in checkpoints, although it may not be effective because we don't have people to man them 24 hours a day. I'm sure most of them were manned but they don't have a lot of resources to pay people to stay there all the time. (Rubyan-Ling, 2015: 18)

Members of the association in England were also in close contact with various other NGOS (non-governmental organizations) and community associations in Sierra Leone during the crisis.

It is, however, important to not idealize the process of return to an ancestral homeland. Return often involves various kinds of challenges relating to reintegration into the society that individuals left a few decades, or even as little as a few years, earlier. There is, at times, a social gulf, or disconnect, when individuals return "home." Sometimes, those who have stayed behind and who did not have the opportunity to migrate abroad resent individuals who have left and have come back. Some come back with money and experiences of living abroad, and end up comparing "backward" life in the ancestral homeland with their seemingly more exciting life elsewhere. Individuals who have left and returned often do not feel comfortable because they have changed as a result of having lived in another country and find that they are not fully accepted in their old surroundings, or by their former friends and social networks. There are now many advice columns for people who are considering returning to their ancestral homeland after having spent years abroad. Case Study Box 9.1 is an excerpt from one such advice blog for "repats" (short for repatriated) people who are planning to return to Nigeria after having lived abroad.

Case Study Box 9.1 You Just Got Back? Here Are Some Tips for You

Repats fill the malls and restaurants of Lagos, so here are some tips for anyone who has recently returned from the United States or Europe. When I was growing up, IJGBs—"I just got backs"—were a rare commodity because in the '80s and '90s hardly anyone ever "got back." It made far more sense to "get away." Everyone who could and many who could not became IJWGAs: "I just wanna get aways." Life, more or less lived staring down AK-47s and in the absence of working phones, electricity, Zinger Burgers and lattes, was pretty awful. Today, it is a different story. Everyone now wants to be an IJGB. There is now even a fancy name for them: "repatriate" or "repat." Loads of Nigerians have been flooding back, tempted by Facebook photos of D'Banj shows and movie screenings and shopping malls and Lagos weddings—and, of course, by that endless stream of "Africa-rising-Nigeria-bouncing" headlines. We can safely classify IJGBs into two camps: the "Temps" and the "Stays." The Temps come every first week of December, leave just after Christmas and are responsible for the overcrowding of malls, cinemas and restaurants. They are easy to spot: shorts-and-singlet-wearing dudes and dudettes wandering around clutching water bottles and complaining about the heat. The Stays are the ones who have moved back for good. They come armed with all sorts: MBAs, non-profit passions, start-up ideas and enough impractical thinking to defuse a nuclear arsenal. It is the Stays the following advice is meant for:

- Life is tougher these days. Once upon a time your accent guaranteed you a job, the sort that came with a company car and apartment. Now you have to compete with homegrown IJGB accents, picked up from *MTV*, *Keeping Up With The Kardashians* and *Sex and the City*.
- Learn Pidgin, and please drop the IJGB accent when speaking Pidgin. Not very many things are more sickening than a gonna-wanna-Pidgin.
- Respect yourself. That means not making a fuss over sums that would be considered chicken change.
- Never forget that this is not and will never be America or London. Drop all the "in America" prefaces to rants and ramblings.
- Eat what you're given, dammit! If you're vegetarian, cook and eat at home. Don't go around complaining how hard it is to find vegetarian pepper soup in town.
- Finally, join an IJGB union. If you're too busy to face-meet to discuss the tragic impossibility of finding "real coffee" in Lagos, join an IJGB BlackBerry Messenger or WhatsApp group.

By Tolu Ogunlesi

Source: http://www.theafricareport.com/North-Africa/repats-ten-stories-of-african-diaspora-who-retunred-home.html

Cohen's ideal type of diaspora often displays a troubled relationship with otherwise tolerant and accepting "host" societies. This is relevant for Jews in the diaspora: many Jews are concerned about declining levels of tolerance in countries of settlement. As we saw in Chapter 7, there is evidence for the emergence of a new and globalized anti-Semitism and that this may lead more Jews to move to Israel. Other communities face hostility and discrimination in their respective host societies. In the 1990s, segments of the Jamaican community in Canada were vilified for their seeming contribution to a rash of drug- and gun-related violence in Toronto.

Another feature of Cohen's (2008) definition that is useful in understanding other communities is the idea that the diaspora can also be a site of creativity. Cohen argues that even though many diaspora communities have histories of traumatic dispersal from original homelands, the places where they eventually settle can also provide the basis for a vibrant and creative cultural life. Jews in the diaspora have made important contributions to education, art, music, medicine, science, and commerce around the world. Cohen (1997: 198) notes that in the early 1990s, Ali Mazrui (1990) pointed out that even though the 15 million Jews worldwide were just 0.2 per cent of the world's population, they accounted for about 25 per cent of the Nobel Prize winners. Researchers interested in other diaspora communities have also noted this seemingly paradoxical feature of diaspora life. Lebanese scholar Albert Hourani (1992, cited in Cohen, 2008: 94) noted that the descendants of Lebanese migrants around the world "boasted a president of Colombia, a prime minister of Jamaica, a majority leader in the US Senate, a Nobel Prize winner for medicine, a president of the [United Kingdom] Royal Society, a world famous heart surgeon and a prizewinning Lebanese-Australian novelist." Cohen (1997: 24) argues that the creativity found in many ethnic diasporas may be the result of the inevitable tensions between ethnic, national, and transnational identities.

A Canadian Diaspora?

Canadians often think of themselves as a country of immigration. As a result, it seems odd to think that there could be a "Canadian diaspora." Yet, there is evidence that Canadians also emigrate, build lives for themselves abroad, yet continue to have strong emotional attachments to Canada—their ancestral homeland (CBC News, 2015). Moreover, organizations and governments are trying to figure out ways to harness our emigrant population for Canadian interests and in doing so are trying to define these emigrants as part of a wider Canadian diaspora (Boyle and Kitchin, 2011). A recent study by the Asia Pacific Foundation estimates that in 2006 there were 2.8 million Canadians living abroad, which was roughly 9 per cent of the total Canadian population. It is estimated that over 1 million Canadians live in the US, 300,000 live in Hong Kong, 73,000 in the United Kingdom, 45,000 in Lebanon, and 27,000 in Australia. Pockets of Canadians are variously dispersed around the world in other countries like China, Egypt, Switzerland, Singapore, and Haiti. If those 2.8 million people lived in Canada, they would be our fifth-largest province (Asia Pacific Foundation, 2011: 11). The study also estimates that the majority of Canadians living overseas are Canadian-born, but that more and more naturalized Canadians (people who became Canadian as a result of moving to the country) are starting to move abroad.

But are Canadians who move abroad actually a diaspora? Jennifer Welsh, an Oxford University professor of international relations who grew up in Saskatchewan thinks so. In much the same way that other diaspora communities invoke romantic images of their distant homelands, Welsh writes:

> In the midst of the open and flat plain in southern Saskatchewan, a gravel road three kilometres long leads down into the lush green of the Qu'Appelle Valley. I have travelled this road many times during my lifetime, as it also meanders down to the Welsh family's summer cottage—which evokes warm memories of Saskatoon berry picking and late-night Scrabble games. Over the years, as I've walked along the road, I have seen multiple versions of that fantastically vast prairie sky: bright blue with a blinding sun, pink and red as the sun slowly sets, pitch black and starlit, and, of course, blurred and buzzing with mosquitoes in late June.
>
> It is here, more than anywhere, that I feel I truly belong. Years of overseas post-secondary education, air travel and remote email correspondence cannot extinguish the strong emotional attachment I have to that particular piece of land. Yet as I write, I am living, working, raising children and paying taxes in another national community. That makes me a full-fledged member of the Canadian diaspora, a group (depending on your definition) that now numbers between 2.5 million and 3 million people. (2011)

Canadians abroad may not display all of the features of Robin Cohen's ideal type of diaspora. Canadians' dispersal abroad, at least since Confederation, has not really been the result of traumatic events in Canada. Most Canadians today probably move for better opportunities abroad, adventure, or because they fall in love with a person from another country, although some, particularly immigrants who have become naturalized Canadians, no doubt move because they face obstacles to advancement in Canada. Canadians do not really face much overt discrimination or hostility in their respective countries of settlement and as a result generally do not have troubled relationships with their host countries. But Canadians may display enough of the features of Cohen's ideal type for a credible case to be made that they are a diaspora. Canadians do seem to display solidarity with other Canadians abroad, they can and do live creative, enriching lives in their countries of settlement (consider Canadian entertainers, producers, and directors in the US), they idealize the ancestral homeland, they have collective memories and myths about their Canadian homeland, and sometimes they return to the "old country." Politically speaking, there is also impetus for thinking about how the Canadian diaspora can become a more recognized part of Canadian policy and consciousness. The federal Department of Foreign

Affairs and International Trade (DFAIT) has launched discussions about what it calls Canada's "global citizens," and in part that discussion focuses on how to mobilize the Canadian diaspora to advance the country's interests abroad. Also in this context, the Asia Pacific Foundation is calling on the federal government to develop more specific policies and programs to cultivate and support our diaspora. Their argument for a Canadian diaspora strategy is outlined in Case Study Box 9.2.

Case Study Box 9.2 Learning from International Practice

A paper commissioned by the Asia Pacific Foundation of Canada surveyed models of diaspora engagement around the globe. The authors, Mark Boyle and Rob Kitchin, identified eight policy interventions that Canada could consider when developing its citizens-abroad strategy:

1. Developing an inclusive definition of Canadians Abroad. Scotland's diaspora strategy aims to include not only individuals who were born in Scotland, but also Ancestral Diaspora (individuals abroad with Scottish heritage) as well as Affinity Diaspora (individuals with connections to Scotland, but no Scottish heritage).

2. Establishing an Emigrant Support Program to extend consular service beyond reactive humanitarian support during natural disasters. Since 2004, the Government of Ireland has administered a program that provides culturally sensitive, frontline welfare services to vulnerable Irish emigrants.

3. Encouraging philanthropic giving to Canada among Canadians Abroad. Over the past 30 years, the Ireland Fund has raised more than €300 million through diaspora networks for domestic projects.

4. Targeting tourism campaigns at diaspora markets. Scotland's Homecoming 2009 was a flagship tourist campaign that sought to secure tourist visits from diasporeans and to use these visits to build longer-term relationships between Scotland and its diaspora.

5. Mapping the full range of Canadian diaspora business networks to determine if additional networks are required. If a new business network is required, Canada could examine models such as Advance Australia, Global Scot, Kea New Zealand, Indus Entrepreneurs Network, and the networks run by Enterprise Ireland.

6. Establishing a high-level forum through which prominent Canadians Abroad can contribute their expertise to Canadian matters of interest and concern. An excellent model is the World Class NZ Network, which brings together very senior and influential New Zealanders and "New Zealand–friendly" experts committed to accelerating the country's development, international competitiveness, and economic growth.

7. Honouring prominent Canadians Abroad to foster "Canadian-mindedness." On Pravasi Bharatiya Divas (Overseas Indians Day) each year, the Government

continued

of India awards overseas Indians who have contributed to enhancing the country's development and global status.

8. Considering the introduction of a new category of citizenship to balance the benefits and liabilities of the Canadians Abroad population. India has recently introduced a new category of citizenship, the Overseas Citizenship of India (OCI). This citizenship extends a number of formally designated citizenship rights to overseas Indians, but not the full set of political rights extended to citizens of India.

The full paper, "A Diaspora Strategy for Canada? Enriching Debate through Heightening Awareness of International Practice," is available at http://www.asiapacific.ca/canadiansabroad.

Source: Asia Pacific Foundation, *Canadians Abroad: Canada's Global Asset.* Asia Pacific Foundation, Vancouver, 2011, p. 57. Retrieved from http://www.asiapacific.ca/sites/default/files/canadians_abroad_final.pdf.

Transnationalism

Basch et al. define transnationalism as a way of describing certain practices in which immigrants appear to be increasingly engaged. In their view, transnationalism refers to

the processes by which immigrants forge and sustain multi-stranded social relations that link together their societies of origin and settlement. We call these processes transnationalism to emphasize that many immigrants today build social fields that cross geographic, cultural and political borders. Immigrants who develop and maintain multiple relationships—familial, economic, social, organizational, religious, and political—that span borders we call "transmigrants." . . . Transmigrants take actions, make decisions, and develop subjectivities and identities embedded in networks of relationships that connect them simultaneously to two or more nation-states. (1994: 7)

Since the publication of *Nations Unbound* by Basch, Glick Schiller, and Szanton Blanc (1994), many empirical studies have been undertaken under the banner of transnationalism, and others have reflected on wider conceptual and theoretical points (Levitt and de la Dehesa, 2003; Portes, 1999; Satzewich and Wong, 2003). Vertovec summarizes this literature by suggesting that there are a number of different ways that transnationalism is defined and analyzed within social science literature. These forms include transnationalism as social morphology or a kind of new community; transnationalism as a type of consciousness; transnationalism as a mode of cultural reproduction; transnationalism as an avenue of capital; and transnationalism as a site of political engagement (Vertovec, 1999: 455).

Transnationalism as social morphology refers to the formation of new kinds of ethnic communities. In some ways, these communities are similar to what Cohen describes as diasporas. In Vertovec's view, transnational ethnic communities are created out of a triadic relationship between globally dispersed but collectively self-identified ethnic groups, the territorial states where these groups live, and the homeland states where they or their ancestors came from (Vertovec, 1999: 449). For example, Italians who have settled outside of Italy can be characterized as a transnational community. They have a strong ethnic group identity that is sustained independently of the specific countries where they live, they have bonds of solidarity with Italians around the world, and they have complicated ties to Italy. Nicholas Harney describes the transnational connections of the Italian community in Canada in the following terms:

> [These connections] also include the personal travels of Italian Canadians to visit kin or to explore Italy with Italian-Canadian tour groups, sports teams, and student exchange programs sponsored by ethnic voluntary organizations. Some hard-working Italian Canadians who laboured, for example, in construction in Canada for thirty years, invest in land and build new homes in their village of birth. (1998:7)

Moreover, Italians living abroad are now able to vote in national elections in Italy and can elect their own legislators to represent their particular interests as a transnational community.

Transnationalism as a type of consciousness refers to the multiple and overlapping identities that individuals now possess. Simmons and Plaza (2006: 142–3) argue that in Canada, many of the children of immigrants from various countries in the Caribbean have developed co-ethnic transnational identities. These hybrid identities are reflected in their "engagement with Caribbean art, music, food, dress, religion, social norms, myths, customs and 'language'" (Simmons and Plaza, 2006: 143). At the same time, these identities are also reflected in things like language code-switching, which involves conversing in "proper" English when talking to authority figures but slipping into patois when talking to close friends. This kind of hybrid identity allows youth whose parents came from the Caribbean to engage both with Canadian society and with the real and imagined societies of their parents or grandparents. Simmons and Plaza (2006: 143) argue further that code-switching is a new form of transnational social incorporation: "one code facilitates better incorporation in mainstream Canadian institutions, jobs, and lifestyles, while the other code facilitates the development of networks of friendship and support within the community."

Some scholars within the field of transnational studies argue that this kind of code-switching, along with the broader development of hybrid, transnational identities, has its social origins in social exclusion in the country of settlement. That is, experiences of racism, social exclusion, and non-acceptance in countries like Canada, the United States, and Britain are factors that encourage members of some groups to retain their ancestral origin identities. If people are made to feel unwelcome or as not truly belonging to the imagined community of the nation, then they seek social and psychological protection and find a sense of belonging in their ethnic communities and ancestral identities (Simmons and Plaza, 2006; Faist, 2000). Though the explanations for why some young men and women who have been born and raised in Western countries travel to the Middle East to join Islamic State extremists are complex and contested, some commentators suggest that the feeling of being excluded from the mainstream is partly responsible. In 2015, a commentator in the British newspaper *The Guardian* suggested, after speaking to a group of young Muslim women in the East End of London, that

> young women in east London felt like no one was listening to them, that no one really cared about their opinions. They felt undervalued and a bit separated from the parts of society that had any influence. Compare that with what ISIS claims to offer; it says it will make teenage girls from east London a part of its "cause," valuing them and their input into society through child bearing and wife duties. (Patel, 2015)

Transnationalism as a mode of cultural reproduction, according to Vertovec (1999: 451), refers to the contemporary fluidity of constructed styles, social institutions, and everyday practices. The intermingling of cultures that is reflected in fashion, music, and films involves a complex process of give-and-take between various national and international traditions. In the area of transnational fashions, for example, scholars are interested in how forms, styles, and materials associated with nationally based heritage intersect with international styles of dress and how these new transnational styles reflect shifting identities and power relations in society (Bryden and Niessen, 1998).

The "Bollywood" film industry is a good example of what authors like Vertovec mean when they refer to transnationalism as a mode of cultural production. Though originally intended for Indian audiences, films produced in India are now widely available in North America and Europe, reflecting the ability of members of Indian communities outside of India to have access to film entertainment. This internationalization of the Bollywood film industry is also leading to changes in film styles. As more Indians in Britain and North America consume this form of entertainment, new "Western" themes, issues, and styles are being introduced into the Bollywood film industry. The worldwide success of the 2008 film *Slumdog Millionaire*, though directed by British director Danny Boyle, may be a reflection of this new internationalization and the intermingling of Hollywood with Bollywood. Musical forms and tastes are also being reconfigured as a result of complex interactions between places of origin and places of settlement. According to Tatla (1999: 68), *bhangra* music, which was originally a form of Punjabi folk dancing, has become a "byword for Asian music, especially in Britain." Tatla argues,

Although it had a humble beginning in the 1960s, several bhangra groups became quite prominent by the 1980s . . . while maintaining their regional roots in Punjabi lyrics, bhangra bands are trying to "cross over" into Western music. British bhangra groups perform in places as far apart as Los Angeles, Frankfurt, and Singapore, whereas Punjab's pop singers make regular appearances in the diaspora. (1999: 68)

When Vertovec speaks of transnationalism as an avenue of capital, he is referring to the increasing international movement of money and resources. The movement of money and resources can take many forms. There are, for example, transnational capitalists who both live their lives and make their investment decisions in the context of networks that not only span their country of origin and their country of settlement but also the globe. Wong and Ho (2006: 249–52) describe Victor Li, the eldest son of Li Ka-Shing (the ninth-richest person in the world in 2012, according to *Forbes* magazine) as one of a growing number of transnational capitalists. Li came to Canada in the 1980s and is a Canadian citizen. His migration to Canada was motivated in part by his family's desire to pursue dispersal as a way of protecting their business interests in the context of the British government's handover of Hong Kong to China in 1999. Li's business interests are both massive and diverse. His companies invest in Canada, Hong Kong, and the global marketplace. One of his conglomerates, Cheung Hong, is involved in property development, real estate, hotels, telecommunications, e-commerce, ports and related services, and energy, to name only a few. It has operations in 40 countries, employs over 175,000 people, and is ranked among the top 100 corporations in the world (Wong and Ho, 2006: 250). While the case of Victor Li may be exceptional in terms of the vast amount of wealth he controls, Wong and Ho (2006) argue that smaller-scale transnational investments on the part of other Chinese Canadians are also an important aspect of capital flows between Canada and Hong Kong, and, more recently, between Canada and mainland China.

Though there is considerable debate about why Vancouver's housing prices keep on rising, Andy Yan, an urban planning researcher, recently showed that in three of Vancouver's most expensive neighbourhoods, 66 per cent of buyers had non-anglicized Chinese names. This implied that they were new immigrants from China and that large capital flows on the part of these transnational immigrants are partly responsible for the increasingly unaffordable homes in the city. Some business analysts suggest that the crash of the Chinese stock market in late 2015 and early 2016 will only increase housing prices in Vancouver as Chinese investors seek safer investments (Shmuel, 2016).

The transnational movement of money and capital is not confined just to large corporations that invest around the world but also includes the money and resources that flow around the world from "ordinary" individuals in support of their families and friends. For many developing countries around the world, including some of the emerging superpowers, remittances are an important part of their respective gross domestic product (GDP). As Table 9.1 shows, India and China each

Table 9.1   Top 10 Migrant Remittance Receiving Countries, 2014 (US$ millions)

Country	US$ millions	% of gross domestic product (GDP)
India	70,389	3.7
China	64,140	0.6
Philippines	28,403	9.8
Mexico	24,866	1.8
France	24,760	0.8
Nigeria	20,921	4.0
Pakistan	17,060	6.3
Germany	15,802	0.4
Bangladesh	14,969	9.2
Vietnam	12,000	6.4

Source: World Bank, 2014. *Remittances Data Inflows*, available at http://econ.worldbank.org/WBSITE/EXTERNAL/EXTDEC/EXTDEC PROSPECTS/0, contentMDK:22759429~pagePK:64165401~piPK:64165026~theSitePK:476883,00.html.

received over \$60 billion (US) in migrant remittances in 2014, while the Philippines, Mexico, and Nigeria each received over \$20 billion (US). Developed countries like Germany, France, and Belgium also receive large amounts in remittances, but they play less of a role in the overall economy than in developing countries like Nigeria and Bangladesh (see also Castles and Miller, 2003: 170; Wong and Ho, 2006: 258). Many ethnic and religious communities encourage individuals who have moved abroad to invest in not-for-profit projects in their ancestral homelands. These investments constitute yet another form of the transnational movement of money and resources. For example, over the past 30 years, Sikhs in North America, Britain, and Malaysia have helped to fund a variety of schools, shrines, health centres, and community welfare agencies, all of which are intended to promote the well-being of communities in the Punjab (Tatla, 1999: 64–5). Since 1991, Ukrainians in North America have helped to fund the construction of churches, the stocking of libraries, and the provision of resources for medical aid as a result of the Chernobyl nuclear accident in Ukraine (Satzewich, 2002). More recently, and in the context of Russia's takeover of Crimea and its occupation of parts of eastern Ukraine, members of the Ukrainian diaspora in Canada have also raised an estimated \$15 million to help supply the Ukrainian armed forces with uniforms, boots, Humvees, and pickup trucks (Mackinnon, 2015). Though this is a drop in the bucket of the overall budget of the Ukrainian armed forces, the money raised nonetheless symbolizes many Ukrainian Canadians' continued attachment to Ukraine and reinforces the long-standing sense that Ukraine is being victimized by its neighbour Russia. Though providing military support to a home country is rather unusual, many other ethnic communities around the world support non-military projects in their respective ancestral homelands. And, of course, many communities mobilize and raise funds to support their countries of origin or ancestry in times of natural disasters. The scale of funding for these kinds of transnationally funded, non-profit projects in various ancestral homelands appears to be substantial but is difficult to quantify precisely because much of the funding goes through informal channels and is not necessarily recorded in government statistics.

Transnationalism as a site of political engagement refers in part to the ways that immigrants and members of ethnic communities continue to engage in the political processes in their respective homelands. As noted above in the case of Italians, this form of transnationalism can involve formal involvement in homeland elections. A related dimension to transnationalism as a site of political engagement is the existence of dual citizenship. Approximately 90 countries around the world currently allow dual citizenship, and it is estimated that 500,000 Canadians currently living in Canada possess dual citizenship (Fong, 2006: A1). Dual citizenship provides certain individuals with citizenship rights and obligations in two countries. For some individuals, the desire for dual citizenship pertains mainly to symbolic ethnicity. Political attachment to an ancestral homeland through the possession of citizenship is simply used to reaffirm a sense of roots or identity, with little or no formal involvement in the homeland. In other cases, however, there are more instrumental reasons for individuals wishing to have and retain dual citizenship. In an age of globalization, dual citizenship can not only facilitate travel but also make investing and doing business easier in both an ancestral and an adopted homeland. Individuals who possess dual citizenship and have business interests in two or more countries may be able to use their multiple citizenships to negotiate more favourable tax policies or to gain access to state subsidies not available to non-citizens.

Political engagement with an ancestral homeland can also occur in the absence of dual citizenship. It can involve support for specific political parties in the homeland, lobbying government officials in countries of settlement, and support for the democratic process more generally. The Ukrainian Canadian Congress, with the financial support of the Canadian government, helped to organize and send individuals of Ukrainian heritage to Ukraine to help monitor the fairness of the parliamentary elections there in 2004 and again in 2006 and 2012. In the 1990s, Croatians in Canada, the United States, Germany, and Australia raised nearly US $4 million in support of the Hrvatska Demokratska Zajednica, one of the main political parties in Croatia (Winland, 2006: 266). And many ethnic groups lobby government officials in their countries of settlement to help support the development of favourable foreign policies toward ancestral homeland governments. For example, the Canadian government was one of the first countries to recognize an independent Ukrainian state in 1991 in part because of lobbying by the Ukrainian-Canadian community in Canada.

A number of important questions have arisen about dual citizenship and transnational political ties. First, the conflict between Israel and Lebanon in the summer of 2006 raised the question of what kinds of obligations countries like Canada have toward their citizens who have citizenship in another country if they appear to have moved away from Canada relatively permanently and have rather tenuous connections to this country. It is estimated that before the conflict began, approximately

50,000 Lebanese Canadians lived in Lebanon. During the conflict, 15,000 Lebanese Canadians were evacuated from Lebanon at a cost to the Canadian government of about $85 million; as many as one half of those evacuated have since returned to Lebanon (Fong, 2006). The issues arising out of the evacuation led Citizenship and Immigration Canada to begin a review of the rights and responsibilities associated with dual citizenship (Fong, 2006).

Second, what do these kinds of transnational political engagements mean with regard to where political loyalties truly lie? That is, when Italian Canadians vote in the election of representatives to the Italian parliament or when Ukrainian Canadians lobby the Canadian government on an issue related to Ukraine, does this mean that members of these communities are less loyal to Canada? What happens if conflicts arise between the Canadian government and the ancestral homeland that an ethnic or immigrant community politically supports or is simply from?

In Canada, some commentators are raising alarms about the apparent excessive influence that diaspora communities have over our foreign policy (Granatstein, 2007). In a recent dire warning to federal politicians, David Carment and Yiagadeesen Samy (2012) argue that "Canada's leaders are opening up the country to exploitation by other countries looking to disrupt our internal affairs, using diasporas to lobby or influence our leaders or bring their conflicts here."

Diaspora politics can also be problematic for the diaspora groups themselves. In Chapter 3 we saw that on occasions when Canada was in conflict with another country, immigrants and ethnic community members who maintained real and imagined political or social relationships with that country were defined as threats to Canada. Perceptions about divided loyalties created concern on the part of Canadian government officials, who feared that some groups' homeland-related activities and identities undermined social and political stability in this country. For example, Japanese Canadians were interned and/or put into prisoner-of-war camps during the Second World War for their real and imagined transnational political ties and identities (Sugiman, 2006). Nearly 8,600 Ukrainians and other peoples were interned in labour camps during the First World War. These were people unlucky enough to have come from the Austro-Hungarian Empire who had yet to take out Canadian citizenship when war broke out with the Triple Alliance in 1914. Ukrainians and others were interned in part because of their perceived political loyalties to the Austro-Hungarian Empire and in part because they were perceived as a potential fifth column, ready to surreptitiously undermine the war effort in this country (Kordan, 2002). In both cases, real and imagined ties to ancestral homelands put immigrants in political jeopardy and resulted in harsh treatment by the federal government.

It is important to note that these kinds of fears have not necessarily dissipated in the early twenty-first century. As we noted in Chapter 7, some Muslim and Arab Canadians worry that their real and imagined interest in maintaining social and political ties with their countries of origin makes them targets of special state surveillance because they are suspected of supporting terrorist organizations and causes (Arat-Koç, 2006). Members of other ethnic and religious communities have also been labelled as terrorists or as supporters of terrorist causes by the media or by governments for their real and imagined support of political causes in their homelands. In North America and Britain, Sikh support for independence for Punjab has historically been of special concern to governments, and the bombing of an Air India flight from Vancouver in 1985 placed segments of the Sikh community in Vancouver under even more scrutiny for its suspected links to terrorist activity (Tatla, 1999: 174–5). As we noted earlier, in the US Samuel Huntington suggests that the Mexican-origin population constitutes a kind of fifth column "contemptuous of American culture," and is prepared to work toward the breakup of the United States where southwestern states like New Mexico, Arizona, and California will unite with northern states of Mexico to be *La Republica del Norte* (Huntington, 2004: 42).

The irony of targeting and putting immigrants and ethnic community members under special surveillance because they maintain either real or imagined interests in the politics of their respective homelands and may lobby the Canadian government for favourable political and economic relationships with their countries of origin is that these interests and this lobbying might actually lead to better social and political integration in Canada. Clearly, there is a difference between support for terrorist causes or the use of violence to achieve political ends in an ancestral homeland and legitimate ethnic mobilization around foreign policy issues. The latter can benefit social and political culture in Canada and other countries of settlement because it helps groups to learn the political ropes and how to make political compromises and it reinforces the values of democracy and pluralism (Wayland, 2006).

Five Critical Comments

The concepts of diaspora and transnationalism have pointed social scientists in useful directions. As we have seen, it is true that some immigrants return to their countries of origin or move on to other locations. Vaira Vike-Frieberga came to Canada as a child from Latvia after the Second World War. She spent most of her adult life as a professor of psychology at the University of Montreal, but she returned to Latvia after her retirement and in 1999 became its president (Wayland, 2006: 27). Many other individuals who left their countries of origin are now returning to participate in the social, economic, and political affairs of those countries. Ellen Johnson-Sirleaf spent nearly a decade in exile before returning to Liberia to successfully run for president. It is also true that some migrant populations eventually become permanent residents and citizens of the state where they settled. Many undocumented Mexican workers who originally entered the United States temporarily have lived in the country for dozens of years. Clearly, where people come from undoubtedly plays a critical role in identity and group formation in their country of settlement. Thus, advocates of both concepts have identified a number of important aspects of immigrant and ethnic group life. At the same time, however, a number of notes of caution should be raised about some of the wider conceptual claims that these approaches make. In the concluding part of this chapter, we want to highlight five particular reservations.

Are "Old" Distinctions Passé?

First, the distinction between *immigrants, migrants, refugees,* and other categories of people who cross international borders is simply not relevant to an earlier phase of migration within the world system. As we pointed out in Chapter 3, the socio-legal distinctions between immigrants, migrants, and illegal immigrants have real consequences, particularly at the level of state policy, citizenship, and access to public resources. In many countries, the distinction between migrants (who only have the right of temporary entry and settlement), immigrants (who have the right of permanent residence in their country of destination), and illegal immigrants is still an important point of differentiation in citizenship rights and associated claims to access to certain public resources (Satzewich, 2006).

Moreover, these socio-legal considerations have an impact on processes of community formation and associated transnational practices—issues that are obviously dear to scholars working within both the diaspora and the transnational frameworks. To state the obvious, migrant workers, like those who come to Canada every year from Mexico or who move from Bangladesh to one of the Gulf states, and have the right of temporary entry but face restrictions on their ability to circulate within particular national labour markets, are forced into being transnational and at the same time face serious external constraints on their ability to become or form part of a relatively permanent diaspora community in the countries where they work. Immigrants, with the right to permanent settlement, have more options and face different sets of constraints and concerns.

Is Transnationalism Historically New?

Second, while Basch et al. (1994) may have been correct in their assumption that "the popular" image of immigrants was one of "uprootedness" and "permanent rupture from their ancestral homelands," earlier research on immigrant and migrant incorporation did recognize the complexity of migratory flows, the fluidity of international boundaries, and migrants' complicated attachment to and relationship with their ancestral homelands. Some authors were silent on transnationalism and the significance of homeland ties and identities, but others did pay attention to "transnationalism," although they may not necessarily have labelled the activities and behaviour as such (Winland, 1998). As some historians have been at pains to point out, immigrants have always had a transnational orientation, although the forms and intensity of transnationalism may have become more complex (Gabaccia, 2000).

For example, American historian Marcus Lee Hansen, author of *The Immigrant in American History* (1940) and *The Atlantic Migration: 1607–1860* (1961) was well aware of transnational connections, the fluidity of international boundaries, and the influence of "home countries" on the lives, experiences, and practices of immigrants in North America. In an overview of the field titled "Immigration as a Field for Historical Research," originally published in 1926, Hansen was acutely aware that European immigrants to the United States had complicated identities and relationships with their ancestral homelands. According to Hansen, immigrants and their descendants had

> on occasion, . . . been more interested in fighting the battles of the old country than in participating in the affairs of the new. . . . Research will probably reveal that the emergence of the new nations of Eastern and Central Europe in consequence of the World War was possible only because there had existed in America, for a generation or two, active colonies of those nationalities, which had kept alive the ideal of independence and could offer financial support and political pressure at the critical moment. (1940: 211–12)

Clearly, earlier work in the field did recognize the fluidity of boundaries and borders, the transitory nature of identity, and the impact of the "homeland" on the lives, consciousness, and social and political organization of immigrants and ethnic groups (Brubaker, 2005). In some ways, criticisms of the so-called traditional work are based on the construction of a straw man.

The usual rejoinder to this historical critique of the concept of transnationalism is that new communications and transportation technologies have made transnational practices more intense, more immediate, and more systematic than in the past. Portes et al. (1999: 225) argue that while previous generations of immigrants engaged in practices that reinforced bonds between their country of origin and their country of settlement, these activities lacked the "regularity, routine involvement, and critical mass characterizing contemporary examples of transnationalism." While they recognize that there are some legitimate examples of transnationalism in the past—particularly "elite-type" transnationalism and long-distance trading relationships—they are largely exceptional cases that are not relevant for the vast majority of Europeans who left their ancestral homelands in the first half of the twentieth century. In their view, "contemporary transnationalism corresponds to a different period in the evolution of the world economy and to a different set of responses and strategies by people in a condition of disadvantage to its dominant logic. Herein lies the import of its emergence" (Portes et al., 1999: 227).

New communication technologies and the broader process of globalization clearly make it easier for individuals and groups to sustain their transnational connections (Karim, 1998). Rather than waiting for a few days or weeks for news from "back home," news today travels instantaneously via various forms of "ethnic media," blogs, YouTube, Facebook, Twitter, and the like. When natural disasters happen back home, fundraising efforts begin almost immediately, and diaspora groups in different countries of settlement can coordinate their activities to make them more effective. Electronic money transfers mean that money can be sent to relatives in a matter of a few hours. Private-sector businesses are now starting to get involved in helping diaspora communities to establish virtual networking and communications capabilities that help them coordinate activities when homelands are affected by various types of disasters (see Peace and Conflict Planners, 2016). However, despite the spread of new communications technologies, few have *systematically* compared the similarities and differences between the "old" ways that immigrants maintained ties with their homelands through letters, telexes, trains, and ships and the new forms of transnationalism facilitated by Facebook, email, and really fast airplanes (but see Glick Schiller, 1999). While it is obvious that communications and transportation technologies have evolved, it is not obvious that these technologies have produced *qualitatively* different kinds of communities, patterns of settlement, and adjustment. In other words, differences between then and now have tended to be asserted rather than demonstrated.

Are Nation-States Irrelevant?

Third, are nation-states really irrelevant in a supposedly transnational world? How important are states versus international norms and conventions in shaping the lives and rights of immigrants? Christian Joppke (1999; Soysal, 2000) argues that within liberal democracies, the main source of immigrant rights still tend to be domestic in nature. While not discounting the role of international human rights norms, regimes, and conventions, Joppke argues that in states with a "robust liberal infrastructure and tradition, there is no need to resort to international norms." In contrast, he suggests that international human rights norms matter mostly in "illiberal or newly liberalizing states." Perhaps the most telling example of Joppke's point is the United Nations Convention on the Protection of the Rights of All Migrant Workers and Members of their Families, which came into force in July 2003. The convention has generated far more interest in "liberalizing states" than in the "developed world." The 66 states that adopted the convention (some have adopted the convention with reservations about specific articles) as of 1 January 2016 include, among others, Azerbaijan, Bangladesh, Belize, Bolivia, Bosnia and Herzegovina, Burkina Faso, Cape Verde, Chile, Colombia, Comoros, Ecuador, Egypt, El Salvador, Ghana, Guatemala, Guinea-Bissau, Kyrgyzstan, Mali, Mexico, Morocco, Paraguay, Philippines, Sao Tome and Principe, Senegal, Seychelles, Sierra Leone, Sri Lanka, Tajikistan, Togo, Turkey, Uganda, and Uruguay. There are a number of notable absences from this list: Australia, Canada, the United States, and all of the European Union countries (Satzewich, 2006). Clearly, one common denominator in the list above is that it is made up of immigrant-sending countries. The question of why advanced, industrialized, immigrant-receiving countries have not signed on to the convention needs to be the subject of further research (Weissbrodt, 1999).

However, their failure to do so points to the limited role that this particular international charter plays in migrant-receiving countries and the continuing relevance of state-based charters, human rights codes, and legislation in shaping the rights that migrants and immigrants have and claim.

Clearly, states and nations still weigh heavily on diaspora and transnational politics and identity. As Anthias (1998: 570) notes, diasporas may finance various kinds of national struggles and projects, and nation-states see their respective diasporas as resources and use real and imagined bonds of ethnicity to secure capital, financial aid, and political influence. States, particularly in the aftermath of 11 September 2001, also continue to spend considerable resources on border control to protect the integrity of the nation-state. Canada and the United States are taking active and cooperative measures to beef up border control and border security, including the sharing of more information.

Is Assimilation Irrelevant?

Fourth, some of the previous work on immigrants and ethnic relations was more relational and nuanced than contemporary critics give it credit for. That is, before the "discovery" of transnationalism, earlier generations of scholars studied how immigrants settled into their new country, their occupational careers, their educational adjustment, their attitudinal, cultural, and structural assimilation, *and* the extent to which they lost or maintained their old-world identities and ties (Alba and Nee, 1999). Some conceptualized the immigrant settlement process as a trade-off between integration and ethnic maintenance. Ironically, however, in searching for evidence of transnational practices, some present-day scholars seem to have forgotten that immigrants and members of ethnic groups who engage in transnational activities or practices have jobs or run businesses in their country of settlement, join trade unions or business associations, vote in and occasionally run in elections, send their children to school, watch television, buy groceries, and take visiting relatives to see Niagara Falls. That is, at the same time that immigrants maintain their transnational or diaspora identities and practices, they also reproduce their conditions of existence in their country of residence and settlement. These routine and everyday non-transnational activities are just as important to understand as voting in an election back home, sending money to relatives, and spending time in the old country. Some contemporary studies of transnationalism leave the impression that all immigrants or ethnic groups do is "be" transnational (Roberts, Frank, and Lozano-Ascencio, 1999).

The concept of diaspora is somewhat insulated from this shortcoming in that it recognizes the dialectical nature of immigrant and ethnic group incorporation. Cohen's (2008) approach recognizes that the material conditions that propel people to leave their countries of origin have an impact on the formation of diaspora consciousness, although he does not systematically examine how the conditions that led people to leave shapes their adjustment to their new homeland. Cohen also recognizes that diasporas often have an uneasy relationship with the host society and that the diaspora can be a site of creativity. Thus, the concept of diaspora may be more useful for recognizing the relational aspects of settlement and continued engagement with a distant homeland than the concept of transnationalism.

Are Marginality and Exclusion Driving Forces of Transnationalism?

Fifth, are marginality and exclusion, in both the country of origin and the country of settlement, responsible for transnationalism? Some scholars seem to be unaware of the contradictions inherent in their own work. That is, while marginalization, exclusion, and blocked mobility are important themes in the analysis of transnationalism, many of the same researchers also acknowledge that there is an "elite"-level transnationalism in which relatively privileged groups participate in the international circulation of capital, commodities, and services. Faist's (2000: 196) example of this kind of transnationalism is "the hypermobile Chinese businessmen in North America." He argues that "these 'astronauts' establish a business, say, in Singapore, but locate their families in Los Angeles, New York or Toronto to maximize the educational opportunities for their children or as a safe haven in the event of political unrest." While it is true that this group of business immigrants in Canada and elsewhere have been racialized, and the children of the "astronauts" may face a certain amount of everyday racism in North America (Li, 1994), it is difficult to argue that these wealthy capitalists and their families face serious economic disadvantages, deprivation, and blocked mobility in Canadian society and that their "disadvantage" in Canada contributes to their transnational identities or practices.

Other research suggests that socially marginal communities are not the only ones engaged in transnational activities (Matthews and Satzewich, 2006). For instance, immigrants from the United States in Canada, while generally economically privileged, appear to engage in many of the same individual and institutional-level transnational practices that other less advantaged immigrants do. According to research conducted by John Hagan (2001) on American war resisters in Canada, many Americans in Canada regularly travel to the United States to visit friends and family or on vacation. Many have gone back to live in the United States for periods of time and then return to Canada. Furthermore, research shows that American immigrants in Toronto have a lower-than-average rate of home ownership in the city, and Murdie and Teixeira (2003: 177) argue that this is due in part to the fact that "Americans employed by US-owned firms view their stay in Toronto as transitory." Also, Americans have one of the lowest rates of citizenship acquisition of all immigrant groups in Canada. It is not implausible to suggest that this is in part because they continue to identify at some level with their ancestral homeland and because, like other transnational immigrants, they want to keep their options open both for themselves and for their children. Americans in Canada have plenty of access to information about their ancestral homeland and can easily follow American economic, political, cultural, and sporting events. Both Democrats Abroad and Republicans Abroad encourage continued political participation in the US by American citizens who have moved abroad (Matthews and Satzewich, 2006). In short, marginality, blocked mobility, and socio-economic deprivation are not the only forces driving transnationalism.

The fundamental forces that drive migration, and associated processes of transnationalism and diaspora formation today, may not be all that different from earlier periods in modern history. People have always moved to improve their economic circumstances for themselves and their families and to find safe places to live, and they are going to continue moved for these reasons in the foreseeable future. The consequences of climate change may be something new added to the mix of pressures to migrate as the combination of rising water levels and increased desertification make parts of the globe less habitable. State borders become more and less porous based on changing political, economic, and military circumstances. Though calls for tighter border control are being made in many Western countries today, as economic conditions improve and population aging and other demographic conditions work their way through individual societies, borders are likely to become more open yet again in the future. Though individuals do integrate and even assimilate into their countries of settlement, they never completely lose touch with friends or relatives back home or become completely disinterested in political and economic developments in places where they come from. How they maintain diasporic and transnational ties and identities is likely to change as a result of ever-evolving transportation and communications technology.

Summary

Over the past 25 years, the concepts of diaspora and transnationalism have become central to scholarly scripts about immigrant and ethnic community life. The concepts share similar critiques of existing literature and display similar concerns about the changing nature of immigrant and ethnic group activities, practices, and community life. For example, when Alejandro Portes et al. (1999: 221) talk about the transnational practices of immigrants that include "the manifold socio-cultural enterprises oriented toward the reinforcement of a national identity abroad or the collective enjoyment of cultural goods," they seem to be talking about the same thing that Robin Cohen (2008) describes as a diaspora's effort to maintain a strong ethnic group consciousness over time.

Despite their common recent histories and common analytical concerns, the concept of *diaspora* has been more sharply criticized than the concept of *transnationalism*. While there have been some efforts to delineate the proper relationship between the concepts of *diaspora* and *transnational*, this chapter has suggested that solutions proposing that diaspora should be thought of as one particular form of transnational community are problematic. The chapter has offered an alternative way of thinking about the relationship between these two important concepts. It has suggested that the two are more compatible than some who work within the transnational perspective imply and that one way to reconcile them is to define *transnationalism* as a set of practices in which diasporas, immigrants, and others engage.

Questions for Critical Thought

1. According to Cohen, what are the main characteristic features of diasporas? Think of a group that you are familiar with and see if it fits his ideal type.

2. What arguments have scholars used to justify their use of the concepts of *diaspora* and *transnationalism*? How convincing are these arguments?

3. What kinds of transnational ties do immigrants have with their various countries of origin? Does transnationalism undermine a commitment to Canada?

4. What, if anything, is historically new about modern forms of transnationalism?

5. How do sociologists explain the apparent growth in transnational activities over the past 25 years?

Debate Questions

1. What could be the role of globalization in promoting transnational identities? How are the two connected?

2. Read Chapter 1 and Chapter 6 again. Are nation-states still important in fostering single-ethnic identities? How do they produce and reproduce such identities?

3. In light of the rise of global transnational identities, should social scientists continue to study how immigrants settle in host societies, their behavioural and structural assimilation, and the extent to which they maintain or lose their old-world identities? Why or why not?

4. Are there any Canadian diasporic communities of which you are aware? Where? Under what circumstances have they developed and how?

Annotated Additional Readings

Asia Pacific Foundation of Canada. 2011. *Canadians Abroad: Canada's Global Asset*. Vancouver: Asia Pacific Foundation of Canada. A thoroughly researched and well-argued case for taking the existence of a Canadian diaspora seriously, the publication contains recommendations for how this diaspora can be harnessed to pursue Canadian national interests abroad.

Basch, Linda, Nina Glick Schiller, and Christine Szanton Blanc. 1994. *Nations Unbound: Transnational Projects, Postcolonial Predicaments and Deterritorialized Nation-States*. Amsterdam: Gordon and Breach. This is a highly influential early statement of the transnational approach. Most of the examples are taken from the American context.

Cohen, Robin. 2008. *Global Diasporas: An Introduction*, 2nd edn. New York: Routledge. Cohen makes a comprehensive case for the utility of the concept of diaspora. The book is wide-ranging in scope and examines various forms of diasporas around the world.

Madibbo, Amal. 2015. *Canada in Sudan, Sudan in Canada: Immigration, Conflict and Reconstruction*. Montreal and Kingston: McGill-Queen's University Press.

Satzewich, Vic, and Lloyd Wong, eds. 2006. *Transnational Communities in Canada*. Vancouver: UBC Press. This is an edited collection containing articles on transnationalism in Canada by some of this country's leading historians, anthropologists, sociologists, geographers, and political scientists.

Related Websites

African Diaspora Policy Center
www.diaspora-centre.org
The African Diaspora Policy Centre (ADPC) is an independent organization that was established in The Netherlands in 2006. ADPC provides a platform that enables African diaspora in Europe to connect more closely with the continent as a collective force, pool their resources, and proactively undertake initiatives for the promotion of peace, better governance, and brain gain in Africa.

Global Networks Journal
www.globalnetworksjournal.com
This is a scholarly journal that publishes research on global networks, transnational affairs and practices, and their relation to wider theories of globalization.

My Journey Home
www.pbs.org/weta/myjourneyhome/andrew/andrew_diaspora_3.html
A moving documentary about the personal stories of three people who returned "home" after living for years in the United States. The documentary challenges the meaning of home and identity for individuals who have transnational ties, connections, and identities.

The Scottish Diaspora Tapestry
www.scottishdiasporatapestry.org
The Scottish Diaspora Forum seeks to develop and deepen understanding of the relationship between Scots abroad and the government of Scotland by posing questions about the vision for the future of the Scots as a global diaspora.

Glossary

Abocide: a term referring to the extermination of Aboriginal people, currently employed in criticizing the implications of Bill C-31, since, it is argued, it might lead to the legal "elimination" of status Indians for successive generations of natives as those who marry non-Indians will lose their status as such.

Ascriptive characteristics: social characteristics with which we are born, such as sex and skin colour.

Assimilation: process by which minority groups adopt the hegemonic culture of a society.

Behavioural assimilation: the acquisition of dominant group cultural values by minority groups.

Bill C-31: a bill of Parliament introduced in 1985 amending the Indian Act that eliminated its enfranchisement and patrilineal provisions, and gave bands the right to decide who are members and who are not.

Blocked social mobility: Porter's argument that ethnic group membership in entrance groups means few opportunities for occupational advancement or upward social mobility.

Charter groups: the so-called founding nations of Canada: the British and the French.

Chinese head tax: an infamous tax on Chinese immigrants introduced in 1885 by the federal government in order to exclude them from coming to Canada.

Collective conscience: Durkheim's idea that pre-modern societies were cohesive because they were based on sameness and the conformity of individual consciousness to the collective. This created social group boundaries and "love for one's own."

Collective ethnic identity: consensus among members of an ethnic group about what constitutes it and differentiates it from other ethnic groups.

Colour-coded vertical mosaic: the argument that "race" or "visibility" have replaced ethnicity in the structure of social, economic, and political inequality in Canada.

Contact hypothesis: the belief that intercultural exchanges and interracial contact among diverse groups reduces prejudice, discrimination, and racism.

Critical race theory (CRT): a diverse body of work that focuses on racial inequalities in the distribution of social goods and services.

Cultural diasporas: formed out of greater geographic areas and exerting cultural influences in the host countries; for example, African-descent Caribbean immigrants in the UK and Canada, or Latin Americans in the US.

Cultural relativism: not evaluating other cultures with criteria derived from our own.

Culture: a set of dynamic social processes and practices; it is a collective response of socially constituted individuals to their ever-changing external conditions, largely determined by social structures.

Deductive criminal profiling: the process of interpreting criminal evidence and other information in order to deduce the social characteristics of the offender.

Democratic racism: a new form of racism in Canadian society that is characterized by the conflict between the prevalent ideologies of democratic principles (justice, equality, fairness, etc.) on one hand, and their co-existence with negative feelings, attitudes, behaviours, prejudice, and discrimination against minorities on the other.

Deracialization of immigration: the elimination of overt racist immigrant selection criteria.

Diachronic dimensions of ethnicity: the homeland, ancestry, and culture associated with one's ethnic group.

Diaspora: a Greek word literally meaning "dispersion," used to refer to members of ethnic groups who have either migrated in large numbers outside their homeland or have been forced out (en masse).

Enfranchisement: the process by which an individual could forcibly lose or voluntarily give up his or her legal status as Indian.

Entrance groups: all other ethnic groups that have immigrated to Canada after the British and the French.

"Eskimos": a derogatory term used by Europeans to refer to Inuit people.

Ethnic enclave: a residential area with a relatively high level of concentration of a single ethnic origin.

Ethnic institutions: educational, religious, economic, and social institutions of ethnic groups that cater to the needs of their members only, separate from mainstream institutions, and socialize their members.

Ethnicity and "race" paradigms: a diverse body of literature primarily concerned with the assimilation, integration, accommodation, conflict, and exclusion of immigrants within particular nation-states. It focuses on inter-group relations within specific political boundaries.

Ethnicized: the construction of difference, and social boundaries, around patterns of real or imagined cultural differences.

Ethnocentrism: the evaluation of other cultures with criteria from our own culture.

Exclusionary movements: racist movements against immigration into Canada.

First Nations: the term used since the 1980s to describe status Indians, i.e., those who have been recognized as natives by governments.

Illegal immigrants: people who immigrate to Canada "illegally," outside the regular immigration process.

Immigration Act of 1910: discriminatory legislation that prohibited entrance to Canada for "the mentally defective," "the diseased," and "the physically defective."

Immigration Act of 1952: legislation that allowed immigration authorities to prohibit immigration to Canada of so-called undesired groups on the basis of their ethnicity, class, culture, "unsuitability," "inability" to assimilate, etc.

Immigration categories: categories of immigrants set by government policies that form the basis for being admitted into Canada, including family class, skilled workers, business immigrants, refugees, etc.

Imperial diasporas: the formation of English, French, and other colonizer diasporas because of imperial conquest. Examples include (1) the English imperial diaspora in Canada, South Africa, or India; and (2) the French imperial diaspora in Canada, Vietnam, or Algeria.

Indian: (a) a misnomer; the term used by Christopher Columbus to describe Aboriginal populations in the Americas, mistakenly thinking he had discovered the Indian continent; (b) a legal term describing certain groups of natives in Canada by the Indian Act.

Indian Act: legislation that defines who is an Indian and governs relations between the federal government and Aboriginal people in Canada.

Individual ethnic identity: the relation of individuals to their own ethnic collectivity.

Inductive criminal profiling: generalizations about an individual criminal based on initial behavioural and demographic characteristics of other offenders who have been studied in the past.

Institutional completeness: Breton's term that denotes the extent to which an ethnic group forms institutions by and for its members.

Institutional racism: racism that is built into and permeates the structure and functions of societal institutions.

Interculturalism: Quebec's version of multiculturalism, which discourages ethnic enclaves but promotes the linguistic assimilation of minority groups.

Islamophobia: fear of people who believe in Islam, based upon prejudices.

Labour diasporas: diasporas formed because of the movement of large numbers of labourers; for example, Pakistani construction workers in Middle Eastern countries like Dubai.

Labour market: a competitive arena in which labour power is sold by workers and bought by employers. Good jobs are found in the primary labour market, bad ones, in the secondary.

Methodological nationalism: the tendency on the part of social scientists to conceptualize social phenomena around the boundaries of the nation-state.

Métis: a French term meaning "half caste," used to describe the descendants of unions between male French-Canadian fur traders and Aboriginal women in sixteenth- and seventeenth-century Canada.

Migrant workers: workers who come to Canada on temporary work visas to perform specific labour tasks (e.g., in seasonal agriculture) but must return to their country of origin when their work is finished.

Monopolistic closure: Weber's concept that refers to social practices of exclusion of "Others" from the distribution of scarce valuable resources such as wealth, high social status, and political power.

Multiculturalism: an ideology and a set of federal government programs that are used to maintain social order and manage ethnic and racial relations in poly-ethnic societies.

Non-status Indians: individuals who lost their legal status as Indians.

Occupational dissimilarity: the net difference between the occupational status of groups and the overall national average.

Orientalism: the biased academic and literary study of Arabs by Europeans.

Over-policing: the claim that the police act overzealously when members of minority groups are crime suspects.

Permanent residents: immigrants, also known as landed immigrants, who have been given permanent residence status in Canada. They can apply for Canadian citizenship after three years of residence in the country.

Racial profiling: taking into account and keeping data on people's "race" in the process of determining whether they are likely to commit a crime.

Racialization: process by which, based on the physical characteristics of people, we categorize human populations into different groups.

Racism: being prejudicial and discriminatory against people because of their biologically different "race."

Reasonable accommodation: Quebec's pluralist notion that government policies and programs should not only tolerate but also accommodate the cultural differences of new immigrants and of minority groups.

Residential schools: a system of schools in which Aboriginal children were placed by government educational authorities in order to assimilate them into the dominant culture.

Royal Proclamation of 1763: King George III's proclamation that laid the foundations of making Crown treaties with Aboriginal peoples in Canada.

Segmented assimilation: the processes whereby new immigrants become integrated into different socio-economic segments of a receiving society.

Selection criteria: criteria set by immigration policy that are associated with different weights (points) such as prospective immigrants' education, work experience, age, knowledge of official languages, "adaptability," etc.

Social class: the structural economic position of social individuals in relation to (a) ownership of money capital, (b) control of the physical means of production, and (c) control of the labour power of others.

Socio-economic hierarchy: social and economic pyramid-like structures in which few social groups of people are on the top and enjoy greater wealth, power, and prestige, and others, the majority of the population, are at the lower layers of these structures.

Structural assimilation: the integration of minority groups into the economic, social, and political life of the host country.

Synchronic dimensions of ethnicity: ways in which an individual and/or collective ethnic identities are defined, evaluated, and treated by others.

Trade diasporas: diasporas formed because of the movement of large numbers of merchants and traders, emerging from developments in international trade. Examples include (1) Greek merchants in Vienna, Odessa, and Trieste during the Ottoman Empire; and (2) Chinese merchants in Southeast Asia during the nineteenth and twentieth centuries,

Transnationalism: a process by which immigrants build multiple social, economic, and cultural relations across geographic and/or political territory boundaries, usually between their country of origin, the host society, and other countries.

Under-policing: the claim that the police do not protect minorities adequately when they are victims of crime.

Vertical mosaic: Porter's metaphor about Canadian society implying that it comprises many ethnic groups (mosaic) but that there is an ethnic hierarchy with the British and the French on the top and all other groups at the bottom of social, economic, and political structures (vertical).

Victim diasporas: ethnic groups who have been forced out of their ancestral homeland through violent persecution and war. Examples include the Jews, Armenians, Kurds, the Greeks of Asia Minor, Palestinians, etc. Ethnic "cleansing" creates victim diasporas.

Zero tolerance: school policies of sanctions against those who "misbehave," often characterized as a reflection of institutional racism since they target minority students disproportionately.

References

Aboriginal Affairs and Northern Development Canada. 2011. *Fact Sheet—2011 National Household Survey Aboriginal Dynamics, Educational Attainment and Labour Market Outcomes*. Ottawa: Aboriginal Affairs and Northern Development Canada.

Aboriginal Justice Inquiry of Manitoba. 1999. *Report*. Winnipeg: Aboriginal Justice Implementation Commission. www.ajic.mb.ca/volume.html.

Abraham, Carolyn. 2005. "Race: Five Years Ago, the Human Genome Project Said Race Didn't Exist. Now, Huge Scientific Projects Are Studying the Genetic Traits of Ethnic Groups. What Happened?" *The Globe and Mail*, 18 June: F1.

Abu-Laban, Yasmeen, and Christina Gabriel. 2002. *Selling Diversity: Immigration, Multiculturalism, Employment Equity and Globalization*. Peterborough: Broadview Press.

———, and Daiva Stasiulis. 1992. "Ethnic Pluralism under Siege: Popular and Partisan Opposition to Multiculturalism," *Canadian Public Policy* 27 (4): 365–86.

Adams, Howard. 1999. *Tortured People: The Politics of Colonization*. Penticton: Theytus Books.

Addis Fortune. 2015. "Ethiopia: Celebrating the Diaspora—Deeds Must Match the Rhetoric," *allAfrica*. http://allafrica.com/stories/201510052703.html.

Agnew, Vijay. 1996. *Resisting Discrimination: Women from Asia, Africa, and the Caribbean and the Women's Movement in Canada*. Toronto: University of Toronto Press.

Agocs, Carol, and Monica Boyd. 1993. "The Canadian Ethnic Mosaic Recast for the 90s," in James Curtis, Edward Grabb, and Neil Guppy, eds, *Social Inequality in Canada: Patterns, Problems, Policies*, 2nd edn, 330–52. Scarborough: Prentice Hall Canada.

Akenson, Donald. 1995. "The Historiography of English Speaking Canada and the Concept of Diaspora: A Sceptical Appreciation," *Canadian Historical Review* 76 (3): 377–410.

Alba, Richard, and Victor Nee. 1999. "Rethinking Assimilation Theory for a New Era of Immigration," in Charles Hirschman et al., eds, *The Handbook of International Migration: The American Experience*. New York: Russell Sage Foundation.

Alboim, Naomi. 2009. *Adjusting the Balance: Fixing Canada's Economic Immigration Policies*. Maytree Foundation. www.maytree.com/policy.

Alfred, Gerald. 1995. *Heeding the Voices of Our Ancestors: Kahnawake Mohawk Politics and the Rise of Native Nationalism*. Toronto: Oxford University Press.

Alfred, Taiaiake. 1999. *Peace, Power and Righteousness: An Indigenous Manifesto*. Toronto: Oxford University Press.

Allahar, Anton. 1998. "Race and Racism: Strategies of Resistance," in Vic Satzewich, ed., *Racism and Social Inequality in Canada*. Toronto: Thompson Educational Publishers.

Allen, Robert. 1993. *His Majesty's Indian Allies: British Indian Policy in the Defence of Canada, 1774–1815*. Toronto: Dundurn Press.

Allport, Gordon. 1954. *The Nature of Prejudice*. Reading, Mass: Addison-Wesley.

Andersen, Kay. 1991. *Vancouver's Chinatown: Racial Discourse in Canada, 1875–1980*. Montreal and Kingston: McGill-Queen's University Press.

Anderson, Alan, and James Frideres. 1980. *Ethnicity in Canada: Theoretical Perspectives*. Scarborough: Butterworths.

Anderson, Kim. 2000. *A Recognition of Being: Reconstructing Native Womanhood*. Toronto: Sumach Press.

Anthias, Floya. 1998. "Evaluating 'Diaspora': Beyond Ethnicity?" *Sociology* 32 (3): 557–80.

Arat-Koç, Sedef. 2006. "Whose Transnationalism? Canada: Clash of Civilizations Discourse, and Arab and Muslim Canadians," in Vic Satzewich and Lloyd Wong, eds, *Transnational Identities and Practices in Canada*. Vancouver: University of British Columbia UBC Press.

Ashcroft, Bill, Gareth Griffiths, and Helen Tiffin, eds. 2006. *The Post-Colonial Studies Reader*, 2nd edn. London: Routledge.

Asia Pacific Foundation of Canada. 2011. *Canadians Abroad: Canada's Global Asset*. Vancouver: Asia Pacific Foundation of Canada.

Assembly of First Nations. 2006. "Key Elements of the Indian Residential Schools Settlement Agreement."

———. 2011. *Fact Sheet—Quality of Life of First Nations, June 2011*. www.afn.ca/uploads/files/factsheets/quality_of_life_final_fe.pdf.

Association of Black Law Enforcers. 2003. "Official Position on 'Racial Profiling' in Canada." Toronto: Association of Black Law Enforcers.

Avery, Donald. 1995. *Reluctant Host: Canada's Response to Immigrant Workers, 1896–1994*. Toronto: McClelland and Stewart.

Aylward, Carol. 1999. *Canadian Critical Race Theory: Racism and the Law*. Halifax, NS: Fernwood Publishing.

Backhouse, Constance. 1999. *Colour-coded: A Legal History of Racism in Canada, 1900–1950*. Toronto: University of Toronto Press.

Bakan, Abigail, and Daiva Stasiulis, eds. 1997. *Not One of the Family: Foreign Domestic Workers in Canada*. Toronto: University of Toronto Press.

Balibar, Etienne, and Immanuel Wallerstein. 1991. *Race, Nation and Class: Ambiguous Identities*. London: Verso.

Bannerji, Himani. 2000. *The Dark Side of the Nation: Essays on Multiculturalism, Nationalism and Gender*. Toronto: Garamond Press.

Banting, Keith, and Will Kymlicka. 2010. "Canadian Multiculturalism: Global Anxieties and Local Debates," *British Journal of Canadian Studies*, 23 (1): 43–72.

Banton, Michael. 1970. "The Concept of Racism," in S. Zubaida, ed., *Race and Racialism*. London: Tavistock.

_____. 1977. *The Idea of Race*. London: Tavistock.

_____. 1979. "Analytical and Folk Concepts of Race and Ethnicity," *Ethnic and Racial Studies* 2: 12–38.

_____. 1987. *Racial Theories*. London: Cambridge University Press.

_____. 2002. *The International Politics of Race*. Cambridge: Cambridge University Press.

Barker, Martin. 1981. *The New Racism*. London: Junction Books.

Basch, Linda, Nina Glick Schiller, and Christina Szanton Blanc. 1994. *Nations Unbound: Transnational Projects, Postcolonial Predicaments and Deterritorialized Nation-states*. Amsterdam: Gordon and Breach Publishers.

Basok, Tanya. 2002. *Tortillas and Tomatoes: Transmigrant Mexican Harvesters in Canada*. Montreal and Kingston: McGill-Queen's University Press.

Basran, Gurcharn, and B. Singh Bolaria. 2003. *The Sikhs in Canada: Migration, Race, Class and Gender*. New Delhi: Oxford University Press.

_____, and Li Zong. 1998. "Devaluation of Foreign Credentials as Perceived by Nonwhite Professional Immigrants," *Canadian Ethnic Studies* 30: 6–23.

Beaujot, Roderic, and Kevin McQuillan. 1982. *Growth and Dualism: The Demographic Development of Canadian Society*. Toronto: Gage.

Bibby, Reginald. 1990. *Mosaic Madness*. Toronto: Stoddart.

Bissoondath, Neil. 1994. *Selling Illusions: The Cult of Multiculturalism*. Toronto: Penguin.

Black, Debra. 2015a. "Citizen-led Initiative Lifeline Syria Working to Bring 1,000 Syrian Refugees to the GTA," *Toronto Star*, 17 June. www.thestar.com/news/gta/2015/06/17/citizen-led-initiative-lifeline-syria-working-to-bring-1000-syrian-refugees-to-the-gta.html.

_____. 2015b. "Wooing the Ethnic Vote," *Toronto Star*, 15 May. www.thestar.com/news/canada/2015/05/15/wooing-the-ethnic-vote.html.

Black, Jerome, and David Hagen. 1993. "Quebec Immigration Politics and Policy: Historical and Contemporary Perspectives," in Alain-G. Gagnon, ed., *Québec: State and Society*, 2nd edn. Toronto: Nelson Canada.

Block, Sheila. 2010. *Ontario's Growing Gap: The Role of Race and Gender*. Ottawa: Canadian Centre for Policy Alternatives.

Bloemraad, Irene. 2006. *Becoming a Citizen: Incorporating Immigrants and Refugees in the United States and Canada*. Berkeley: University of California Press.

Bolaria, B. Singh, and Peter Li. 1988. *Racial Oppression in Canada*, 2nd edn. Toronto: Garamond Press.

Boldt, Menno. 1993. *Surviving as Indians: The Challenge of Self-government*. Toronto: University of Toronto Press.

Bonacich, Edna. 1972. "A Theory of Ethnic Antagonism: The Split Labour Market," *American Sociological Review* 37: 547–59.

_____. 1976. "Advanced Capitalism and Black–White Relations in the United States: A Split Labour Market Interpretation," *American Sociological Review* 41: 34–51.

_____. 1979. "The Past, Present and Future of Split Labour Market Theory," in Cora Bagley Marrett and Cheryl Leggon, eds, *Research in Race and Ethnic Relations: A Research Annual* 1: 17–64. Greenwich, CT: JAI Press.

Bonnett, Alastair. 1998. "How the British Working Class Became White: The Symbolic (Re) formation of Racialized Capitalism," *Journal of Historical Sociology* 11 (3): 316–40.

———. 2000. *Anti-Racism*. London: Routledge.

Borden, Sam. 2015. "Russia Tackles Racism, While Playing It Down, Ahead of World Cup," *New York Times*, 2 November. www.nytimes.com/2015/11/03/sports/soccer/russian-soccer-denies-racism-problem-even-as-it-vows-to-solve-it.html.

Borjas, George. 1999. *Heaven's Door: Immigration Policy and the American Economy*. Princeton, NJ: Princeton University Press.

Borowski, Allan, and Alan Nash. 1994. "Business Immigration," in Howard Adelman et al., eds, *Immigration and Refugee Policy: Australia and Canada Compared* (Vol. 1). Carleton, Aus.: Melbourne University Press.

Borrows, John. 1997. "Wampum at Niagara: The Royal Proclamation, Canadian Legal History, and Self-Government," in Michael Asch, ed., *Aboriginal and Treaty Rights in Canada*. Vancouver: University of British Columbia Press.

Bose, Pablo, 2007. "Development and Diasporic Capital: Nonresident Indians and the State," in Luin Goldring and Sailaja Krishnamurti, eds, *Organizing the Transnational: Labour, Politics and Social Change*. Vancouver: University of British Columbia Press.

Bouchard, Genevieve, and Barbara Wake Carroll. 2002. "Policy-Making and Administrative Discretion: The Case of Immigration in Canada," *Canadian Public Administration* 45 (2): 239–57.

Bouchard, Gérard, and Charles Taylor. 2008. *Building the Future: A Time for Reconciliation*. Gouvernement du Québec. Consultation Commission on Accommodation Practices Related to Cultural Differences. www.accommodements.qc.ca/documentation/rapports/rapport-final-integral-en.pdf.

Boult, Adam. 2015. "Trolls' Racist Comments Get Plastered on Billboards Near Their Homes," *The Telegraph*, 23 Nov. www.telegraph.co.uk/news/worldnews/southamerica/brazil/12026054/Trolls-racist-comments-get-plastered-on-billboards-near-their-homes.html.

Bourhis, Richard. 2003. "Measuring Ethnocultural Diversity Using the Canadian Census," *Canadian Ethnic Studies* 35 (1): 9–32.

Boyd, Monica. 1992. "Gender, Visible Minority, and Immigrant Earnings Inequality: Reassessing an Employment Equity Premise," in Vic Satzewich, ed., *Deconstructing a Nation: Immigration, Multiculturalism and Racism*

in '90s Canada*, 279–321. Halifax, NS: Fernwood Press.

———. 2002. "Educational Attainments of Immigrant Offspring: Success or Segmented Assimilation?" *International Migration Review*, 36 (4): 1037—60.

———, John Goyder, Frank E. Jones, Hugh A. McRoberts, Peter C. Pineo, and John Porter. 1981. "Status Attainment in Canada: Findings of the Canadian Mobility Study," *Canadian Review of Sociology and Anthropology* 18 (5): 657–73.

———, and Doug Norris. 2001. "Who are the 'Canadians'? Changing Census Responses, 1986–1996," *Canadian Ethnic Studies* 33 (1): 1–24.

Boyle, Mark, and Rob Kitchin. 2011. *A Diaspora Strategy for Canada? Enriching Debate through Heightening Awareness of International Practice*. Vancouver: Asia Pacific Foundation of Canada.

Brenner, Marie. 2015. "The Troubling Question in the French Jewish Community: Is It Time to Leave?" *Vanity Fair*, 31 July. www.vanityfair.com/news/2015/07/anti-semitism-france-hostage-hyper-cacher-kosher-market.

Breton, Raymond. 1964. "Institutional Completeness of Ethnic Communities and the Personal Relations of Immigrants," *American Journal of Sociology* 70: 193–205.

———. 1991. *The Governance of Ethnic Communities: Political Structures and Processes in Canada*. New York: Greenwood Press.

———, and Howard Roseborough. 1971. "Ethnic Differences in Status," in Bernard R. Blishen, Frank E. Jones, Kaspar D. Naegele, and John Porter, eds, *Canadian Society: Sociological Perspectives*, 540–68. Toronto: MacMillan Canada.

British Columbia Civil Liberties Association. 2010. *Racial Profiling*. Vancouver: BC Civil Liberties Association.

Brown, Rupert. 1995. *Prejudice: Its Social Psychology*. Oxford: Blackwell Publishers.

Brubaker, Rogers. 2005. "The 'Diaspora' Diaspora," *Ethnic and Racial Studies* 28 (1): 1–19.

Bruquetas-Callejo, Maria, Blanca Gares-Mascarenas, Rinus Penninx, and Peter Scholten. 2006. "Policymaking Related to Immigration and Integration: The Dutch Case," IMISCOE Working Paper: Country Report. www.imiscoe.org.

Bryden, Anne, and Sandra Niessen, eds. 1998. *Consuming Fashion: Adorning the Transnational Body*. Oxford: Berg Publishers.

Brym, Robert J., and Bonnie Fox. 1989. *From Culture to Power: The Sociology of English Canada*. Toronto: Oxford University Press.

Calliste, Agnes. 1987. "Sleeping Car Porters in Canada: An Ethnically Submerged Split Labour Market," *Canadian Ethnic Studies* 19 (1): 1–20.

Cameron, David. 2012. "PM's Speech at Munich Security Conference." www.number10.gov. uk/news/pms-speech-at-munich-security-conference/.

Canada. 1947. *Debates of the House of Commons*. 1 May: 2644–6.

_____. 1993. *Indian Treaties and Surrenders, From no. 281 to no. 483* (Vol. 3). Saskatoon: Fifth House Publishers.

_____ 2016. "Determine your eligibility-Sponsor your parents and grandparents." http://www.cic.gc.ca/english/immigrate/sponsor/pgp-apply-who.asp.

_____ Department of Justice. 2002. *Immigration and Refugee Protection Regulations*. http://laws.justice.gc.ca/en/I2.5/SOR-2002-227/239632.html.

Canadian Race Relations Foundation. 2001. "Canada's Immigration Polices: Contradictions and Shortcomings," *CRRF Perspectives: Focus on Immigration and Refugee Issues* Autumn/Winter. www.crr.ca/en/Publications/ePubHome.htm.

Carens, Joseph. 2000. *Culture, Citizenship and Community: A Contextual Exploration of Justice and Evenhandedness*. Oxford: Oxford University Press.

Carment, David, and Yiagadeesen Samy. 2012. "The Dangerous Game of Diaspora Politics," *The Globe and Mail*, 10 February.

Carter, Sarah. 1990. *Lost Harvests: Prairie Indian Reserve Farmers and Government Policy*. Montreal and Kingston: McGill-Queen's University Press.

Castles, Stephen, and Godula Kosack. 1973. *Immigrant Workers and Class Structure in Western Europe*. London: Oxford University Press.

_____, and _____. 1984. *Immigrant Workers and Class Structure in Western Europe*, 2nd edn. Oxford: Oxford University Press.

_____, and Mark Miller. 2003. *The Age of Migration: International Population Movements in the Modern World*, 3rd edn. New York: Guilford.

Cawley, John, Karen Conneely, James Heckman, and Edward Vytlacil. 1997. "Cognitive Ability, Wages, and Meritocracy," in Bernie Devlin et al., eds, *Intelligence, Genes and Success: Scientists Respond to The Bell Curve*. New York: Springer-Verlag.

CBC News. 2003. "Ahenakew Charged with Spreading Hate. www.cbc.ca/news/canada/story/2003/06/11/ahenakew_charge030611.html.

_____ "What Is a Hate Crime?" www.cbc.ca/news/canada/story/2011/06/15/f-hate-crimes.html.

_____. 2014. "Canadian Attitudes toward Immigrants Conflicted, Poll Says." www.cbc.ca/news/canada/canadian-attitudes-toward-immigrants-conflicted-poll-says-1.2826022.

_____. 2015. "Wayne Gretzky Endorses Harper Despite Not Being Allowed to Vote." www.cbc.ca/news/politics/gretzky-harper-1.3234136.

Centre for the Study of Living Standards. 2012. *Aboriginal Labour Market Performance in Canada: 2007–2011*. Ottawa: Centre for the Study of Living Standards.

Chaudhry, Irfan. 2015. "#Hashtagging Hate: Using Twitter to Track Racism Online," *First Monday* 20 (2). http://journals.uic.edu/ojs/index.php/fm/article/view/5450/4207.

_____. 1980. *The Canadian Odyssey: The Greek Experience in Canada*. Toronto: McClelland and Stewart.

Chimbos, Peter. 1980. *The Canadian Odyssey: The Greek Experience in Canada*. Toronto: McClelland and Stewart.

Chua, Amy, and Rubenfeld, Jed. 2014. *The Triple Package: How Three Unlikely Traits Explain the Rise and Fall of Cultural Groups in America*. New York: Penguin Press.

Citizenship and Immigration Canada. 2002. *Business Immigration Program Statistics*.

_____. 2015. *Refugees and Asylum*. www.cic.gc.ca/english/refugees/index.asp.

Citizenship and Immigration Canada. 2016. "Refugee System in Canada." www.cic.gc.ca/english/refugees/canada.asp.

Clatworthy, Stuart. 2013. "Indian Registration, Membership and Population Change in First Nations Communities," in Jerry White, Susan Wingert, Dan Beavon, and Paul Maxim, eds, *Aboriginal Policy Research* (Vol. 5, pp. 99–120). Toronto: Thompson Educational Publishers.

Clement, Wallace. 1975. *The Canadian Corporate Elite: An Analysis of Economic Power*. Toronto: McClelland and Stewart.

_____, and John Myles. 1994. *Relations of Ruling*. Montreal: McGill-Queen's University Press.

Cohen, Robin. 1995. "Rethinking 'Babylon': Iconoclastic Conceptions of the Diasporic

Experience," *New Community* 21 (1): 5–18.

_____. 1997. *Global Diasporas: An Introduction.* Seattle: University of Washington Press.

_____. 2008. *Global Diasporas: An Introduction*, 2nd edn. New York: Routledge.

Collins, Jock. 1988. *Migrant Hands in a Distant Land: Australia's Post-war Immigration.* Sydney: Pluto Press.

Commission des droits de la personne et des droits de la jeunesse. 2011. *Racial Profiling and Systemic Discrimination of Racialized Youth: Report of the Consultation on Racial Profiling and Its Consequences.* Quebec City: Commission des droits de la personne et des droits de la jeunesse.

Congress of Aboriginal Peoples. 2014. "Who Are the Metis?" http://abo-peoples.org/f-a-q/.

Connolly, Kate. 2010. "Angela Merkel Declares Death of German Multiculturalism," *The Guardian*, 17 October.

Cooke, Martin, Daniel Beavon, and Mindy McHardy. 2004. "Measuring the Wellbeing of Aboriginal People: An Application of the United Nations Human Development Index to Registered Indians in Canada, 1981–2001." Ottawa: Indian and Northern Affairs Canada.

Correctional Service Canada. 2013. "Aboriginal Offender Statistics." www.csc-scc.gc.ca/aboriginal/002003-1010-eng.shtml.

Cox, David, and Patrick Glenn. 1994. "Illegal Immigration and Refugee Claims," in Howard Adelman et al., eds, *Immigration and Refugee Policy: Australia and Canada Compared* (Vol. 1). Carleton, Victoria: Melbourne University Press.

Cox, Oliver Cromwell. 1948. *Caste, Class and Race: A Study in Social Dynamics.* New York: Doubleday.

Croucher, Sheila. 2012. Americans Abroad: A Global Diaspora?" *The Journal of Transnational American Studies* 4 (2): 1–33.

Crowley, Brian Lee. 1995. "Property, Culture, and Aboriginal Self-government," in Helmar Cuneo, Carl, and James E. Curtis. 1975. "Social Ascription in the Educational and Occupational Status Attainment of Urban Canadians," *Canadian Review of Sociology and Anthropology* 12 (1): 6–24.

Cuneo, Carl and James Curtis. 1975. "Social Ascription in the Educational and Occupational Status Attainment of Urban Canadians," *Canadian Review of Sociology*, 12 (1): 6–24.

Curry, Bill. 2005. "The Government Responds: Indian Affairs Minister Announces Plan to Relocate Settlement, Improve Sanitation," *The Globe and Mail*, 28 October: A1.

Curtis, Bruce. 2001. *The Politics of Population: State Formation, Statistics and the Census of Canada, 1840–1875.* Toronto: University of Toronto Press.

Daniels, Harry. 1998. "Bill C-31: Abocide Bill." Paper presented at the Native Women's Association of Canada Conference on Bill C-31. Ottawa, March.

Daniels, Michael, Bernie Devlin, and Kathryn Roeder. 1997. "Of Genes and IQ," in Bernie Devlin et al., eds, *Intelligence, Genes and Success: Scientists Respond to The Bell Curve.* New York: Springer-Verlag.

Darroch, Gordon. 1979. "Another Look at Ethnicity, Stratification and Social Mobility in Canada," *Canadian Journal of Sociology* 4 (1): 1–24.

Davies, Scott, and Neil Guppy. 1998. "Race and Canadian Education," in Vic Satzewich, ed., *Racism and Social Inequality in Canada: Concepts, Controversies and Strategies of Resistance*, 131–55. Toronto: Thompson Educational Publishing.

Denis, Wilfrid. 1999. "Language Policy in Canada," in Peter Li, ed., *Race and Ethnic Relations in Canada*, 2nd edn. Toronto: Oxford University Press.

de Silva, Arnold. 1992. *Earnings of Immigrants: A Comparative Analysis.* Economic Council of Canada.

Devlin, Bernie, Stephen E. Fienberg, Daniel P. Resnick, and Kathryn Roeder, eds. 1997. *Intelligence, Genes, and Success: Scientists Respond to The Bell Curve.* New York: Springer-Verlag.

Devortez, Don, and Samuel Laryea. 1998. *Canadian Human Capital Transfers: The USA and Beyond.* Metropolis Working Paper series no. 98-18. Vancouver: Vancouver Centre of Excellence.

Diamond, Jeremy. 2015. "Donald Trump: Ban All Muslim Travel to US," www.cnn.com/2015/12/07/politics/donald-trump-muslim-ban-immigration/.

Dickason, Olive. 1992. *Canada's First Nations: A History of Founding Peoples from Earliest Times.* Toronto: McClelland and Stewart.

Ditchburn, Jennifer. 2014. "Reports Contradict Stephen Harper's View on Aboriginal Women Victims." www.cbc.ca/news/aboriginal/reports-contradict-stephen-harper-s-view-on-aboriginal-women-victims-1.2754542.

Driedger, Leo. 1975. "In Search of Cultural Identity Factors: A Comparison of Ethnic

Students," *Canadian Review of Sociology and Anthropology* 12: 150–62.

_____. 1996. *Multi-ethnic Canada: Identities and Inequalities*. Toronto: Oxford University Press.

Du Bois, W.E.B. 1998[1899]. *The Philadelphia Negro: A Social Study*. Philadelphia: University of Pennsylvania Press.

_____. 1992 [1935]. *Black Reconstruction in America, 1860–1880*. New York: The Free Press.

Dua, Enakshi. 2004. "Racializing Imperial Canada: Indian Women and the Making of Ethnic Communities," in Marlene Epp, Franca Iacovetta, and Frances Swyripa, eds, *Sisters or Strangers: Immigrant, Ethnic, and Racialized Women in Canadian History*, 71–85. Toronto: University of Toronto Press.

_____. 2009. "On the Effectiveness of Anti-Racist Policies in Canadian Universities: Issues of Implementation of Policies by Senior Administrators," in Frances Henry and Carol Tator, eds, *Racism in the Canadian University*. Toronto: University of Toronto Press.

Dufour, Christian. 1992. "A Little History," excerpt from *Le défi québécois*, in William Dodge, ed, *Boundaries of Identity*. Toronto: Lester Publishing.

Dunk, Thomas. 1991. *It's a Working Man's Town: Male Working-class Culture*. Montreal and Kingston: McGill–Queen's University Press.

Durham, First Earl of. 1963. *The Durham Report*. Toronto: McClelland and Stewart.

Durkheim, Émile. 1964 [1893]. *The Division of Labour in Society*. New York: Free Press.

Dyck, Noel. 1991. *What Is the Indian "Problem": Tutelage and Resistance in Canadian Indian Administration*. St. John's NFL: Institute of Social and Economic Research.

Economic Council of Canada. 1991. *New Faces in the Crowd: Economic and Social Impacts of Immigration*. Ottawa: Ministry of Supply and Services.

The Economist. 2014. "Japan's Demography: The Incredibly Shrinking Country," 25 March. www.economist.com/blogs/banyan/2014/03/japans-demography.

European Union. 2010. *Racism, Ethnic Discrimination and Exclusion of Migrants and Minorities in Sport: A Comparative View of the Situation in the European Union*. Vienna, Austria: European Union Agency for Fundamental Rights.

Faist, Thomas. 2000. "Transnationalism in International Migration: Implications for the Study of Citizenship and Culture," *Ethnic and Racial Studies* 23 (2): 189–222.

Fanon, Frantz. 1961. *The Wretched of the Earth*. New York: Grove Press.

_____. 1967. *Black Skin, White Masks*. New York: Grove Press.

Farmer, Nathan. 2005. "Kingston Police Chief Apologizes for Force's Systemic Racism." http://friendsofgrassynarrows.com/item.php?427F.

Feagin, Joe R., and Hernán Vera. 1995. *White Racism*. New York: Routledge.

Fitzpatrick, Meagan. 2013. "Harper on Terror Arrests: Not a Time for 'Sociology,'" CBC *news* www.cbc.ca/news/politics/harper-on-terror-arrests-not-a-time-for-sociology-1.1413502.

Flanagan, Thomas. 2000. *First Nations, Second Thoughts*. Kingston and Montreal: McGill-Queen's University Press.

Fleras, Augie. 2012. *Unequal Relations: An Introduction to Race, Ethnic and Aboriginal Dynamics in Canada*, 7th edn. Toronto: Pearson Education.

_____. 2015. Immigration Canada: Evolving Realities and Emerging Challenges in a Postnational World. Vancouver: University of British Columbia Press.

_____, and Jean Leonard Elliott. 1996. *Unequal Relations: An Introduction to Race, Ethnic and Aboriginal Dynamics in Canada*. Toronto: Prentice Hall Canada.

Fong, Petti. 2005. "BC Teen Pleads Guilty in School Beating Death," *The Globe and Mail*, 27 October: A11.

_____. 2006. "Immigrant Groups Fear Dual-Citizenship Review," *The Globe and Mail*, 19 October: A1.

Forcese, Dennis. 1997. *The Canadian Class Structure*, 4th edn. Toronto: McGraw-Hill Ryerson.

Foster, Lorne. 2008. "Foreign Trained Doctors in Canada: Cultural Contingency and Cultural Democracy in the Medical Profession," *International Journal of Criminology and Sociological Theory* 1 (1): 1–25.

_____. 2009. "Lawyers of Colour and Racialized Immigrants with Foreign Legal Degrees: An Examination of the Institutionalized Process of Social Nullification," *International Journal of Criminology and Sociological Theory* 2 (1): 189–217.

Francis, Diane. 2002. *Immigration: The Economic Case*. Toronto: Key Porter Books.

Fraser, Steven. 1995. "Introduction," in Steven Fraser, ed., *The Bell Curve Wars: Race,*

Intelligence and the Future of America. New York: Basic Books.

Frideres, James, and René Gadacz. 2004. *Aboriginal Peoples in Canada*, 7th edn. Toronto: Pearson Education Canada.

_____, and _____. 2012. *Aboriginal Peoples in Canada*, 9th edn. Toronto: Pearson.

Friesen, Joe. 2005. "Another Funeral, This One Well-Guarded," *The Globe and Mail*, 28 November: A11.

Fulford, Robert. 2006. "How We Became a Land of Ghettos," *National Post*, 12 June: A19.

Furi, Megan, and Jill Wherrett. 2003. *Indian Status and Band Membership Issues*. Ottawa: Parliamentary Research Branch, Library of Parliament.

Gabaccia, Donna. 2000. *Italy's Many Diasporas*. Seattle: University of Washington Press.

Gagnon, Alain-G., ed. 2004. *Québec: State and Society*, 3rd edn. Peterborough: Broadview Press.

Gains, Cork. 2011. "White Coaches Prefer White Quarterbacks, Black Coaches Prefer Black Quarterbacks, *Business Insider*, 14 September. http://articles.businessinsider.com/2011-09-14/sports/30153148_1_black-quarterbacks-head-coaches-white-quarterbacks.

Galabuzi, Grace-Edward. 2006. *Canada's Economic Apartheid: The Social Exclusion of Racialized Groups in the New Century*. Toronto: Canadian Scholars Press.

Gibbon, Edward. 1998. *The Decline and Fall of the Roman Empire*. Hertfordshire: Wordsworth.

Gillis, Wendy, Jim Rankin, and Patty Winsa. 2015. "Ontario Sets Strict New Limits on Police Street Checks," *Toronto Star*, 28 Oct. www.thestar.com/news/crime/2015/10/28/province-to-unveil-limits-on-carding.html.

Gimpel, James, and James Edwards. 1999. *The Congressional Politics of Immigration Reform*. Boston: Allyn and Bacon.

Giroux, France. 1997. "Le nouveau contrat nationalist: Est-il possible dans une démocratie pluraliste? Examen comparatif des situations française, canadienne et québécoise," *Politique et société* 16 (3).

Glick Schiller, Nina. 1999. "Transmigrants and Nation-states: Something Old and Something New in the US Immigrant Experience," in Charles Hirschman et al., eds, *The Handbook of International Migration: The American Experience*. New York: Russell Sage Foundation.

Goldberg, David Theo, ed. 1990. *Anatomy of Racism*. Minneapolis: University of Minnesota Press.

_____. 1993. *Racist Culture: Philosophy and the Politics of Meaning*. Oxford: Blackwell Publishers.

Gordon, Milton. 1964. *Assimilation in American Life: The Role of Race, Religion, and National Origins*. New York: Oxford University Press.

Granatstein, Jack. 2007. *Whose War Is It? How Canada Can Survive in the Post-9/11 World*. Toronto: HarperCollins.

Goyder, John C., and James E. Curtis. 1979. "Occupational Mobility over Four Generations," in James E. Curtis and William G. Scott, eds, *Social Stratification: Canada*, 221–33. Scarborough: Prentice Hall Canada.

Graves, Frank. 2015. "The OKOS Poll: Are Canadians Getting More Racist?" ipolitics, 12 March. http://ipolitics.ca/2015/03/12/the-ekos-poll-are-canadians-getting-more-racist/.

Gulf Research Centre. 2013. "Gulf Labour Markets and Migration." http://gulfmigration.eu/media/graphs/GLMM%20-%20Website%20-%20GCC%20Graph%201%20-%2008%20Nov%202013.pdf.

Guillaumin, Colette. 1995. *Racism, Sexism, Power and Ideology*. London: Routledge.

Hagan, John. 2001. *Northern Passage: American War Resisters in Canada*. Cambridge, MA: Harvard University Press.

Hamilton, Graeme. 2015. "Still Warriors: Kahanawake Mohawks Are Ready to Take Up Arms to Defend Their Beliefs (and Those Gambling Operations)," *National Post*, 10 July. http://news.nationalpost.com/news/canada/still-warriors-kahnawake-mohawks-are-ready-to-take-up-arms-to-defend-their-beliefs.

Hansen, Marcus Lee. 1940. *The Immigrant in American History*. New York: Harper and Row.

_____. 1961. *The Atlantic Migration: 1607–1860*. New York: Harper and Row.

Hardcastle, Leonie, Andrew Parkin, Alan Simmons, and Nobuaki Suyama. 1994. "The Making of Immigration and Refugee Policy: Politicians, Bureaucrats and Citizens," in Howard Adelman et al., eds, *Immigration and Refugee Policy: Australia and Canada Compared* (Vol. 1). Carleton, Aust.: Melbourne University Press.

Harney, Nicholas. 1998. *Eh, Paesan! Being Italian in Toronto*. Toronto: University of Toronto Press.

Harris, Cecil. 2003. *Breaking the Ice: The Black Experience in Professional Hockey*. Toronto: Insomniac Press.

Harvey, Frank. 2000. "Primordialism, Evolutionary Theory and Ethnic Violence in the Balkans: Opportunities and Constraints for Theory and Policy," *Canadian Journal of Political Science*, 33 (1): 37–65.

Harvey, Julien. 1985. "Une impasse, le multiculturalism?" Texte présenté a la Conférence fédérale-provinciale sur le multiculturalisme, Winnipeg.

Hawkins, Freda. 1988. *Canada and Immigration: Public Policy and Public Concern*, 2nd edn. Montreal and Kingston: McGill-Queen's University Press.

———. 1989. *Critical Years in Immigration: Canada and Australia Compared*. Montreal: McGill-Queen's University Press.

Hennebry, Jenna. 2012. *Permanently Temporary? Agricultural Migrant Workers and Their Integration in Canada*. Montreal. Institute for Research on Public Policy.

Henry, Frances. 1999. "Two Studies of Racial Discrimination," in James Curtis, Edward Grabb, and Neil Guppy, eds, *Social Inequality in Canada: Patterns, Problems, and Policies*, 3rd edn, 226–35. Scarborough: Prentice Hall Canada.

———, and Effie Ginzberg. 1985. *Who Gets the Work? A Test of Racial Discrimination in Employment*. Toronto: Urban Alliance on Race Relations and the Social Planning Council of Metropolitan Toronto.

———, and ———. 1988. "Racial Discrimination in Employment," in James Curtis, Ed ward Grabb, Neil Guppy, and Sid Gilbert, eds, *Social Inequality in Canada: Patterns, Problems, Policies*, 214–20. Scarborough: Prentice-Hall Canada.

———, and Carol Tator. 1999. "State Policy and Practices as Racialized Discourse: Multiculturalism, the Charter, and Employment Equity," in Peter Li, ed., *Race and Ethnic Relations in Canada*. Toronto: Oxford University Press.

———, and ———. 2010. *The Colour of Democracy: Racism in Canadian Society*, 4th edn. Toronto: Nelson Canada.

Herberg, Edward N. 1989. *Ethnic Groups in Canada: Adaptations and Transitions*, 2nd edn. Scarborough: Nelson Canada.

Hernandez-Ramdwar, Camille. 2009. "Caribbean Students in the Academy: We've Come a Long Way?" in Frances Henry and Carol Tator, eds, *Racism in the Canadian University*. Toronto: University of Toronto Press.

Herodotus. 1998. *Histories*. Hertfordshire, UK: Wordsworth.

Herrnstein, Richard, and Charles Murray. 1994. *The Bell Curve: Intelligence and Class Structure in American Life*. New York: Free Press.

Hier, Sean, and Joshua Greenberg. 2002. "News Discourse and the Problematization of Chinese Migration to Canada," in Frances Henry and Carol Tator, eds, *Discourses of Domination: Racial Bias in the Canadian English-language Press*. Toronto: University of Toronto Press.

Hill Collins, Patricia. 2000. *Black Feminist Thought: Knowledge, Consciousness, and the Politics of Empowerment*. New York: Routledge.

Hirschfeld Davis, Julie. 2015. "Obama's Twitter Debut, @POTUS, Attracts Hate-Filled Posts," *New York Times*, 21 May. www .nytimes.com/2015/05/22/us/politics/ obamas-twitter-debut-potus-attracts-hate -filled-posts.html?hp&action=click&- pgtype=Homepage&module=second -column-region&region=top-news&WT .nav=top-news&_r=1.

Hooten, Ernest. 1946. *Up from the Ape*. New York: MacMillan.

Hou, Feng, and T.R. Balakrishnan. 1999. "The Economic Integration of Visible Minorities in Contemporary Canadian Society," in James Curtis, Edward Grabb, and Neil Guppy, eds, *Social Inequality in Canada: Patterns, Problems, and Policies*, 3rd edn, 214–25. Scarborough: Prentice Hall Canada.

Hourani, Albert. 1992. 'Introduction' in Albert Hourani and Nadim Shehadi, eds., *The Lebanese in the World: A Century of Emigration*. London: Centre for Lebanese Studies.

Howard-Hassmann, Rhoda. 1999. "'Canadian' as an Ethnic Category: Implications for Multiculturalism and National Unity," *Canadian Public Policy* 25 (4): 531.

Harles, John. 2004. "Immigrant Integration in Canada and the United States," *American Review of Canadian Studies* 34 (2): 223–58.

Hum, Derek, and Wayne Simpson. 2007. "Revisiting Equity and Labour: Immigration, Gender, Minority Status, and Income in Canada," in Sean Hier and Singh Bolaria, eds, *Race and Racism in 21st Century Canada: Continuity, Complexity, and Change*, 89–109. Peterborough: Broadview Press.

Humphreys, Adrian. 2012. "Violent Racist Gang Expands into Edmonton." http://news .nationalpost.com/2012/04/17/

violent-racist-gang-expands-into-edmonton/.

Huntington, Samuel. 2004. "The Hispanic Challenge," *Foreign Policy* 141 (March–April): 30–45.

Huntley, Audrey, and Fay Blaney. 1999. *Bill C-31: Its Impacts, Implications, and Recommendations for Change in British Columbia—Final Report*. Vancouver: Aboriginal Women's Action Network and Vancouver Status of Women.

Hussain, Murtaza. 2013. "What the World Can Learn from Canadian Multiculturalism," www.aljazeera.com/indepth/opinion/2013/09/2013915111722311111.html.

Hutchinson, Brian. 2011. "Blood and Honour 'White Supremacists' Charged over String of Assaults on Minorities." http://news.nationalpost.com/2011/12/09/white-supremacists-who-allegedly-set-fire-to-filipino-man-charged-over-hate-crimes/.

Iacovetta, Franca. 1992. *Such Hardworking People: Italian Immigrants in Postwar Canada*. Toronto: University of Toronto Press.

———, and Robert Ventresca. 2000. "Redress, Collective Memory and the Politics of History," in Franca Iacovetta, Roberto Perin, and Angelo Principe, eds, *Enemies Within: Italian and Other Internees in Canada and Abroad*. Toronto: University of Toronto Press.

Immigration, Refugees and Citizenship Canada 2016. "Designated Countries of Origin." www.cic.gc.ca/english/refugees/reform-safe.asp.

Innovation, Science and Economic Development Canada. 2014. "Seizing Canada's Moment," https://www.ic.gc.ca/eic/site/icgc.nsf/eng/07481.html.

Inuit Tapiriit Kanatami. 2004a. "The Case for Inuit Specific: Renewing the Relationship between the Inuit and Government of Canada." Ottawa: Inuit Tapiriit Kanatami.

———. 2004b. "The Inuit Tapiriit Kanatami: The Origin of the ITK." www.tapirisat.ca/.

Isaacs, Harold. 1975. "Basic Group Identity: The Idols and the Tribe," in Nathan Glazer and Daniel Patrick Moynihan, eds, *Ethnicity: Theory and Experience*. Cambridge: Harvard University Press.

Isajiw, Wsevolod W. 1999. *Understanding Diversity: Ethnicity and Race in the Canadian Context*. Toronto: Thompson Educational Publishing.

Israeli Ministry of Foreign Affairs. 2015. "Global Forum for Combating Anti-semitism Closes."

http://mfa.gov.il/MFA/PressRoom/2015/Pages/Global-Forum-for-Combating-Antisemitism-closes-14-May-2015.aspx.

Jacobson, Matthew Frye. 1998. *Whiteness of a Different Color: European Immigrants and the Alchemy of Race*. Cambridge, MA: Harvard University Press.

Jakubowski, Lisa. 1997. *Immigration and the Legalization of Racism*. Halifax, NS: Fernwood Press.

James, Carl. 2005. *Race in Play: Understanding the Socio-cultural Worlds of Student Athletes*. Toronto: Canadian Scholars Press.

Jedwab, Jack. 2003. "Coming to Our Census: The Need for Continuing Inquiry into Canadians' Ethnic Origins," *Canadian Ethnic Studies* 35 (1): 33–50.

———, and Vic Satzewich. 2015. "Introductory Essay: John Porter's *The Vertical Mosaic*, 50 Years Later," in John Porter, *The Vertical Mosiac: An Analysis of Social Class and Power in Canada (50th Anniversary Edition)*. Toronto: University of Toronto Press.

Jelinek, Otto. 1986. "Welcoming Remarks to the Multiculturalism Means Business Conference." Toronto, 18 May.

Jhappan, Radha. 1996. "Post-modern Race and Gender Essentialism or a Post-mortem of Scholarship," *Studies in Political Economy* 51 (3): 15–63.

———. 2005. "Broken Gates: How People Smugglers are Beating the System," *The Globe and Mail*, 20 April: A1.

Jimenez-Pardo, Johanna. 2014. "Inside *Justice at Last*: Understanding the Numbers," *Assembly of First Nations, State of Claims* (Vol. 1), Spring.

Johnson, James H., Jr, Walter C. Farrell, Jr, and Chandra Guinn. 1999. "Immigration Reform and the Browning of America: Tensions, Conflicts and Community Instability in Metropolitan Los Angeles," in Charles Hirschman et al., eds, *The Handbook of International Migration: The American Experience*. New York: Russell Sage Foundation.

Johnson, Lisa. 2011. "Seeing Red: High School Controversy Leads to Some Serious Hate," *Planet S* 10 (3). www.planetsmag.com/story.php?id=617.

Joppke, Christian. 1999. "How Immigration is Changing Citizenship: A Comparative View," *Ethnic and Racial Studies* 22 (4): 629–52.

———. 2009. *Veil: Mirror of Identity*. Cambridge: Polity Press.

Jull, Stephen. 2000. "Youth Violence, Schools, and the Management Question: Discussion of Zero Tolerance and Equity in Public Schooling," *Canadian Journal of Educational Administration and Policy* 17.

Juteau, Danielle. 2002. "The Citizen Makes an Entrée: Redefining the National Community in Quebec," *Citizenship Studies* 6 (4): 441–58.

Kalbach, Madeline, and Warren Kalbach. 2000. *Perspectives on Ethnicity in Canada*. Toronto: Harcourt Canada.

Kallen, Evelyn. 2003. *Ethnicity and Human Rights in Canada*, 3rd edition. Toronto: Oxford University Press.

Karim, Karim. 1998. "From Ethnic Media to Global Media: Transnational Communication Networks among Diasporic Communities." Ottawa: Heritage Canada. www.transcomm. ox.ac.uk/working%20papers/karim.pdf.

Karmis, Demetrios. 2004. "Pluralism and National Identity(ies) in Contemporary Quebec: Conceptual Clarifications, Typology, and Discourse Analysis," in Alain-G. Gagnon, ed., *Québec: State and Society*, 3rd edn, 69–96. Peterborough: Broadview Press.

Keenan, Greg. 2015. "TPP Deal Is Bad for Auto Sector, Ford Canada Chief Says," *The Globe and Mail*, 25 October. www.theglobeand-mail.com/report-on-business/international-business/trans-pacific-partnership-deal-bad-for-auto-sector-ford-canada-head-says/article26968929/.

Kelly, Karen. 1995. "Visible Minorities: A Diverse Group," *Canadian Social Trends* 37 (Summer): 2–8.

Khayati, Khalid. 2008. *From Victim Diaspora to Transborder Citizenship: Diaspora Formation and Transnational Relations among Kurds in France and Sweden*. Ph.D. dissertation, Linkopings University, Sweden.

Kinder, Donald, and David Sears. 1981. "Prejudice and Politics: Symbolic Racism versus Racial Threats to the Good Life," *Journal of Personality and Social Psychology* 40: 414–31.

Kirkham, Della. 1998. "The Reform Party of Canada: A Discourse on Race, Ethnicity and Equality," in Vic Satzewich, ed., *Racism and Social Inequality in Canada: Concepts, Controversies and Strategies of Resistance*. Toronto: Thompson Educational Publishing.

Knowles, Valerie. 1992. *Strangers at Our Gates: Canadian Immigration and Immigration Policy, 1540–1990*. Toronto: Dundurn Press.

Kobayashi, Audrey. 2009. "Now You See Them, How You See Them: Women of Colour in Canadian Academia," in Frances Henry and Carol Tator, eds, *Racism in the Canadian University*. Toronto: University of Toronto Press.

_____, and Linda Peake. 2000. "Racism out of Place: Thoughts on Whiteness and an Anti-Racist Geography in the New Millennium," *Annals of the Association of American Geographers* 90 (2): 392–403.

Kordan, Bohdan. 2000. *Ukrainian Canadians and the Canadian Census, 1981–1996*. Saskatoon: Heritage Press.

_____. 2002. *Enemy Aliens, Prisoners of War*. Montreal and Kingston: McGill-Queen's University Press.

Koser, Khalid. 2001. "The Smuggling of Asylum Seekers into Western Europe: Contradictions, Conundrums and Dilemmas," in David Kyle and Rey Koslowski, eds, *Global Human Smuggling: Comparative Perspectives*. Baltimore: Johns Hopkins University Press.

Krahn Harvey, Graham Lowe, and Karen Hughes. 2007. *Work, Industry, and Canadian Society*, 5th edn. Toronto: Nelson Canada. Kukushkin, Vadim. 2009. *Immigrant-Friendly Communities: Making Immigration Work for Employers and Other Stakeholders in Small-Town Canada*. Ottawa: Conference Board of Canada.

Kyle, David. 1999. "The Otavalo Trade Diaspora: Social Capital and Transnational Entrepreneurship," *Ethnic and Racial Studies* 22(2): 422–46.

Kymlicka, Will. 1998. "The Theory and Practice of Canadian Multiculturalism." Paper presented to the Canadian Federation of the Social Sciences and Humanities, 23 November: 1–10. /www.fedcan.ca/english/ fromold/ breakfast-kymlicka1198.cfm.

_____. 2010. *The Current State of Multiculturalism in Canada and Research Themes on Canadian Multiculturalism, 2008–2010*. www .cic.gc.ca/english/resources/publications/ multi-state/index.asp.

_____. 2012. "Multiculturalism: Success, Failure, and the Future." Washington, DC: Migration Policy Institute.

Lapchick, Ron, and Leyroy Robinson. 2015. "The 2015 Racial and Gender Report Card: National Football League," The Institute for Diversity and Ethics in Sports. www .tidesport.org/.

Lautard, Hugh, and Neil Guppy. 1990. "The Vertical Mosaic Revisited: Occupational

Differentials among Canadian Ethnic Groups," in Peter Li, ed., *Race and Ethnic Relations in Canada*, 189–208. Toronto: Oxford University Press.

———, and ———. 2007. "Occupational Inequality among Canadian Ethnic Groups, 1931 to 2001," in Robert J. Brym, ed., *Society in Question*, 5th edn. Toronto: Nelson Canada.

Lawrence, Bonita. 2004. *"Real" Indians and Others: Mixed-blood Urban Native Peoples and Indigenous Nationhood*. Lincoln: University of Nebraska Press.

Leslie, Keith. 2005. "NDP Wants Safe Schools Act Repealed: Claim It Helps Gangs Recruit." www.canada.com/components/printstory/.

Levant, Ezra. 2008. "David Ahenakew, Celebrity." http://ezralevant.com/2008/11/david-ahenakew-celebrity.html.

Lévesque, Stéphane. 1999. "Rethinking Citizenship and Citizenship Education: A Canadian Perspective for the 21st Century." Paper presented at the Citizenship Research Network Symposium, Fourth International Metropolis Conference, Georgetown University, Washington, DC, 129.

Levitt, Cyril. 1994. "Is Canada a Racist Country?" in Sally F. Zerker, ed., *Change and Impact: Essays in Canadian Social Sciences*, 304–16. Jerusalem, IS: Magnes Press, Hebrew University.

Levitt, Peggy, and Raphael de la Dehesa. 2003. "Transnational Migration and the Redefinition of the State: Variations and Explanations," *Ethnic and Racial Studies* 26 (4): 587–611.

Lewis, Oscar. 1959. *Five Families: Mexican Case Studies in the Culture of Poverty*. New York: Oxford University Press.

———. 1966. "The Culture of Poverty," *Scientific American* 215: 19–25.

Lewycky, Laverne. 1992. "Multiculturalism in the 1990s and into the 21st Century: Beyond Ideology and Utopia," in Vic Satzewich, ed., *Deconstructing a Nation: Immigration, Multiculturalism and Racism in '90s Canada*. Halifax, NS: Fernwood Press.

Li, Peter. 1988. *Ethnic Inequality in a Class Society*. Toronto: Thompson Educational Publishing.

———. 1992. "Race and Gender as Bases of Class Fractions and the Effects on Earnings," *Canadian Review of Sociology and Anthropology* 29 (4): 488–510.

———. 1994a. "A World Apart: The Multicultural World of Visible Minorities and the Art World of Canada," *Canadian Review of Sociology and Anthropology* 31(4): 365–91.

———. 1998a. *The Chinese in Canada*, 2nd edn. Toronto: Oxford University Press.

———. 1998b. "The Market Value and Social Value of Race," in Vic Satzewich, ed., *Racism and Social Inequality in Canada: Concepts, Controversies and Strategies of Resistance*, 115–30. Toronto: Thompson Educational Publishing.

———, ed. 1999. *Race and Ethnic Relations in Canada*, 2nd edn. Toronto: Oxford University Press.

———. 2003. *Destination Canada: Immigration Debates and Issues*. Toronto: Oxford University Press.

———. 2012. "Differences in Employment Income of University Professors," *Canadian Ethnic Studies* 44 (2): 39–48.

Lian, Jason Z., and Ralph Matthews. 1998. "Does the Vertical Mosaic Still Exist? Ethnicity and Income in Canada, 1991," *Canadian Review of Sociology and Anthropology* 35 (4): 461–81.

Linder, Douglas. 2001. "Famous American Trials: Los Angeles Police Officers' (Rodney King Beating) Trials, 1992 & 1993," http://law2.umkc.edu/faculty/projects/ftrials/lapd/lapd.html.

Liodakis, Nikolaos. 1998. "The Activities of Hellenic-Canadian Secular Organizations in the Context of Canadian Multiculturalism," *Études Helléniques/Hellenic Studies* 6 (1): 37–58.

———. 2002. "The Vertical Mosaic Within: Class, Gender and Nativity within Ethnicity." Unpublished PhD dissertation, Department of Sociology, McMaster University, Hamilton, ON.

———, and Vic Satzewich. 2003. "From Solution to Problem: Multiculturalism and 'Race Relations' as New Social Problems," in Wayne Antony and Les Samuelson, eds, *Power and Resistance: Critical Thinking about Canadian Social Issues*, 3rd edn, 145–68. Halifax, NS: Fernwood Press.

Lorimer, Douglas. 1978. *Colour, Class and the Victorians: English Attitudes to the Negro in the Mid-Nineteenth Century*. New York: Holmes and Meier Publishers.

Louie, Vivian S. 2004. *Compelled to Excel: Immigration, Education, and Opportunity among Chinese Americans*. Stanford, CA: Stanford University Press.

Luciuk, Lubomir, ed. 1994. *Righting an Injustice: The Debate Over Redress for Canada's First National Internment Operations*. Toronto: Justinian Press.

Luxen, Micah. 2015. "#BBCTrending: Is Winnipeg Canada's most racist city?," BBC News, www.bbc.com/news/blogs-trending-30941647.

McAll, Christopher. 1990. *Class, Ethnicity and Social Inequality*. Montreal: McGill-Queen's University Press.

McConahay, J. 1986. "Modern Racism, Ambivalence, and the Modern Racism Scale," in J. Dovidio and S. Gaertner, eds, *Prejudice, Discrimination, and Racism*. New York: Academic Press.

Macdonald, Nancy. 2015. "Welcome to Winnipeg: Where Canada's Racism Problem Is at Its Worst," *Maclean's*, 22 January. www.macleans.ca/news/canada/welcome-to-winnipeg-where-canadas-racism-problem-is-at-its-worst/.

McElwee, Sean. 2013. "The Case for Censoring Hate Speech on the Internet," *Arts. Mic* http://mic.com/articles/55553/the-case-for-censoring-hate-speech-on-the-internet.

McIntosh, Peggy. 1988. "White Privilege and Male Privilege: A Personal Account of Coming to See Correspondences through Work in Women's Studies," Working Paper no. 189, Wellesley College.

Mackinnon, Mark. 2015. "Bypassing Official Channels, Canada's Ukrainian Diaspora Finances a War against Russia, *The Globe ad Mail*, 26 February. www.theglobeandmail.com/news/world/ukraine-canadas-unofficial-war/article23208129/.

McLaren, Angus. 1990. *Our Own Master Race: Eugenics in Canada, 1885–1945*. Toronto: McClelland and Stewart.

McSheffrey, Elizabeth. 2015. "Track Foreign Buying of Real Estate, Says Chinese Canadian Group," *Vancouver Observer*. www.vancouverobserver.com/news/track-foreign-buying-real-estate-says-chinese-canadian-group).

Makabe, Tamoko. 1981. "The Theory of the Split Labour Market: A Comparison of the Japanese Experience in Brazil and Canada," *Social Forces* 59: 786–809.

Malloy, Jonathan. 2003. "To Better Service Canadians: How Technology is Changing the Relationship between Members of Parliament and Public Servants," *New Directions*, no. 9. Toronto: Institute of Public Administration.

Mamdani, Mahmood. 2001. *When Victims Become Killers: Colonialism, Nativism, and the Genocide in Rwanda*. Princeton, NJ: Princeton University Press.

Mandelbaum, Michael. 2000. "Introduction," in Michael Mandelbaum, ed, *The New European Diasporas: National Minorities and Conflict in Eastern Europe*. New York: Council on Foreign Relations Press.

Marger, Martin. 1997. *Race and Ethnic Relations: American and Global Perspectives*. Belmont, CA: Wadsworth Publishing.

Marx, Karl. [1859] 1970. *A Contribution to the Critique of Political Economy*. New York: International Publishers.

Mason, David. 1986. "Controversies and Continuities in Race and Ethnic Relations Theory," in John Rex and David Mason, eds, *Theories of Race and Ethnic Relations*. London: Cambridge University Press.

Massey, Douglas. 1999. "Why Does Immigration Occur? A Theoretical Synthesis," in Charles Hirschman et al., eds, *The Handbook of International Migration: The American Experience*. New York: Russell Sage Foundation.

Matthews, Kim, and Vic Satzewich. 2006. "The Invisible Transnationals: American Immigrants in Canada," in Vic Satzewich and Lloyd Wong, eds, *Transnational Identities and Practices in Canada*. Vancouver: University of British Columbia Press.

Mazrui, Ali. 1990. *Cultural Forces in World Politics*. London: James Currey.

Media Awareness Network. 2010. "Deconstructing Hate Sites." www.media-awareness.ca/english/issues/online_hate/deconst_online_hate.cfm.

Meerman-Scott, David. 2012. "The Second Most Important Communication Revolution in History," *WebInkNow*. www.webinknow.com/2012/12/the-second-most-important-communication-revolution-in-history.html.

Métis National Council. 2014. "Métis Registration Guide." www.metisnation.ca/wp-content/uploads/2011/04/M%C3%A9tis-Registration-Guide.pdf.

Miles, Robert. 1982. *Racism and Migrant Labour*. London: Routledge and Kegan Paul.

———. 1984. *White Man's Country: Racism in British Politics*. London: Pluto Press.

———. 1993. *Racism after "Race Relations."* London: Routledge.

———, and Malcolm Brown. 2003. *Racism*, 2nd edn. London: Routledge.

———, and Rudy Torres. 1996. "Does 'Race' Matter? Transatlantic Perspectives on Racism after 'Race Relations,'" in V. Amit-Talai and C. Knowles, eds, *Re-situating*

Identities: The Politics of Race, Ethnicity and Culture, 24–46. Peterborough: Broadview Press.

Mimms, Sarah. 2015. "What Rachel Dolezal Left Behind," *National Journal*. www.nationaljournal.com/politics/rachel-dolezal-spokane-naacp-20150706.

Mitchell, Katharyne. 2004. *Crossing the Neoliberal Line: Pacific Rim Migration and the Metropolis*. Philadelphia PA: Temple University Press.

Mitchell, Marybelle. 1996. *From Talking Chiefs to a Native Corporate Elite: The Birth of Class and Nationalism among Canadian Inuit*. Montreal and Kingston: McGill-Queen's University Press.

Mohawk Council of Kanawàke, 2007. "Kanawa:ke Membership Law," www.kahnawake.com/.

Molotov, Alexander. 2012. "Not a Good Year for 'Blood and Honour' Canada." http://vancouver.mediacoop.ca/story/not-good-year-neo-nazi-blood-and-honour-canada/10321.

Montagu, Ashley. 1964. *Man's Most Dangerous Myth*. New York: World Publishing.

_____. 1972. *Statement on Race*. Oxford: Oxford University Press.

Monture, Patricia. 2009. "'Doing Academia Differently': Confronting 'Whiteness' in the University," in Frances Henry and Carol Tator, eds, *Racism in the Canadian University*. Toronto: University of Toronto Press.

Moodley, Kogila. 1983. "Canadian Multiculturalism as Ideology," *Ethnic and Racial Studies* 6 (3): 320–31.

Morley Johnson, Daniel. 2011. "From the Tomahawk Chop to the Road Block," *American Indian Quarterly* 35 (1): 104–35.

Murdie, Robert, and Carlos Teixeira. 2003. "Towards a Comfortable Neighbourhood and Appropriate Housing: Immigrant Experiences in Toronto," in Paul Anisef and Michael Lanphier, *The World in a City*. Toronto: University of Toronto Press.

Nadeau, Mary-Jo. 2005. *The Making and Unmaking of a Parliament of Women: Nation, Race and the Politics of the National Action Committee on the Status of Women (1972–1992)*. PhD dissertation, York University, Toronto.

Nagel, Joane. 2003. *Race, Ethnicity and Sexuality: Intimate Intersections, Forbidden Frontiers*. New York: Oxford University Press.

Nagler, Mark. 1975. *Natives without a Home*. Toronto: Longmans.

Nakhaie, Reza, ed. 1999. *Debates on Social Inequality: Class, Gender and Ethnicity in Canada*. Toronto: Harcourt Canada.

_____. 2000. "Ownership and Management Position of Canadian Ethnic Groups in 1973 and 1989," in Madeline A. Kalbach and Warren Kalbach, eds, *Perspectives on Ethnicity in Canada*. Toronto: Harcourt Canada.

_____. 2004. "Who Controls Canadian Universities? Ethnoracial Origins of Canadian University Administrators and Faculty's Perception of Mistreatment," *Canadian Ethnic Studies* 26 (1): 92–110.

_____. 2015. "Economic Benefits of Self-Employment for Canadian Immigrants," *Canadian Review of Sociology* 52(4): 377–401.

Nangia, Parveen. 2013. "Discrimination Experienced by Landed Immigrants in Canada," Working Paper no. 2013/7. Toronto: Ryerson Centre for Immigration and Settlement.

National Post. 2007. "Mayrand Flouts Will of Parliament with Interpretation of Elections Act." www.nationalpost.com/news/story.html?id=27a9995c-e915-4f09-9ec1-763cf8251532&k=88632, 10 September.

Nishnawabe-Aski Legal Services, 2015. "Gladue Report." www.nanlegal.on.ca/article/gladue-report-252.asp.

Nobles, Melissa. 2000. *Shades of Citizenship: Race and the Census in Modern Politics*. Stanford, CA: Stanford University Press.

Noh, Samuel, and Violet Kaspar. 2003. "Diversity and Immigrant Health," in Paul Anisef and Michael Lanphier, eds, *The World in a City*. Toronto: University of Toronto Press.

Noivo, Edite. 1998. "Neither 'Ethnic Heroes' Nor 'Racial Villains': Inter-minority Group Racism," in Vic Satzewich, ed., *Racism and Social Inequality in Canada: Concepts, Controversies and Strategies of Resistance*. Toronto: Thompson Educational Publishing.

Ocadunfa, Sola. 2006. "Nigeria's Counting Controversy." BBC News. http://news.bbc.co.uk/go/pr/fr/-/1/hi/world/africa/4512240.stm.

Odunfa, Sola. 2006. "Nigeria's counting controversy," *BBC Focus on Africa*, March 26. http://news.bbc.co.uk/2/hi/africa/4512240.stm.

OECD. 2015. "Foreign-born Population (Indicator)." Doi:10.1787/5a368e1b-en

Office of the Correctional Investigator for Canada. 2014. *Annual Report for 2013–14*. Ottawa: Correctional Investigator Canada.

Ogmundson, Richard. 1991. "Perspective on the Class and Ethnic Origins of Canadian Elites: A Methodological Critique of the Porter/Clement/Olsen Tradition," *Canadian Journal of Sociology* 15 (2): 165–77.

———. 1993. "At the Top of the Mosaic: Doubts about the Data," *American Review of Canadian Studies* Autumn: 373–86.

———, and J. McLaughlin. 1992. "Trends in the Ethnic Origins of Canadian Elites: The Decline of the BRITS?" *Canadian Review of Sociology and Anthropology* 29 (2): 227–42.

Omatsu, Maryka. 1992. *Bittersweet Passage: Redress and the Japanese Canadian Experience.* Toronto: Between the Lines Press.

Omi, Michael, and Howard Winant. 1986. *Racial Formation in the United States.* London: Routledge.

Ontario Human Rights Commission. 2005a. *Disproportionate Impact of "Zero Tolerance" Discipline.* www.ohrc.on.ca/en_text/consultations/safe-schools-submission.

———. 2005b. *The Existence of Racial Profiling.* Toronto: Ontario Human Rights Commission.

Ontario Ministry of Education, 2016. "Progressive Discipline," http://edu.gov.on.ca/eng/safeschools/discipline.html.

Ooka, Emi, and Barry Wellman. 2000. *Does Social Capital Pay Off More within or between Ethnic Groups? Analysing Job Searches in Five Toronto Ethnic Groups.* Toronto: Centre of Excellence for Research on Immigration and Settlement.

Oppal, Wally. 2012. *Forsaken: The Report of the Missing Women Commission of Inquiry. Executive Summary.* British Columbia: Missing Women Commission of Inquiry.

Ornstein, Michael. 1981. "The Occupational Mobility of Men in Ontario," *Canadian Review of Sociology and Anthropology* 18 (2): 181–215.

———. 1983. *Accounting for Gender Differentials in Job Income in Canada: Results from a 1981 Survey.* Ottawa: Minister of Supply and Services.

Osborne, John. 1991. "'Non-preferred' People: Inter-war Ukrainian Immigration to Canada," in Lubomir Luciuk and Stella Hryniuk, eds, *Canada's Ukrainians: Negotiating an Identity,* 81–102. Toronto: University of Toronto Press.

Ostrovsky, Yuri. 2008. "Earnings Inequality and Earnings Instability of Immigrants in Canada." Ottawa: Statistics Canada.

Analytical Studies, Research Paper Series. Catalogue no. 11F0019M, No. 309.

Park, Robert. 1914. "Racial Assimilation in Secondary Groups," *American Journal of Sociology* 607.

Parsons, Talcott. 1991. *The Social System.* London: Routledge.

Patel, Humaira. 2015. "Without More Support, Muslim Girls May Well Be Tempted by ISIS's HR Department," *The Guardian,* 24 February. www.theguardian.com/commentisfree/2015/feb/24/muslim-girls-isis-teenage-east-london

Peace and Conflict Planners. 2016. "Projects: Diaspora Communications Response Centres." www.pcpcanada.com/projects/.

Pendakur, Krishna. 2005. "Visible Minorities in Canada's Workplaces: A Perspective on the 2017 Projection." Research on Immigration and Integration in the Metropolis Working Paper no. 05-11. Vancouver: Vancouver Centre of Excellence.

———, and Ravi Pendakur. 1996. "Earnings Differentials among Ethnic Groups in Canada." Ottawa: Strategic Research and Analysis, Department of Canadian Heritage.

———, and ———. 2011. "Aboriginal Income Disparity in Canada," *Canadian Public Policy* 37 (1): 61–83.

Peritz, Ingrid. 2011. "Gatineau's Values Guide for Immigrants Stirs Controversy," *The Globe and Mail,* 4 December.

Perreaux, Les. 2015. "Quebec Crackdown on Violent Extremism Reopens Secularism Debate," *The Globe and Mail,* 10 June. www.theglobeandmail.com/news/national/quebec-introduces-action-plan-to-combat-violent-radicalization/article24901428/).

Petryshyn, Jaroslav. 1991. "Sifton's Immigration Policy," in Lubomir Luciuk and Stella Hryniuk, eds, *Canada's Ukrainians: Negotiating an Identity,* 17–29. Toronto: University of Toronto Press.

Pettigrew, Thomas. 1998. "Intergroup Contact Theory," *Annual Review of Psychology* 49: 65–85.

Pettipas, Katherine. 1994. *Severing the Ties That Bind: Government Repression of Indigenous Ceremonies on the Prairies.* Winnipeg: University of Manitoba Press.

Phillips, Paul. 1967. *No Power Greater: A Century of Labour in BC.* Vancouver: BC Federation of Labour.

Picot, Garnett, and Feng Hou. 2011. *Divergent Trends in Citizenship Rates among Immigrants in Canada and the United States.* Ottawa. Statistics Canada.

Pizarro, Marcos. 1998. "Chicana/o Power! Epistemology and Methodology for Social Justice and Empowerment in Chicana/o Communities," *Qualitative Studies in Education* 11 (1): 57–80.

Poirier, Agnes. 2009. "Britain Could Never Debate the Burka Like France," *Times Online.* www.timesonline.co.uk/tol/comment/columnists/guest_contributors/article6565064.ece.

Ponting, J. Rick, and Roger Gibbins. 1980. *Out of Irrelevance: A Sociopolitical Introduction to Indian Affairs in Canada.* Scarborough: Butterworths.

Porter, John. 2015 [1965]. *The Vertical Mosaic: An Analysis of Social Class and Power in Canada,* 50th anniversary edn. Toronto: University of Toronto Press.

_____. 1985. "Canada: The Societal Context of Occupational Allocation," in Monica Boyd, John Goyder, Frank E. Jones, Hugh A. McRoberts, Peter C. Pineo, and John Porter, *Ascription and Achievement: Studies in Mobility and Status Attainment in Canada,* 29–65. Ottawa: Carleton University Press.

Portes, Alejandro. 1995. "Children of Immigrants: Segmented Assimilation and Its Determinants," in Alejandro Portes, ed., *The Economic Sociology of Immigration.* New York: Russell Sage Foundation.

_____. 1999. "Conclusion: Towards a New World—The Origins and Effects of Transnational Activities," *Ethnic and Racial Studies* 22 (2): 463–77.

_____, Luis Guarnizo, and Patricia Landolt. 1999. "The Study of Transnationalism: Pitfalls and Promise of an Emergent Research Field," *Ethnic and Racial Studies* 22 (2): 217–37.

_____, and Min Zhou. 1993. "The New Second Generation: Segmented Assimilation and Its Variants among Post-1965 American Youth," *Annals of the American Academy of Political and Social Science* 530 (November): 74–96.

Pratt, Anna. 2005. *Securing Borders: Detention and Deportation in Canada.* Vancouver: University of British Columbia Press.

Powers, Lucas. 2015. "Conservatives Pledge Funds, Tip Line to Combat 'Barbaric Cultural Practices.'" CBC News, 2 October. www.cbc.ca/news/politics/canada-election-2015-barbaric-cultural-practices-law-1.3254118.

Preston, Valerie, Lucia Lo, and Shunguang Wang. 2003. "Immigrants' Economic Status in Toronto; Triumph and Disappointment," in Paul Anisef and Michael Lanphier, eds, *The World in a City.* Toronto: University of Toronto Press.

Principe, Angelo. 2000. "A Tangled Knot: Prelude to 10 June 1940," in Franca Iacovetta et al., eds, *Enemies Within: Italian Canadians and Other Internees in Canada and Abroad.* Toronto: University of Toronto Press.

Quigley, Tim. 1994. "Some Issues in Sentencing of Aboriginal Offenders," in Richard Goose et al., eds, *Continuing in Poundmaker and Riel's Quest.* Saskatoon, SK: Purich Publishing.

Ralston, Helen. 1991. "Race, Class, Gender and Work Experience of South Asian Immigrant Women in Atlantic Canada," *Canadian Ethnic Studies* (23): 129–39.

Ramos, Howard. 2012. "Does How You Measure Representation Matter? Assessing the Persistence of Canadian Universities' Gendered and Colour Coded Vertical Mosaic," *Canadian Ethnic Studies* 44 (2): 13–37.

Rankin, Jim, et al. 2002. "Singled Out: An Investigation into Race and Crime," *Toronto Star* 26 October: A6.

Reis, Michele. 2004. "Theorizing Diaspora: Perspectives on 'Classical' and 'Contemporary' Diaspora," *International Migration* 42 (2): 41–60.

Reitz, Jeffrey G. 1980. *The Survival of Ethnic Groups.* Toronto: McGraw-Hill Ryerson.

_____. 1990. "Ethnic Concentrations in Labour Markets and Their Implications for Ethnic Inequality," in Raymond Breton et al., eds, *Ethnic Identity and Inequality: Varieties of Experience in a Canadian City.* Toronto: University of Toronto Press.

_____. 2001. "Immigrant Skill Utilization in the Canadian Labour Market: Implications of Human Capital Research," *Journal of International Migration and Integration* 2 (3): 347–78.

_____. 2008. "Tapping Immigrants' Skills," in Robert Brym, ed., *Society in Question,* 5th edn, 130–40. Toronto: Thomson Nelson.

_____, and Raymond Breton. 1994. *The Illusion of Difference: Realities of Ethnicity in Canada and the United States.* Toronto: CD Howe Institute.

Rich, Camille Gear. 2015. "Rachel Dolezal Has a Right to Be Black." www

.cnn.com/2015/06/15/opinions/rich-rachel-dolezal/.

Richards, John. 1995. "A Comment," in Helmar Drost, Brian Lee Crowley, and Richard Schwindt, eds, *Market Solutions for Native Poverty*. Toronto: CD Howe Institute.

Richmond, Anthony. 1967. *Post-war Immigrants in Canada*. Toronto: University of Toronto Press.

Roberts, Barbara. 1988. *Whence They Came: Deportation from Canada 1900–1935*. Ottawa: University of Ottawa Press.

Roberts, Bryan, Beanne Frank, and Fernando Lozano-Acencio. 1999. "Transnational Migrant Communities and Mexican Migration to the US," *Ethnic and Racial Studies* 22 (2): 238–66.

Roberts, Lance, and Rodney Clifton. 1982. "Exploring the Ideology of Canadian Multiculturalism," *Canadian Public Policy* 8 (1): 88–94.

Rodriguez, Nestor. 1999. "US Immigration and Changing Relations between African Americans and Latinos," in Charles Hirschman et al., eds, *The Handbook of International Migration: The American Experience*. New York: Russell Sage Foundation.

Roediger, David. 1991. *The Wages of Whiteness*. New York: Verso.

Rosen, Bernard C. 1956. "The Achievement Syndrome: A Psychocultural Dimension of Social Stratification," *American Sociological Review* 21: 203–11.

_____. 1959. "Race, Ethnicity, and the Achievement Syndrome," *American Sociological Review* 24: 47–60.

Rosen, Jeffrey, and Charles Lane. 1995. "The Sources of the Bell Curve," in Steven Fraser, ed., *The Bell Curve Wars: Race, Intelligence and the Future of America*. New York: Basic Books.

Roy, Patricia. 1989. *A White Man's Province: British Columbia Politicians and Chinese and Japanese Immigrants, 1858–1914*. Vancouver: University of British Columbia Press.

Royal Commission on Aboriginal Peoples. 1996a. *Bridging the Cultural Divide: A Report on Aboriginal People and Criminal Justice in Canada*. Ottawa: Supply and Services Canada.

_____. 1996b. *Report, Volume 1: Looking Forward, Looking Back*. Ottawa: Supply and Services Canada.

Royal Commission on Bilingualism and Biculturalism. 1969. *Report* (Vol. 3a). Ottawa: Queen's Printer.

Royal Commission on Equality in Employment. 1984. *Report*. Ottawa: Supply and Services Canada.

Rubyan-Ling, David. 2015. "Briefing Paper: Diaspora Communications and Health Seeking Behaviour in the Time of Ebola: Findings from the Sierra Leonean Community in London." www.ebola-anthropology.net/wp-content/uploads/2015/11/Diaspora-communication-and-health-seeking-behaviour1.pdf.

Ruck, Martin, and Scot Wortley. 2002. "Racial and Ethnic Minority Students: Perceptions of School Disciplinary Practices: A Look at Some Canadian Findings," *Journal of Youth and Adolescence* 31 (3): 185–95.

Rudin, Ronald. 1993. "English-speaking Quebec: The Emergence of a Disillusioned Minority," in Alain-G. Gagnon, ed., *Québec: State and Society*, 2nd edn. Toronto: Nelson Canada.

Rushton, J. Philippe. 1988. "Race Differences in Behaviour: A Review and Evolutionary Analysis," *Personality and Individual Differences* 9: 1009–24.

_____, and A. Bogaert. 1987. "Race Differences in Sexual Behavior: Testing an Evolutionary Hypothesis," *Journal of Research in Personality* 21: 529–51.

Safran, William. 1991. "Diasporas in Modern Societies: Myths of Homeland and Return," *Diaspora* 1 (1): 83–99.

Said, Edward W. 1978. *Orientalism*. New York: Pantheon.

Sanchez, George. 1999. "Face the Nation: Race, Immigration and the Rise of Nativism in Late Twentieth-Century America," in Charles Hirschman et al., eds, *The Handbook of International Migration: The American Experience*. New York: Russell Sage Foundation.

Satzewich, Vic. 1989. "Racisms: The Reactions to Chinese Migrants in Canada at the Turn of the Century," *International Sociology* 4 (3): 311–27.

_____. 1991. *Racism and the Incorporation of Foreign Labour: Farm Labour Migration to Canada since 1945*. London: Routledge.

_____. 1998b. "Race, Racism and Racialization: Contested Concepts," in Vic Satzewich, ed., *Racism and Social Inequality in Canada: Concepts, Controversies and Strategies of Resistance*. Toronto: Thompson Educational Publishing.

_____. 1999. "The Political Economy of Race and Ethnicity," in Peter Li, ed., *Race and Ethnic Relations in Canada*, 2nd edn, 311–46. Toronto: Oxford University Press.

_____. 2000. "Whiteness Limited: Racialization and the Social Construction of 'Peripheral Europeans,'" *Histoire sociale/ Social History* 32 (66): 271–90.

_____. 2002. *The Ukrainian Diaspora.* London: Routledge.

_____. 2006. "The Economic Rights of Migrant and Immigrant Workers in Canada and the United States," in Rhoda Howard-Hassmann and Claude Welch, eds, *Economic Rights in Canada and the United States.* Philadelphia: University of Pennsylvania Press.

_____. 2007. "Whiteness Studies: Race, Diversity and the New Essentialism," in Sean Hier and B. Singh Bolaria, eds, *Race & Racism in 21st Century Canada: Continuity, Complexity and Change.* Peterborough: Broadview Press.

_____. 2015. *Points of Entry: How Canada's Visa Officers Decide Who Gets In.* Vancouver: University of British Columbia Press.

_____, and Nik Liodakis. 2007. *"Race" and Ethnicity in Canada: A Critical Introduction,* 1st edn. Toronto: Oxford University Press.

_____, and Linda Mahood. 1994. "Indian Affairs and Band Governance: Deposing Indian Chiefs in Western Canada," *Canadian Ethnic Studies* 26 (1): 40–58.

_____, and William Shaffir. 2009. "Racism versus Professionalism: Claims and Counter-claims about Racial Profiling," *Canadian Journal of Criminology and Criminal Justice* 51 (2): 199–226.

_____, and Lloyd Wong. 2003. "Immigration, Ethnicity, and Race: The Transformation of Transnationalism, Localism, and Identities," in Wallace Clement and Leah Vosko, eds, *Changing Canada: Political Economy as Transformation.* Montreal and Kingston: McGill-Queen's University Press.

_____, and _____, eds. 2006. *Transnational Communities in Canada.* Vancouver: University of British Columbia Press.

_____, and Terry Wotherspoon. 2000. *First Nations: Race, Class and Gender Relations.* Regina: Canadian Plains Research Centre.

Schissel, Bernard, and Terry Wotherspoon. 2003. *The Legacy of School for Aboriginal People: Education, Oppression and Emancipation.* Toronto: Oxford University Press.

Schoenfeld, Stewart, William Shaffir, and Morton Weinfeld. 2006. "Canadian Jewry and Transnationalism: Israel, Anti-Semitism and the Jewish Diaspora," in Vic Satzewich and Lloyd Wong, eds, *Transnational Identities and Practices in Canada.* Vancouver: University of British Columbia Press.

Sharma, Nandita. 2001. "On Being *not* Canadian: The Social Organization of 'Migrant Workers' in Canada," *Canadian Review of Sociology and Anthropology* 38 (4): 415–39.

_____. 2006. *Home Economics: Nationalism and the Making of "Migrant Workers" in Canada.* Toronto: University of Toronto Press.

Sheffer, Gabriel. 2003. *Diaspora Politics: At Home Abroad.* Cambridge: Cambridge University Press.

Shepard, R. Bruce. 1991. "Plain Racism: The Reaction against Oklahoma Black Immigration to the Canadian Plains," in Ormond McKague, ed., *Racism in Canada.* Saskatoon, SK: Fifth House Publishers.

Shmuel, John. 2016. "Why China's Stock Market Crash is Going to Send More Money into Vancouver Housing," *Financial Post,* 7 January. http://business.financialpost.com/investing/global-investor/why-chinas-stock-market-crash-is-going-to-send-more-money-into-vancouver-housing.

Shull, Steven. 1993. *A Kinder, Gentler Racism? The Reagan–Bush Civil Rights Legacy.* Armonk, NY: M.E. Sharpe.

Siegfried, André. 1966. *The Race Question in Canada.* Toronto: McClelland and Stewart.

Siggner, Andrew, and Evelyn Peters. 2014. "The Non-Status Indian Population Living Off Reserve in Canada: A Demographic and Socio-Economic Profile." *Aboriginal Policy Studies* 3(3): 86–108.

Silman, Janet. 1987. *Enough is Enough: Aboriginal Women Speak Out.* Toronto: The Women's Press.

Simmons, Alan. 1998. "Racism and Immigration Policy," in Vic Satzewich, ed., *Racism and Social Inequality in Canada: Concepts, Controversies and Strategies of Resistance.* Toronto: Thompson Educational Publishing.

_____, and Dwaine Plaza. 2006. "The Caribbean Community in Canada: Transnational Connections and Transformations," in Vic Satzewich and Lloyd Wong, eds, *Transnational Identities and Practices in Canada.* Vancouver: University of British Columbia Press.

Small, Steven. 1994. *Racialized Barriers: The Black Experience in the United States and England.* New York: Routledge.

Smith, Dorothy. 1987. *The Everyday World as Problematic.* Boston: Northeastern University Press.

Smith, Graham. 1999. "Transnational Politics and the Politics of the Russian Diaspora," *Ethnic and Racial Studies* 22 (2): 500–23.

Smith, Madeline. 2015. "A Call to Action: Black Lives Matter Toronto Continues the Fight Against Racism," *The Globe and Mail*, 31 July. www.theglobeandmail.com/news/toronto/a-call-to-action-black-lives-matter-toronto-continues-the-fight-against-racism/article25809106/.

Smylie, Janet, et al. 2011. *Our Health Counts: Urban Aboriginal Health Database Research Project*. Hamilton: De dwa da dehs nye>s/ Aboriginal Health Centre.

Soave Strategy Group. 2006. *The Impact of Undocumented Workers on the Residential Construction Industry in the Greater Toronto Area*. Toronto: Labourers' International Union of North America.

Sokol, Sam. 2015. "Government Anti-Semitism Conference Endorses Net Censorship," *Jerusalem Post*, 14 May. www.jpost.com/Israel-News/Government-anti-Semitism-conference-endorses-net-censorship-403123.

Solomon, R. Patrick, and Howard Palmer. 2004. "Schooling in Babylon, Babylon in School: When Racial Profiling and Zero Tolerance Converge," *Canadian Journal of Educational Administration and Policy* 33: 1–16.

Solomos, John. 1986. "Varieties of Marxist Conceptions of 'Race,' Class and the State: A Critical Analysis," in John Rex and David Mason, eds, *Theories of Race and Ethnic Relations*. London: Cambridge University Press.

Sowell, Thomas. 1989. "Affirmative Action: A Worldwide Disaster," *Commentary* 12: 21–41.

Soysal, Yasmeen N. 2000. "Citizenship and Identity: Living in Diasporas in Post-war Europe?" *Ethnic and Racial Studies* 23 (1): 1–15.

Spener, David. 2001. "Smuggling Migrants through South Texas: Challenges Posed by Operation Rio Grande," in David Kyle and Rey Koslowski, eds, *Global Human Smuggling: Comparative Perspectives*. Baltimore, MD: Johns Hopkins University Press.

Srivastava, Sarita. 2007. "Troubles with 'Anti-Racist Multiculturalism': The Challenges of Anti-Racist and Feminist Activism," in S. Hier and B. Singh Bolaria, eds, *Race and Racism in 21st Century Canada: Continuity, Complexity, and Change*. Peterborough: Broadview Press.

St. Germain, Jill. 2001. *Indian Treaty Making Policy in the United States and Canada, 1867–1877*. Toronto: University of Toronto Press.

Stalker, Peter. 2000. *Workers without Frontiers—The Impact of Globalisation on International Migration*. Geneva: International Labour Organization.

Standing Senate Committee on Aboriginal Peoples. 2013. *"The People Who Own Themselves": Recognition of Métis identity in Canada*. Ottawa: Senate of Canada.

Stasiulis, Daiva. 1980. "The Political Structuring of Ethnic Community Action," *Canadian Ethnic Studies* 12 (3): 19–44.

———. 1990. "Theorizing Connections: Gender, Race, Ethnicity, and Class," in Peter Li, ed., *Race and Ethnic Relations in Canada*, 269–305. Toronto: Oxford University Press.

———. 1999. "Feminist Intersectional Theorizing," in Peter Li, ed., *Race and Ethnic Relations in Canada*, 2nd edn, 347–97. Toronto: Oxford University Press.

———, and Abigail Bakan. 2005. *Negotiating Citizenship: Migrant Women in Canada and the Global System*. Toronto: University of Toronto Press.

Statistics Canada. 2003a. *Ethnic Diversity Survey*. Ottawa: Supply and Services Canada.

———. 2003b. *Ethnic Diversity Survey: Portrait of a Multicultural Society*. Ottawa: Statistics Canada.

———. 2006. Census of Population.

———. 2011. *Aboriginal Peoples in Canada: First Nations People, Métis and Inuit*. Ottawa: Statistics Canada. www12.statcan.gc.ca/nhs-enm/2011/as-sa/99-011-x/99-011-x2011001-eng.cfm.

Steeves, Valerie. 2014. *Young Canadians in a Wired World, Phase III: Encountering Racist and Sexist Content Online*. Ottawa: MediaSmarts. http://mediasmarts.ca/sites/mediasmarts/files/publication-report/full/ycwwiii_encountering_racist_sexist_content_online.pdf.

Stevenson, Garth. 2005. "Remarks." Panel discussion of the Institute of Intergovernmental Relations, Department of Political Science, Brock University, St Catharines, ON, 14 May.

Stoffman, Daniel. 2002. *Who Gets In: What's Wrong with Canada's Immigration Program—And How To Fix It*. Toronto: Macfarlane Walter and Ross.

Sugiman, Pamela. 2006. "Unmaking a Transnational Community: Japanese Canadian Families in Wartime Canada," in Vic Satzewich and Lloyd Wong, eds, *Transnational*

Identities and Practices in Canada. Vancouver: University of British Columbia Press.

Sullivan, Steve. 2014. "The Sociology of Stephen Harper." http://ipolitics.ca/2014/08/27/the-sociology-of-stephen-harper/.

Swartz, Daniel. 2015. "Cultural Genocide Label for Residential Schools Has No Legal Implications, Expert Says." www.cbc.ca/news/aboriginal/cultural-genocide-label-for-residential-schools-has-no-legal-implications-expert-says-1.3110826.

Synnott, Anthony, and David Howes. 1996. "Canada's Visible Minorities: Identity and Representation," in V. Amit-Talai and C. Knowles, eds, *Re-situating Identities: The Politics of Race, Ethnicity and Culture.* Peterborough: Broadview Press.

Taguieff, Pierre-André. 1999. "The New Cultural Racism in France," in Martin Bulmer and John Solomos, eds, *Racism.* Oxford: Oxford University Press.

Tatla, Darshan Singh. 1999. *The Sikh Diaspora: The Search for Statehood.* Seattle: University of Washington Press.

Taylor, Keeanga-Yamahtta. 2008. "W.E.B. Du Bois, Black Reconstruction in America 1860-1880," *International Socialist Review* 57 (January–February).

Tepperman, Lorne. 1975. *Social Mobility in Canada.* Toronto: McGraw-Hill Ryerson.

Thatcher, Richard. 2004. *Fighting Firewater Fictions: Moving Beyond the Disease Model of Alcoholism in First Nations.* Toronto: University of Toronto Press.

Thomas, William, and Florian Znaniecki. 1920. *The Polish Peasant in Europe and America.* Boston: Gorham Press.

Thompson, Leonard. 1985. *The Political Mythology of Apartheid.* New Haven, CN: Yale University Press.

Titley, Brian. 1986. *A Narrow Vision: Duncan Campbell Scott and the Administration of Indian Affairs in Canada.* Vancouver: University of British Columbia Press.

Toronto Star. 2005. "Cast Aside by France." 10 November.

_____. 2007. "Election Chief Stands Firm on Veil Rules." 10 September.

Truth and Reconciliation Commission of Canada. 2015. *Honouring the Truth, Reconciling for the Future: Summary of the Final Report of the Truth and Reconciliation Commission of Canada.* Ottawa: Truth and Reconciliation Commission of Canada.

UNHCR. 2014. "UNHCR Global Report 2014." www.unhcr.org/5575a7840.html.

United Nations. 1993. "Declaration on the Elimination of Violence Against Women," General Assembly: 85th Plenary meeting. http://www.un.org/documents/ga/res/48/a48r104.htm.

_____. 1995. "Fourth World Conference on Women," http://www.un.org/womenwatch/daw/beijing/platform/.

_____. Department of Economic and Social Affairs. 2013. Trends in International Migrant Stock: The 2013 Revision. http://esa.un.org/unmigration/migrantstocks2013.htm?mtotals.

Valentine, Charles. 1968. *Culture and Poverty.* Chicago: University of Chicago Press.

Valpy, Michael. 2005. "As Riots Rage across France, Troubling Parallels Emerge among Children of Canada's Visible Minority Youth," *The Globe and Mail,* 12 November: A1, A5.

_____. 2006. "Westerners Face Up to Their Fear of the Veil," *The Globe and Mail,* 23 October: A16.

van den Berghe, Pierre. 1981. *The Ethnic Phenomenon.* New York: Elsevier.

_____. 1986. "Ethnicity and the Sociobiology Debate," in J. Rex and D. Mason, eds, *Theories of Race and Ethnic Relations.* Cambridge: Cambridge University Press.

Van Hear, Nicholas. 1998. *New Diasporas: The Mass Exodus, Dispersal and Regrouping of Migrant Communities.* Seattle: University of Washington Press.

Vertovec, Stephen. 1999. "Conceiving and Researching Transnationalism," *Ethnic and Racial Studies* 22 (2): 447–62.

Vlassis, George Demetrios. 1942. *The Greeks in Canada.* Ottawa.

Voyageur, Cora. 2008. *Firekeepers of the Twenty-First Century: First Nations Women Chiefs.* Montreal and Kingston: McGill-Queen's University Press.

Voyer, Jean-Pierre. 2004. "Foreword to Special Issue on the Role of Social Capital in Immigrant Integration," *Journal of International Migration and Integration* 5 (2): 159–64.

Wagley, Charles, and Marvin Harris. 1959. *Minorities in the New World.* New York: Columbia University Press.

Wahlsten, Douglas. 1997. "The Malleability of Intelligence Is Not Constrained by Heritability," in Bernie Devlin et al., eds, *Intelligence, Genes and Success: Scientists Respond to* The Bell Curve. New York: Springer-Verlag.

Waldram, James, Ann Herring, and T. Kue Young. 1995. *Aboriginal Health in Canada:*

Historical, Cultural and Epidemiological Perspectives. Toronto: University of Toronto Press.

Wallerstein, Immanuel. 1974. *The Modern World-System I*. New York: Academic Press.

———. 1979. *The Capitalist World Economy*. London: Cambridge University Press.

Warburton, Rennie. 2007. "Canada's Multicultural Policy: A Critical Realist Narrative," in S. Hier and B. Singh Bolaria, eds, *Race and Racism in 21st Century Canada: Continuity, Complexity, and Change*. Peterborough: Broadview Press.

Ward, Peter. 2002. *White Canada Forever: Popular Attitudes and Public Policy towards Orientals in British Columbia*, 3rd edn. Montreal and Kingston: McGill-Queen's University Press.

Waters, Mary C. 2000. *Black Identities: West Indian Dreams and American Realities*. Cambridge: Harvard University Press.

Wayland, Sarah. 2006. "The Politics of Transnationalism: Comparative Perspectives," in Vic Satzewich and Lloyd Wong, eds, *Transnational Identities and Practices in Canada*. Vancouver: University of British Columbia Press.

Weber, Max. 1958. *The Protestant Ethic and the Spirit of Capitalism*. New York: Scribner.

———. 1978. *Economy and Society* (Vol. I and II), Guenther Roth and Claus Wittich, eds. Berkeley: University of California Press.

Webster, Yehudi. 1994. *The Racialization of America*. London: Palgrave Macmillan.

Weinfeld, Morton. 1988. "Ethnic and Race Relations," in James Curtis and Lorne Tepperman, eds, *Understanding Canadian Society*, 587–616. Toronto: McGraw-Hill Ryerson.

———. 2001. *Like Everyone Else . . . But Different: The Paradoxical Success of Canadian Jews*. Toronto: McClelland and Stewart.

Weissbrodt, David. 1999. "Comprehensive Examination of Thematic Issues Relating to the Elimination of Racial Discrimination." Working Paper, Sub-Commission on Prevention of Discrimination and Protection of Minorities. Geneva: United Nations Commission on Human Rights.

Welsh, Jennifer. 2011. "Our Overlooked Diaspora," *Literary Review of Canada*. March.

Wente, Margaret. 2009. "Ban the Burka? No, But . . . ," *The Globe and Mail*. www.theglobeandmail.com/news/opinions/banthe-burka-no-but/article1195738/.

West, Cornell. 1993. *Keeping Faith: Philosophy and Race in America*. London: Routledge.

Whitaker, Reginald. 1993. "From the Quebec Cauldron to the Canadian Cauldron," in Alain-G. Gagnon, ed., *Québec: State and Society*, 2nd edn. Toronto: Nelson Canada.

Widdowson, Frances, and Albert Howard. 2008. *Disrobing the Aboriginal Industry: The Deception behind Indigenous Cultural Preservation*. Montreal and Kingston: McGill-Queen's University Press.

Williams, Cara. 2008. *Women in Canada: A Gender Based Statistical Report*. Ottawa: Statistics Canada.

Wimmer, Andreas, and Nina Glick Schiller. 2002. "Methodological Nationalism and Beyond: Nation-State Building, Migration and the Social Sciences," *Global Networks* 2 (4): 301–34.

Winland, Daphne. 1998. "Our Home and Native Land? Canadian Ethnic Scholarship and the Challenge of Transnationalism," *Canadian Review of Sociology and Anthropology* 35 (4): 555–77.

———. 2006. "Raising the Iron Curtain: Transnationalism and the Croatian Diaspora since the Collapse of 1989," in Vic Satzewich and Lloyd Wong, eds, *Transnational Identities and Practices in Canada*. Vancouver: University of British Columbia Press.

Winn, Conrad. 1985. "Affirmative Action and Visible Minorities: Eight Premises in Quest of Evidence," *Canadian Public Policy* 11 (4): 684–700.

———. 1988. "The Socio-economic Attainment of Visible Minorities: Facts and Policy Implications," in James Curtis, Edward Grabb, Neil Guppy, and Sid Gilbert, eds, *Social Inequality in Canada: Patterns, Problems, Policies*, 195–213. Scarborough: Prentice Hall Canada.

Winsa, Patty. 2015. "Proposed Class-action Lawsuit Alleges Racial Profiling by Durham Police," *Toronto Star*, 7 January. www.thestar.com/news/crime/2015/01/07/proposed_classaction_lawsuit_alleges_racial_profiling_by_durham_police.html.

Wong, Lloyd, and Connie Ho. 2006. "Chinese Transnationalism: Class and Capital Flows," in Vic Satzewich and Lloyd Wong, eds, *Transnational Identities and Practices in Canada*. Vancouver: University of British Columbia Press.

———, and Nancy Netting. 1992. "Business Immigration to Canada: Social Impact and Racism," in Vic Satzewich, ed., *Deconstructing a Nation: Immigration, Multiculturalism and Racism in '90s Canada.* Halifax: Fernwood Press.

_____, and Vic Satzewich. 2006. "Introduction: The Meaning and Significance of Transnationalism," in Vic Satzewich and Lloyd Wong, eds, *Transnational Identities and Practices in Canada.* Vancouver: University of British Columbia Press.

Woodsworth, J.S. 1972. *Strangers within Our Gates: Or Coming Canadians.* Toronto: University of Toronto Press.

Wortley, Scot. 2005. *Bias Free Policing: The Kingston Data Collection Project, Preliminary Results.* Toronto: Centre of Excellence for Research on Immigration and Settlement.

_____, and Julian Tanner. 2003. "Data, Denials and Confusion: The Racial Profiling Debate in Toronto," *Canadian Journal of Criminology and Criminal Justice* 45 (3): 1–9.

Wright, Erik Olin. 1983. *Class, Crisis and the State,* 2nd impression. London: Verso.

Wylie, Alison. 2003. "Why Standpoint Matters," in Robert Figueroa and Sandra Haring, eds., *Science and Other Cultures.* New York: Routledge.

Yeoh, Brenda, and Weiqiang Lin. 2012. "Rapid Growth in Singapore's Immigrant Population Brings Policy Challenges," Migration Policy Institute. www.migration-policy.org/article/rapid-growth-singapores-immigrant-population-brings-policy-challenges.

Zhou, Min. 1999. "Segmented Assimilation: Issues, Controversies and Recent Research on the New Second Generation," in Charles Hirschman et al., eds, *The Handbook of International Migration: The American Experience.* New York: Russell Sage Foundation.

Index

Note: Page numbers in italics indicate figures and illustrations.

abocide, 220-1

Aboriginal conditions, 224-7; education, 226; employment, 226; health, 224-5; housing, 225; imprisonment, 226-7; income, 225-6; water/ sanitation, 225. *See also entry below*

Aboriginal conditions, explanations for, 227-36; cultural, 228-32; socio-biological, 227-8; structural, 232-3; "weight of history" argument, 233-6

Aboriginal/non-Aboriginal relations, 65-73; assimilation and, 70-3, 230-1; marriage/status and, 218-19, 221, 222, 223, 237; opposing views of, 233-6; residential school system and, 71-3, 233, 234, 235; Royal Proclamation and, 66-9; treaties and, 67-70, 240

Aboriginal people, 212-41; alcoholism among, 227-8; assimilation of, 70-3, 230-1; compared to non-Aboriginal people, 224-7; culture of, vi, 70-2, 228-32; distinctions between, 213-24; explanations for conditions of, 227-36; gender divisions of, 236-8; labelling/naming of, 212, 213; land claims by, 61-2, 239-40; leadership issues/class divisions of, 238-40; legal/justice system and, 51-2, 226-7, 230, 231, 232-3; multiculturalism and, 166; populations of, 213, 214; in Quebec, 174; racism toward, 180-2; sports racism and, 196-7; treaties with, 67-70, 240; as university faculty members, 193-4. *See also* First Nations; Inuit; Métis; non-status Indians

Aboriginal women, 236-8; as chiefs, 237-8; compared to non-Aboriginal women, 226; crimes against, 1-3; marriage/status of, 218-19, 221, 222, 223, 237; as missing/murdered, in BC, 198-9

Abu-Laban, Yasmeen: and Christina Gabriel, 96, 106; and Daiva Stasiulis, 164

Acknowledgment, Commemoration and Education (ACE) Program, 80-1

Act to Encourage the Gradual Civilization of the Indian Tribes of Canada (1857), 70

Adams, Howard, 238-9

Ahenakew, David, 183-4

Air India bombing, vi, 265

Alba, Richard, and Victor Nee, 38

Alfred, Taiaiake, 222, 223-4, 231, 233-4

Allport, Gordon, 37

Amnesty International, 101

Anderson, Kim, 212, 234, 237

Anthias, Floya, 247, 269

anti-Semitism, 174, 207-9, 255; in Canada, 183-4, 207; global, 189, 208-9

apartheid, 46-7

apologies/redress, for racist treatment of ethnic groups, 62-3, 79-81

Arabs, 141, 142; Orientalism and, 54; racism toward/ suspicion of, 2, 205, 206, 264-5

Arat-Koç, Sedef, 205, 206

Aryan Nations (white supremacist group), 182, 183

ascriptive characteristic: race as, 9-10

Asia Pacific Foundation, 255-6; on Canadian diaspora engagement, 257-8

Assembly of First Nations (AFN), 183, 217, 237, 238

assimilation, 6; of Aboriginal peoples, 70-3, 230-1; as ethnicity/"race" theory, 35-9; relevance of, 245-6, 247, 269-70; seven stages of, 36-7. *See also entry below*

assimilation, types of: behavioural, 40, 124; segmented, 38; structural, 40, 124

Association of Black Law Enforcers (ABLE), 203-4

Atlanta Braves, 196

Austro-Hungarian Empire, 6, 264

Baeumler, Alfred, 11

Banting, Keith, and Will Kymlicka, 169-70

Banton, Michael, 10-11, 18, 19, 27

Barker, Martin: *The New Racism*, 19-20, 22

Barthes, Roland, 53

Basch, Linda, Nina Glick Schiller, and Christina Szanton Blanc: *Nations Unbound*, 258, 266

Bédard, Yvonne, 219

Bedford Road Collegiate (Saskatoon), sports teams of, 197

behavioural assimilation, 40, 124

bhangra music, 260-1

Bibby, Reginald: *Mosaic Madness*, 162-3

Bill C-31 (Indian Act amendments), issues/problems resulting from, 219-24; band membership codes/ blood quantum rules, 223-4; long-term decline in status Indian population, 220-1, *221*; rejection of reinstated persons, 222-3

Bill 101 (Charter of the French Language, Quebec), 62, 172

Bissoondath, Neil: *Selling Illusions: The Cult of Multiculturalism in Canada*, 161-2, 163

Black Action Defence Committee, 202

Black Lives Matter, 204

Blair, Tony, 205

Block, Sheila, 130

blocked social mobility, 39, 40-1, 124, 127

Bloemraad, Irene, 170

Blood and Honour (white supremacist group), 182-3

Boldt, Menno, 238

Bollywood film industry, 260

Boston Bruins, 195

Botengan, Kelly, 108-9

Bouchard, Gérard, and commission co-chaired by, 174-5

Bowman, Brian, 181

Boyd, Monica, 39, 129

Boyle, Danny, 260

Boyle, Mark, and Rob Kitchin, 257-8

Brant, Clare, 228

Breton, Raymond, 9

Britain, 63-4, 105, 186; control of immigrants from, 74, 76; India and, 78-9, 260; Islamophobia/Muslim exclusion in, 205, 244, 259-60; multiculturalism in, 152-3, 166; new racism in, 19-20; Sikhs in, 262, 265

British Canadians, 127, 128, 129, 139, 142; as charter group, 87, 124–5, 144, 153–4; as "founding nation," 63, 174
British Columbia Civil Liberties Association, 202
British Columbia Public Interest and Advocacy Centre, 138
British North America Act (1867), 217
Brubaker, Rogers, 248
burka, 205, 243–5
Bush, George H.W., 21, 33
Business Immigration Program, 105–6

Calliste, Agnes, 47
Cameron, David, 152–3
Canada: Aboriginal/non-Aboriginal relations in, 65–73; census-taking in, 84–9; diaspora of, 255–8; French/English relations in, 62, 63–5; immigration history in, 73–84; multiculturalism in, 22–3, 152–71; social inequality in, 122–48; US immigrants in, 75–6, 270–1
Canada, racism in, 180–210; as democratic, 22–3; public opinion on, 184–7; split labour market and, 47. See also racism
Canada Fair Employment Practices Act (1953), 47
Canada Research Chairs Program, 252
"Canadian," as ethnic origin, 86–7
Canadian Association of Refugee Lawyers, 101
Canadian Centre for Policy Alternatives, 130
Canadian Charter of Rights and Freedoms, 100, 155–6, 183
Canadian Civil Liberties Association, 101
Canadian Council for Refugees, 101
Canadian Islamic Congress, 175
Canadian Museum for Human Rights, 181
Canadian Race Relations Foundation, 104
Caribbean immigrants, 20, 26, 38–9, 49, 82–3; class composition of, 145–6; diaspora of, 251; as live-in caregivers, 107; as seasonal agricultural workers, 82–3, 96, 115–16, 190; transnationalism of, 259
Caring for Children Pathway (Caregiver Program), 107
Caring for People with High Medical Needs Pathway (Caregiver Program), 107
Carnegie, Herb, 195
census, Canadian, 84–9; as used to study social inequality, 124, 128–35, 139–40, 144–7
Charest, Jean, 175
Charlie Hebdo (French magazine), attack on offices of, 157, 208
charter groups (British and French Canadians), 87, 124–5, 144, 153–4
Charter of Quebec Values, proposed (Bill 60), 176–7; protests against, 176, 176
Charter of the French Language (Quebec; Bill 101), 62, 172
Chaudhry, Irfan, 188–9
Cheshire, Coye, 35
Cheung Hong (conglomerate), 261
Chicago School of sociology: assimilation studies by, 35–9
Chinese Americans, 38, 42, 106, 123, 270
Chinese Canadians: as early immigrants, 62, 77–8, 81, 97; hostility toward, 48, 106, 270; transnationalism of, 261–2, 270; in vertical mosaic, 129, 142, 144–5
Chinese head tax, 62, 77–8
Chinese Immigration Act: (1885), 77; (1923), 77–8, 81

Christie Pits (Toronto), anti-Jewish riot at, 207
Chua, Amy, and Jed Rubenfeld, 123
Citizenship and Immigration, Department of, 82
Civil Rights Commission (US), 21
class. See social class
Clemente, Qara, 109
Cleveland Indians, 196
Closs, William, 201–2, 204
code-switching, 259–60
Cohen, Robin, 249, 250–2, 255, 256, 259, 269–70
collective conscience, 4
collective ethnic identity, 6
colour-coded vertical mosaic, 123, 128–35; immigrants and, 131–5
Commission des droits de la personne et des droits de la jeunesse (Quebec), 202
Community Historical Recognition Program (CHRP), 81
conflict theory, 42–3. See also political economy, as ethnicity/"race" theory
Congress of Aboriginal Peoples, 215–16, 220, 238
Conseil des communautés culturelles et de l'immigration (Quebec), 173
Conservative Party of Canada, 162, 163
Constitution Act (1982), 155–6, 183, 213, 215. See also Canadian Charter of Rights and Freedoms
Consultation Commission on Accommodation Practices Related to Cultural Differences (CCAPRCD), 174–5
contact hypothesis, 37, 160
Cox, Oliver Cromwell, 44
Criminal Code, 51, 171; hate crimes in, 183–4
criminal profiling: deductive, 203; inductive, 203. See also racial profiling
critical race theory (CRT), 50–1; as applied to First Nations jury experience, 51–2
cultural diasporas, 245, 251
cultural relativism, 154; multiculturalism and, 162–4, 168
culture, 6–7, 33; assimilation and, 6, 35–9; socio-economic success and, 39–42

Daniels, Harry, 220–1, 223
Darroch, Gordon, 127
dating websites, 34–5
Davin, Nicholas Flood, 72
deductive criminal profiling, 203
democratic racism, 22–3
deracialization of immigration, 82–4
Derrida, Jacques, 53
Dhalla, Ruby, 108–9
diachronic dimensions of ethnicity, 7
diasporas: assimilation and, 245–6, 269–70; Canadian, 255–8; in context of socio-legal distinctions, 266; features of, 250–1; genealogy of, 246–50; Jewish, 249, 251, 252, 255; nation-states and, 247, 268–9; returnees from, 253, 254; return movements within, 251, 252–3, 255; social media and, 253; types of, 251. See also entry below
diasporas, types of: cultural, 245, 251; imperial, 251; labour, 251; trade, 251; victim, 250, 251, 252
Dion, Stéphane, 206
Dolezal, Rachel, 17
Driedger, Leo, 36
Drouin, André, 175

Dua, Enakshi, 194–5
dual citizenship, 263
Du Bois, W.E.B., 44–5; *The Philadelphia Negro*, 44
Dufour, Christian: *Le défi québécois*, 166
Dunbar, William, 10
Durham, John Lambton, First Earl of, 64
Durham Regional Police Services Board, 202
Durkheim, Émile, 4
Dyck, Noel, 231–2, 233
Eagleburger, Lawrence, 33

earnings inequalities, 128; as colour-coded, 123, 128–35; among/within ethnic groups, 146–7, 158; ethnicity/class and, 144–6; of immigrants, 131–5; university education/teaching positions and, 126, 130–5, 141. *See also* social mobility, of ethnic groups; vertical mosaic
Eastern Europe, immigrants from, 76–7
economic immigrants, 101–10; business class, 105–6; live-in caregivers, 96, 107–9; provincial nominees, 96, 108–10; skilled workers, 102–4
Edmonton Eskimos, 197
Education Act (Ontario), 192
Elections Canada, 205–6
Elmenyawi, Salam, 177
empires, 6; Austro-Hungarian, 6, 264; British, 78–9
enfranchisement, of "status" Indians, 218–19, 237
entrance groups, 124, 144
Equal Employment Opportunity Commission (US), 21
"Eskimos," 197, 213. *See also* Inuit
Esseghaier, Chiheb, 1
Ethiopia: diaspora of, 248–9
ethnic conflict: in former Yugoslavia, 33; in Rwanda, 33; in South Sudan, 26
ethnic enclaves, 166–7, 171
ethnic identity: collective, 6; individual, 6–7
ethnic institutions, 7–9; completeness of, 7–8; as political, 9; as predating multiculturalism, 9
ethnicity, 3–9; class and, 139, 144–6; culture/identity and, 6–7, 33; dimensions of, 7; early sociological approaches to, 3–6; institutions of, 7–9; language and, 4, 6, 7, 8–9; social inequality and, 123–42, 158; socio-biology and, 32
ethnicity and "race": on Canadian census, 84–9; concepts of, 3–26; immigration and, 75–9, 82–4; paradigms of, 247; as relational concepts, 43–9. *See also entry below*
ethnicity and "race," theories of, 30–58; conflict theory/political economy, 42–9; critical race theory, 50–2; culture/assimilation, 35–9; culture/socio-economic success, 39–42; intersectional analysis, 49–50; post-colonialism, 53–5; primordialism/socio-biology, 32–5; "whiteness," 55–7
ethnicity and "race" paradigms, 247
ethnicization, 2
ethnic origin: "Canadian" as, 86–7; as reported on 2011 census, 85–7
ethnic shopping malls, 48
ethnocentrism, 154
European Union, 198
European Union Monitoring Center (EUMC), 209
exclusionary movements, 46

Facebook, 34, 253, 254, 267–8; racism on, 180, 189
Fair Housing and Equal Opportunity Program (US), 21
family class immigrants, 110–13; determining "real" relationships of, 111, 112
Fanon, Frantz, 54–5
Feagin, Joe R., and Hernán Vera, 24, 25
female circumcision, 171, 175
Filipino Canadians: in vertical mosaic, 145, 146–7; violence against, 25–6, 183; workplace issues of, 107, 108–9, 138
Filipino Canadian Youth Alliance, 109
Fiore, Andrew T., 34, 35
First Nations, 213, 216–18; land claims by, 61–2; as "non-status" Indians, 213, 218–19; on Ontario juries, 51–2; as "status" Indians, 213–14, 216–23. *See also* Aboriginal conditions, *and entries following*; Bill C-31 (Indian Act amendments), issues/problems resulting from; "status," of First Nations people
Fisher, Helen, 34
Flanagan, Thomas, 235
Fleras, Augie, 155–7; and Jean Leonard Elliott, 171
Fontaine, Tina, 1–2
Foreign Affairs and International Trade, Department of (DFAIT), 256–7
Foucault, Michel, 53
France, 9, 63, 169, 186, 250, 262; anti-Semitism in, 207–8, 209; burka/niqab ban in, 205, 243; new racism in, 20
Freedom of Information and Protection of Privacy Act (Ontario), 201
French Canadians, 40–1, 87, 127, 129, 139, 145, 215; as charter group, 87, 124–5, 144, 153–4; as "founding nation," 63, 165–6, 174. *See also entry below*
French/English relations, 62, 63–5; Conquest and, 62, 63; Quiet Revolution and, 64–5; racialized understandings of, 64
Frimpong, Emmanuel, 196
Fujian (China), undocumented migrants from, 116
Fulford, Robert, 166–7

Galabuzi, Grace-Edward: *Canada's Economic Apartheid: The Social Exclusion of Racialized Groups in the New Century*, 130
Gatineau, Quebec, 176
gender: multiculturalism and, 158–9, 171; "race," class, and, 49–50. *See also* women
Germany, 209, 262, 263; multiculturalism in, 9, 152, 153. *See also* Nazi Germany
Global Forum for Combating Anti-Semitism, 189
Goldberg, David Theo, 17–18, 43, 160
Gordo, Magdalene, 108–9
Gordon, Milton, 36–7
Greek Canadians, 8, 26, 40, 41, 144–5; earnings of, 125, 129, 141–2, 147
Gutenberg, Johannes, 187

Hagan, John, 270
Hamilton Regional Indian Centre, 217
Hampton, Howard, 192
Hansen, Marcus Lee: *The Immigrant in American History*, 267
Haplotype Project, 15
Harney, Nicholas, 259

Harper, Stephen, 1–2, 3, 62, 80–1, 206
Harvey, Frank, 33
Henry, Frances, and Carol Tator, 22–3, 24, 104
Herodotus: *Histories*, 3, 4
Hérouxville, Quebec, 175–6
Herrnstein, Richard, and Charles Murray: *The Bell Curve: Intelligence and Class Structure in American Life*, 13–15
Hier, Sean, and Joshua Greenberg, 117
hijab, 174
Hill Collins, Patricia, 50
Hitler, Adolf, 82, 182, 184
Holliday, George, 30
Holocaust, 82
Hong Kong, 105, 106
Hourani, Albert, 255
Howard-Hassmann, Rhoda, 167–8
Hrvatska Demokratska Zajednica (Croatian political party),
Hudson's Bay Company: Cowichan sweater appropriated by, xii
Human Genome Project, 15–16
Huntington, Samuel, 245–6, 265
Hussain, Murtaza, 169

Iacobucci, Frank, 51–2
illegal immigrants, 116–19
Immigrant Investor Capital Fund, 105
Immigrant Investor Venture Capital Pilot Program, 105
immigrants: Canadian attitudes toward, 185–7; devalued educational credentials of, 135; earnings inequalities of, 128–35; occupational attainment of, 125–7, 135; success stories of, v, 136–7; top 10 sources of, 93, 94; unattractive jobs filled by, 96–7, 122, 126
immigrants, economic, 101–10; business class, 105–6; live-in caregivers, 96, 107–9; provincial nominees, 96, 108–10; skilled workers, 102–4
immigrants, marginal, 113–19; non-status, 116–19; temporary workers, 93, 96–7, 108–9, 114–16, 138
immigration, 73–84, 92–119; categories of, 98–113; early controls on, 73–9; from 1860 to 2013 (graph), 73; factors explaining, 93–8, 127; humanitarianism/ nation-building and, 98; later deracialization of, 82–4; marginal, 113–19; points system of, 102–4, 105, 109, 111; political aspects of, 75; political economy of, 95–7; population concerns and, 97; postwar, 81–3; Quebec and, 65, 171–7; "race"/ethnicity and, 75–9, 82–4
Immigration Act (1910), 74–5
Immigration Act (1952), 82–3
Immigration and Refugee Board (IRB), 100–1
immigration categories, 98–113; admissions by, 99; economic, 101–10; family class, 110–13; refugees, 99–101
immigration officers: exercise of discretion by, 102–4, 192
Immigration Reform and Control Act (US), 118
imperial diasporas, 251
India: immigration from, 62–3, 78–9; remittances to, 261–2; transnational culture of, 260–1. *See also* Indo-Canadians
"Indian" (term), 212. *See also* First Nations; non-status Indians
Indian Act, 70, 214, 218; amendments to, 219–24. *See also* Bill C-31 (Indian Act amendments), issues/ problems resulting from

Indian Affairs, Department of, 71, 218
Indian Affairs and Northern Development, Department of, 214
Indigenous and Northern Affairs Canada, 214
individual ethnic identity, 6–7
Indo-Canadians: Air India bombing and, vi, 265; ethnic violence and, 25–6
inductive criminal profiling, 203
inequality. *See* social inequality
institutional completeness, 7–8
institutional racism, 75–6, 189–90, 198–204
interculturalism, 65, 171–4
International Covenant on Civil and Political Rights, 219
Internet: racism on, 180, 187–9
intersectional analysis, 49–50
Inuit, 213, 214; land claims issues of, 239–40
Inuit Tapiriit Kanatami, 214
Islamic State (ISIS), 260
Islamophobia, 2, 174, 204–7, 244, 264–5
Israel: criticism of, 208; Law of Return to, 252
Italian Canadians, 26, 164; class composition of, 124, 139, 144–5; earnings of, 128, 129, 141–2; transnationalism of, 259, 263, 264; wartime internment of, 62, 79, 80–1
Ivison, John, 206

Jamaican Canadians, 255
James, Carl, 197–8
Japan: demographic problems of, 97
Japanese Canadians, 62, 79, 164
Jaser, Raed, 1
Jelinek, Otto, 156
Jewish Canadians, 8, 175; in vertical mosaic, 124, 127, 128, 144–5, 146. *See also entry below*; anti-Semitism
Jewish diaspora, 249, 251, 252, 255
Johnson-Sirleaf, Ellen, 265
Joppke, Christian, 268
Jull, Stephen, 191–2

Kahnawake Mohawks: membership code/blood quantum rules of, 223–4
Kallen, Evelyn, 6–7, 104
Kenney, Jason, 93
Khayati, Khalid, 250
Kinder, Donald, and David Sears, 21, 22
King, Rodney, 30–1
Kingston (Ontario) Police, 201–2, 204
Knox, Robert: *The Races of Men*, 10–11
Kobayashi, Audrey, 193; and Linda Peake, 56–7
Komagata Maru (ship), 62–3, 79
Kono District Development Association, 253
Ku Klux Klan, 18, 182, 188
Kurdish diaspora, 250

labour diasporas, 251
labour market, 123, 124, 125–35; capitalist split in, 46–7; earnings inequalities in, 128–35; immigrants and, 36, 38–40, 131–5; occupational attainment/ dissimilarity and, 125–7, 135
Lacan, Jacques, 53
language: code-switching in, 259–60; colonialism and, 55; ethnicity and, 4, 6, 7, 8–9; multiculturalism and,

155, 156, 160, 165-6, 168, 171-3; nationality and, 4, 6, 21; in Quebec, 62, 64-5, 171-3
Latvia, 265
Lautard, Hugh, and Neil Guppy, 127
Lavell, Jeannette, 219
Lawrence, Bonita, 221, 224
Lebanese Canadians, 263-4
Lebanese diaspora, 255
Lee-Chin, Michael, xi
Levant, Ezra, 184
Lévesque, René, 62, 166, 172
Lévesque, Stéphane, 173
Lewis, Oscar, 40
Li Ka-Shing, 261
Li, Peter, 41, 48, 111, 131, 165, 187; B. Singh Bolaria and, 45-6
Li, Victor, 261
Lian, Jason Z., and Ralph Matthews, 129-30, 142
Liberal Party of Canada, 154-5, 164-5
Liberal Party of Quebec, 172, 176-7
Liberia, 265
Lin, Jeremy, 196
Live-in Caregiver Program, 96, 107-8; Dhalla case and, 108-9; streams of, 107
Los Angeles Riots, 25, 31
Louie, Vivian S., 39, 42
Lovelace, Sandra, 219
McIntosh, Peggy, 57

McLachlin, Beverley, 71
marriage/relationships: Aboriginal women's status and, 218-19, 221, 222, 223, 237; dating websites and, 34-5; of family class immigrants, 110-13; interracial, 78
Marson, Mike, 195
Martin, Paul, 80
Marx, Karl, 42-3, 44
Marxist theory, 49
Match.com, 34
Mayrand, Marc, 205-6
Meisel, John, 124
Mendelsohn, Gerald A., 34-5
Merkel, Angela, 152, 153
methodological nationalism, 247
Métis, 213, 215-16; of Saint Laurent, Manitoba, 216-17
Métis National Council (MNC), 215, 219, 238
Mexican immigrants: Quebec and, 65; remittances by, 262; as seasonal agricultural workers, 96, 115-16, 190; as temporary foreign workers, 138, 266; in US, 117, 245-6, 265
migrant workers, 93, 94, 96, 108-9, 114-16, 190; Canada's increasing dependence on, 114; exploitation of, 116; UN convention on, 268-9
Miles, Robert: and Malcolm Brown, 16, 206-7; and Rudy Torres, 16
Ministère de l'Immigration (Quebec), 172
Ministère de l'Immigration et des Communautés culturelles (Quebec), 174
Ministère des Communautés culturelles et de l'Immigration (Quebec), 172
Ministère des Relations avec les citoyens et de l'Immigration (Quebec), 173-4

Missing Women Commission of Inquiry (BC), 198-9
Mitchell, Marybelle, 239-40
monopolistic closure, 5
Montagu, Ashley, 45
Monture, Patricia, 193-4, 195
Mulroney, Brian, 80
multiculturalism, 9, 22-3, 36, 152-71; anti-racist workshops and, 160; Canadian attitudes toward, 185-7; citizenship and, 156-7; as contested concept, 157-68, 171; evolution of, as federal policy, 155-7; as facilitating integration, 167-8, 169-70; folkloric aspects of, 155, 156-7, 161-2, 165, 177; funding of, 160; gender and, 158-9, 171; as ineffective against social inequality, 157-60; integrative, 157; language and, 155, 156, 160, 165-6, 168, 171-3; Liberal Party and, 154-5, 164-5; meanings of, in Canadian society, 153-5; PC Party and, 156, 163-4; as pluralistic, 153-4, 156, 162-3, 166, 168; problematic success of, 160-7; Quebec's responses to, 65, 165-6, 171-7; responses to critics of, 167-8, 171. See also entry below
multiculturalism, perceived problems caused by success of, 160-7; hardening of stereotypes, 161-2; indirect support for intolerance/terrorism, 166-7; marginalization of ethnocultural issues, 164-5; promotion of cultural relativism, 162-4, 168; undermining of francophone and Aboriginal claims, 165-6
Multiculturalism Act, 156
Multiculturalism and Citizenship, Department of, 157, 164
Multiculturalism Means Business Conference (Toronto, 1986), 156
multinationalism, 6
Muslim Canadians, 8, 157, 171; in Quebec, 174, 175-7
Muslim Council of Montreal, 177
Muslims: immigration/integration of, 243-6; racism toward/suspicion of, 2, 174, 204-7, 244, 264-5
Muslim women: attire of, 169, 174, 205-6, 243-5; sense of exclusion felt by, 260

Nakhaie, Reza, 135, 139, 141, 194
Nangia, Parveen, 184-5
National Alliance of Philippine Women in Canada (NAPWC), 108-9
National Collegiate Athletic Association (NCAA), 197
National Football League (NFL), 197; "Rooney Rule" of, 198
National Front (France), 20
National Hockey League (NHL), 195, 196
National Household Survey (NHS), 85-9
National Indian Brotherhood, 217
nationality, 5-6; language and, 4, 6, 21; as subsumed by empires, 6
National Organization of Immigrant and Visible Minority Women (NOIVMW), 159
nation-state, 5-6; diasporas/transnationalism and, 245, 247, 258, 268-9; as focus of study, 247
Nazi Germany, 82; scientific racism in, 11, 207; white supremacist groups and, 182-3, 188
Netherlands: anti-Semitism in, 209; retreat from multiculturalism in, 244
New Democratic Party (NDP) of Ontario, 160
New France, conquest of, 62, 63

New York Knicks, 196
Nigeria: advice for "repats" in, 253, 254; census-taking in, 89
niqab, 169, 205–6, 243–4
Nobles, Melissa, 140
Noivo, Edite, 26
Non-Immigrant Employment Authorization Program (NIEAP), 114–15
non-status immigrants, 116–19; control/deportation of, 118–19; exploitation of, 118; as failed refugee claimants, 118; as human smuggling victims, 117; as visa over-stayers, 117–18
non-status Indians, 213, 218–19
Nunziata, John, 164

Obama, Barack, 188
occupational attainment, 125–7, 135
occupational dissimilarity, 127
Odidi, Isa and Amina, 136–7
Official Language Act (Quebec; Bill 22), 172
Ontario Anti-Racism Secretariat (OARS), 160
Ontario Coalition of Visible Minority Women (OCVMW), 159
Ontario Human Rights Commission, 192, 200–1
Oppal, Wally, 199
O'Ree, Willie, 195
Orientalism, 54
Orlando, Florida: attack on LGBT nightclub in, 244–5
Otavalo (Ecuador), trade diaspora of, 251
Other(s), 2; Self vs, 3–4, 53–5; white/black dichotomy and, 55–7
Ouellette, Robert Falcon, 180–1
over-policing, 198, 199–200

Pacetti, Massimo, 81
Paris: terrorist attacks in, 157, 206, 208
Parizeau, Jacques, 177
Park, Robert, 35, 36
Parti Québécois, 62, 172, 176, 177
Peel Police Services Board, 202
permanent residents, 98–9
Peter, Karl, 154
Pickton, Robert, 198–9
pluralism, multiculturalism and, 153–4, 156, 162–3; Aboriginal people and, 166; as leading to relativism, 162–3, 168; in Quebec, 172, 174
points system, immigration, 102–4, 105, 109, 111; for skilled workers, 102, 103
policing, racism in, 198–204; over-policing, 198, 199–200; racial profiling, 190, 199–204; under-policing, 198–9
Polish peasants, study of, 35–6
political economy, as ethnicity/"race" theory, 42–9; capitalism/class relations and, 44–7; conflict theory and, 42–3; local economic hostilities/tensions and, 47–9
political economy, of immigration, 95–7
Porter, John, The Vertical Mosaic, 123–5; on assimilation/blocked social mobility, 39, 40–1, 124, 127; criticisms of, 125–8; on ethnic class divisions, 139, 144. See also vertical mosaic
Portes, Alejandro, 38, 267

post-colonialism, 53–5
Powley case (Supreme Court of Canada), 216
primordialism, 32–3; dating websites and, 34–5; sociobiology and, 32
Progressive Conservative (PC) Party of Canada, 156, 163–4
Protestant ethic, 6
Provincial Nominee Program (PNP), 96, 108–10; selection criteria for, 109

Quebec, 62, 63–5; "founding nations" concept and, 63, 165–6, 174; French language in, 62, 64–5, 171–3; immigration policy/control in, 65, 171–7; interculturalism in, 65, 171–4; municipal controversies in, 175–6; proposed Charter of Values in, 176–7; reasonable accommodation in, 174–5; referendums in, 62. See also French Canadians; French/English relations
Quebec Act, 63
Québec interculturel (citizenship program), 174
Quiet Revolution, 64–5
Quigley, Tim, 199–200
"race," 9–18; on Canadian census, 84–9; class, gender, and, 49–50; as colonial construct, 10; criminal behaviour and, 199–204; immigration and, 75–9, 82–4; racialization and, 16–18; science and, 10–18; UNESCO's statement on, 12. See also "race" science
"race," theories of. See ethnicity and "race," theories of
"race" science, 10–18; early history of, 10–11; Human Genome Project and, 15–16; modern versions of, 13–15; in Nazi Germany, 11, 207; racialization and, 16–18; UNESCO's attempt to discredit, 12–13
racialization, 2, 16–18
racial profiling, 190, 199–204
racism, 18–26, 180–210; capitalism/class relations and, 44–9; democratic, 22–3; institutional, 75–6, 189–90, 198–204; on Internet/social media, 180, 187–9; in legal/justice system, 50–2; new forms of, 19–23, 182; organized, 182–4; in policing, 190, 198–204; religious hatred and, 204–9; scientific, 10–13; in sports, 195–8; subtle/coded forms of, 50–1; surveys/public opinion on, 184–7; at universities, 193–5, 207; white/non-white, 24–6; zero tolerance of, 190–2
railways, Canadian: racist employment practices at, 47
Ramos, Howard, 126
Reagan, Ronald, 21
reasonable accommodation, 174–5
Reform Party of Canada, 162, 163
refugees, 99–101; Conservative government policies on, 100–1; "safe-third-country" principle and, 101; Syrian, 100, 251; unsuccessful, as non-status immigrants, 118
Reitz, Jeffrey, 135
religious hatred: anti-Semitism, 207–9; Islamophobia, 204–7
remittances, 261–3, 268
residential schools, 71–3, 233, 234, 235
Rich, Camille Gear, 17
Richards, John, 229, 234
Rodriguez, Nestor, 20–1
Rosen, Bernard C., 40, 41
Rosenfeld, Michael J., 34–5

Royal Canadian Mounted Police (RCMP), 206, 214
Royal Commission on Aboriginal Peoples, 228–9, 230, 232
Royal Commission on Equality in Employment, 129
Royal Proclamation (1763), 66–9
Ruck, Martin, and Scot Wortley, 191
Runnymede Trust (UK), 204–5
Rushton, Philippe, 14–15
Russia: Ukraine and, 262
Rwanda, genocide in, 33

Safe Schools Act (Ontario), 190–2
Said, Edward: *Orientalism*, 54
Saint Laurent, Manitoba, 216–17
San Bernardino, California: terrorist attack in, 244–5
Saputo, Lino, v
Sarkozy, Nicolas, 205, 243
Saskatoon Indian and Métis Friendship Centre, 217
Satzewich, Vic, 112; and William Shaffir, 202–3
Schoenfeld, Stewart, William Shaffir, and Morton
    Weinfeld, 208
scientific racism, 10–13. *See also* "race" science
Scotland: diaspora strategy of, 252, 257
Seasonal Agricultural Workers Program, 96, 115–16, 190
segmented assimilation, 38
selection criteria, for provincial nominee immigrants, 109
Self: vs Other, 3–4, 53–5; white/black dichotomy and,
    55–7
September 11, 2001, terrorist attacks of, 157, 204, 269
Siegfried, André: *The Race Question in Canada*, 64
Sierra Leone, diaspora of: Ebola outbreak and, 253
Sifton, Clifford, 76–7
Sikhs, xii, 262, 265; *Komagata Maru* incident and, 62–3, 79
SIKLAB-Ontario (migrant workers' organization), 108–9
Simmonds, Wayne, 196
Simmons, Alan, and Dwaine Plaza, 259
Sinclair, Murray, 71
Singh case (Supreme Court of Canada), 100
skilled workers, as immigrants, 102–4; express entry
    system for, 102–3
slavery, 44–5, 53
Slumdog Millionaire (film), 260
Smythe, Conn, 195
soccer: racism in, 196
social class: "race," gender, and, 49–50; ethnicity and, 139,
    144–6; inequality and, 124–5, 139, 142–7
social inequality, 122–48; census data and, 124, 128–35,
    139–40, 144–7; class and, 124–5, 139, 142–7;
    ethnicity and, 123–42, 158. *See also* earnings
    inequalities; social mobility, of ethnic groups;
    vertical mosaic
social media, 253, 267–8; racism on, 180, 187–9
social mobility, of ethnic groups, 123–5; as blocked, 39,
    40–1, 124, 127; convergence in, 125–8; in earnings,
    123, 128–35; in occupational attainment, 125–7,
    135. *See also* earnings inequalities; social inequality;
    vertical mosaic
socio-biology, 32; as explanation for Aboriginal
    conditions, 227–8
socio-economic hierarchy, 122. *See also* vertical mosaic
socio-economic success: culture and, 39–42
South Africa: apartheid in, 46–7
split labour market, 46–7

sports, issues of racism in, 195–8; choice of sports, 197–8;
    coaching, 198; early colour bar, 195; player abuse/
    racial slurs, 196; player positions, 197; team names/
    mascots, 196–7
Srivastava, Sarita, 159–60
Standing Senate Committee on Aboriginal Peoples, 216
Stasiulis, Daiva, 49–50, 158, 164; and Abigail Bakan,
    107–8
"status," of First Nations people, 213–14, 216–23; early
    definition of, 218; enfranchisement provisions and,
    218–19, 237; fallout from government changes to,
    219–24; women's challenges to, 218, 219, 237. *See
    also* Bill C-31 (Indian Act amendments), issues/
    problems resulting from
Stoffman, Daniel, 93, 95, 96, 98, 101
Stormfront (white supremacist group), 182, 188
Straw, Jack, 205, 244
Stronach, Frank, xi
structural assimilation, 40, 124
Sun Life, 62
Supreme Court of Canada, 51, 100; Aboriginal people
    and, 213, 214, 216, 219
surveys on racism, 184–7; social distance, 185–7;
    victimization, 184–5
synchronic dimensions of ethnicity, 7
Synnott, Anthony, and David Howes, 140–1
Syrian refugees, 100, 251

Taguieff, Pierre-André, 20
Tatla, Darshan Singh, 260–1
Taylor, Charles, and commission co-chaired by, 174–5
Taylor, Lindsay Shaw, 35
Temporary Foreign Worker Program, 93, 96–7, 108–9,
    114–16, 138
terrorism: multiculturalism and, 166–7; recent wave of,
    in Europe, 157, 206, 208
Thatcher, Margaret, 19–20
Thatcher, Richard, 227–8, 232, 235–6
Thomas, W.I., 35–6; and Florian Znaniecki: *The Polish
    Peasant in Europe and America*, 35–6
Tim Hortons: discrimination at, 138
Tongson, Richelyn, 108–9
Toronto Maple Leafs, 195
Toronto Police Service, 201
trade diasporas, 251
transnationalism, 258–65; assimilation and, 245–6, 247,
    269–70; as avenue of capital, 261–3, 268; business
    class immigrants and, 106; in context of socio-legal
    distinctions, 266; genealogy of, 246–50; as historical
    phenomenon, 266–8; marginality/exclusion and,
    259–60, 270–1; as mode of cultural reproduction,
    260–1; nation-states and, 245, 247, 258, 268–9;
    as site of political engagement, 263–5; as social
    morphology, 259; as type of consciousness, 259–60
Trans-Pacific Partnership, 126
treaties, with Aboriginal peoples, 67–70; continuing
    relevance of, 69–70, 240; map of, 68
Trudeau, Justin, 62–3
Trudeau, Pierre Elliott, 154–5, 173
Trump, Donald, 245
Truth and Reconciliation Commission of Canada, 72, 233
Twitter, 267; racism on, 188–9

Ukrainian Canadians, 62, 79, 85–6, 264
Ukrainian diaspora: in Canada, 262; in Europe, 251; in North America, 248–9
under-policing, 198–9
United Nations Committee to Eliminate Racial Discrimination, 140
United Nations Convention on the Protection of the Rights of All Migrant Workers and Members of their Families, 268–9
United Nations Declaration on the Elimination of Violence against Women, 171
United Nations Educational, Scientific, and Cultural Organization (UNESCO), 12–13; *Statement on Race* by, 12
United Nations High Commissioner for Refugees (UNHCR), 99–100
United Nations Human Rights Committee, 219
United States: census-taking in, 89; exploitative labour practices in, 44–6; immigrants from, 75–6, 270–1; new racism in, 20–1; war of independence in, 63–4, 67
universities: racism at, 193–5, 207; vertical mosaic and, 126, 130–5, 141
University of Chicago. *See* Chicago School of sociology
University of Illinois team mascot, 196–7

Vancouver, 79, 92, 110–11, 189; business immigration to, 106; ethnic violence in, 25–6; hate crime in, 183; housing prices in, 48, 106, 119, 261; Sikh community in, xii, 265
Vancouver Olympic Games, xii
Vancouver Police Department, 198–9
van den Berghe, Pierre: *The Ethnic Phenomenon*, 32, 33
vertical mosaic, 123–5; charter groups and, 124–5; class and, 124–5, 139, 142–7; as colour-coded, 123, 128–35; ethnic convergence and, 125–8; immigrants and, 131–5; problems with ethnic/racial approach to, 136–42; university education and, 130–5, 141
Vertovec, Stephen, 260–1
victim diasporas, 250, 251, 252
Vietnamese refugees: as boatpeople, 251; in Toronto and Boston, 170
Vike-Frieberga, Vaira, 265
"visible minority" (term), 140
Vlassis, George D., 40

volk (people), 5–6
Voltaire, 63
Voyageur, Cora, 237–8

Warburton, Rennie, 158
Washington Redskins, 196
Waters, Mary, 38–9
Weber, Max, 4–6, 42–3, 124
Weiner, Gerry, 164
Weinfeld, Morton, 128, 207, 208
Welsh, Jennifer, 256
Wente, Margaret, 244
"whiteness," 55–7; of Europeans, 56; gaze/privilege of, 56–7
white supremacist groups, 182–3, 188
Widdowson, Frances, and Albert Howard: *Disrobing the Aboriginal Industry: The Deception Behind Indigenous Cultural Preservation*, 229, 231
Wimmer, Andreas, and Nina Glick Schiller, 247
Winn, Conrad, 128, 129
Winnipeg: anti-Aboriginal racism in, 180–2
women: in Aboriginal society, 236–8; early immigration issues of, 74, 78; earnings of, 129–31, 142, 146–7, 226; as live-in caregivers, 107–9; multiculturalism and, 158–9, 171; "race"/class/language issues faced by, 49–50; violence against, 1–3, 171, 175, 198–9. *See also* Aboriginal women; marriage/relationships; Muslim women
Wong, Lloyd: and Connie Ho, 261; and Nancy Netting, 106
Woodsworth, J.S., 75–6
World Conference on Women (Beijing, 1995), Declaration of, 171
World Cup, 196
Wortley, Scot, 191, 202

Yan, Andy, 261
York University (Toronto), 171
Yugoslavia, former: ethnic conflict in, 33

Zero Tolerance for Barbaric Cultural Practices Act, 169, 206, 244
zero tolerance of racism, in schools, 190–2
Znaniecki, Florian. *See* Thomas, W.I.